T0366617

LOEB CLASSICAL LIBRARY

FOUNDED BY JAMES LOEB 1911

EDITED BY
JEFFREY HENDERSON

PLAUTUS

IV

LCL 260

PLAUTUS

THE LITTLE CARTHAGINIAN · PSEUDOLUS · THE ROPE

EDITED AND TRANSLATED BY

WOLFGANG DE MELO

HARVARD UNIVERSITY PRESS

CAMBRIDGE, MASSACHUSETTS

LONDON, ENGLAND

2012

First published 2012

LOEB CLASSICAL LIBRARY® is a registered trademark
of the President and Fellows of Harvard College

Library of Congress Control Number 2010924480
CIP data available from the Library of Congress

ISBN 978-0-674-99986-2

*Composed in ZephGreek and ZephText by
Technologies 'N Typography, Merrimac, Massachusetts.
Printed on acid-free paper and bound by
The Maple-Vail Book Manufacturing Group*

CONTENTS

To my wife and daughter

PREFACE

To an editor of Plautus, every play and every volume presents its own challenges. The greatest challenge in this volume, which comprises the *Poenulus*, the *Pseudolus*, and the *Rudens*, was the Punic passages in Latin script in the first play. Punic is a Semitic language that cannot be rendered in the Latin alphabet without problems. And as if it were not difficult enough to understand passages that are written in an ill-suited script and that moreover belong to a language whose finer grammatical points are still a matter of debate, the texts themselves are more corrupt than other passages of Plautus; the reason is that copyists naturally make more mistakes if they do not know the language of the texts they are copying.

The old Loeb edition of Plautus by Paul Nixon left the Punic passages untranslated, and most Latinists still ignore them today, as if they were an irrelevant oddity. However, our knowledge of Phoenician and Punic has increased to such an extent over the last fifty years that such a procedure is hardly justifiable today. Much of the Semitist literature on Punic in general and Plautine Punic in particular is inaccessible to the average Latinist for two reasons: the grammatical categories and terminology differ from Latin, and there is a tendency to render Punic in the Hebrew/Aramaic script, since unlike the Latin alphabet it has all the necessary consonant signs. Even those Latinists with access to the relevant literature often find it impossible to differentiate between what is certain, uncertain but plausible, and purely speculative. I have left the Punic passages untranslated in the English version of the *Poenulus* because they will not have been intelligible to most Romans; but I have explained them as far as possible in an appendix to the play. This appendix has two aims: on the one hand I hope that my treatment of the Punic passages will make them intelligible to those who know no Semitic languages; and on the other hand I have tried to show clearly what can be known and what has to remain unknown.

I am very grateful for the invaluable help I received from two specialists in Semitic, Kevin Cathcart and John Healey; both answered various queries and read the section I wrote on the Punic passages. Anna Morpurgo Davies also read this part of the book and saved me from inaccuracies and inconsistencies. It is with great fondness that I remember the Hebrew lessons Rüdiger Feuerstein gave me more than a decade ago. When there were not enough students to continue with the regular course, we would meet every Tuesday night and he would give me one-to-one tuition out of pure love for the subject. Without this background in a Semitic language I would not have been able to tackle the Punic texts.

Despite all the inevitable difficulties, work on this volume was also very satisfying. Each of the three plays is a masterpiece and has its own highlights. In the *Poenulus*, Plautus' charming and humane description of the Carthaginian Hanno, who goes on a trip around the world to find his long-lost daughters, is deeply moving; it is all the more so when we consider that Rome and Carthage had been at war in the recent past. In the *Pseudolus*, great entertainment is provided by the nasty and villainous pimp Ballio and his opponent, the bold and clever slave Pseudolus, who eventually brings about the pimp's downfall. The *Rudens* combines both farcical and sentimental elements; the argument between the pimp and his guest is as funny as the recovery of Daemones' lost daughter is touching.

This volume would not be what it is without support from colleagues, family, and friends. On the Latin side, Jim Adams and Peter Brown continued to answer queries on all sorts of problems. Panagiotis Filos helped me with idiosyncratic Greek. And as before, John Trappes-Lomax read the entire volume and commented on both the Latin and the English. Both his critical acumen and his kindness have shaped this book in more ways than I can say here. As always, my family and friends have supported me throughout, no one more so than my wife and my daughter, to whom this book is lovingly dedicated.

POENULUS

INTRODUCTORY NOTE

It was not uncommon in antiquity for plays to have more than one name. Among the fragmentary comedies attributed to Plautus, one is called both *Caecus*, "The Blind Man," and *Praedones*, "The Bandits." Similarly, the *Casina* may have had *Sortientes*, "Men Casting Lots," as an alternative title. Our play was called *Poenulus*, "The Little Carthaginian," already in antiquity (see Varro *ling.* 7.69), but some scholars have claimed that it had *Patruus*, "The Uncle," as an alternative title. Both titles would refer to Hanno, a Carthaginian traveling around the world in search of his long-lost daughters. The second name would have been given to the play because Hanno is the "uncle"[1] of Agorastocles, a young man madly in love with one of Hanno's daughters.

However, the grounds for assuming *Patruus* as an alternative title are inconclusive at best. In l. 53 we are told that the Greek name of the play is *Karkhedonios*, "The Carthaginian," and in l. 54 the words "Plautus," "porridge-eater" (*pultiphagonides*), and "uncle" (*patruus*) occur. *Pace* Copley, "porridge-eater" must jokingly refer to Plautus rather than Hanno, as Plautus makes fun of

---

[1] This is what he is referred to in the play. He is Agorastocles' first cousin once removed.

Romans having this dietary staple elsewhere (*Most.* 828). There are two major objections to taking *patruus* as the title of the play: first, its position in between the name "Plautus" and his epithet "porridge-eater" is awkward, and second, *patruus* stands in the nominative like the other two nouns, not in the accusative, as one would expect. For these reasons it makes more sense to take *patruus* as jocularly referring to Plautus as well and to assume, with Geppert, that a line was lost between what are now ll. 53 and 54.

Therefore, it is best to reckon with a single Latin title, *Poenulus*, as translation of the name of the original, *Karkhedonios*. Plautus does not say who wrote the original, but we know that both Menander and Alexis wrote plays with this title. Menander's *Karkhedonios* has nothing in common with the Plautine *Poenulus*; in Menander's comedy, a Carthaginian man pursues a girl and claims to be an Athenian citizen, being registered in an Attic township. The play by Alexis, on the other hand, is highly likely to be the original of the *Poenulus*. Thus fr. 105 Kassel-Austin corresponds to l. 1318 of the *Poenulus*; in both cases someone is accused of being unmanly. While this correspondence is not sufficient proof because the fragment consists of only two words, further evidence comes from the correspondence between *Poen.* 522–23 and 525 with an unattributed but long fragment of Alexis (265 Kassel-Austin), which can therefore be assigned to his *Karkhedonios*. In both passages it is stated that fast walking is suitable for slaves, while free men ought to walk at a leisurely pace.

Since the *Poenulus* has played a major role in the discussion of *contaminatio*, the content of the play needs to be outlined in some detail. It combines elements of the

3

standard intrigue that a clever slave concocts against a pimp for his young master and of a recognition play. The background of the comedy is narrated in the prologue. There were two wealthy first cousins in Carthage, called Iahon and Hanno. Iahon had a son, but this son, Agorastocles, was kidnapped and sold in Calydon. The man who bought him, Antidamas, had no wife or children himself. Ironically, even though he was Hanno's friend, he never realized that he had bought and adopted his cousin's son. Antidamas died and bequeathed great wealth to Agorastocles. Hanno, Iahon's cousin, had two daughters, Anterastilis and Adelphasium. Like Agorastocles, both were kidnapped when young, and together with their nurse Giddenis, who was abducted as well, they were sold to a pimp called Lycus. When Lycus moved to Calydon, Agorastocles fell in love with Adelphasium, the elder sister. Both Iahon and his wife died, but Hanno decided to go traveling until he found his daughters and nephew again.

The play is set in Calydon with good reason. In Athens only Athenian citizens could be adopted, so that an important premise of the *Poenulus*, the adoption of Agorastocles by Antidamas, would be impossible to maintain in an Athenian setting. The law of Calydon presumably differed in this respect. Incidentally, in l. 372 Milphio promises Adelphasium that Agorastocles will make her an Athenian citizen. This sentence was in all likelihood introduced by Plautus rather than the Greek playwright, but it does not really make the comedy inconsistent: Athenian citizenship means no more than "best citizenship."

In the prologue (l. 66) it is stated that Agorastocles was seven years old when he was kidnapped, but in ll. 902 and

987 his age is given as six at the time. However, this does not mean that Plautus took these conflicting passages from different Greek plays without noticing the clash; rather, it seems more likely that Plautus encountered different, equivalent Greek expressions but translated some of them wrongly. For instance, the statement that Agorastocles was seven could go back to a Greek phrase that said he was in his seventh year (and thus six years old), while the two statements that he was six would go back to a Greek phrase that said straightforwardly that he was six years old.

The play itself presents us with the events during the Aphrodisia, a festival of Aphrodite/Venus, the goddess of love. Agorastocles complains to his slave Milphio that he is denied access to Adelphasium by Lycus. Milphio suggests tricking the pimp. Collybiscus, a farm overseer belonging to Agorastocles, is to dress up as a foreign soldier and to bring money to the pimp in order to buy dinner, wine, and sexual services. Agorastocles then has to come with witnesses and ask Lycus whether he has received his slave. The pimp will naturally deny this and hence be guilty of perjury and receiving stolen property. The punishment will be so immense that the pimp will have to hand over his property, including Adelphasium. Agorastocles agrees to the plan.

However, the plan is not executed immediately because Agorastocles and Milphio spot Adelphasium, Anterastilis, and a servant girl accompanying them. They are going to the temple of Venus to sacrifice because on this day they will become prostitutes; so far, neither girl has been intimate with men. The audience can witness Agorastocles' passionate love as well as Adelphasium's rather cool behavior toward him, which is not without reason: she is upset that Agorastocles has not bought her and set her free, despite being wealthy.

What is commonly referred to as the second act is a single short scene (ll. 449–503). We encounter the pimp for the first time. He is angry because the priests have told him that his sacrifice is unacceptable to Venus, and as a result he blasphemes. Lycus is followed by the soldier Antamynides,[2] a customer met at the festival; like other soldiers in comedy, he is boastful and obviously a liar. The two go into the pimp's house in order to wait for the girls to return.

The third act begins with the return of Agorastocles from the forum. He brings advocates with him. These advocates are presented as poor, litigious freedmen who dislike everybody, but who side with Agorastocles because their hatred for the pimp is greater than their dislike of Agorastocles. Milphio brings along Collybiscus, who is by now dressed up as a soldier and properly instructed as to what he should do. Agorastocles and Milphio go into their house, and the advocates call out Lycus. The pimp is delighted to have a second customer and receives his money, while Agorastocles, who has been called out again, observes the transaction from a distance. Not much later,

[2] The name is derived from Greek *antamynomai*, "defend oneself"/"requite"; the name fits because a soldier needs to defend himself and because Antamynides takes revenge on Lycus. The manuscripts spell the name *Antamoenides*; Greek *y* was rendered as *u* by Plautus, and since archaic Latin *oe* became *u*, the manuscript spelling seems to be a hypercorrection.

Agorastocles and the advocates go to the pimp again. As planned, Agorastocles asks him if his slave and money are at his place, and when Lycus denies it, Agorastocles and the advocates tell him that Collybiscus is not a soldier but an overseer belonging to Agorastocles. Collybiscus confesses immediately. The pimp is distressed and goes to the forum to consult his friends; the advocates also leave, grumbling against Agorastocles despite having their wish fulfilled.

The fourth act is short again and only comprises ll. 817–929; moreover, ll. 923–29 are probably to be excluded as a doublet of what immediately precedes. Milphio meets Syncerastus, one of the pimp's slaves, who tells him that Adelphasium and Anterastilis are freeborn Carthaginians and that Agorastocles can ruin the pimp by asserting their freedom. Milphio is happy that Agorastocles has this opportunity and is keen to carry out this second trick.

It is only at the beginning of the fifth act that we meet Hanno, the pivotal figure in our play. Hanno's entire entrance monologue is in Punic, a language not many in the audience will have understood. There are in fact two Punic versions of the entrance monologue, each ten verses long (ll. 930–39 and 940–49), followed by a Latin version thereof, also ten lines long (ll. 950–60, without the spurious l. 954). Of the two Punic versions, the second follows Plautine orthographic conventions and must be the original one; it is, however, by and large unintelligible and was already corrupt in antiquity. This makes it likely that the first Punic text, which follows later spelling conventions, is a scholar's attempt to replace the older, incomprehensible text. In all likelihood Hanno recited not only the second Punic entrance monologue but also the Latin version. Gratwick has argued that the Latin text is unnecessary for understanding what is going on because the staging will have made things clear, so that the Latin version should be regarded as a later addition. But this seems improbable: only a very attentive spectator would have been able to follow at this point, and Plautus is a playwright who prefers to spell things out for his audience.

The Punic entrance monologue is not the only piece of Punic the audience encounters in the play. As most Romans were unable to understand the language, I have left the passages untranslated in the English version of the play but have explained them—insofar as they can be explained—in an appendix.

Hanno encounters Agorastocles and Milphio and addresses them in Punic. Milphio offers to translate because his master has forgotten the language entirely, but as he himself knows no more than a few words of Punic, his translations become more and more absurd until he has to give up, at which point Hanno effortlessly switches to Latin. Agorastocles is keen to help Hanno because he hails from Carthage himself, and soon Hanno realizes that Agorastocles is none other than his first cousin's son. Milphio tells Hanno that Agorastocles loves a Carthaginian girl owned by a pimp; Hanno should pretend that she is his daughter so that Agorastocles can set her free. All three go to the pimp's house. The woman who answers the door is Giddenis, who instantly recognizes her master, Hanno. Hanno promises Agorastocles to give him his daughter Adelphasium in marriage. When the two sisters return from the sacrifice, they do not recognize their father because they have not seen him since they were small; Hanno reveals himself to them, and everyone is overjoyed. Antamynides appears, sees the girl he has hired embracing a foreigner in exotic dress, and is angry. However, on learning what has happened he is pleased as well. As soon as the pimp returns, Agorastocles, Hanno, and the soldier want to drag him to court; he yields and promises to pay everyone his due.

At this point the manuscripts contain a spurious ending (ll. 1355–71), which probably goes back to a later revival production. Its main purpose seems to have been to shorten the original ending; the pimp is willing to give up the girls and pay his debts to the soldier, who did not get his entertainment. The meter, iambic senarii, is entirely untypical of Plautine endings.

The next part, ll. 1372–97, is also a part of a spurious ending; again it is in iambic senarii and overlaps in content with the true Plautine ending (ll. 1398–1422), which is in trochaic septenarii, the appropriate meter. Here too the pimp has to give up the girls and compensate Agorastocles and Antamynides.

Many scholars have considered the *Poenulus* a contaminated play based on two Greek originals rather than one. The main reason is the existence of two tricks, either of which would be sufficient to free the girls and give Agorastocles his heart's desire. What is more, the first trick was already successful (see ll. 815–16) when the second trick is begun, which makes this second trick rather superfluous.

However, matters are more complicated than that. The first trick can in reality give Agorastocles no more than a strong bargaining position. In addition, the trial cannot take place on the day of the play, for during religious festivals legal proceedings were not allowed in either Greece or Rome, and Lycus can still prostitute the girls until summoned to court. Presumably the first trick was not as successful in the Greek original as it is in the Latin play, where Plautus, as so often, emphasizes the role of the clever slave. Plautine workmanship can also be spotted in the legal ramifications of the first trick. In Greece, the pimp would only have had to pay a double penalty, as actually stated in l. 1351, which must come from the Greek original; in Rome, on the other hand, the pimp would have become a bond slave of Agorastocles, as mentioned in l. 564. Similarly, in l. 621 the advocates call themselves Aetolian citizens, but we know that they are freedmen; in Greece freedmen did not become citizens, so that this line actually reflects Roman legal practices rather than Aetolian ones.

There are good arguments for assuming that the second trick is a purely Plautine invention and does not go back to the Greek original containing the first trick or to any other Greek play. To begin with, as the two girls are foreigners, the only way a Greek audience would assume that they could be freed on the basis of their free birth is if there were a treaty between Carthage and the Aetolian League, of which Calydon was a part. Since there is no evidence for such a treaty, Lycus has not actually violated Greek law by buying Adelphasium and Anterastilis. The second trick only works if the girls are treated as Romans in Rome, so it must be Plautine. Hanno too is treated as a Roman in Rome: in 189 BC a treaty of friendship was established between Rome and Carthage, which would allow him to appeal to the authorities against the pimp, but he would still need a patron to represent him; Plautus presents him as able to appeal by himself (ll. 1102–3), which he could not do as a foreigner.

There are further indications that the second trick is Plautine rather than Greek in origin. For instance, for more than fifty lines Agorastocles stands around idly while Milphio and Hanno discuss strategy (ll. 1077–1135); such a situation would violate Greek stage conventions. Similarly, Milphio's characterization of the girls as not only slaves but also prostitutes is inaccurate (l. 1094); so far they have not worked in the trade. Perhaps even odder is Milphio's failure to mention to Hanno that the girls are Carthaginian or that he has already tricked the pimp. All this is in line with Plautine techniques of composition, which value individual scenes more highly than the coherence of the play as a whole, but not with Greek New Comedy, where consistency is more important than the humor of individual scenes.

If these arguments are correct, it is likely that when Hanno was discovered to be the girls' father in the Greek play, Agorastocles did not wait for the trial but seized the girls immediately, just as Aeschinus does in Terence's *Adelphoe*, which is based on a play by Menander (although it also contains a passage from Diphilus). By contrast, to Plautus the revelation that the girls are Hanno's daughters immediately suggested legal proceedings against the pimp.

The way Plautus paints Hanno is truly astonishing. Since Hanno is a Carthaginian, and hence part of a nation that had always been a rival of Rome, whether in war or in peace, one would expect, or at least not be surprised by, his unsympathetic portrayal. Yet the play contains practically no racial or ethnic slurs.[3] Franko emphasizes that the Greek title, *Karkhedonios*, or "The Carthaginian," refers only to Hanno's place of birth, whereas the name *Poenulus* literally means "the little Carthaginian" and thus adds not only an ethnic dimension but also a note of contempt conveyed in part by the diminutive suffix. However, not too much should be made of this, since the distinction between origin and ethnicity was not as strictly drawn in antiquity as it is today, and the diminutive may actually simply be affectionate or refer to Hanno's stature. Those who have tried to find negative evaluations of Carthaginians in the *Poenulus* have generally given more weight to the depiction of Hanno in the prologue. Hanno's method of searching for his daughters is described as consisting of visits to brothels around the Mediterranean, where he hires nights with prostitutes and then proceeds to ask them about their parentage (ll. 106–10). According to Franko, the risk that he might be sleeping with his own daughters does not seem to bother him. Again I cannot agree: presumably Hanno made his inquiries before sleeping with the girls, if indeed he did sleep with them, which should not be taken for granted, especially since he is an old man. Hanno's unconventional method of looking for his daughters should not be treated as an attempt by Plautus to ridicule the foreigner; his procedure makes sense because kidnapped girls were quite likely to end up as prostitutes. The Hanno we encounter later in the play is certainly not a lewd figure; his entrance begins with a

[3] A mildly negative view of Carthaginians is expressed in ll. 112–13.

solemn prayer and he behaves with great dignity. It is notable that all the verbal abuse Hanno has to endure comes from Milphio, a slave who has just been revealed as a fraud, and from Antamynides, a pompous, lying, and cowardly soldier. Hanno is consistently lauded for his piety, a virtue which Romans claimed Carthaginians did not possess. So despite making the occasional joke about the foreigner, Plautus has presented him in a very positive light.

The date of the first production of the *Poenulus* can be established relatively accurately. In l. 525 it is said that the state is at peace and that its enemies have been conquered. In all likelihood, an explicit statement to this effect would not have been inserted after a minor victory. Perhaps Plautus is alluding to the four triumphs that were held in 189 BC. The general tenor of the play, which shows a positive attitude toward Carthaginians, points in the same direction. The second Punic War, in which Rome faced one of its most formidable opponents in the Carthaginian Hannibal, ended in 201, and it is inconceivable that Plautus would have been able to stage the *Poenulus* with its Carthaginian hero during the war or in its immediate aftermath. However, a peace treaty was made with Carthage in 189, the year of the four triumphs, so that it is quite likely that our play came onstage in this year or shortly after. The year 189 also marks the end of the Aetolian war; since Agorastocles is an Aetolian, we have another indication that this is when the *Poenulus* was first produced. A possible *terminus ante quem* can be derived from l. 694, where Antiochus is referred to in such a way as to give the impression that he was still alive during the first production. Since Antiochus died in 187, the play was probably

13

staged in 189, 188, or 187; but it seems sensible not to read too much into l. 694. Finally, another historical allusion is made by Agorastocles' advocates in ll. 663–65. They claim that the man they are bringing along did military service for King Attalus in Sparta, but that the city is now taken. This account is garbled and no more than an invention of the advocates; Attalus I of Pergamum was not king of Sparta and died in 197, and Flaminius attacked Nabis and thereby Sparta only two years after the death of Attalus. If we ignore this last allusion, the least we can state with certainty is that the *Poenulus* was produced in Plautus' final years; and perhaps it is legitimate to narrow the span of time during which the first production took place to the years 189 to 187.

SELECT BIBLIOGRAPHY

Editions and Commentaries

Gratwick, A. S. (1968), *The* Poenulus *of Plautus and Its Attic Original*, 2 vols. (diss. Oxford).

Maurach, G. (1975), *Plauti* Poenulus: *Einleitung, Textherstellung und Kommentar* (Heidelberg).

Criticism

Arnott, W. G. (1959), "The Author of the Greek Original of the *Poenulus*," in *Rheinisches Museum* NS 102: 252–62.

——— (1970), "Studies in Comedy, II: Toothless Wine," in *Greek, Roman, and Byzantine Studies* 11: 43–47.

Baier, T. (ed.) (2004), *Studien zu Plautus'* Poenulus (Tübingen).

Copley, F. O. (1970), "Plautus, *Poenulus*, 53–55," in *American Journal of Philology* 91: 77–78.

Franko, G. F. (1996), "The Characterization of Hanno in Plautus' *Poenulus*," in *American Journal of Philology* 117: 425–52.

Gratwick, A. S. (1972), "Plautus, *Poenulus* 967–81: Some Notes," in *Glotta* 50: 228–33.

Jocelyn, H. D. (1990), "Plautus, *Poenulus* 200–202 and the *ballistarium*," in *Liverpool Classical Monthly* 15: 5–8.

Traina, A. (1966), "Note Plautine (III): *NINNIVM* (*Poen.* 371)," in *Rivista di filologia e di istruzione classica* NS 94: 50–53.

POENVLVS

ARGVMENTVM

Puer septuennis surripitur Carthagine.
Osor mulierum emptum adoptat hunc senex
Et facit heredem. eius cognatae duae
Nutrixque earum raptae. mercatur Lycus,
5 Vexatque amantem. at ille cum auro uilicum
Lenoni optrudit, ita eum furto alligat.
Venit Hanno Poenus, gnatum hunc fratris repperit
Suasque agnoscit quas perdiderat filias.

THE LITTLE CARTHAGINIAN

PLOT SUMMARY

A seven-year-old boy is kidnapped from Carthage. Having
bought him, an old misogynist adopts him and makes him his
heir. Two female relatives of the young man and their nurse
are kidnapped. Lycus buys them and torments the young man, 5
who loves one. But that young man palms off his overseer with
gold on the pimp and in this way implicates him in theft. The
Carthaginian Hanno comes, finds the young man to be his
nephew, and recognizes his daughters, whom he had lost.

PERSONAE

AGORASTOCLES adulescens
MILPHIO seruos
ADELPHASIVM puella
ANTERASTILIS puella
LYCVS leno
ANTAMYNIDES miles
ADVOCATI
COLLYBISCVS uilicus
SYNCERASTVS seruos
HANNO Poenus
GIDDENIS nutrix
PVER
ANCILLA

SCAENA

Calydone

---

1 Not advocates in the modern sense ("lawyers"), but legal assistants.

CHARACTERS

AGORASTOCLES a young man; Carthaginian by birth, Calydonian by upbringing
MILPHIO a slave; works for Agorastocles
ADELPHASIUM a girl; Carthaginian slave of Lycus, loved by Agorastocles
ANTERASTILIS a girl; Adelphasium's sister
LYCUS a pimp; a newcomer in the city of Calydon
ANTAMYNIDES a soldier; interested in Anterastilis
ADVOCATES[1] litigious freedmen siding with Agorastocles
COLLYBISCUS an overseer; works for Agorastocles
SYNCERASTUS a slave; works for Lycus, but dislikes him
HANNO a Carthaginian; father of Adelphasium and Anterastilis
GIDDENIS a nurse; abducted long ago together with Adelphasium and her sister
SLAVE BOY son of Giddenis, belongs to Hanno
SLAVE GIRL belongs to Lycus, accompanies Adelphasium and Anterastilis to the temple

STAGING

The stage represents a street in Calydon. The house of Lycus is on the left, that of Agorastocles on the right. The street leads to the city center on the right and to the temple of Venus and the harbor on the left.

PROLOGVS

Achillem Aristarchi mihi commentari lubet:
ind' mihi principium capiam, ex ea tragoedia,
"sileteque et tacete atque animum aduortite,
audire iubet uos imperator" . . . histricus,
5   bonoque ut animo sedeant in subselliis
et qui esurientes et qui saturi uenerint:
qui edistis, multo fecistis sapientius,
qui non edistis, saturi fite fabulis;
nam quoi paratum est quod edit, nostra gratia
10 nimia est stultitia sessum impransum incedere.
"exsurge, praeco, fac populo audientiam."
iam dudum exspecto si tuom officium scias:
exerce uocem quam per uiuisque et clues.
nam nisi clamabis, tacitum te obrepet fames.
15 age nunc reside, duplicem ut mercedem feras.
"bonum factum est, edicta ut seruetis mea."
scortum exoletum ne quis in proscaenio
sedeat, neu lictor uerbum aut uirgae muttiant,
neu dissignator praeter os obambulet
20 neu sessum ducat, dum histrio in scaena siet.

> 5 sedeate *P*, sedeant ς
> 13 colis *P*, clues *Lindsay in apparatu*, te alis *Leo*
> 16 factum esse *P*, factumst *Pylades*

PROLOGUE

Enter the SPEAKER OF THE PROLOGUE *from the right, followed by a herald.*

I wish to rehearse the *Achilles* by Aristarchus;[2] from there, from that tragedy, I'll take my beginning: "be silent and be quiet and pay attention; you are ordered to listen by the commander of" . . . actors; and both those who've come hungry and those who've come full should sit on their benches with goodwill. You who have eaten have behaved far more wisely. You who haven't eaten, fill yourselves with tales:[3] it's great folly for a man who has something that he could eat to come to sit without breakfast for our sake. "Rise, herald, make the people all ears." For a while now I've been waiting with interest to see if you know your duty. Exercise your voice, through which you live and have a reputation; if you won't shout, hunger will creep upon you while you're quiet. (*The herald proclaims silence.*) Go on, now sit down so as to get double pay. (*The herald obeys.*) "It is proper for you to observe my edicts."[4] No male prostitute is to sit in the space in front of the stage; neither lictor[5] nor rods are to utter a single word; no usher is to walk in front of someone's face or show someone his seat while an actor is onstage.

[2] Greek writer of tragedies, contemporary of Sophocles. His *Achilles* was translated by Ennius and performed in Rome.

[3] In the Latin, a pun on *făbulae*, "tales," and *făbulae*, "little beans."   [4] Formula used by the praetor, a Roman official.

[5] Attendant of Roman magistrates, carrying rods and an ax.

diu qui domi otiosi dormierunt, decet
animo aequo nunc stent uel dormire temperent.
serui ne opsideant, liberis ut sit locus,
uel aes pro capite dent; si id facere non queunt,
25   domum abeant, uitent ancipiti infortunio,
ne et hic uarientur uirgis et loris domi,
si minus curassint, quom eri reueniant domum.
nutrices pueros infantis minutulos
domi ut procurent neue spectatum afferant,
30   ne et ipsae sitiant et pueri pereant fame
neue esurientes hic quasi haedi obuagiant.
matronae tacitae spectent, tacitae rideant,
canora hic uoce sua tinnire temperent,
domum sermones fabulandi conferant,
35   ne et hic uiris sint et domi molestiae.
quodque ad ludorum curatores attinet,
ne palma detur quoiquam artifici iniuria
neue ambitionis causa extrudantur foras,
quo deteriores anteponantur bonis.
40   et hoc quoque etiam quod paene oblitus fui:
dum ludi fiunt, in popinam, pedisequi,
irruptionem facite; nunc dum occasio est,
nunc dum scriblitae aestuant, occurrite!
haec quae imperata sunt pro imperio histrico,
45   bonum hercle factum pro se quisque ut meminerit.
ad argumentum nunc uicissatim uolo
remigrare, ut aeque mecum sitis gnarures.
eius nunc regiones, limites, confinia
determinabo: ei rei ego finitor factus sum:

29 neu quae (que *CD*) *P*, neue *Pylades*   afferat *P*, afferant
Pylades   44 quae imperata *P, transp. Camerarius*

POENULUS

Those who have slept at leisure at home for too long ought now to stand with goodwill or else refrain from sleeping. Let no slaves occupy seats so that the free may have a place, or let them pay money for their freedom. If they can't do this, let them go home and avoid a double thrashing, so that they won't get checkered with rods here and with whips at home if they haven't done their chores when their masters return home. Let the nurses attend to tiny babies at home and not bring them to watch the play, so that the nurses themselves won't be thirsty and the children won't die from hunger or disturb us by wailing here like little goats because of their hunger. Let the married women watch quietly and laugh quietly, let them refrain from tinkling with their ringing voices, and let them take their chattering conversations home, so that they won't be a nuisance to their husbands here as well as at home. And as for the organizers of the games, let the palm not be given to any artist unfairly and let them not be thrown out so that others benefit from corruption and so that the worse can be placed ahead of the good. And this, too, which I almost forgot: while the games are taking place, footmen, storm the eating house; attack now while you have the opportunity, now while the cheese tarts[6] are hot! It is proper that everyone should remember for himself these orders issued by virtue of the actor's authority. Now in turn I wish to come back to the plot summary so that you may be as knowledgeable as me. I shall now determine its spaces, boundaries, and surroundings; for this I've been made

[6] A popular, simple dish; the recipe can be found in Cato *agr.* 78.

49 sum factus finitor *P, transp. Muretus*

50 sed nisi molestum est, nomen dare uobis uolo
comoediai; sin odio est, dicam tamen,
siquidem licebit per illos quibus est in manu.
53 Καρχηδόνιος uocatur haec comoedia;
53ᵃ ***
latine Plautus patruos pultiphagonides.
55 nomen iam habetis. nunc rationes ceteras
accipite; nam argumentum hoc hic censebitur:
locus argumento est suom sibi proscaenium,
uos iuratores estis. quaeso, operam date.
Carthaginienses fratres patrueles duo
60 fuere, summo genere et summis ditiis;
eorum alter uiuit, alter est emortuos.
propterea apud uos dico confidentius,
quia mi pollictor dixit qui eum pollinxerat.
sed illi seni qui mortuost, ⟨ei⟩ filius
65 unicus qui fuerat ab diuitiis a patre
puer septuennis surrupitur Carthagine,
sexennio prius quidem quam moritur pater.
quoniam periisse sibi uidet gnatum unicum,
conicitur ipse in morbum ex aegritudine:
70 facit illum heredem fratrem patruelem suom,
ipse abit ad Accheruntem sine uiatico.
ill' qui surrupuit puerum Calydonem auehit,
uendit eum domino hic diuiti quoidam seni,
cupienti liberorum, osori mulierum.
75 emit hospitalem is filium imprudens senex
puerum illum eumque adoptat sibi pro filio
eumque heredem fecit quom ipse obiit diem.
is illic adulescens habitat in illisce aedibus.
reuortor rursus denuo Carthaginem:
80 si quid mandare uoltis aut curarier,

24

land surveyor. But if you don't object, I want to give you the   50
name of the comedy; if it does annoy you, I'll still say it, if in-
deed I'm allowed to by those in whose hands this is. This com-
edy is called *Karchedonios*; in Latin uncle porridge-eater Plau-
tus ***. You already have the name. Now receive the remaining   55
declarations; for this plot summary will be examined as a dec-
laration of property. The plot summary has as place where it's
examined its own space in front of the stage: you are the of-
ficials who receive sworn declarations. Please pay attention.
There were two first cousins from Carthage, from a very great   60
family and with very great riches. One of them is alive, the
other is dead. I'm stating this before you so confidently for the
simple reason that the undertaker who prepared him for burial
told me so himself. But as for that old man who died, the
only son he had is kidnapped from his wealth and from his fa-   65
ther from Carthage as a seven-year-old boy, six years before his
father dies; when he sees that his only son was lost, he himself
falls ill from grief. He makes that cousin of his his heir and he   70
himself goes to the Underworld without any travel provisions.
The one who kidnapped the boy takes him away to Calydon and
sells him to a certain rich old master here who wants to have
children but hates women. Without knowing it, this old man,   75
in buying that boy, buys the son of his family friend, adopts him
as his son, and makes him his heir when he himself dies. This
young man lives there, in that house. (*points to it*) I'm returning
to Carthage again. If you want to entrust anything to me or   80

53[a] *lacunam indicat Geppert*   54 latine Patruom ⟨uortit⟩ Pul-
tiphagonides *Trappes-Lomax per litteras*

   64 ei *add. Acidalius*

   71 abiit *P*, abit *Lachmann* (*fortasse* abiit [ad] Accheruntem)

   80 amandare *P*, mandare *Saracenus*

argentum nisi qui dederit, nugas egerit;
uerum qui dederit, magis maiores [nugas] egerit.
sed illi patruo huius qui uiuit senex,
Carthaginiensi duae fuere filiae,
85   altera quinquennis, altera quadrimula:
cum nutrice una periere a Magaribus.
eas qui surrupuit in Anactorium deuehit,
uendit eas omnis, et nutricem et uirgines,
praesenti argento homini, si leno est homo,
90   quantum hominum terra sustinet sacerrumo.
uosmet nunc facite coniecturam ceterum
quid id sit hominis quoi Lyco nomen siet.
is ex Anactorio, ubi prius habitauerat,
huc commigrauit in Calydonem hau diu,
95   sui quaesti causa. is in illis habitat aedibus.
earum hic adulescens alteram efflictim perit,
suam sibi cognatam, imprudens, nec scit quae siet
neque eam umquam tetigit, ita eum leno macerat;
nec quicquam cum ea fecit etiamnum stupri
100 nec duxit umquam, neque ille uoluit mittere:
quia amare cernit, tangere hominem uolt bolo.
illam minorem in concubinatum sibi
uolt emere miles quidam qui illam deperit.
sed pater illarum Poenus, postquam eas perdidit,
105 mari te⟨rraque⟩ usquequaque quaeritat.
ubi quamque in urbem est ingressus, ilico
omnis meretrices, ubi quisque habitant, inuenit;
dat aurum, ducit noctem, rogitat postibi

---

82 nugas *del. Pylades*   94 commigrauit in Calydonem *P*, in
Calydonem commigrauit *Pylades*
   99–100 *secl. Guyet*   105 te⟨rraque⟩ *Geppert*

26

want anything to be taken care of, then unless someone gives me money he'll behave like a fool; but the man who does give me money will behave like an even bigger fool. But this chap's Carthaginian uncle, who is alive, but old, had two daughters, one 85 five years old, the other four; they disappeared from Magara[7] together with their nurse. The man who kidnapped them brings them to Anactorium[8] and sells them all for cash, the nurse and the girls, to the most detestable human being —if a pimp 90 counts as a human being—whom the earth sustains. As for the rest, you can now guess for yourselves what sort of creature it is that has the name Lycus.[9] Not long ago he moved from Anactorium, where he had lived before, here to Calydon, to ply 95 his trade. He lives in that house. (*points to it*) This young chap is madly in love with one of the girls, his own relative, completely unaware of this fact; he doesn't know who she is and he's never touched her: that's how the pimp wears him out. He hasn't had any intercourse with her yet and he's never hired her, 100 nor would the pimp send her to him. Because he can see that he is in love, he wants to catch him with a throw of the net. A certain soldier, who is passionately in love with that younger one, wants to buy her to become his concubine. But ever since their Carthaginian father lost them, he's been looking for them 105 everywhere by sea and by land. Whenever he enters a city, he immediately finds out where all the prostitutes live. He pays money, hires her for a night, and then asks where she's from

7 A suburb of Carthage.
8 A city in Aetolia.
9 The Greek word for "wolf."

und' sit, quoiatis, captane an surrupta sit,
110   quo genere gnata, qui parentes fuerint.
ita docte atque astu filias quaerit suas.
et is omnis linguas scit, sed dissimulat sciens
se scire: Poenus plane est. quid uerbis opust?
is heri huc in portum naui uenit uesperi,
115   pater harunc; idem huic patruos adulescentulo est:
iamne hoc tenetis? si tenetis, ducite;
caue dirumpatis, quaeso, sinite transigi.
ehem, paene oblitus sum relicuom dicere.
ille qui adoptauit hunc sibi pro filio,
120   is illi Poeno huius patruo hospes fuit.
[is hodie huc ueniet reperietque hic filias
et hunc sui fratris filium, ut quidem didici ego.
ego ibo, ornabor; uos aequo animo noscite.]
hic qui hodie ueniet reperiet suas filias
125   et hunc sui fratris filium. dehinc ceterum
ualete, adeste. ibo, alius nunc fieri uolo:
quod restat, restant alii qui faciant palam.
ualete atque adiuuate ut uos seruet Salus.

ACTVS I

I. i: AGORASTOCLES. MILPHIO

AGO   saepe ego res multas tibi mandaui, Milphio,
130   dubias, egenas, inopiosas consili,
quas tu sapienter, docte et cordate et cate

121–23 *secl. Lindsay*

28

and what country she comes from, whether she was captured
in war or kidnapped, what family she comes from, and who her   110
parents were. In this way he looks for his daughters cleverly
and smartly. He also knows all languages, but he knowingly
pretends not to know: he's an out-and-out Carthaginian. What
need is there for words? Yesterday evening he came here into
the harbor by ship, the father of these girls; the same man is   115
the uncle of this young chap. Have you got it? If you've got it,
pull;[10] make sure you don't break it off, please, let it glide
through. Oh, I almost forgot to tell you the rest. The man who
adopted this chap as his son was a family friend of that Cartha-   120
ginian, the uncle of the young man. [Today he'll come here and
find his daughters here and his nephew, as I've learned. I'll go
and get into my costume; you must get to know the play with
goodwill.] The man who comes today will find his daughters
here and his nephew. As for the rest, fare well and pay atten-   125
tion. I'll go, I want to become someone else now. There remain
others who will reveal the remainder to you. Fare well and
support us, so that Salvation may keep you safe.

Exeunt the SPEAKER OF THE PROLOGUE *and the herald to the
right.*

ACT ONE

Enter AGORASTOCLES *and* MILPHIO *from the former's house.*

AGO Milphio, I've often entrusted you with many uncer-
tain and needy affairs which lacked counsel and which   130
you have intelligently, cleverly, sensibly, and shrewdly

[10] Reference to a dance in which the participants hold a rope.

29

mihi reddidisti opiparas opera tua.
quibus pro benefactis fateor deberi tibi
et libertatem et multas gratas gratias.

135 MIL scitum est, per tempus si obuiam est, uerbum uetus.
nam tuae blanditiae mihi sunt, quod dici solet,
gerrae germanae, αἱ δὲ κολλῦραι λύραι.
nunc mihi blandidicus es: heri in tergo meo
tris facile corios contriuisti bubulos.

140 AGO amans per amorem si quid feci[t], Milphio,
ignoscere id te mi aequom est.

MIL   hau uidi magis.
em, nunc ego amore pereo. sine te uerberem,
item ut tu mihi fecisti, ob nullam noxiam:
postid locorum tu mihi amanti ignoscito.

145 AGO si tibi lubido est aut uoluptati, sino:
suspende, uinci, uerbera; auctor sum, sino.

MIL si auctoritatem postea defugeris,
ubi dissolutus tu sies, ego pendeam.

AGO egone istuc ausim facere, praesertim tibi?
150 quin si feriri uideo te, extemplo dolet.

MIL mihi quidem hercle.

AGO   immo mihi.

MIL   istuc mauelim.
sed quid nunc tibi uis?

AGO   quor ego apud te mentiar?
amo immodeste.

MIL   meae istuc scapulae sentiunt.

AGO at ego hanc uicinam dico Adelphasium meam,
155 lenonis huius meretricem maiusculam.

MIL iam pridem equidem istuc ex te audiui.

140 fecit *P*, feci ς   142 et *P*, em *Ussing*

30

made sumptuous for me through your efforts. For these good turns I admit that you're owed freedom and many thankful thanks.

MIL An old saying is neat if it fits the occasion; yes, your flattery is, as they say, pure poppycock, but loaves are the real lyres.[11] Today you flatter me; yesterday you easily wore out three ox hides[12] on my back.   135

AGO If in my love I did something out of love, Milphio, you ought to forgive me for it.   140

MIL A likely story! There, now I'm the one dying from love. Let me beat you the way you beat me, for no offense at all; after that you must forgive me because I'm in love.

AGO If you wish or desire it, I let you do it. Hang me up, bind me, beat me: I authorize you, I permit you.   145

MIL If you evade your authorization later on when you're set free, I'd be the one hanging.

AGO Would I dare to do this, especially to you? No, if I see you being beaten, it' very painful at once.   150

MIL Yes, for me.

AGO No, for me.

MIL I'd prefer that. But what do you want now?

AGO Why should I lie to you? I'm in love beyond self-control.

MIL My shoulder blades are aware of that.

AGO But I'm talking about this neighbor of mine, Adelphasium, the prostitute of that pimp here, the one who's a little older than the other.   155

MIL I heard that from you long ago.

11 I.e., empty words mean nothing, while presents mean true praise.

12 Whips were made from ox hide.

AGO   differor

cupidine eius. sed lenone istoc Lyco,

illius domino, non lutum est lutulentius.

MIL   uin tu illi nequam dare nunc?

AGO   cupio.

MIL   em me dato.

160 AGO   abi dierectus.

MIL   dic mihi uero serio:

uin dare malum illi?

AGO   cupio.

MIL   em eundem me dato:

utrumque faxo habebit, et nequam et malum.

AGO   iocare.

MIL   uin tu illam hodie sine [damno et] dispendio

tuo tuam libertam facere?

AGO   cupio, Milphio.

165 MIL   ego faciam ut facias. sunt tibi intus aurei

trecenti nummi Philippi?

AGO   sescenti quoque.

MIL   satis sunt trecenti.

AGO   quid eis facturu's?

MIL   tace.

totum lenonem tibi cum tota familia

dabo hodie dono.

AGO   qui id facturu's?

MIL   iam scies.

170   tuos Collybiscus nunc in urbe est uilicus;

eum hic non nouit leno. satin intellegis?

AGO   intellego hercle, sed quo euadas nescio.

MIL   non scis?

163 damno et *del. Gruterus*

AGO   I'm being torn apart by my desire for her. But dirt isn't dirtier than that pimp Lycus, her master.

MIL   Do you want to give him trouble now?

AGO   Yes, I do.

MIL   There, give him me.

AGO   Go and hang yourself! 160

MIL   Tell me honestly and seriously: do you want to give him a hard time?

AGO   I'm keen on it.

MIL   There, give him the same me. I'll make sure that he has both trouble and a hard time.

AGO   You're joking.

MIL   Do you want to make her your freedwoman today without expense on your part?

AGO   Yes, I do, Milphio.

MIL   I'll make you do it. Do you have three hundred gold 165 Philippics inside?

AGO   Even six hundred.

MIL   Three hundred is enough.

AGO   What are you going to do with it?

MIL   Be quiet. I'll give you the entire pimp with his entire household as a present today.

AGO   How are you going to do that?

MIL   You'll soon know. Your overseer Collybiscus is in town 170 now; the pimp here doesn't know him. Do you understand?

AGO   I do understand, but I don't know what you're getting at.

MIL   You don't know?

	AGO	non hercle.
	MIL	at ego iam faxo scies.
		ei dabitur aurum, ut ad lenonem deferat
175		dicatque se peregrinum esse ex alio oppido:
		se amare uelle atque opsequi animo suo;
		locum sibi uelle liberum praeberier
		ubi nequam faciat clam, ne quis sit arbiter.
		leno ad se accipiet auri cupidus ilico:
180		celabit hominem et aurum.
	AGO	consilium placet.
	MIL	rogato seruos ueneritne ad eum tuos.
		ill' me censebit quaeri: continuo tibi
		negabit. quid tu? dubitas quin extempulo
		dupli tibi, auri et hominis, fur leno siet?
185		neque id unde efficiat habet: ubi in ius uenerit,
		addicet praetor familiam totam tibi.
		ita decipiemus fouea lenonem Lycum.
	AGO	placet consilium.
	MIL	immo etiam, ubi expoliuero
		magis hoc tum demum dices: nunc etiam rude est.
190	AGO	ego in aedem Veneris eo, nisi quid uis, Milphio.
		Aphrodisia hodie sunt.
	MIL	scio. AGO oculos uolo
		meos delectare munditiis meretriciis.
	MIL	hoc primum agamus quod consilium cepimus.
		abeamus intro, ut Collybiscum uilicum
195		hanc perdoceamus ut ferat fallaciam.
	AGO	quamquam Cupido in corde uorsatur, tamen

---

13 Roman official with mainly judicial functions.

14 The annual feast of Aphrodite, Venus in Latin, the goddess of love.

AGO No.

MIL But I'll let you know now. Collybiscus will be given the
money so as to bring it to the pimp and say that he's a 175
stranger from another town; that he wants to make love
and enjoy himself; that he wants to be given a free space
where he can act naughtily in secret, so that no one is a
witness. Keen on the money, the pimp will receive him
at once: he'll be concealing man and money. 180

AGO I like the plan.

MIL You must then ask whether your slave has come to him.
He'll believe that I am the one being looked for; he'll
deny it at once. What do you think? Do you doubt that
the pimp will instantly be a thief liable for twice the sum
to you, for money and man? And he doesn't have the 185
means to settle. When he comes to court, the praetor[13]
will adjudge the entire household to you. In this way
we'll deceive the pimp Lycus and make him fall into a
trap.

AGO I like the plan.

MIL Yes, when I've polished it, you'll say so even more. Now
it's still crude.

AGO I'm going to the temple of Venus, unless you want any- 190
thing, Milphio. It's the Aphrodisia[14] today.

MIL I know.

AGO I want to feast my eyes on the pretty get-up of the pros-
titutes.

MIL Let's first attend to the plan we've made. Let's go inside
in order to instruct the overseer Collybiscus on how to 195
play his part in this deception.

AGO However busy Cupid is in my heart, I'll still obey you.

tibi auscultabo.

MIL   faciam ut facto gaudeas.
      inest amoris macula huic homini in pectore,
      sine damno magno quae elui ne utiquam potest.

200   itaque hic scelestus est homo leno Lycus,
      quoi iam infortuni intenta ballista est probe,
      quam ego hau multo post mittam e ballistario.
      sed Adelphasium eccam exit atque Anterastilis.
      haec est prior quae meum erum dementem facit.

205   sed euocabo. heus, i foras, Agorastocles,
      si uis uidere ludos iucundissumos.

AGO   quid istuc tumulti est, Milphio?

MIL   em amores tuos,
      si uis spectare.

AGO   o multa tibi di dent bona,
      quom hoc mi optulisti tam lepidum spectaculum!

I. ii: ADELPHASIVM. ANTERASTILIS. ANCILLA.
MILPHIO. AGORASTOCLES

210 ADE   negoti sibi qui uolet uim parare,
      nauem et mulierem, haec duo comparato.
      nam nullae magis res duae plus negoti
      habent, forte si occeperis exornare,
      [neque umquam sat istae duae res ornantur]

215   neque is ulla ornandi satis satietas est.
      atque haec, ut loquor, nunc domo docta dico.
      nam nos usque ab aurora ad hoc quod diei est,
      [postquam aurora illuxit, numquam concessamus,]
      ex industria ambae numquam concessamus

214 satis hae *P*, sat istae *Hermann*   *uersum del. Ritschl*
218 *del. Acidalius*

MIL   I'll make sure you're happy about what's done.

Exit AGORASTOCLES into his house.

MIL   This chap has the stain of love in his breast, which cannot
      be washed off without great loss in any way. So it's this   200
      crooked pimp Lycus against whom the missile of trouble
      is aimed properly now, which I'll send out from the cat-
      apult shortly. But look, Adelphasium is coming out, and
      Anterastilis, too. It's this first one that's driving my mas-
      ter crazy. But I'll call him out. (*into the house*) Hey, come   205
      out, Agorastocles, if you want to see a gorgeous show.

Enter AGORASTOCLES from his house.

AGO   What's that uproar, Milphio?
MIL   There, your sweetheart, if you want to watch her.
AGO   Oh! May the gods give you many good things for bring-
      ing me such a lovely sight!

*Enter ADELPHASIUM and ANTERASTILIS from the pimp's
house, followed by a slave girl; they are all dressed nicely and
carrying gifts. None of them notices Agorastocles and Milphio,
who overhear and comment on their conversation.*

ADE   A man who wants to create a lot of trouble for himself   210
      should get himself a ship and a woman, these two: no two
      things are more troublesome if you happen to start fitting
      them out, [nor are those two things ever sufficiently fit-
      ted out,] nor do they ever have a sufficient sufficiency of   215
      fitting out. And in saying this, I speak from my own ex-
      perience: from dawn to this time of day, [ever since the
      crack of dawn we've never ceased,] both of us have dili-

220	lauari aut fricari aut tergeri aut ornari,
	poliri, expoliri, pingi, fingi; et una
	binae singulis quae datae ancillae nobis,
	eae nos lauando, eluendo operam dederunt,
	aggerundaque aqua sunt uiri duo defessi.
225	apage sis, negoti quantum in muliere una est.
	sed uero duae, sat scio, maxumo uni
	populo quoilubet plus satis dare potis sunt,
	quae noctes diesque omni in aetate semper
	ornantur, lauantur, tergentur, poliuntur.
230	postremo modus muliebris nullus est.
231	neque umquam lauando et fricando
231ᵃ	scimus facere neniam.

nam quae lauta est nisi perculta est, meo quidem
   animo quasi illuta est.

ANTE miror equidem, soror, te istaec sic fabulari
      quae tam callida et docta sis et faceta.

| 235 | nam quom sedulo munditer nos habemus, |
| | uix aegreque amatorculos inuenimus. |

ADE ita est. uerum hoc unum tamen cogitato:
    modus omnibus rebus, soror, optumus est habitu.
    nimia omnia nimium exhibent negoti hominibus ex se.

240 ANTE soror, cogita, amabo, item nos perhiberi
       quam si salsa muriatica esse autumantur,
       sine omni lepore et sine suauitate:
       nisi multa aqua usque et diu macerantur,
       olent, salsa sunt, tangere ut non uelis.

245	item nos sumus,
245ᵃ	eius seminis mulieres sunt,
	insulsae admodum atque inuenustae
	sine munditia et sumptu.

gently never ceased to wash or scrub or dry or dress, 220
smooth, polish, paint ourselves, and do up our hair; and
with us we had two slave girls each that we were given
—they took care of washing and bathing us; and from
bringing us water two men got exhausted. Away with the 225
amount of trouble that's in a single woman! But two,
I know that well enough, can keep any one enormous
people you please busy; night and day at all times they
always make themselves up, wash, dry, and polish them-
selves. In short, there is no such thing as female mod- 230
eration. We never know how to put an end to washing
and rubbing. Yes, a woman that's washed is, to my mind,
unwashed as it were, unless she's highly polished.

ANTE I really am surprised, my sister, that you say that like this,
even though you're so clever and smart and witty. Af- 235
ter all, even though we eagerly keep ourselves tidy, we
barely and with difficulty find lovers.

ADE Yes. But think of this one thing nonetheless: moderation
is the best thing to have in all situations, my sister. An
excess of everything creates from it an excess of trouble
for man.

ANTE My sister, please consider that we're talked about in the 240
same way as salted fish is said to be too salty, without any
attraction and without sweetness; unless they're soaked
with a lot of water throughout and for a long time, they
stink, they're too salty, so that you don't want to touch
them. We are like that, women are of that stock, quite 245
unappetizing and unattractive without neatness and ex-
pense.

---

222 nobis ancillae *P, transp. Bothe*   233 miro[r] *Geppert*
238 optimum *P,* optimus *Leo*

	MIL	coqua est haec quidem, Agorastocles, ut ego opinor:
		scit muriatica ut maceret.
	AGO	quid molestu's?
250	ADE	soror, parce, amabo: sat est istuc alios
		dicere nobis, ne nosmet in nostra etiam uitia loquamur.
	ANTE	quiesco.
	ADE	ergo amo te. sed hoc nunc responde
		mihi: sunt hic omnia
254		quae ad deum pacem oportet ades-
254ᵃ		se?
	ANTE	omnia accuraui.
255	AGO	diem pulchrum et celebrem et uenustatis plenum,
		dignum Venere pol, quoi sunt Aphrodisia hodie.
	MIL	ecquid gratiae, quom huc foras te euocaui?
		iam num me decet donari
		cado uini ueteris? dic dare. nil respondes?
260		lingua huic excidit, ut ego opinor.
		quid hic, malum, astans opstipuisti?
	AGO	sine amem, ne opturba ac tace.
	MIL	taceo.
	AGO	si tacuisses, iam istuc "taceo" non gnatum foret.
	ANTE	eamus, mea soror.
	ADE	eho amabo, quid illo nunc properas?
	ANTE	rogas?
		quia erus nos apud aedem Veneris mantat.
	ADE	maneat pol. mane.
265		turba est nunc apud aram. an te ibi uis inter istas uor-
		sarier
		prosedas, pistorum amicas, reginas alicarias,
		miseras schoeno delibutas seruilicolas sordidas,

259 dari *P*, dare *Dousa*   266 reginas *T*, reliquias *BC*

MIL Agorastocles, she's a cook, I think: she knows how to soak salted fish.

AGO Why are you being a nuisance?

ADE My sister, please stop: it's enough that others say that to 250
us, without us talking against ourselves as well.

ANTE I'm quiet.

ADE Then thank you. But answer me this now: is everything here that ought to be here in order to gain the gods' favor?

ANTE I've got everything ready.

AGO (*to himself*) O beautiful day, festive and full of charm, 255
worthy indeed of Venus, in whose honor the Aphrodisia is celebrated today.

MIL Do I get any thanks for calling you out here? Shouldn't I be presented with a jar of old wine now? Say that you'll give me one. You aren't giving me any answer? (*to the* 260
audience) His tongue has fallen out, I think. (*to Ago-rastocles*) Why the blazes are you standing here dumb-founded?

AGO Let me be in love, stop interrupting me and be quiet.

MIL I'm quiet.

AGO If you'd been quiet, your "I'm quiet" wouldn't have been born.

ANTE Let's go, my dear sister.

ADE Hey, please, why are you rushing there now?

ANTE You ask? Because our master is waiting for us at the temple of Venus.

ADE Let him wait. Wait. Now there's a crowd at the altar. You 265
don't want to mingle there with those prostitutes ad-vertising themselves outside, do you? The girlfriends of millers, the queens of the groat mills, wretched, smeared

PLAUTUS

quae tibi olant stabulum statumque, sellam et sessibu-
    lum merum,
quas adeo hau quisquam umquam liber tetigit nec
    duxit domum,
270   seruolorum sordidulorum scorta diobolaria?
MIL   i in malam crucem! tun audes etiam seruos spernere,
propudium? quasi bella sit, quasi eampse reges ducti-
    tent,
monstrum mulieris, tantilla tanta uerba funditat,
quoius ego nebulai cyatho septem noctes non emam.
275 AGO   di immortales omnipotentes, quid est apud uos pul-
    chrius?
quid habetis qui mage immortalis uos credam esse
    quam ego siem
qui haec tanta oculis bona concipio? nam Venus non
    est Venus:
hanc equidem Venerem uenerabor me ut amet posthac
    propitia.
Milphio, heus [Milphio], ubi es?
MIL   assum apud te eccum.
AGO   at ego elixus sis uolo.
280 MIL   enim uero, ere, facis delicias.
AGO   de tequidem haec didici omnia.
MIL   etiamne ut ames eam quam numquam tetigeris?
AGO   nihil id quidem est:
deos quoque edepol et amo et metuo, quibus tamen
    apstineo manus.

279 Milphio *del. Bothe*

[15] A fragrant plant (botanical name *Cymbopogon schoenanthus*),
similar in appearance to grass.   [16] Different ways of soliciting are

42

with the juice of camel's hay,[15] mean, dirty? The ones who smell of the brothel and standing outside, of chair and seat,[16] whom moreover no free man has ever touched or taken home, the two-obol prostitutes of filthy slaves? 270

MIL (*as if to Adelphasium*) Go and be hanged! Do you actually dare to look down on slaves, you shameful creature? (*muttering to himself*) As if she were pretty, as if kings were in the habit of hiring her, that monstrosity of a woman, such a tiny creature pours forth such big words! I wouldn't buy seven nights with her for a ladleful of fog.

AGO Immortal, almighty gods, what is more beautiful among 275 you? What do you have because of which I should believe you to be more immortal than I am, who perceive these stupendous goods with my eyes? Yes, Venus isn't Venus: this girl I'll venerate as Venus so that she may show me her favor and love from now on. Milphio, hey, where are you?

MIL I'm here to serve you.

AGO But I wish the cook would serve you up.[17]

MIL Really, master, you're making fun of me. 280

AGO I for one have learned all this from you.

MIL Is it possible that you love a girl that you've never touched?

AGO That doesn't mean anything: I also love and fear the gods, who I keep my hands away from nonetheless.

referred to: being in a brothel, walking the streets, and sitting outside the brothel or behind the window front.

[17] The pun is difficult to reproduce. Milphio says *assum* in the meaning "I am present"; as the word can also mean "roasted," Agorastocles states that he prefers him boiled.

ANTE eu ecastor! quom ornatum aspicio nostrum ambarum, paenitet

exornatae ut simus.

ADE   immo uero sane commode;

285   nam pro erili et nostro quaestu satis bene ornatae sumus.

non enim potis est quaestus fieri, ni sumptus sequitur, scio,

et tamen quaestus non consistet, si eum sumptus superat, soror.

eo illud satiust, satis quod [satis est] habitu[s], ⟨hau satis est quod⟩ plus quam sat est.

AGO ita me di ament, ut illa me amet malim quam di, Milphio.

290   nam illa mulier lapidem silicem subigere ut se amet potest.

MIL pol id quidem hau mentire, nam tu es lapide silice stultior

qui hanc ames.

AGO   at uide sis, cum illac numquam limaui caput.

MIL curram igitur aliquo ad piscinam aut ad lacum, limum petam.

AGO quid eo opust?

MIL   ego dicam: ut illi et tibi limem caput.

295 AGO i in malam rem!

MIL   ibi sum equidem.

AGO   pergis?

MIL   taceo.

AGO   at perpetuo uolo.

288 [satis est] habitu[s], ⟨hau satis est quod⟩ *Leo*
295 perg—*A*, pergis ς, perdis *P*

ANTE Goodness! When I look at our dresses, I'm unhappy about how we're made up.

ADE No, we're made up quite appropriately: we're made up 285
well enough for our master's and our income. No income
can be generated unless expenditure accompanies it, I
know that, and yet the income will not remain if the
expenditure outweighs it, my sister. That's why what is
enough to have is better; what is more than enough is
not enough.

AGO As truly as the gods may love me, I'd prefer being loved
by her to being loved by the gods, Milphio: that woman 290
could force a flintstone to love her.

MIL You aren't lying in this: your love for her shows that
you're more stupid than a flintstone.[18]

AGO But do look, I've never rubbed my head with her admir-
ingly.[19]

MIL Then I'll run somewhere to a pond or a lake and get some
mire.

AGO What's that necessary for?

MIL I'll tell you: so that I can rub her head and yours admir-
ingly.

AGO Go to hell! 295

MIL I'm there already.

AGO You're continuing?

MIL I'm silent.

AGO But I want you to be silent for good.

---

[18] Also a term of abuse for a stupid person.

[19] *Caput limare*, "rub one's head," is a metaphor for kissing. I have added "admiringly" in the translation in order to reproduce the pun with *limus*, "mire, mud."

MIL enim uero, ere, meo me lacessis ludo et delicias facis.

ANTE satis nunc lepide ornatam credo, soror, te tibi uiderier;
      sed ubi exempla conferentur meretricum aliarum, ibi tibi
      erit cordolium si quam ornatam melius forte aspexeris.

300 ADE inuidia in me numquam innata est nec malitia, mea soror.
      bono med esse ingenio ornatam quam auro multo mauolo:
      aurum, id fortuna inuenitur, natura ingenium bonum.
      [bonam ego quam beatam me esse nimio dici mauolo.]
      meretricem pudorem gerere magis decet quam puram:

305   [magisque id meretricem, pudorem quam aurum gerere, condecet.]
      pulchrum ornatum turpes mores peius caeno collinunt,
      lepidi mores turpem ornatum facile factis comprobant.

AGO eho tu, uin tu facinus facere lepidum et festiuom?

MIL   uolo.

AGO potesne mi auscultare?

MIL   possum.

AGO   abi domum ac suspende te.

310 MIL quam ob rem?

AGO   quia iam numquam audibis uerba tot tam suauia.
      quid tibi opust uixisse? ausculta mihi modo ac suspende te.

MIL siquidem tu es mecum futurus pro uua passa pensilis.

AGO at ego amo hanc.

MIL   at ego esse et bibere.

ADE   eho tu, quid ais?

303 *del. Ritschl*   305 *del. Guyet*

46

MIL   Really, master, you're provoking me at my own game and making fun of me.

ANTE   I believe that you consider yourself dressed nicely enough now, my sister; but when comparisons with the other prostitutes are made, then you'll suffer from heartache if by chance you spot one who is better dressed.

ADE   Jealousy or malice has never been a characteristic of 300
mine, my dear sister. I'd rather be adorned with a good nature than with much gold; gold comes through luck, but a good nature comes from within. [I'd much rather be called good than rich.] It's more suitable for a prostitute to wear modesty than purple. [And it's more appro- 305
priate for a prostitute to wear modesty than gold.] A bad character defiles a pretty dress more than filth, a good character easily ennobles an ugly dress through its actions.

AGO   (*still to Milphio*) Hey you, do you want to do a charming and cheerful deed?

MIL   Yes, I do.

AGO   Can you obey me?

MIL   Yes, I can.

AGO   Go home and hang yourself.

MIL   What for?   310

AGO   Because now you'll never again hear so many words as sweet as these. What do you need to have lived for? Just obey me and hang yourself.

MIL   Yes, if you hang beside me like a bunch of raisins.

AGO   But I love this girl.

MIL   But I love eating and drinking.

ADE   (*still to Anterastilis*) Hey you, what do you say?

ANTE   quid rogas?

ADE   uiden tu? pleni oculi sorderum qui erant, iam splen-
      dent mihi?

315 ANTE immo etiam medio oculo paulum sordet. cedo sis, de-
      teram.

AGO   ut quidem tu huius oculos illutis manibus tractes aut
      teras?

ANTE nimia nos socordia hodie tenuit.

ADE   qua de re, opsecro?

ANTE quia non iam dudum ante lucem ad aedem Veneris
      uenimus,
      primae ut inferremus ignem in aram.

ADE   aha! non facto est opus:

320   quae habent nocturna ora, noctu sacruficatum ire oc-
      cupant.
      prius quam Venus expergiscatur, prius deproperant
      sedulo
      sacruficare; nam uigilante Venere si ueniant eae,
      ita sunt turpes, credo ecastor Venerem ipsam e fano fu-
      gent.

AGO   Milphio.

MIL   edepol Milphionem miserum! quid nunc uis tibi?

325 AGO opsecro hercle, ut mulsa loquitur!

MIL   nil nisi laterculos,
      sesumam papaueremque, triticum et frictas nuces.

AGO   ecquid amare uideor?

MIL   damnum, quod Mercurius minime amat.

AGO   namque edepol lucrum ⟨ullum⟩ amare nullum ama-
      torem addecet.

ADE   eamus, mea germana.

    315 dexteram Ω, deteram *Scaliger*   328 ullum *add. Brix*

ANTE   What do you ask?

ADE   Can you see? Are my eyes, which were full of dirt, shiny now?

ANTE   No, in the middle of the eye there is still a speck of dirt.   315
       Come here, I'll wipe it for you.

AGO   (*as if to Anterastilis*) Should you really handle or rub her eyes with dirty hands?

ANTE   Excessive indolence has held us in its grip today.

ADE   Indolence about what, please?

ANTE   Because we didn't go to the temple of Venus a long time ago, before sunlight, so that we'd be the first to put fire onto the altar.

ADE   Ah! There's no need to do so; girls who have faces as ugly   320
       as night are the first to go to sacrifice at night. Even before Venus gets up, they eagerly hurry to sacrifice: ugly as they are, if they came while Venus was awake, I do believe they'd drive Venus herself out of her temple.

AGO   Milphio!

MIL   Poor Milphio! What do you want now?

AGO   Please, how her lips drip honey!   325

MIL   Yes, nothing but biscuits, sesame and poppy, wheat and ground nuts.

AGO   Do I seem to be in love at all?

MIL   Yes, with loss, which Mercury[20] doesn't love at all.

AGO   Indeed, no lover ought to love any gain.

ADE   Let's go, my dear sister.

[20] The god of commerce.

	ANTE	age sis, ut lubet.
	ADE	sequere hac.
	ANTE	sequor.
330	MIL	eunt hae.
	AGO	quid si adeamus?
	MIL	adeas.
	AGO	primum prima salua sis,

et secunda tu [in] secundo salue in pretio; tertia
salue extra pretium.

	ANC	tum pol ego et oleum et operam perdidi.
	AGO	quo te agis?
	ADE	egone? in aedem Veneris.
	AGO	quid eo?
	ADE	ut Venerem propitiem.
	AGO	eho, an irata est?
	ADE	propitia hercle est.
	AGO	uel ego pro illa spondeo.
335		quid tu ais?
	ADE	quid mihi molestu's, opsecro?
	AGO	aha, tam saeuiter!
	ADE	mitte, amabo.
	AGO	quid festinas? turba nunc illi est.
	ADE	scio.

sunt illi aliae quas spectare ego et me spectari uolo.

	AGO	qui lubet spectare turpis, pulchram spectandam dare?
	ADE	quia apud aedem Veneris hodie est mercatus mere-
		tricius:
340		eo conueniunt mercatores, ibi ego me ostendi uolo.
	AGO	inuendibili merci oportet ultro emptorem adducere:

331 in *del. Camerarius*

50

ANTE Go on, please, as you wish.

ADE Follow me this way.

ANTE Yes.

MIL They're going.   330

AGO What if we approach them?

MIL Do.

AGO (*to Adelphasium*) First my greetings to the one who goes
     first, (*to Anterastilis*) then my greetings of second
     rank to you who come second; (*to the servant*) my greet-
     ings without any rank at all to you, the third.

MAID Then I've wasted both lamp oil and effort.

AGO (*to Adelphasium*) Where are you going?

ADE I? To the temple of Venus.

AGO Why there?

ADE In order to make Venus well disposed.

AGO Hey, she's not angry, is she?

ADE She's certainly well disposed.

AGO If you wish, I can guarantee that on her behalf. What do   335
     you say? (*grabs her*)

ADE Why are you annoying me, please?

AGO Ah, so fierce!

ADE Let go, please. (*pushes him away*)

AGO Why are you in a rush? There's a crowd there now.

ADE I know. There are others there whom I want to see and
     be seen by.

AGO Why do you wish to watch ugly ones and show a pretty
     one?

ADE Because at the temple of Venus there's a prostitute fair
     today; there the merchants come together, there I want   340
     to be presented.

AGO For ware that can't be sold one ought to take the initia-

proba merx facile emptorem reperit, tam etsi in ap-
    struso sita est.
quid ais tu? quando illi apud me mecum palpas et
    λαλεῖς?
ADE   quo die Orcus Accherunte mortuos amiserit.
345 AGO   sunt mihi intus nescioquot nummi aurei lymphatici.
ADE   deferto ad me, faxo actutum constiterit lymphaticum.
MIL   bellula hercle!
AGO   i dierecte in maxumam malam crucem!
MIL   quam magis aspecto, tam magis est nimbata et nugae
    merae.
ADE   segrega sermonem. taedet.
AGO   age, sustolle hoc amiculum:
350 ADE   pura sum, comperce amabo me attrectare, Agorasto-
    cles.
AGO   quid agam nunc?
ADE   si sapias, curam hanc facere compendi potest.
AGO   quid? ego non te curem? quid ais, Milphio?
MIL   ecce odium meum!
quid me uis?
AGO   quor mi haec irata est?
MIL   quor haec irata est tibi?
quor ego id curem? namque istaec magis mea est cura-
    tio.
355 AGO   iam hercle tu periisti, nisi illam mihi tam tranquillam
    facis

343 palpas et lallas *A*, caput et corpus copulas *P*   *fortasse* [caput
et] corpus copulas *aut* παίζεις καὶ λαλεῖς
352 nunc Ω, non *Acidalius*

tive in bringing a buyer; good ware easily finds a buyer, even if it's placed out of view. What do you say? When are you cuddling and chitchatting there at my place?

ADE On the day Orcus[21] sends the dead out of the Underworld.

AGO Inside I have some gold coins jingling madly. 345

ADE Bring them to me, I'll make sure that the madness stops at once.

MIL Really pretty!

AGO (*to Milphio*) Go and be hanged!

MIL The more I look at her, the stormier and trashier she is. (*walks over to the servant girl and starts flirting*)

ADE (*to Agorastocles*) Break off the conversation. I'm fed up.

AGO Go on, lift up this little cloak. (*grabs her*)

ADE I'm pure, please refrain from groping me, Agorastocles. 350

AGO (*dejectedly*) What should I do now?

ADE If you're wise, you can spare yourself this worry.

AGO (*to Adelphasium*) What? I shouldn't worry about you now?[22] (*to Milphio*) What do you say, Milphio?

MIL Look, my nuisance! What do you want from me?

AGO Why is she angry with me?

MIL Why is she angry with you? Why should I care about that? (*pointing to the servant*) That girl there is what I care about.

AGO This instant you're dead, unless you make her as calm 355

---

[21] The god of the Underworld.

[22] Adelphasium meant that Agorastocles need not worry about the continuation of their relationship: by setting her free he would unite them for good. Agorastocles misunderstands and believes that she does not want him to look after her, i.e., that she wants to break up with him.

		quam mare olim est quom ibi alcedo pullos educit
		suos.
	MIL	quid faciam?
	AGO	exora, blandire, palpa.
	MIL	faciam sedulo.
		sed uide sis ne tu oratorem hunc pugnis pectas postea.
	AGO	non faciam.
	ADE	non aequos in me es, sed morare et male facis.
360		bene promittis multa ex multis: omnia in cassum ca-
		dunt.
		liberare iurauisti me hau semel sed centiens:
		dum te exspecto, neque ego usquam aliam mihi paraui
		copiam
		neque istuc usquam apparet; ita nunc seruio nihilo mi-
		nus.
		i, soror. apscede tu a me.
	AGO	perii! ecquid agis, Milphio?
365	MIL	mea uoluptas, mea delicia, mea uita, mea amoenitas,
		meus ocellus, meum labellum, mea salus, meum
		sauium,
		meum mel, meum cor, mea colustra, meus molliculus
		caseus—
	AGO	mene ego illaec patiar praesente dici? discrucior miser,
		nisi ego illum iubeo quadrigis cursim ad carnuficem
		rapi.
370	MIL	—noli, amabo, suscensere ero meo causa mea.
		ego faxo, si non irata es, ninnium, pro te dabit

357 palpa *A*, expalpa *P Nonius*

toward me as the sea is at the time when the halcyon
hatches its young ones there.[23]

MIL What should I do?

AGO Persuade her, flatter her, coax her.

MIL I'll do my best. But please make sure that you don't comb
this orator with your fists afterward.

AGO I won't do so.

ADE (*to Agorastocles*) You aren't fair toward me, but you
waste my time and treat me badly. You make a lot of nice   360
promises one after another; they all come to nothing.
Not once but a hundred times you've sworn to free me.
While I was waiting for you, I didn't acquire any other
support for myself anywhere and your promise never
materializes. So now I'm just as much a slave as I was
before. (*to Anterastilis*) Come, my sister. (*to Agorasto-
cles*) You, go away from me.

AGO I'm dead! Won't you do something, Milphio?

MIL (*to Adelphasium*) My darling, my pleasure, my life, my   365
charm, apple of my eye, my lip, my salvation, my kiss, my
honey, my heart, my beestings, my soft little cheese—

AGO (*interrupting*) Should I tolerate those things being said
in my presence? Poor me, I'm being tortured, unless I
have that chap dragged to the hangman by a chariot at
top speed.

MIL (*still to Adelphasium*)—please don't be angry with my   370
master for my sake. If you're not angry, my little doll, I'll
make sure that he'll pay for you and that he'll make you

---

[23] The time when halcyons, often identified with kingfishers, were
believed to hatch their eggs in nests floating on the sea is one week
before and one after the winter solstice (December 14–28). During this
period the sea was said to be particularly calm.

ac te faciet ut sis ciuis Attica atque libera.
quin adire sinis? quin tibi qui bene uolunt, bene uis
    item?
si ante quid mentitust, nunciam dehinc erit uerax tibi.
375   sine te exorem, sine prehendam auriculis, sine dem
    sauium.

ADE apscede hinc sis, sycophanta par ero.
MIL   at scin quo modo?
iam hercle ego faciam ploratillum, nisi te facio propi-
    tiam,
atque hic ne me uerberetillum faciat, nisi te propitio,
380   male formido: noui ego huius mores morosi malos.
    quam ob rem amabo, mea uoluptas, sine te hoc exora-
    rier.

AGO non ego homo trioboli sum, nisi ego illi mastigiae
exturbo oculos atque dentes. em uoluptatem tibi!
em mel, em cor, em labellum, em salutem, em sauium!
MIL impias, ere, te: oratorem uerberas.
AGO   iam istoc magis.
385 [etiam ocellum addam et labellum et linguam.
MIL   ecquid facies modi?]
AGO sicine ego te orare iussi?
MIL   quo modo ergo orem?
AGO   rogas?
sic enim diceres, sceleste: "huius uoluptas, te opsecro,
huius mel, huius cor, huius labellum, huius lingua,
    huius sauium,
huius delicia, huius salus amoena, huius festiuitas;
390   huius colustra, huius dulciculus caseus," mastigia;

381 non Ω, ne *Gratwick*   385 *del. Leo*
386 orare *A*, orares *P*

56

a free citizen of Athens. Why don't you let him approach you? Why don't you wish those well who wish you well? Even if he told you any lie before, he'll be truthful to you from now on. Let me persuade you, let me grab you by 375 the ears, let me give you a kiss.[24]

ADE   Go away, will you, you impostor equal to your master!

MIL   But do you know how? I'll shed tears now if I don't make you well disposed, and I'm terribly afraid that this chap will give me a beating unless I make you well disposed. I know the bad character of this unreasonable person. So 380 please, my darling, let yourself be persuaded to do this.

AGO   I'm not worth a triobol piece unless I knock out this whipping stock's eyes and teeth. (*hits Milphio*) There's your darling! There's your honey, there's your heart, there's your lip, there's your salvation, there's your kiss!

MIL   You're staining yourself morally, master: you're beating an envoy.

AGO   All the more so for that statement! (*hits him again*) [I'll 385 also add the apple of the eye and the lip and tongue.

MIL   Aren't you ever going to stop?]

AGO   Did I tell you to plead like this?

MIL   Then how should I plead?

AGO   You ask? Well, you should have spoken like this, you criminal: "his darling, I entreat you, his honey, his heart, his lip, his tongue, his kiss, his pleasure, his charming salvation, his joy; his beestings, his sweet little cheese," 390

[24] Grabbing someone's ears precedes kissing and is often synonymous with it.

390ᵃ   ["huius cor, huius studium, huius sauium," mastigia;]
    omnia illa, quae dicebas tua esse, ea memorares mea.

MIL opsecro hercle te, uoluptas huius atque odium meum,
    huius amica mammeata, mea inimica et maleuola,
    oculus huius, lippitudo mea, mel huius, fel meum,
395 ut tu huic irata ne sis aut, si id fieri non potest,
    capias restim ac te suspendas cum ero et uostra familia.
    nam mihi iam uideo propter te uictitandum sorbilo,
    itaque iam quasi ostreatum tergum ulceribus gestito
    propter amorem uostrum.

ADE   amabo, men prohibere postulas
400 ne te uerberet magis quam ne mendax me aduorsum
    siet?

ANTE aliquid huic responde, amabo, commode, ne incommo-
    dus
    nobis sit. nam detinet nos de nostro negotio.

ADE uerum. etiam tibi hanc amittam noxiam unam, Agoras-
    tocles.
    non sum irata.

AGO   non es?

ADE   non sum.

AGO   da ergo, ut credam, sauium.
405 ADE mox dabo, quom ab re diuina rediero.

AGO   i ergo strenue.

ADE sequere me, soror.

AGO   atque audin?

ADE   etiam?

AGO   Veneri dicito
    multum meis uerbis salutem.

ADE   dicam.

390ᵃ *del. Acidalius*

58

  you whipping stock; ["his heart, his desire, his kiss," you
  whipping stock;] all the things that you said were yours
  you should have called mine.

MIL (*to Adelphasium*) I entreat you, his darling and object of
  my hate, his full-breasted girlfriend and my enemy and
  opponent, apple of his eye and my eyesore, his honey
  and my gall, not to be angry with him or, if that's impos- 395
  sible, to take a rope and to hang yourself with your mas-
  ter and household. Yes, I can see now that because of you
  I have to keep myself alive one sip at a time, and so I now
  carry around my back striped like an oyster from weals
  because of your love.

ADE Please, do you expect me to prevent him from beating 400
  you any more than from lying to me?

ANTE Please give him some pleasant answer so that he won't
  be a nuisance to us: he's keeping us from our business.

ADE (*to Anterastilis*) True. (*to Agorastocles*) Again I'll let you
  get away with this one crime, Agorastocles. I'm not
  angry.

AGO You aren't?

ADE No, I'm not.

AGO Then give me a kiss so that I may believe you.

ADE I'll give you one in due course when I come back from 405
  the sacrifice.

AGO Then go quickly.

ADE Follow me, my sister. (*turns to go*)

AGO And can you hear me?

ADE Again?

AGO Give my best regards to Venus.

ADE Yes.

AGO   atque hoc audi.

ADE   quid est?

AGO paucis uerbis rem diuinam facito. atque audin? respice.
      respexit. idem edepol Venerem credo facturam tibi.

I. iii: AGORASTOCLES. MILPHIO

410 AGO quid nunc mi es auctor, Milphio?

MIL   ut me uerberes
      atque auctionem facias: nam impunissume
      tibi quidem hercle uendere hasce aedis licet.

AGO quid iam?

MIL   maiorem partem in ore habitas meo.

AGO supersede istis uerbis.

MIL   quid nunc uis tibi?

415 AGO trecentos Philippos Collybisco uilico
      dedi dudum, prius quam me euocauisti foras.
      nunc opsecro te, Milphio, hanc per dexteram
      perque hanc sororem laeuam perque oculos tuos
420   perq' meos amores perque Adelphasium meam
      perque tuam libertatem—

MIL   em nunc nihil opsecras.

AGO —mi Milphidisce, mea Commoditas, mea Salus,
      fac quod facturum te promisisti mihi,
      ut ego hunc lenonem perdam.

MIL   perfacile id quidem est.
      i, adduce testis tecum; ego intus interim

419 *uersum del. Ussing*

---

[25] Agorastocles puns on the double meaning of the verb *respicere*: when he says to Adelphasium that she should do so, he simply means

AGO   And listen to this.

ADE   What is it?

AGO   Make your sacrifice with few words. (*as the girls are leaving*) And can you hear me? Look well at me. (*Adelphasium briefly looks back*) She did look well at me. I do believe Venus will do the same to you.[25]

Exeunt ADELPHASIUM, ANTERASTILIS, *and the* SLAVE GIRL *to the left.*

AGO   What do you advise me to do now, Milphio?   410

MIL   To beat me and hold an auction: you can sell this house without any ill effects at all.

AGO   How so?

MIL   You spend most of your time in my face.[26]

AGO   Put an end to those words.

MIL   What do you want now?

AGO   I gave three hundred Philippics to the overseer Collybis- 415
cus a while ago, before you called me out. Now I entreat
you by this right hand, Milphio, and by its sister, this left
one, and by your eyes and by my love and by my Adel-
phasium and by your freedom—   420

MIL   (*interrupting*) There, now you aren't entreating me at all.

AGO   —my dear little Milphio, my Opportunity, my Salvation, do what you promised me you would, so that I can ruin this pimp.

MIL   That's very easy. Go, bring witnesses with you. Mean-

that she should look back; but the word also has the meaning "to treat kindly," and this is what he promises that Venus will do.

[26] By beating him.

425		iam et ornamentis meis et sycophantiis
		tuom exornabo uilicum. propera atque abi.
	AGO	fugio.
	MIL	meum est istuc magis officium quam tuom.
	AGO	egone, egone, si istuc lepide effexis—
	MIL	i modo.
	AGO	—ut non ego te hodie—
	MIL	abi modo.
	AGO	—emittam manu—
430	MIL	i modo.
	AGO	—non hercle meream—
	MIL	oh!
	AGO	uah!
	MIL	abi modo.
	AGO	—quantum Accherunte est mortuorum—
	MIL	etiamne abis?
	AGO	—nec quantum aquai est in mari—
	MIL	abiturun es?
	AGO	—nec nubes omnes quantum est—
	MIL	pergin pergere?
	AGO	—nec stellae in caelo—
	MIL	pergin auris tundere?
435	AGO	—neque hoc neque illud neque—enim uero serio—
		neque hercle uero—quid opust uerbis? quippini?
		quod uno uerbo—dicere hic quiduis licet—
		neque hercle uero serio—scin quo modo?
		ita me di amabunt—uin bona dicam fide?
440		quod hic inter nos liceat—ita me Iuppiter—
		scin quam uidetur? credin quod ego fabuler?
	MIL	si nequeo facere ut abeas, egomet abiero;

	while now I'll get your overseer ready with my get-up	425
	and tricks. Hurry and leave.	
AGO	I'm running away.	
MIL	This is my job more than yours.	
AGO	If you sort this out nicely, I, I—	
MIL	(*interrupting*) Just go!	
AGO	—if today I don't—	
MIL	(*interrupting*) Just go!	
AGO	—set you free—	
MIL	(*interrupting*) Just go!	430
AGO	—I really wouldn't deserve—	
MIL	(*interrupting*) Oh!	
AGO	Bah!	
MIL	Just go!	
AGO	—as many as there are dead people in the Under- world—	
MIL	(*interrupting*) Won't you go away?	
AGO	—nor as much as there is water in the sea—	
MIL	(*interrupting*) Will you not go away?	
AGO	—nor all the clouds there are—	
MIL	(*interrupting*) Are you continuing to go on?	
AGO	—nor stars in the sky—	
MIL	(*interrupting*) Are you continuing to beat my ears?	
AGO	—neither this nor that nor—seriously—honestly—what need is there for words? Why not? With a single word— one can say anything here—nor, in honest truth—do you know how? As truly as the gods will love me—do you want me to speak in good faith? What here among us one can—as truly as Jupiter—do you know how firmly it's decided? Don't you believe what I say?	435 440
MIL	If I can't make you go away, I'll go away myself; your	

nam isti quidem hercle orationi Oedipo
opust coniectore, qui Sphingi interpres fuit.
445 AGO illic hinc iratus abiit. nunc mihi cautio est
ne meamet culpa meo amori obiexim moram.
ibo atque arcessam testis, quando iubet Amor
me oboedientem esse seruo liberum.

ACTVS II

II. i: LYCVS. ANTAMYNIDES

LYC di illum infelicent omnes qui post hunc diem
450 leno ullam Veneri umquam immolarit hostiam
quiue ullum turis granum sacruficauerit.
nam ego hodie infelix dis meis iratissumis
sex immolaui agnos nec potui tamen
propitiam Venerem facere uti esset mihi.
455 quoniam litare nequeo, abii illim ilico
456 iratus, uotui exta prosecarier;
456^a neque ea poricere uolui, quoniam non bona
456^b haruspex dixit: deam esse indignam credidi.
eo pacto auarae Veneri pulchre adii manum.
quando id quod sat erat satis habere noluit,
ego pausam feci. sic ago, sic me decet.
460 ego faxo posthac di deaeque ceteri
contentiores mage erunt atque auidi minus,

447 amor iubet *P, transp. Luchs*
456^a–56^b *uersus non feruntur in A, del. Geppert*

---

[27] The Sphinx, a creature that is part woman, part lion, and part
bird, asked passersby a riddle, and anyone who could not answer was

speech needs Oedipus as interpreter, who was the translator for the Sphinx.[27]

Exit MILPHIO *into the house of Agorastocles.*

AGO He's left angrily. Now I need to be on my guard so that 445
I won't delay my love through my own fault. I'll go and
summon witnesses, since Love commands me, a free
man, to obey my slave.

Exit AGORASTOCLES *to the right.*

ACT TWO

Enter LYCUS *from the left.*

LYC May all the gods ruin the pimp who after this day ever 450
offers a single victim to Venus or who sacrifices a single
grain of incense: poor me, when my gods were in a rage
I offered six lambs today and still couldn't bring it about
that Venus would be well disposed to me. Since I was 455
unable to get a good omen, I immediately went away
from there angrily and forbade the innards to be cut up;
nor did I want to offer them, since the soothsayer pronounced them bad. I thought the goddess didn't deserve
them. In this way I beautifully tricked greedy Venus. As
she didn't want to be satisfied with what was satisfactory,
I stopped. That's what I do, that's what suits me. I'll make 460
sure that from now on the other gods and goddesses will
be more contented and less avaricious when they know

devoured. Oedipus was the only one who could solve her riddle, which
made her kill herself.

quom scibunt Veneri ut adierit leno manum.
condigne haruspex, non homo trioboli,
omnibus in extis aibat portendi mihi
465 malum damnumque et deos esse iratos mihi.
quid ei diuini aut humani aequom est credere?
mina mihi argenti dono postilla data est.
sed quaeso, ubinam illic restitit miles modo
qui hanc mihi donauit, quem ego uocaui ad prandium?
470 sed eccum incedit.

ANTA   ita ut occepi dicere,
lenulle, de illac pugna Pentetronica,
quom sexaginta milia hominum uno die
uolaticorum manibus occidi meis—

LYC uolaticorum hominum?

ANTA   ita dico quidem.

475 LYC an, opsecro, usquam sunt homines uolatici?

ANTA fuere. uerum ego interfeci.

LYC   quo modo
potuisti?

ANTA   dicam. uiscum legioni dedi
fundasque; eo praesternebant folia farferi.

LYC quoi rei?

ANTA   ad fundas uiscus ne adhaeresceret.

480 LYC perge. optume hercle periuras. quid postea?

ANTA in fundas uisci indebant grandiculos globos,
eo illos uolantis iussi funditarier.
quid multa uerba? quemquem uisco offenderant,

---

471 pentetronica Ω, Ptenornithica *Gronovius*, Ptenolatronica *Leo*,
alii alia
479 ne ad fundas uiscus adhaeresceret Ω, *transp. Bothe*

how the pimp tricked Venus. Equally worthily, the sooth-
sayer, a man not worth three obols, said that in all the
innards bad luck and loss were shown for me and that   465
the gods were angry with me. In what divine or human
matter is it right to trust him? After that I was given
a silver mina as a present. But please, where on earth
did that soldier stop now who gave me that present and
whom I invited for lunch? But look, he's coming along.   470

Enter ANTAMYNIDES *from the left.*

ANTA As I began to tell you, my little pimp, about that Pente-
tronian[28] battle, when I killed sixty thousand flying men
with my hands in one day—
LYC (*interrupting*) Flying men?
ANTA That's what I'm saying.
LYC Please, there aren't flying men anywhere, are there?   475
ANTA There were. But I killed them.
LYC How could you do that?
ANTA I'll tell you. I gave birdlime and slings to my legion;[29]
within they placed coltsfoot leaves.
LYC What for?
ANTA So that the birdlime wouldn't stick to the slings.
LYC Continue. You're perjuring yourself perfectly. What   480
next?
ANTA They put largish blobs of birdlime into the slings, and
with that I told them to shoot down those flying men.
Why should I use many words? Those who they hit with

[28] An invented place-name.
[29] Military unit of 4,200 to 6,000 soldiers; Antamynides claims to
be a military leader.

484–
85

       tam crebri ad terram reccidebant quam pira.
       ut quisque acciderat, eum necabam ilico
       per cerebrum pinna sua sibi quasi turturem.

LYC   si hercle istuc umquam factum est, tum me Iuppiter
       faciat ut semper sacruficem neque umquam litem.

490 ANTA an mi haec non credis?

LYC   credo, ut mi aequom est credier.
       age eamus intro.

ANTA   dum exta referuntur, uolo
       narrare tibi etiam unam pugnam.

LYC   nil moror.

ANTA ausculta.

LYC   non hercle auscultabo.

ANTA   quo modo?
       colaphis quidem hercle tuom iam dilidam caput,

495   nisi aut auscultas aut . . . is in malam crucem.

LYC   malam crucem ibo potius.

ANTA   certumne est tibi?

LYC   certum.

ANTA   tum tu igitur die bono, Aphrodisiis,
       addice tuam mi meretricem minusculam.

LYC   ita res diuina mihi fuit: res serias

500   omnis extollo ex hoc die in alium diem.

ANTA profestos festos habeam decretum est mihi.

LYC   nunc hinc eamus intro. sequere hac me.

ANTA   sequor.
       in hunc diem iam tuos sum mercennarius.

    484–85 accidebant *P*, aecidebant *uel* recidebant *A*

the birdlime fell back on the ground as thickly as pears. 485
As soon as each one fell down, I killed him on the spot
with his own feather through his brains like a turtle-
dove.

LYC If that ever happened, then may Jupiter make sure that
I always sacrifice and never get a good omen.

ANTA You don't believe me, do you? 490

LYC I believe you just as much as I deserve to be believed.[30]
Come on, let's go in.

ANTA While the innards are being brought back, I want to tell
you about one more battle.

LYC No thanks.

ANTA Listen!

LYC No, I won't listen.

ANTA How's that? I'll smash your head to pieces with blows
right now, unless you either listen or . . . go and be 495
hanged.

LYC I'd rather go and be hanged.

ANTA Are you sure?

LYC Yes.

ANTA Then assign your younger prostitute to me on this auspi-
cious day, the Aphrodisia.

LYC The way my sacrifice went, I'll postpone all serious mat- 500
ters from this day to another.

ANTA I'm resolved to treat feast days as business days.

LYC Now let's go in. Follow me this way.

ANTA Yes. For this day now I'm your hired servant.

Exeunt LYCUS and ANTAMYNIDES into the former's house.

[30] Lycus admits that pimps cannot be trusted.

ACTVS III

III. i: AGORASTOCLES. ADVOCATI

AGO ita me di ament, tardo amico nihil est quicquam
    nequius,
505 praesertim homini amanti, qui quicquid agit properat
    omnia.
sicut ego hos duco aduocatos, homines spissigradissu-
    mos,
tardiores quam corbitae sunt in tranquillo mari.
atque equidem hercle dedita opera amicos fugitaui
    senes:
scibam aetate tardiores, metui meo amori moram.
510 nequiquam hos procos mi elegi loripedes, tardissumos.
quin si ituri hodie estis, ite, aut ite hinc in malam cru-
    cem.
sicine oportet ire amicos homini amanti operam da-
    tum?
nam istequidem gradus succretust cribro pollinario;
nisi cum pedicis condidicistis istoc grassari gradu.
515 ADVO heus tu, quamquam nos uidemur tibi plebeii et pau-
    peres,
si nec recte dicis nobis, diues de summo loco,
diuitem audacter solemus mactare infortunio.
nec tibi nos obnoxii [sumus] istuc quid tu ames aut
    oderis:
quom argentum pro capite dedimus, nostrum dedimus,
    non tuom;
520 liberos nos esse oportet. nos te nihili pendimus,
ne tuo nos amori seruos [tuos] esse addictos censeas.

ACT THREE

Enter AGORASTOCLES *and his* ADVOCATES *from the right; in the ensuing dialogue, Agorastocles typically addresses all advocates, but only one of them replies as their spokesman.*

AGO   (*to the audience*) As truly as the gods may love me, nothing is more useless than a slow friend, especially for a 505 lovesick man, who rushes everything he does. For instance, I'm bringing along these advocates, the most slow-moving of men, slower than freight ships are on a calm sea. And I deliberately avoided my elderly friends: I knew they'd be slower because of their age, and I feared delay for my love. But I've gained no advantage 510 by choosing these attendants for myself, leaden-footed, very slow ones. (*to the advocates*) If you're going today, go, or go and be hanged! Should friends walk like this in order to support a lovesick man? That step of yours has been sifted through a flour sieve;[31] unless you learned to walk with shackles at that pace.

ADVO Hey you, even though we seem low-class and poor to 515 you, if you insult us, you rich man of good birth, we usually boldly punish the rich man with trouble. We aren't bound by what you love or hate. When we paid money for our freedom, we paid our own money, not yours. We 520 ought to be free. We don't care about you, so don't believe we are bond slaves to your love. It's more appropri-

[31] Because of its small size.

---

504 inequius *P*, nequius *uel* inaequius *edd.*
518 sumus *del. Bothe*   521 tuos *del. Pylades*

liberos homines per urbem modico magis par est gradu
ire, seruile esse duco festinantem currere.
praesertim in re populi placida atque interfectis hosti-
bus
525   non decet tumultuari. sed si properabas magis,
pridie nos te aduocatos huc duxisse oportuit.
ne tu opinere, hau quisquam hodie nostrum curret per
uias
nec nos populus pro cerritis insectabit lapidibus.
AGO at si ad prandium me in aedem uos dixissem ducere,
530   uinceretis ceruom cursu uel gralatorem gradu;
nunc uos quia mihi aduocatos dixi et testis ducere,
podagrosi estis ac uicistis cocleam tarditudine.
ADVO an uero non iusta causa est quor curratur celeriter
ubi bibas, edas de alieno quantum uis usque ad fatim,
535   quod tu inuitus numquam reddas domino de quoio
ederis?
sed tamen cum eo cum quiqui, quamquam sumus pau-
perculi,
est domi quod edimus, ne nos tam contemptim con-
teras.
quicquid est pauxillulum illuc, nostrum id omne, non
tuom est,
nec nos quemquam flagitamus nec nos quisquam flagi-
tat.
540   tua causa nemo nostrorum est suos rupturus ramites.
AGO nimis iracundi estis: equidem haec uobis dixi per io-
cum.

523 seruile B, seruili D, seruuli C (*fortasse recte*)
534 uelis CD, om. B, ueis *edd.*
538 intus est P, non tuomst *Bentley*

ate for free men to walk through the city with measured step; whereas I believe it to be right for slaves to run in a hurry. Especially when the state is at peace and our enemies have been killed, one ought not to make a com- 525 motion. But if you were in such a rush, you ought to have brought us here as advocates the day before. Just so that you don't get a false impression, none of us will run through the streets today and the people won't assail us as madmen with stones.

AGO But if I'd said I was taking you to the temple[32] to lunch, you'd have beaten a hind in its run or a stilt-walker 530 in his step; now that I've said I was taking you as my advocates and witnesses, you are gouty and have beaten a snail in its sluggishness.

ADVO Well, isn't there a just cause for running quickly to a place where you can drink and eat out of someone else's pocket as much as you want until you're full, something 535 you need never return against your will to the master from whose food you've eaten? But still, taking this and any other consideration into account,[33] even though we're somewhat poor, we have something to eat at home, so don't trample us down so contemptuously. Whatever that little something is, it's all ours, not yours, and we don't demand anything from anyone, nor does anyone demand anything from us. None of us is going to rupture 540 his lungs for your sake.

AGO You're too angry: I for one said these things to you in jest.

[32] In temples animals were sacrificed, and most of the meat was consumed by those making the sacrifices and by their guests.

[33] A technical term of legal language.

ADVO per iocum itidem dictum habeto quae nos tibi respon-
      dimus.

AGO opsecro hercle, operam celocem hanc mihi, ne corbi-
      tam date;

    attrepidate saltem, nam uos approperare hau postulo.

545 ADVO si quid tu placide otioseque agere uis, operam damus.

    si properas, cursores meliust te aduocatos ducere.

AGO scitis rem, narraui uobis quod uostra opera mi opus
      siet,

    de lenone hoc qui me amantem ludificatur tam diu,

    ei paratae ut sint insidiae de auro et de seruo meo.

550 ADVO omnia istaec scimus iam nos, si hi spectatores sciant;

    horunc hic nunc causa haec agitur spectatorum fabula:

    hos te satius est docere, ut, quando agas, quid agas sci-
      ant.

    nos tu ne curassis: scimus rem omnem, quippe omnes
      simul

    didicimus tecum una, ut respondere possimus tibi.

555 AGO ita profecto est. sed agite igitur, ut sciam uos scire rem,

    expedite, [et] mihi quae uobis dudum dixi dicite.

ADVO itane? temptas an sciamus? non meminisse nos ratu's

    quo modo trecentos Philippos Collybisco uilico

    dederis, quos deferret huc ad lenonem inimicum tuom,

560   isqu' se ut assimularet peregrinum [esse] aliunde ex
      alio oppido?

    ubi is detulerit, tu eo quaesitum seruom aduentes
      tuom

    cum pecunia.

AGO   meministis memoriter, seruastis me.

543–46 *del. Leo*   556 et *del. Lambinus*
560 esse *del. Bothe*

ADVO Regard what we replied to you as said in jest as well.

AGO Please, give me speedboat help, not cargo-ship help; at
least stir yourselves: I don't expect you to hurry.

ADVO If you want to do something gently and leisurely, we'll 545
help you. If you're in a hurry, you'd better take runners
as advocates.

AGO You know the situation, I've told you what I need your
help for, about the pimp here, who has been tricking me,
the lover, for so long, so that a trap has been prepared
for him concerning my gold and my slave.

ADVO We know all those things already, if these spectators 550
know them. This play is now being staged here for the
sake of these spectators; it's better for you to teach them,
so that they know what you're doing when you're doing
it. Don't bother about us: we know the entire business,
since we all learned it together with you, so that we could
answer you.

AGO That's indeed how it is. But go on then, so that I may 555
know that you know the business, explain and tell me
what I told you a while ago.

ADVO Really? You're testing if we know it? Didn't you think
we'd remember how you gave your overseer Collybiscus
three hundred Philippics, which he was to bring here to
the pimp, your enemy, and that he should pretend to 560
be a stranger from somewhere else, from another city?
When he has brought it, you are to arrive there looking
for your slave and your money.

AGO You remember it memorably, you've saved me.

---

561 quaesitum seruom *P, transp. Bothe*   aduentes *P,* aduenies
Bothe

ADVO ill' negabit: Milphionem quaeri censebit tuom;
id duplicabit omne furtum. leno addicetur tibi.
565 ad eam rem nos esse testis uis tibi.
AGO   tenetis rem.
ADVO uix quidem hercle, ita pauxilla est, digitulis primoribus.
AGO hoc cito et cursim est agendum. propera iam quantum
      potest.
ADVO bene uale igitur. te aduocatos meliust celeris ducere;
tardi sumus nos.
AGO   optume itis, pessume hercle dicitis.
570 quin etiam deciderint femina uobis in talos uelim.
ADVO at edepol nos tibi in lumbos linguam atque oculos in
      solum.
AGO heia! hau uostrum est iracundos esse quod dixi ioco.
ADVO nec tuom quidem est amicis per iocum iniuste loqui.
AGO mittite istaec. quid uelim uos scitis.
ADVO   callemus probe:
575 lenonem ut periurum perdas, id studes.
AGO   tenetis rem.
eugae! opportune egrediuntur Milphio una et uilicus.
basilice exornatus cedit et fabre ad fallaciam.

III. ii: MILPHIO. COLLYBISCVS.
AGORASTOCLES. ADVOCATI
MIL iam tenes praecepta in corde?

577 cedit *A*, incedit *P*

ADVO He'll deny it; he'll think you're looking for your Milphio. That will double the value of the entire theft. The pimp will be handed over to you by court order. For this business you want us to be your witnesses. 565

AGO You've got it.

ADVO We hardly need our fingertips for it, that's how small it is.

AGO This needs to be done in a rush and a hurry. (*to one of them*) Now be as quick as possible.

ADVO Goodbye, then. It's better for you to bring fast advocates along; we are slow.

AGO You're walking very well, and speaking very badly. What's more, I wish your thighs had fallen down onto your ankles. 570

ADVO But we wish your tongue had fallen onto your loins and your eyes onto the ground.

AGO Goodness! You shouldn't be angry about what I said in jest.

ADVO And you shouldn't insult your friends in jest.

AGO Stop those things. You know what I want.

ADVO We understand it well: you're keen to ruin the perjuring pimp. 575

AGO You've got it. (*looking at his house*) Hurray! Just in the nick of time Milphio and the overseer are coming out together. He's strutting along dressed up magnificently and cunningly for the trick.

Enter MILPHIO and COLLYBISCUS from the house of Agorastocles, the latter wearing a cloak, broad-brimmed hat, and sword and carrying a wallet around his neck.

MIL Have you got my instructions in mind now?

PLAUTUS

COL pulchre.
MIL uide sis calleas.
COL quid opust uerbis? callum aprugnum callere aeque non
sinam.
580 MIL fac modo ut condocta tibi sint dicta ad hanc fallaciam.
COL quin edepol condoctior sum quam tragoedi aut comici.
MIL probus homo est.
AGO adeamus propius.
MIL assunt testes?
AGO tot quidem.
MIL non potuisti adducere homines magis ad hanc rem ido-
neos.
nam istorum nullus nefastust: comitiales sunt meri;
585 ibi habitant, ibi eos conspicias quam praetorem sae-
pius.
hodie iuris coctiores non sunt qui litis creant
quam hi sunt qui, si non est quicum litigent, litis
emunt.
ADVO di te perdant!
MIL uos quidem hercle . . . cum eo cum quiqui tamen
et bene et benigne facitis quom ero amanti operam
datis.
590 sed isti iam sciunt negoti quid sit?
AGO omne in ordine.
MIL tum uos animum aduortite igitur. hunc uos lenonem
Lycum
nouistis?

582 assunt testes *Agorastocli*, tot quidem *Milphioni dat P, corr.
Leo*
587 nihil Ω, non *Kienitz*

78

COL	Beautifully.
MIL	Do make sure you're smart.
COL	What need is there for words? I won't let a stuck pig smart equally.[34]
MIL	Just make sure that you have your words memorized for this trick.
COL	Yes, I have them better memorized than tragic or comic actors do.
MIL	He's a decent chap.
AGO	(*to the advocates*) Let's go closer. (*approaches Milphio*)
MIL	Are the witnesses present?
AGO	So many. (*points*)
MIL	You couldn't have brought men more suitable for this business: none of them is a public-holiday man, they're pure public-business men; that's where they live, that's where you can spot them more frequently than the praetor. Today there are no men more cooked in law who create lawsuits than these people, who buy lawsuits if there's no one to have a lawsuit with.
ADVO	May the gods ruin you!
MIL	(*to the advocates*) No, you . . . are acting well and kindly, taking this and any consideration into account nonetheless, by helping my lovesick master. (*to Agorastocles*) But do they know already what business this is?
AGO	All from beginning to end.
MIL	(*to the advocates*) Then pay attention. Do you know the pimp Lycus here?

Line numbers: 580, 585, 590

---

[34] Lit. "I won't let a boar's hide be equally smart." The pun is difficult to reproduce: Milphio uses *callere* in the meaning "be clever," while Collybiscus makes a joke of it and uses it in the meaning "be thick."

ADVO   facile.

COL   at pol ego eum qua sit facie nescio.
eum mihi uolo demonstretis hominem.

ADVO   nos curabimus.
satis praeceptum est.

AGO   hic trecentos nummos numeratos habet.

595 ADVO ergo nos inspicere oportet istuc aurum, Agorastocles,
ut sciamus quid dicamus mox pro testimonio.

COL   agite, inspicite.

ADVO   aurum est profecto hic, spectatores, comicum:
macerato hoc pingues fiunt auro in barbaria boues;
uerum ad hanc rem agundam Philippum est: ita nos as-
    simulabimus.

600 COL   sed ita assimulatote quasi ego sim peregrinus.

ADVO   scilicet,
et quidem quasi tu nobiscum adueniens hodie oraueris
liberum ut commonstraremus tibi locum et uolupta-
    rium
ubi ames, potes, pergraecere.

COL   eu edepol mortalis malos!

AGO   ego enim docui.

MIL   quis te porro?

COL   agite intro abite, Agorastocles,

605 ne hic uos mecum conspicetur leno neu fallaciae
praepedimentum obiciatur.

ADVO   hic homo sapienter sapit.
facite quod iubet.

AGO   abeamus. sed uos—

ADVO   satis dictum est. abi.

---

[35] Lupines, used for feeding cattle in Italy, need to be soaked be-
cause they contain alkaloids.

ADVO Of course.

COL But I don't know what he looks like. (*to the advocates*) I
      want you to show me this chap.

ADVO We'll take care of it. We've been instructed enough.

AGO This chap has three hundred Philippics counted out.

ADVO Then we ought to inspect that gold, Agorastocles, so   595
      that we know what to say as witness statement in due
      course.

COL Go on, inspect it.

ADVO There's indeed comic gold here, spectators: when it's
      been soaked, oxen become fat from it in barbarian land.[35]
      But for doing this business it's Philippic; so we shall pre-
      tend.

COL But pretend that I'm a stranger myself.   600

ADVO Of course, and that on your arrival today you asked us to
      show you a free and pleasurable place where you could
      make love, drink, and live in Greek style.

COL Goodness, what sly people!

AGO Yes, I taught them.

MIL Who taught you in turn?

COL (*to Agorastocles and Milphio*) Come on, go inside, Ago-
      rastocles, so that the pimp doesn't see you with me and   605
      so that no hindrance obstructs our trick.

ADVO (*to Agorastocles and Milphio*) This chap is very smart.
      Do what he tells you.

AGO Let's go away.

Exit MILPHIO *into the house of Agorastocles.*

AGO But you—

ADVO (*interrupting*) Enough has been said. Go away.

	AGO	abeo.
	ADVO	quaeso, di immortales, quin abis?
	AGO	abeo.
	ADVO	sapis.
609	COL	st!
609ᵃ		tace.
	ADVO	quid est?
	COL	fores hae fecerunt magnum flagitium modo.
610	ADVO	quid ⟨id⟩ est flagiti?
	COL	crepuerunt clare.
	ADVO	di te perduint!
		pone nos recede.
	COL	fiat.
	ADVO	nos priores ibimus.
	COL	faciunt scurrae quod consuerunt: pone sese homines locant.
	ADVO	illic homo est qui egreditur leno.
	COL	bonus est, nam similis mali est.
		iam nunc ego illic egredienti sanguinem exsugam procul.

III. iii: LYCVS. ADVOCATI. COLLYBISCVS

615	LYC	iam ego istuc reuortar, miles: conuiuas uolo
		reperire nobis commodos qui una sient;
		interibi attulerint exta, atque eadem mulieres
		iam ab re diuina credo apparebunt domi.
		sed quid huc tantum hominum incedunt? ecquidnam afferunt?

610 id *add. Acidalius*

82

AGO   Yes, I'm going.

ADVO Please, immortal gods, why won't you go away?

AGO   I'm going away.

ADVO You're wise.

Exit AGORASTOCLES into his house.

COL   Hush! Be quiet.

ADVO What is it?

COL   This door has just made a major faux pas.

ADVO What faux pas is that?   610

COL   It's rumbled[36] loudly.

ADVO May the gods ruin you! Step behind us.

COL   Yes.

ADVO We'll go in front.

COL   They do what men about town usually do: they place
      people behind themselves.[37]

ADVO That chap who is coming out is the pimp.

COL   He's a good one; for he resembles a bad one. Now I'll
      suck his blood out from a distance while he's coming
      out.

Enter LYCUS from his house.

LYC   (*into the house*) I'll return to you in a moment, soldier. I   615
      want to find us agreeable guests to be with us. In the
      meantime they'll bring the innards, and at the same time
      the women will soon appear at home from their sacrifice,
      I believe. (*to himself*) But why is such a large number of

---

[36] The verb *crepare* is ambiguous between making a creaking
sound (said of doors) and farting.   [37] A euphemism for wishing
to be the passive partner in anal intercourse.

620	et ill' chlamydatus quisnam est qui sequitur procul?
ADVO	Aetoli ciues te salutamus, Lyce,
622	quamquam hanc salutem ferimus inuiti tibi et
622ᵃ	quamquam bene uolumus leniter lenonibus.
LYC	fortunati omnes sitis, quod certo scio
	nec fore nec Fortunam id situram fieri.
625 ADVO	istic est thesaurus stultis in lingua situs,
	ut quaestui habeant male loqui melioribus.
LYC	uiam qui nescit qua deueniat ad mare,
	eum oportet amnem quaerere comitem sibi.
	ego male loquendi uobis nesciui uiam:
630	nunc uos mihi amnes estis; uos certum est sequi:
	si bene dicetis, uostra ripa uos sequar,
	si male dicetis, uostro gradiar limite.
ADVO	malo bene facere tantundem est periculum
	quantum bono male facere.
LYC	qui uero?
ADVO	scies.
635	malo si quid bene facias, [id] beneficium interit;
	bono si quid male facias, aetatem expetit.
LYC	facete dictum! sed quid istuc ad me attinet?
ADVO	quia nos honoris tui causa ad te uenimus,
	quamquam bene uolumus leniter lenonibus.
640 LYC	si quid boni apportatis, habeo gratiam.
ADVO	boni de nostro tibi nec ferimus nec damus
	nec pollicemur neque adeo uolumus datum.
LYC	credo hercle uobis: ita uostra est benignitas.
	sed quid nunc uoltis?

622ᵃ *uersum cum* et *uersus prioris del.* Bentley
629 *uersum del.* Maurach
635 id *del.* Bentley

people coming here? Are they bringing anything? And 620
who on earth is that man in a cloak who is following at a
distance?

ADVO (*advancing, leaving Collybiscus in the background*) We,
Aetolian citizens, give you our greeting, Lycus, even
though we bring you this greeting unwillingly and even
though we wish pimps well only in moderation.

LYC May you all be happy, which I know for sure won't be the
case, nor will Fortune allow it to happen.

ADVO Fools have your kind of repository in their tongue, so 625
that they regard it as profitable to insult their betters.

LYC A man who doesn't know the way by which he can reach
the sea ought to seek a river as his companion. I didn't
know the way to insult you; now you're my rivers, I'm 630
determined to follow you. If you speak politely, I'll follow
you on your bank; if you speak rudely, I'll keep to your
course.

ADVO Doing a bad man a good turn is as risky as doing a good
man a bad turn.

LYC How so?

ADVO You'll find out. If you do a bad man a good turn, the good 635
deed perishes; if you do a good man a bad turn, it follows
you for a lifetime.

LYC A witty saying! But what does that have to do with me?

ADVO Because we've come to you out of regard for you, even
though we wish pimps well only in moderation.

LYC If you bring me some good, I'm grateful to you. 640

ADVO From what belongs to us we aren't bringing or giving or
promising you any good, nor do we want any good to be
given to you.

LYC I do believe you; that's what your kindness is like. But
what do you want now?

ADVO   hunc chlamydatum quem uides,
645   ei Mars iratust.
COL   capiti uostro istuc quidem!
ADVO nunc hunc, Lyce, ad te diripiundum adducimus.
COL   cum praeda hic hodie incedet uenator domum:
      canes compellunt in plagas lepide lupum.
LYC   quis hic est?
ADVO   nescimus nos quidem istum qui siet;
650   nisi dudum mane ut ad portum processimus,
      atque istum e naui exeuntem oneraria
      uidemus. adiit ad nos extemplo exiens;
      salutat, respondemus.
COL   mortalis malos!
      ut ingrediuntur docte in sycophantiam!
655 LYC quid deinde?
ADVO   sermonem ibi nobiscum copulat.
      ait se peregrinum esse, huius ignarum oppidi;
      locum sibi uelle liberum praeberier
      ubi nequam faciat. nos hominem ad te adduximus.
      tu si te di amant, agere tuam rem occasio est.
660 LYC itane?
ADVO   ille est cupiens, aurum habet.
LYC   praeda haec mea est.
ADVO potare, amare uolt.
LYC   locum lepidum dabo.
ADVO at enim hic clam, furtim esse uolt, ne quis sciat
      neue arbiter sit. nam hic latro in Sparta fuit,

      660 ille est cupiens *dat Lyco P, aduocatis Seyffert*

86

ADVO This man in a cloak you can see, Mars is angry with   645
him.[38]
COL May that fall onto *your* heads!
ADVO Now, Lycus, we're bringing him to you to be plun-
dered.
COL (*aside, pointing at himself*) This hunter will go home
with a catch today: the dogs are driving the wolf into the
nets in a delightful way.
LYC (*to the advocates*) Who is he?
ADVO We actually don't know who he is; but when we went   650
towards the harbor a while ago, early, we saw him leave
a cargo ship. On leaving he approached us at once. He
greets us, we reply.
COL (*aside*) What sly mortals! How cleverly they're embark-
ing on the trick!
LYC (*to the advocates*) What next?   655
ADVO He starts a conversation with us there. He says he's a
stranger and doesn't know this city; he'd like to be given
a free space where he can do naughty things. We've
brought him to you. If the gods love you, you have the
opportunity to do what's to your advantage.
LYC Really?   660
ADVO He's keen and has gold.
LYC This booty is mine.
ADVO He wants to drink and make love.
LYC I'll give him a lovely place.
ADVO But he wants to be concealed and in secret, so that no
one may know or be a witness: he was a mercenary in

[38] Mars, the god of war, is angry with Collybiscus, the pretend
soldier, because he had to desert from the army and because he will
now be plundered by Lycus.

		ut quidem ipse nobis dixit, apud regem Attalum;
665		ind' nunc aufugit, quoniam capitur oppidum.
	COL	nimis lepide de latrone, de Sparta optume.
	LYC	di deaeque uobis multa bona dent, quom mihi
		et bene praecipitis et bonam praedam datis.
	ADVO	immo ut ipse nobis dixit, quo accures magis,
670		trecentos nummos Philippos portat praesidi.
	LYC	rex sum, si ego illum hodie ad me hominem allexero.
	ADVO	quin hic quidem tuos est.

LYC   opsecro hercle hortamini,
                   ut deuortatur ad me in hospitium optumum.
       ADVO nec nos hortari nec dehortari decet
675   hominem peregrinum: tuam rem tu ages, si sapis.
             nos tibi palumbem ad aream usque adduximus:
             nunc te illum meliust capere, si captum esse uis.
       COL   iamne itis? quid quod uobis mandaui, hospites?
       ADVO cum illoc te meliust tuam rem, adulescens, loqui:
680   illic est ad istas res probus quas quaeritas.
       COL   uidere equidem uos uellem quom huic aurum darem.
       ADVO illinc procul nos istuc inspectabimus.
       COL   bonam dedistis mihi operam.
       LYC   it ad me lucrum.
       COL   illud quidem quorsum asinus caedit calcibus.
685 LYC   blande hominem compellabo. hospes hospitem
             salutat. saluom te aduenire gaudeo.

---

665 nunc *P*, huc *Camerarius*

---

39 A made-up historical event; Attalus I of Pergamum (died in 197) was never ruler of Sparta.

40 I.e., no profit at all, but rather harm.

Sparta with King Attalus;[39] at least that's what he himself has told us. From there he's fled now that the city is taken. 665

COL (*aside*) Terribly delightful about the mercenary, perfect about Sparta.

LYC May the gods and goddesses give you many good things for giving me good instructions and good booty.

ADVO Well, just so that you take greater care, as he himself has told us, he's carrying three hundred Philippics as funds. 670

LYC I'm a king, if I lure him to me today.

ADVO He's yours.

LYC Please encourage him to put up with me in most agreeable quarters.

ADVO We ought not to encourage or discourage a stranger: look after your own business yourself, if you're wise. We've led the pigeon up to the net for you; now it's better that you should catch it if you want it caught. (*turning to go*) 675

COL (*to the advocates*) Are you going already? What about my commission to you, kind strangers?

ADVO You'd better discuss your business with that chap, young man; he is reliable for the things you look for. 680

COL I'd like you to see it when I give him the gold.

ADVO We'll observe it from there, from a distance.

COL You've done me a good service.

LYC (*aside*) Profit is coming my way.

COL (*overhearing him, aside*) Yes, that sort of profit after which the donkey kicks with its hooves.[40]

LYC (*aside*) I'll address him coaxingly. (*to Collybiscus*) A friend is greeting a friend. I'm happy that you've arrived safely. 685

	COL	multa tibi di dent bona, quom me saluom esse uis.
	LYC	hospitium te aiunt quaeritare.
	COL	quaerito.
	LYC	ita illi dixerunt qui hinc a me abierunt modo,
690		te quaeritare a muscis.
	COL	minime gentium.
	LYC	quid ita?
	COL	quia ⟨a⟩ muscis si mi hospitium quaererem,
		adueniens irem in carcerem recta uia.
		ego id quaero hospitium ubi ego curer mollius
		quam regi Antiocho oculi curari solent.
695	LYC	edepol ne tibi illud possum festiuom dare,
		siquidem potes esse te pati in lepido loco,
		in lecto lepide strato lepidam mulierem
		complexum contrectare—
	COL	is, leno, uiam.
	LYC	—ubi tu Leucadio, Lesbio, Thasio, Chio,
700		uetustate uino edentulo aetatem irriges;
		ibi ego te repplebo usque unguentum geumatis;
		quid multa uerba? faciam, ubi tu laueris,
		ibi ut balineator faciat unguentariam.
		sed haec latrocinantur quae ego dixi omnia.
705	COL	quid ita?
	LYC	quia aurum poscunt praesentarium.

691 a *add.* ʂ
695 illum *P*, illud ʂ

COL May the gods give you many good things for wanting me safe.

LYC They say you're looking for hospitality.

COL Yes.

LYC The people who have just left me have told me that you 690
want hospitality with no risk of gate-crashers.[41]

COL Not at all.

LYC How so?

COL Because if I were looking for hospitality with no risk of
gate-crashers, I'd have gone directly to jail on my arrival.
I'm looking for the kind of hospitality where I'm taken
care of more gently than the eyes of King Antiochus.[42]

LYC Yes, I can give you that charming sort of thing, if indeed 695
you can bear being in a delightful place and fondling a
delightful lady in your embrace on a delightfully laid-out
couch—

COL (interrupting) You're on the right track, pimp.

LYC —where you can lubricate your life with wine from Leu- 700
cas, Lesbos, Thasos, and Chios,[43] wine which is toothless
from old age.[44] There I'll keep filling you with tasters of
perfumes; what need is there for words? I'll see to it that
where you've bathed there the bathman will open a per-
fume store. But all these things I said are mercenaries.

COL How so? 705

LYC Because they demand gold, cash down.

---

[41] Lit. "flies." Flies symbolize overcurious people, as in *Merc.* 361,
where the signification is spelled out. [42] Ruler of the Seleucid
Empire, which comprised Syria; died in 187.

[43] Four Greek islands; Leucas is in the Ionian Sea, the others are
in the Aegean Sea. [44] I.e., the wine has lost its original tartness
and is mellowed by age.

COL quin hercle accipere tu non mauis quam ego dare.
ADVO quid si euocemus huc foras Agorastoclem,
    ut ipsus testis sit sibi certissumus?
    heus tu, qui furem captas, egredere ocius,
710   ut tute inspectes aurum lenoni dari.

III. iv: AGORASTOCLES. ADVOCATI.
COLLYBISCVS. LYCVS

AGO quid est? quid uoltis, testes?
ADVO   specta ad dexteram.
    tuos seruos aurum ipsi lenoni dabit.
COL age, accipe hoc sis: hic sunt numerati aurei
    trecenti nummi qui uocantur Philippei.
715   hinc me procura; propere hosce apsumi uolo.
LYC edepol fecisti prodigum promum tibi.
    age, eamus intro.
COL   te sequor. LYC age, age, ambula,
    ibi quae relicua alia fabulabimur.
COL eadem narrabo tibi res Spartiaticas.
720 LYC quin sequere me ergo.
COL   abduc intro. addictum tenes.
AGO quid nunc mi auctores estis?
ADVO   ut frugi sies.
AGO quid si animus esse non sinit?
ADVO   esto ut sinit.
AGO uidistis leno quom aurum accepit?
ADVO   uidimus.

710 dare *P*, darei *Bentley*

COL   You aren't keener to receive than I am to give.

ADVO (*aside*) How about calling out Agorastocles, so that he
      himself may be his star witness? (*into the house of Ago-*
      rastocles) Hey you, who are trying to catch the thief,
      come out quickly, so that you yourself can see the money   710
      being given to the pimp.

Enter AGORASTOCLES from his house.

AGO   (*quietly*) What is it? What do you want, witnesses?

ADVO (*quietly*) Look to the right. Your slave will give the gold
      to the pimp himself.

COL   (*to Lycus, handing over his wallet*) Go on, please take
      this; here there are three hundred counted gold coins
      called Philippics. Look after me with this; I want it to be 715
      used up quickly.

LYC   You've made an extravagant man your dispenser. Come
      on, let's go in.

COL   I'm following you.

LYC   Come on, come on, walk, there we'll talk about the re-
      maining details.

COL   At the same time I'll tell you my Spartan stories.

LYC   Then follow me.   720

COL   Take me in. You're holding a bond slave.

Exeunt LYCUS and COLLYBISCUS into the former's house.

AGO   What do you advise me to do now?

ADVO To be decent.

AGO   What if my mind doesn't allow it?

ADVO Be the way it allows you.

AGO   Did you see it when the pimp took the gold?

ADVO We did.

AGO eum uos meum esse seruom scitis?
ADVO   sciuimus.
725 AGO rem aduorsus populi saepe leges?
ADVO   sciuimus.
AGO em istaec uolo ergo uos commeminisse omnia,
    mox quom ad praetorem usus ueniet.
ADVO   meminimus.
AGO quid si recenti re aedis pultem?
ADVO   censeo.
AGO si pultem, non recludet?
ADVO   panem frangito.
730 AGO si exierit leno, quid tum? hominem interrogem
    meus seruos ad eum ueneritne?
ADVO   quippini?
AGO cum auri ducentis nummis Philippis?
ADVO   quippini?
AGO ibi extemplo leno errabit.
ADVO   qua de re?
AGO   rogas?
    quia centum nummis minus dicetur.
ADVO   bene putas.
735 AGO alium censebit quaeritari.
ADVO   scilicet.
AGO extemplo denegabit.
ADVO   iuratus quidem.
AGO homo furti sese astringet—
ADVO   hau dubium id quidem est.

730 quid tum A, censeo C¹, *censent* C²D, censerit B, censen *Leo*
732–34 *del. Maurach*

AGO Do you know that he is my slave?

ADVO We do.

AGO A matter against frequent laws of the people?   725

ADVO We've found out.

AGO There, so I want you to remember all this soon when
     need arises before the praetor.

ADVO We remember.

AGO What if I batter the door while the matter is fresh?

ADVO I think so.

AGO If he ignores the batter?[45]

ADVO Break bread.

AGO If the pimp comes out, what then? Should I ask him   730
     whether my slave has come to him?

ADVO Why not?

AGO With two hundred gold Philippics?

ADVO Why not?

AGO There the pimp will instantly make a mistake.

ADVO What about?

AGO (*to one of them*) You ask? Because the figure given will
     be one hundred Philippics too low.

ADVO You're calculating well.

AGO He'll think I'm looking for someone else.   735

ADVO Of course.

AGO He'll deny it at once.

ADVO And that on oath.

AGO He'll implicate himself in theft—

ADVO (*interrupting*) There's no doubt about it.

---

[45] Lit. "If I knock, won't he open?" The advocates pun on the dou-
ble meaning of *pultem*; Agorastocles uses it as subjunctive of *pultare*,
"knock"; the advocates pretend that he uses it as accusative of *puls*,
"spelt porridge" ("if he won't open the porridge?").

AGO	—quantumquantum ad eum erit delatum.
ADVO	quippini?
AGO	Diespiter uos perduit!
ADVO	te quippini?
740 AGO	ibo et pultabo ianuam.
ADVO	ita, quippini?
AGO	tacendi tempus est, nam crepuerunt fores.
	foras egredier uideo lenonem Lycum.
	adeste quaeso.
ADVO	quippini? ⟨sine⟩ si uoles
	operire capita, ne nos leno nouerit,
745	qui illi malae rei tantae fuimus illices.

III. V: LYCVS. AGORASTOCLES. ADVOCATI

LYC	suspendant omnes nunciam se haruspices
	quam ego illis posthac quod loquantur creduam,
	qui in re diuina dudum dicebant mihi
750	malum damnumque maxumum portendier:
	is explicaui meam rem postilla lucro.
AGO	saluos sis, leno.
LYC	di te ament, Agorastocles.
AGO	magis me benigne nunc salutas quam antidhac.
LYC	tranquillitas euenit quasi naui in mari:
	utquomque est uentus exim uelum uortitur.
755 AGO	ualeant apud te quos uolo; atque hau te uolo.
LYC	ualent ut postulatum est, uerum non tibi.
AGO	mitte ad me, si audes, hodie Adelphasium tuam,
	die festo celebri nobilique Aphrodisiis.
LYC	calidum prandisti prandium hodie? dic mihi.

742 egredier *B*, egredie *T*, egredietur *CD*, egrediri *Brix*
743 sine *add. Geppert*

96

AGO —of however much was brought to him.

ADVO Why not?

AGO May Jupiter ruin you!

ADVO Why not you?

AGO I'll go and knock at the door.   740

ADVO Yes, why not? (*Agorastocles knocks*)

AGO It's time to be quiet: the door has creaked. I can see the pimp Lycus coming out. Please be present.

ADVO Why not? Let us cover our heads, if you wish, so that the pimp won't recognize us, as we've lured him into such 745 big trouble. (*They step aside*)

Enter LYCUS *from his house, holding the wallet of Collybiscus.*

LYC Now all soothsayers can hang themselves rather than that I should believe anything they say from now on; a while ago, during the sacrifice, they told me that very great trouble and loss were indicated: I settled my busi- 750 ness with profit afterward.

AGO My greetings, pimp.

LYC May the gods love you, Agorastocles.

AGO Now you're greeting me more kindly than before.

LYC Calm has come as for a ship at sea; whatever the wind is like, the sail turns accordingly.

AGO May the ones at your place be well whom I want to be 755 well; and I don't want you to be well.

LYC They're well, as wished, but not for your benefit.

AGO Send your Adelphasium to me today, if you please, on the celebrated and noble feast day, the Aphrodisia.

LYC Did you eat a hot lunch today? Tell me.

760	AGO	quid iam?
	LYC	quia os nunc frigefactas, quom rogas.
	AGO	hoc age sis, leno. seruom esse audiui meum
		apud te.
	LYC	apud me? numquam factum reperies.
	AGO	mentire. nam ad te uenit aurumque attulit.
		ita mi renuntiatum est, quibus credo satis.
765	LYC	malus es, captatum me aduenis cum testibus.
		tuorum apud me nemo est nec quicquam tui.
	AGO	mementote illud, aduocati.
	ADVO	meminimus.
	LYC	hahahae! iam teneo quid sit, perspexi modo.
		hi qui illum dudum conciliauerunt mihi
770		peregrinum Spartanum, id nunc his cerebrum uritur,
		me esse hos trecentos Philippos facturum lucri.
		nunc hunc inimicum quia esse sciuerunt mihi,
		eum allegarunt suom qui seruom diceret
		cum auro esse apud me; composita est fallacia
775		ut eo me priuent atque inter se diuidant.
		lupo agnum eripere postulant. nugas agunt.
	AGO	negasne apud te esse aurum nec seruom meum?
	LYC	nego: et negando, si quid refert, aruio.
	ADVO	periisti, leno. nam iste est huius uilicus
780		quem tibi nos esse Spartiatem diximus,
		qui ad te trecentos Philippeos modo detulit.
		idque in istoc adeo aurum inest marsuppio.
	LYC	uae uostrae aetati!
	ADVO	id quidem <in> mundo est tuae.
	AGO	age omitte actutum, furcifer, marsuppium:

783 in *add. Pylades*

AGO   How so?   760

LYC   Because now you're cooling your mouth by asking that question.

AGO   Pay attention, pimp, will you? I've heard that my slave is at your place.

LYC   At my place? You'll never find that this has happened.

AGO   You're lying: he came to you and brought you gold. This has been reported to me by people I trust well enough.

LYC   (*spotting the advocates*) You're a crook, you're coming   765 with witnesses to try and catch me. No one and nothing of yours is with me.

AGO   Remember that, advocates.

ADVO   We remember.

LYC   Hahaha! Now I've got what this is, I've just seen through it. Those who a while ago procured that stranger from   770 Sparta for me now have an itch in their brains about me making a profit of these three hundred Philippics. Now because they knew that this chap is my enemy, they've sent him to say that his slave is at my place with gold. A trick has been set up in order to deprive me of it and to   775 divide it among themselves. They expect to snatch away the lamb from the wolf. They're wasting their time.

AGO   Do you deny that my gold and my slave are with you?

LYC   Yes, I do deny it; and I'm hoarse from denying it, for that matter.

ADVO   You're ruined, pimp: that chap is his overseer, the one   780 who we told you was from Sparta and who just now brought three hundred Philippics to you. And what's more, this gold is in that wallet.

LYC   Bad luck to you!

ADVO   That's in store for you.

AGO   (*to Lycus*) Come on, let go of the wallet at once, you

785   manufesto fur es. mihi quaeso hercle operam date
          dum me uideatis seruom ab hoc abducere.

LYC   nunc pol ego perii certo, haud arbitrario.
          consulto hoc factum est mihi ut insidiae fierent.
          sed quid ego dubito fugere hinc in malam crucem
790   prius quam hinc optorto collo ad praetorem trahor?
          eheu! quom ego habui hariolos, haruspices;
          qui si quid bene promittunt, perspisso euenit,
          id quod mali promittunt, praesentarium est.
          nunc ibo, amicos consulam quo me modo
795   suspendere aequom censeant potissumum.

    III. vi: AGORASTOCLES. COLLYBISCVS. ADVOCATI

AGO   age tu progredere, ut [testes] uideant te ire istinc foras.
          estne hic meus seruos?

COL   sum hercle uero, Agorastocles.

AGO   quid nunc, sceleste leno?

ADVO   quicum litigas
      apscessit.

AGO   utinam hinc abierit malam crucem!
800 ADVO ita nos uelle aequom est.

AGO   cras supscribam homini dicam.

COL   numquid me?

AGO   apscedas, sumas ornatum tuom.

COL   non sum nequiquam miles factus; paululum
          praedae intus feci: dum lenonis familia
          dormitat, extis sum satur factus probe.
805   apscedam hinc intro.

    793 praesentarium est *P*, praesentari (*unde* praesentarii *Lindsay*)
est *Nonius*
    796 testes *del. Bentley*

criminal: you're a thief caught red-handed. (*takes the* 785
wallet; then to the advocates) Please assist me until you
can see me taking the slave away from him.

Exit AGORASTOCLES into the pimp's house.

LYC   Now I'm ruined for certain, not doubtfully. This was
done on purpose so as to lay a trap for me. But why don't
I run off to hang myself before I'm dragged off to the 790
praetor with a noose around my neck? Poor me, since I
had prophets and soothsayers! If they promise anything
good, it comes very slowly; the bad they promise is at
hand. Now I'll go and consult my friends what they think 795
is the best way for me to hang myself.

Exit LYCUS to the right.
*Enter AGORASTOCLES and COLLYBISCUS from the pimp's
house.*

AGO   (*to Collybiscus*) Come on, you, come forward so that
they can see you coming out. (*to the advocates*) Isn't this
my slave?

COL   I am indeed, Agorastocles.

AGO   Well then, crooked pimp?

ADVO The man you're having a lawsuit with has gone.

AGO   May he have gone to be hanged!

ADVO It's right for us to wish so. 800

AGO   Tomorrow I'll write him a lawsuit.

COL   Do you want anything from me?

AGO   Go and take your get-up.

COL   I didn't become a soldier for nothing; I took a little bit
of booty inside: while the pimp's household was sleeping,
I filled myself properly with the innards. I'll go in. 805

AGO   factum a uobis comiter.
        bonam dedistis, aduocati, operam mihi.
        cras mane, quaeso, in comitio estote obuiam.
        tu sequere me intro. uos ualete.

ADVO   et tu uale.
        iniuriam illic insignite postulat:

810   nostro seruire nos sibi censet cibo.
        uerum ita sunt ⟨morati⟩ isti nostri diuites:
        si quid bene facias, leuior pluma est gratia,
        si quid peccatum est, plumbeas iras gerunt.

815   domos abeamus nostras, sultis, nunciam,
        quando id quoi rei operam dedimus impetrauimus,
        ut perderemus corruptorem ciuium.

ACTVS IV

IV. i: MILPHIO

MIL   exspecto quo pacto meae techinae processurae sient.
        studeo hunc lenonem perdere, qui meum erum mise-
           rum macerat,
        is me autem porro uerberat, incursat pugnis, calcibus:

820   seruire amanti miseria est, praesertim qui quod amat
           caret.
        attat! e fano recipere uideo se Syncerastum,
        lenonis seruom; quid habeat sermonis auscultabo.

811 morati *add. Palmer*
818 iut *B*, ut *CD*, qui ς

AGO (*to the advocates*) You've been very kind. Advocates, you've done me a good turn. Please meet me tomorrow morning in the assembly place. (*to Collybiscus*) You, follow me inside. (*to the advocates*) You, fare well.

Exeunt AGORASTOCLES *and* COLLYBISCUS *into the former's house.*

ADVO (*calling after Agorastocles*) And farewell to you. (*to the audience*) He wants to do us an injustice in a striking way: he believes we serve him while providing our own 810 rations. But that's the way our rich men are: if you do them a good turn, the thanks is lighter than a feather; if you make a mistake, their anger is as heavy as lead. Please, let's go home now since we've succeeded in what 815 we were after, in ruining the corruptor of citizens.

Exeunt the ADVOCATES *to the right.*

ACT FOUR

Enter MILPHIO *from the house of Agorastocles.*

MIL I'm waiting to see how my tricks will work out. I'm keen to ruin this pimp, who is torturing my wretched master, and he beats me in turn and attacks me with fists and heels; it's misery to be the slave of a lovesick man, espe- 820 cially of one who doesn't have the object of his love. (*looks around*) Goodness! I can see Syncerastus, the pimp's slave, returning from the shrine; I'll listen to what sort of things he's saying.

IV. ii: SYNCERASTVS. MILPHIO

SYN   satis spectatum est deos atque homines eius neglegere
        gratiam,
    quoi homini erus est consimilis uelut ego habeo hunc
        huius modi.
825   nec periurior nec peior alter usquam est gentium
    quam erus meus est, nec tam luteus nec tam caeno col-
        litus.
    ita me di ament, uel in lautumiis uel in pistrino maue-
        lim
    agere aetatem praepeditus latere forti ferreo
    quam apud lenonem hunc seruitutem colere. quid illuc
        est genus,
830   quae illic hominum corruptelae fiunt! di uostram fi-
        dem!
    quoduis genus ibi hominum uideas quasi Acheruntem
        ueneris,
    equitem, peditem, libertinum, furem an fugitiuom
        uelis,
    uerberatum, uinctum, addictum: qui habet quod det,
        ⟨ut⟩ut homo est,
    omnia genera recipiuntur; itaque in totis aedibus
835   tenebrae, latebrae, bibitur, estur quasi in popina, hau
        secus.
    ibi tu uideas litteratas fictilis epistulas,
    pice signatas, nomina insunt cubitum longis litteris:
    ita uinariorum habemus nostrae dilectum domi.
MIL   omnia edepol mira sunt nisi erus hunc heredem facit,
840   nam id quidem, illi, uti meditatur, uerba faciet mortuo.
    et adire lubet hominem et autem nimis eum ausculto
        lubens.

Enter SYNCERASTUS *from the left, carrying vessels; he is too preoccupied to notice anyone.*

SYN It's clear enough that gods and men don't care for the goodwill of a man whose master is like the one I have. No 825 one is a greater perjurer or criminal anywhere on earth than my master is, nor as dirty or smeared with excrement. As truly as the gods may love me, I'd rather spend my life tied to a heavy iron block in the quarries or the mill than be a slave at this pimp's. What breed is that, what 830 corruptions of men happen there! Gods, your protection! There you can see any type of man, as if you'd come to the Underworld, whether you want a nobleman, ordinary citizen, freedman, thief, or run-away, a beaten one, a bound one, a bond slave: a man who has something to pay, whatever he's like, all types are taken in. And so in the whole house there's darkness, hiding places, one 835 drinks and eats as in a tavern, no differently. There you can see clay letters[46] with inscriptions on them, signed with pitch, and there are names on them in letters an ell long: that's the way we have a recruitment of wine vessels in our house.

MIL (*aside*) It's all very strange unless his master has made him his heir: the way he's rehearsing, he'll deliver the 840 eulogy for him when he's dead. I'd love to approach him, and yet I listen to him with great pleasure.

[46] The amphoras.

---

833 <ut>ut *Gulielmus*
840 facit emortuo *P*, faciet mortuo *Ussing*

SYN   haec quom hic uideo fieri, crucior: pretiis emptos max-
       umis
       apud nos expeculiatos seruos fieri suis eris.
       sed ad postremum nihil apparet: male partum male
       disperit.

845   MIL   proinde habet orationem quasi ipse sit frugi bonae,
       qui ipsus hercle ignauiorem potis est facere Ignauiam.

SYN   nunc domum haec ab aede Veneris refero uasa, ubi
       hostiis
       erus nequiuit propitiare Venerem suo festo die.

MIL   lepidam Venerem!

SYN   nam meretrices nostrae primis hostiis

850   Venerem placauere extemplo.

MIL   o lepidam Venerem denuo!

SYN   nunc domum ibo.

MIL   heus, Synceraste!

SYN   Syncerastum qui uocat?

MIL   tuos amicus.

SYN   haud amice facis qui cum onere offers moram.

MIL   at ob hanc moram tibi reddam operam ubi uoles, ubi
       iusseris.
       habe rem pactam.

SYN   si futurum est, do tibi operam hanc.

MIL   quo modo?

855   SYN   ut enim ubi mihi uapulandum sit, tu corium sufferas.
       apage, nescio quid uiri sis.

MIL   malus sum.

SYN   tibi sis.

MIL   te uolo.

SYN   at onus urget.

SYN   When I see this happening, I'm tortured: slaves bought for very high prices to lose their savings to the disadvantage of their masters here at our place! But in the end it's in vain: what's been acquired in a bad way disappears in a bad way.

MIL   (*aside*) He's giving a speech as if he himself were any 845 good, he who could make Laziness lazier himself.

SYN   Now I'm bringing these vessels home from the temple of Venus, where my master couldn't make Venus well disposed with his sacrificial animals on her feast day.

MIL   (*aside*) Well done, Venus!

SYN   Well, our prostitutes at once made Venus favorable with 850 their first sacrificial animals.

MIL   (*aside*) Well done again, Venus!

SYN   Now I'll go home.

MIL   Hey, Syncerastus!

SYN   Who is calling Syncerastus?

MIL   Your friend.

SYN   You're not behaving in a friendly way since you cause me delay when I'm carrying a burden.

MIL   But in return for this delay I'll give you my assistance when you want and when you command. Accept this agreement.

SYN   On this condition I'll give you my assistance.

MIL   How do you mean?

SYN   Well, when I have to get a beating, you must offer your 855 hide instead. Back off, I don't know what sort of man you are.

MIL   I'm a bad one.

SYN   Be so for yourself.

MIL   I want to speak to you.

SYN   But my burden is weighing me down.

MIL	at tu appone et respice ad me.
SYN	fecero,
	quamquam haud otium est.
MIL	saluos sis, Synceraste.
SYN	o Milphio,
	di omnes deaeque ament—
MIL	quemnam hominem?
SYN	nec te nec me, Milphio:

860   neque erum meum adeo.

MIL	quem ament igitur?
SYN	aliquem id dignus qui siet.
	nam nostrorum nemo dignust.
MIL	lepide loquere.
SYN	me decet.
MIL	quid agis?
SYN	facio quod manufesti moechi hau ferme solent.
MIL	quid id est?
SYN	refero uasa salua.
MIL	di te et tuom erum perduint!
SYN	me non perdent; illum ut perdant facere possum, si ue-
	lim,

865   meum erum ut perdant, ni mihi metuam, Milphio.

MIL	quid id est? cedo.
SYN	malus es?
MIL	malus sum.
SYN	male mihi est.
MIL	memora⟨dum⟩, num esse aliter decet?
	quid est quod male sit tibi, quoi domi sit quod edis,
	quod ames affatim,
	nec triobolum ullum amicae das et ductas gratiis?

860 id *A, om. P*   866 memora num *A*, memorandum *P*,
memora⟨dum⟩ num *Geppert*

MIL	Well, put it down and look at me.
SYN	Okay, even though I don't have spare time. (*puts down the vessels*)
MIL	My greetings, Syncerastus.
SYN	O Milphio, may all the gods and goddesses love—
MIL	(*after waiting for a moment*) Well, whom?
SYN	Neither you nor me, Milphio; and what's more, my master neither.
MIL	Then whom should they love?
SYN	Someone who deserves it: none of us does.
MIL	You're talking in a charming way.
SYN	So I should.
MIL	What are you up to?
SYN	I'm doing what adulterers caught in the act usually don't do.
MIL	What's that?
SYN	I'm carrying my utensils[47] back safe and sound.
MIL	May the gods ruin you and your master!
SYN	Me they won't ruin; I can make sure that they ruin him, if I wish, that they ruin my master, if I weren't afraid for myself, Milphio.
MIL	What's that? Tell me.
SYN	Are you a bad one?
MIL	Yes, I'm a bad one.
SYN	I'm feeling bad.
MIL	Tell me, should it be any different? How come you're feeling bad? At home you have what you can eat and what you can love to your heart's content, and you don't pay even three obols to your girlfriend and you hire her for free.

[47] *Vasa* can refer to vessels as well as the male sexual organs.

SYN   Diespiter me sic amabit—

MIL   ut quidem edepol dignus es.

870   SYN   —ut ego hanc familiam interire cupio.

MIL   adde operam, si cupis.

SYN   sine pinnis uolare hau facile est: meae alae pinnas non
           habent.

MIL   nolito edepol deuellisse: iam his duobus mensibus
           uolucres tibi erunt tuae hirquinae.

SYN   i malam rem!

MIL   i tu atque erus.

SYN   uerum. enim qui homo eum norit, norit. cito homo
           peruorti potest.

875   MIL   quid iam?

SYN   quasi tu tacitum habere quicquam potis sis.

MIL   rectius
          tacitas tibi res sistam quam quod dictum est mutae
          mulieri.

SYN   animum inducam facile ut tibi istuc credam, ni te
           nouerim.

MIL   crede audacter meo periclo.

SYN   male credam et credam tamen.

MIL   scin tu erum tuom meo ero esse inimicum capitalem?

SYN   scio.

880   MIL   propter amorem—

SYN   omnem operam perdis.

MIL   quid iam?

SYN   quia doctum doces.

MIL   quid ergo dubitas quin lubenter tuo ero meus quod
           possiet

875 tacere uero *A*, tacere *P*, tacitum habere *Leo*
881 meus quod *P*, meus quid *A*

110

SYN So love me Jupiter—

MIL (*interrupting*) In the way you deserve.

SYN —as I wish this household to perish.   870

MIL Add your effort, if you wish for it.

SYN It's not easy to fly without feathers; my wings[48] don't have feathers. (*lifts his arms*)

MIL Don't pluck them; within the next two months your goaty armpits will be fully fledged.

SYN Go and be hanged!

MIL You go and your master!

SYN True. Yes, those who know him, know him. He can be overthrown quickly.

MIL What's that?   875

SYN As if you could keep anything quiet.

MIL I'll keep your affairs quiet more properly than what's been said to a dumb woman.

SYN I'd easily persuade myself to trust you in this, if I didn't know you.

MIL Trust me boldly at my own risk.

SYN I'll trust you at my peril and yet I'll trust you.

MIL Do you know that your master is a mortal enemy of my master?

SYN I do.

MIL Because of his love—   880

SYN (*interrupting*) You're wasting all your effort.

MIL How come?

SYN Because you're telling me what I already know.

MIL Then why do you doubt that my master would love to do

---

[48] Latin *ala* can mean "wing" as well as "armpit."

facere faciat male, eius merito? tum autem si quid tu
  adiuuas,
eo facilius facere poterit.

SYN   at ego hoc metuo, Milphio.
MIL quid est quod metuas?
SYN   dum ero insidias paritem, ne me perduim.
885   si erus meus me esse elocutum quoiquam mortali sciat,
           continuo is me ex Syncerasto Crurifragium fecerit.
MIL numquam edepol mortalis quisquam fiet e me certior,
       nisi ero meo uni indicasso, atque ei quoque ut ne
          enuntiet
       id esse facinus ex ted ortum.
SYN   male credam et credam tamen.
890   sed hoc tu tecum tacitum habeto.
MIL   Fide non melius creditur.
       loquere—locus occasioque est—libere: hic soli sumus.
SYN erus si tuos uolt facere frugem, meum erum perdet.
MIL   qui id potest?
SYN facile.
MIL   fac ergo id "facile" noscam ego, ut ille possit noscere.
SYN quia Adelphasium, quam erus deamat tuos, ingenua est.
MIL   quo modo?
895 SYN eodem quo soror illius altera Anterastilis.
MIL cedo qui id credam.
SYN   quia illas emit in Anactorio paruolas
       de praedone Siculo.
MIL   quanti?
SYN   duodeuiginti minis,
       duas illas et Giddenenem nutricem earum tertiam.

as much harm as he can do to your master, which is what he deserves? Then, if you help him in any way, he'll be able to do so all the more easily because of it.

SYN   But I'm afraid of this, Milphio.

MIL   What is it that you're afraid of?

SYN   Of ruining myself while preparing a plot against my master. If my master knows that I told any living soul, he'll   885
turn me from Syncerastus to Shinbreak at once.

MIL   Never will any living soul get any news from me; but I'll report it only to my master, and tell him in addition that he mustn't pass on that this deed has originated from you.

SYN   I'll trust you at my peril and yet I'll trust you. But keep   890
this to yourself.

MIL   Good Faith isn't more trustworthy. Speak freely—it's the right place and occasion: here we're alone.

SYN   If your master wants to do something useful, he'll ruin my master.

MIL   How can he do so?

SYN   Easily.

MIL   Then let me learn this "easily," so that he can learn it.

SYN   Because Adelphasium, whom your master is in love with, is freeborn.

MIL   How so?

SYN   In the same way as the other one, her sister Anteras-   895
tilis.

MIL   Tell me how I can believe this.

SYN   Because he bought them in Anactorium from a Sicilian pirate when they were little.

MIL   For how much?

SYN   For eighteen minas, the two of them and Giddenis, their nurse, as a third. And the man who sold them said he was

	et ille qui eas uendebat dixit se furtiuas uendere:
900	ingenuas Carthagine aibat esse.
MIL	di uostram fidem!

      nimium lepidum memoras facinus. nam erus meus
        Agorastocles
      ibidem gnatust, ind' surruptus fere sexennis, postibi
      qui eum surrupuit huc deuexit meoque ero eum hic
        uendidit.
      is in diuitias homo adoptauit hunc quom diem obiit
        suom.

905 SYN omnia memoras quo id facilius fiat: manu eas asserat,
      suas popularis, liberali causa.
MIL   tacitus tace modo.
SYN profecto ad incitas lenonem rediget, si eas abduxerit.
MIL quin prius disperibit faxo quam unam calcem ciuerit.
      ita paratum est.
SYN   ita di faxint ne apud lenonem hunc seruiam!
910 MIL hercle qui meus collibertus faxo eris, si di uolent.
SYN ita di faxint! numquid aliud? me morare, Milphio.
MIL ualeas beneque ut tibi sit.
SYN   pol istuc tibi et tuo est ero in manu.
      uale et haec cura clanculum ut sint dicta.
MIL   non dictum est. uale.
SYN at enim nihil est, nisi dum calet hoc agitur.
MIL   lepidu's quom mones.
915 et ita hoc fiet.
SYN   proba materies data est, si probum adhibes fabrum.

906 tacitus *Milphioni dat Camerarius*, Syncerasto Ω
908 unam Ω, unum *Nonius*
910 quin hercle conlibertus meus *A*, qui hercle conlibertus meus
P, hercle qui meus conlibertus *Fleckeisen*   eris *P*, tu eris *A*

114

selling kidnapped girls; he said they were freeborn, from 900
Carthage.

MIL Gods, your protection! You're telling me absolutely de-
lightful news: my master Agorastocles was born in the
same place, kidnapped from there at around six years,
and after that the man who kidnapped him brought him
here and sold him here to my master, who adopted him
and made him his heir when he passed away.

SYN You're telling everything whereby it can happen more 905
easily. Let him lay his hand on them, his compatriots, to
assert their freedom.

MIL Just be very quiet.

SYN He'll indeed checkmate the pimp if he takes them
away.

MIL No, I'll make sure that he perishes before moving a
single piece; that's what I've prepared.

SYN May the gods bring it about, so that I won't be a slave at
this pimp's!

MIL Seriously, I'll make sure that you're a freedman together 910
with me if the gods wish it.

SYN May the gods bring it about! Anything else? You're de-
laying me, Milphio.

MIL Farewell and be well.

SYN That's in your and your master's hands. Farewell and
make sure that this was said in secret.

MIL It wasn't said at all. Goodbye.

SYN But it's nothing unless it's done while it's hot.

MIL It's charming of you to remind me. And that's how it'll be 915
done.

SYN You've been given decent raw material, if you use a de-
cent workman.

115

MIL   potin ut taceas?

SYN   taceo atque abeo.

MIL   mihi commoditatem creas.

       illic hinc abiit. di immortales meum erum seruatum
         uolunt

       et hunc disperditum lenonem: tantum eum instat exiti.

       satine prius quam unum est iniectum telum, iam instat
         alterum?

920   ibo intro haec ut meo ero memorem. nam huc si ante
         aedis euocem,

       quae audiuistis modo, nunc si eadem hic iterum
         iterem, inscitia est.

       [ero] uni potius ero odio intus quam hic sim uobis om-
         nibus.

       [di immortales, quanta clades, quanta aduentat calami-
         tas

       hodie ad hunc lenonem! sed ego nunc est quom me
         commoror.

925   ita negotium institutum est, non datur cessatio;

       nam et hoc docte consulendum quod modo concredi-
         tum est

       et illud autem inseruiendum est consilium uernaculum.

       remora si sit, qui malam rem mihi det merito fecerit.

       nunc intro ibo: dum erus adueniat a foro, opperiar
         domi.]

    922 ero *del. Guyet*   intus ero obio (odio D^4) *P*, intro ero *A*, ero
odio intus *scripsi*
    923–29 *del. Weise*
    923 clades *P*, tur(ba) *A*

MIL   Can't you be quiet?
SYN   I'm quiet and I'm leaving.

Exit SYNCERASTUS into the pimp's house.

MIL   (*calling after him*) You're creating a real opportunity for
      me! (*to the audience*) He's left. The immortal gods want
      my master saved and this pimp ruined, to judge from
      what great ruin is threatening him. Does a second missile
      really threaten him already before the first one has been
      shot? I'll go inside in order to tell my master about this: 920
      if I were to call him out in front of the house, it would
      be stupidity if I were to repeat again the same things
      here which you've just heard. I'd rather annoy one per-
      son inside than all of you here. [Immortal gods, what
      ruin and what destruction is coming to this pimp today!
      But now is the time that I'm wasting my time. That's   925
      how the business has been begun, there's no room for
      hesitation: what's just been entrusted to me needs to be
      planned cleverly, and on the other hand that homegrown
      plan needs to be looked after. If there were any delay, a
      man who gave me a big thrashing would do so deserv-
      edly. Now I'll go inside; I'll wait at home for my master
      to come from the forum.]

Exit MILPHIO into the house of Agorastocles.

ACTVS V

v. i: HANNO

930 HAN [yth alonim u alonuth si corathi sy macom syth
chy mlachthi in ythmum ysthyalm ych ibarcu mysehi.
li pho caneth yth bynuthi iad aed in byn ui
by marob sy llohom alonim uy by mysyrthohom.
byth lymmoth ynnochoth uulech antidamas chon
935 ys si dobrim chy fel yth chil ys chon chen liful.
yth binim ys dybur ch innochoth u Agorastocles.
ythem anechi hy chirs aelichot sith nasot.
bynny id li chi ily gubulim lasibitthim.
bodi aly thera ynnynny yslym mon choth iusim.]
940 yth alonim u alonuth si corathi is thymchy macom syth
combaepumamitalmetlotiambeat
iulecantheconaalonimbalumbar dechor
bats****hunesobinesubicsillimbalim
esseantidamossonalemuedubertefet
945 donobun*huneccilthumucommucroluful
altanimauosduberithemhuarcharistolem
sittesedanecnasotersahelicot
alemusdubertimurmucopsuistiti

ACT FIVE

Enter HANNO *from the right, followed by porters carrying heavy luggage and wearing earrings. All are wearing loose tunics.*

Hanno speaks a Punic entrance monologue (ll. 940–49), presumably followed by the Latin version (ll. 950–60). The Punic monologue in ll. 930–39 is a more recent doublet of the other Punic version. All Punic words are left untranslated, as they were incomprehensible to most of the Roman audience, and put in italics to mark them as foreign; an explanation of the Punic passages, insofar as one is possible, is provided in an appendix to this play.

HAN   [*yth alonim u alonuth si corathi sy macom syth*   930
     chy mlachthi in ythmum ysthyalm ych ibarcu mysehi.
     li pho caneth yth bynuthi iad aed in byn ui
     by marob sy llohom alonim uy by mysyrthohom.
     byth lymmoth ynnochoth uulech antidamas chon
     ys si dobrim chy fel yth chil ys chon chen liful.   935
     yth binim ys dybur ch innochoth u Agorastocles.
     ythem anechi hy chirs aelichot sith nasot.
     bynny id li chi ily gubulim lasibitthim.
     bodi aly thera ynnynny yslym mon choth iusim.]
     yth alonim u alonuth si corathi is thymchy macom syth   940
     combaepumamitalmetlotiambeat
     iulecantheconaalonimbalumbar dechor
     bats****hunesobinesubicsillimbalim
     esseantidamossonalemuedubertefet
     donobun*huneccilthumucommucroluful   945
     altanimauosduberithemhuarcharistolem
     sittesedanecnasotersahelicot
     alemusdubertimurmucopsuistiti

aocca anec lictor bode si ussilim limmim co iusim.
950 deos deasque ueneror qui hanc urbem colunt
ut quod de mea re huc ueni rite uenerim,
measque hic ut gnatas et mei fratris filium
reperire me siritis, di uostram fidem!
[quae mihi surruptae sunt et fratris filium.]
955 sed hic mihi antehac hospes Antidamas fuit;
eum fecisse aiunt sibi quod faciundum fuit.
eius filium esse hic praedicant Agorastoclem:
ad eum hospitalem hanc tesseram mecum fero;
is in hisce habitare monstratust regionibus.
960 hos percontabor qui hinc egrediuntur foras.

     V. ii: AGORASTOCLES. MILPHIO. HANNO

AGO ain tu tibi dixe Syncerastum, Milphio,
eas esse ingenuas ambas surrupticias
Carthaginiensis?

MIL   aio, et, si frugi esse uis,
eas liberali iam asseres causa manu.
965 nam tuom flagitium est tuas te popularis pati
seruire ante oculos, domi quae fuerint liberae.

HAN pro di immortales, opsecro uostram fidem!
quam orationem hanc aures dulcem deuorant?
creta est profecto horunc hominum oratio.
970 ut mi apsterserunt omnem sorditudinem!

954 *del. Lindemann*
969 horum Ω, haec horunc *Geppert*

120

aocca anec lictor bode si ussilim limmim co iusim.

I pray to the gods and goddesses who inhabit this city 950
that as for the thing I came here for, I've come righ-
teously, and that you let me find my daughters here and
my brother's son; gods, your protection! [Daughters who
were stolen from me, and my brother's son.] But here I 955
had Antidamas as my guest-friend before; they say he
did what he had to do. People claim that his son Agoras-
tocles lives here; to him I'm bringing this shard of hos-
pitality[49] with me. This was pointed out as the area where
he lives. I'll ask these people who are coming out. 960

Enter AGORASTOCLES *and* MILPHIO *from the former's house
without noticing anyone.*

AGO   Did you say that Syncerastus told you, Milphio, that both
are freeborn, kidnapped Carthaginians?

MIL   I do, and if you want to behave properly, you'll lay your
hand on them in order to assert their freedom: it's a 965
disgrace for you to let your compatriots be slaves in front
of your eyes, women that were free at home.

HAN   (*aside*) Immortal gods, I implore your protection! What
sweet speech do my ears devour? The speech of these
people is indeed fuller's earth.[50] How they've cleaned my 970
ears![51]

---

[49] A piece of pottery was broken, and each party forming part of a
contract of hospitality kept one. When a family member visited the host
family, he could prove his identity by showing his shard, which would
fit together with theirs.   [50] Fuller's earth was used for cleaning
clothes.   [51] Lit. "how they've wiped all dirt off me." *Sorditudo*, a
nonce-formation, means "dirt," but puns with *surdus*, "deaf." Hanno
has heard something interesting and is all ears now.

	AGO	si ad eam rem testis habeam, faciam quod iubes.
	MIL	quid tu mihi testis? quin tu insistis fortiter?
		aliqua Fortuna fuerit adiutrix tibi.
	AGO	incipere multo est quam impetrare facilius.
975	MIL	sed quae illaec auis est quae huc cum tunicis aduenit?
		numnam in balineis circumductust pallio?
	AGO	facies quidem edepol Punica est. gugga est homo.
	MIL	seruos quidem edepol ueteres antiquosque habet.
	AGO	qui scis?
	MIL	uiden homines sarcinatos consequi?
980		atque ut ⟨ego⟩ opino[r] in manibus digitos non habent.
	AGO	quid iam?
	MIL	quia incedunt cum anulatis auribus.
	HAN	adibo ⟨ego⟩ hosce atque appellabo Punice.
		si respondebunt, Punice pergam loqui;
		si non, tum ad horum mores linguam uortero.
985	MIL	quid ais tu? ecquid commeministi Punice?
	AGO	nil edepol. nam qui scire potui, dic mihi,
		qui illim sexennis perierim Carthagine?

980 ut opinor digitos in manibus Ω, ut ⟨ego⟩ opino[r] in manibus
digitos *Weise*   982 ego *add. Reiz*

---

[52] Hanno's sleeves flutter like a bird's wings.

[53] Neither speaker assignment nor the meaning of *gugga* is clear.
GG' is attested as the name of a profession in a Punic inscription; since
the inscription leaves it unclear what that profession is, and since
Hanno has clearly traveled, I have translated the word as "tradesman,"
a term which Agorastocles may be familiar with despite not speaking
Punic. Gratwick prefers to give the last sentence to Milphio and to
regard *gugga* as the name of a bird. In Greek the *gyges* is the bittern,
but Gratwick prefers to see in the bird the purple heron, which would

AGO	If I had witnesses for this, I'd do what you tell me.
MIL	Witnesses? Nonsense! Why don't you proceed boldly? Fortune will somehow support you.
AGO	It's much easier to begin something than to succeed.
MIL	But who is that bird[52] that's coming here with the tunics? 975 Was he cheated out of his cloak in the baths?
AGO	His appearance is certainly Carthaginian. The chap's a tradesman.[53]
MIL	He certainly has old and ancient slaves.
AGO	How do you know?
MIL	Can't you see that men with backpacks are following?[54] And I think they don't have fingers on their 980 hands.
AGO	How so?
MIL	Because they come along with rings in their ears.
HAN	(aside) I'll approach them and address them in Punic. If they reply, I'll continue to speak Punic. If not, then I'll adapt my language to their customs.
MIL	(to Agorastocles) What do you say? Do you remember 985 any Punic?
AGO	None at all: how could I know any, tell me, given that I was stolen from Carthage at the age of six?

introduce a rather complex pun: Phoenicians traded in purple, and hence Hanno can be seen as a purple heron; the heron was also called the "treacherous bird" by the Romans, and this association would introduce negative stereotyping of Carthaginians.

[54] They cannot walk upright because of the heavy weight and hence look like old men. In addition there is a pun because *sarcina*, "patched-up bundle," implies that the carriers have been "mended" because of their old age.

	HAN	pro di immortales! plurumi ad illunc modum
		periere pueri liberi Carthagine.
990	MIL	quid ais tu?
	AGO	quid uis?
	MIL	uin appellem hunc Punice?
	AGO	an scis?
	MIL	nullus me est hodie Poenus Poenior.
	AGO	adi atque appella quid uelit, quid uenerit,
		qui sit, quoiatis, unde sit: ne parseris.
	MIL	auo. quoiates estis aut quo ex oppido?
995	HAN	anno byn mytthymbal carthadati anech.
	AGO	quid ait?
	MIL	Hannonem se esse ait Carthagine,
		Carthaginiensis Mytthymbalis filium.
	HAN	auo.
	MIL	salutat.
	HAN	donni.
	MIL	doni uolt tibi
		dare hic nescioquid. audin pollicitarier?
1000	AGO	saluta hunc rursus Punice uerbis meis.
	MIL	auo donni inquit hic tibi uerbis suis.
	HAN	mehar bocca.
	MIL	istuc tibi sit potius quam mihi.
	AGO	quid ait?
	MIL	miseram esse praedicat buccam sibi.
		fortasse medicos nos esse arbitrarier.

---

55 Milphio's "translations" are based on Latin words that sound
similar to what Hanno says in Punic. In my translation I have preferred
to translate the Latin literally, which means the similarities of sound
are by and large lost.

124

HAN	(*aside*) Immortal gods! A lot of freeborn children were stolen from Carthage that way.	
MIL	What do you say?	990
AGO	What do you want?	
MIL	Do you want me to address him in Punic?	
AGO	Do you know any?	
MIL	No Carthaginian is more Carthaginian than me today.	
AGO	Go and ask him what he wants, why he's come, who he is, from what country, from which region: don't spare your questions.	
MIL	(*to Hanno*) *Auo.* What country are you people from, or from what town?	
HAN	*Anno byn mytthymbal carthadati anech.*	995
AGO	(*to Milphio*) What does he say?	
MIL	He says he's Hanno from Carthage, the son of Mytthymbal the Carthaginian.	
HAN	*Auo.*	
MIL	(*to Agorastocles*) He's greeting you.	
HAN	*Donni.*	
MIL	(*to Agorastocles*) He wants to make some donation[55] to you. Can you hear him promise it?	
AGO	Greet him in turn in Punic in my name.	1000
MIL	(*to Hanno*) *Auo donni*, he says to you in his name.	
HAN	*Mehar bocca.*	
MIL	(*to Hanno*) May you have that rather than me.	
AGO	What does he say?	
MIL	He states that his jaw hurts. Perhaps he thinks we're doctors.	

125

1005	AGO	si ⟨ita⟩ est, nega esse; nolo ego errare hospitem.
	MIL	audin tu?
	HAN	rufe ynny cho is tam.
	AGO	sic uolo
		profecto uera cuncta huic expedirier.
		roga numquid opus sit.
	MIL	tu qui zonam non habes,
		quid in hanc uenistis urbem aut quid quaeritis?
1010	HAN	mu phursa?
	AGO	quid ait?
	HAN	mi uulech ianna?
	AGO	quid uenit?
	MIL	non audis? mures Africanos praedicat
		in pompam ludis dare se uelle aedilibus.
	HAN	lech lachannani limini chot.
	AGO	quid nunc ait?
	MIL	ligulas, canalis ait se aduexisse et nuces:
1015		nunc orat operam ut des sibi, ut ea ueneant.
	AGO	mercator credo est.
	HAN	assam.
	MIL	aruinam quidem.
	HAN	palu umer; gad etha.
	AGO	Milphio, quid nunc ait?
	MIL	palas uendundas sibi ait et mergas datas,
		ad messim credo, nisi quid tu aliud sapis,
1020		[ut hortum fodiat atque ut frumentum metat.]
	AGO	quid istuc ad me?

1005 ita *add. Camerarius*
1020 *del. Hasper*

126

AGO If it's like that, tell him that we aren't; I don't want a 1005
     stranger to be mistaken.

MIL (*to Hanno*) Can you hear?

HAN *Rufe ynny cho is tam.*

AGO (*to Milphio*) Indeed, I want everything explained to him
     truthfully like this. Ask him if he needs anything.

MIL (*to Hanno*) You who don't have a belt! Why did you all
     come into this city or what are you looking for?

HAN *Mu phursa?* 1010

AGO What does he say?

HAN *Mi uulech ianna?*

AGO Why has he come?

MIL Can't you hear? He states that he wants to present Afri-
     can mice for the parade at the games of the aediles.[56]

HAN *Lech lachannani limini chot.*

AGO What does he say now?

MIL He says he's brought spoons, funnels, and nuts; now he 1015
     asks you to help him so that they can be sold.

AGO I believe he's a merchant.

HAN *Assam.*

MIL (*to Hanno*) Yes, of lard.[57]

HAN *Palu umer; gad etha.*

AGO Milphio, what does he say now?

MIL He says he's been given spades and reaping boards to
     sell, for the harvest, I think, unless you have some other
     idea, [so that he may dig up the garden and harvest the 1020
     corn.]

AGO How does that concern me?

---

[56] Roman officials in charge of games, buildings, and markets.

[57] Milphio mistakes the Punic word *assam* for a Latin homophone
meaning "roasted."

	MIL	certiorem te esse uolt,
		ne quid clam furtim se accepisse censeas.
	HAN	mu phonnim si corathi.
	MIL	hem! caue sis feceris
		quod hic te orat.
	AGO	quid ait aut quid orat? expedi.
1025	MIL	sub cratim ut iubeas se supponi atque eo
		lapides imponi multos, ut sese neces.
	HAN	gune bal samem ierasan.
	AGO	narra, quid est?
		quid ait?
	MIL	non hercle nunc quidem quicquam scio.
	HAN	at ut scias, nunc dehinc latine iam loquar.
1030		seruom hercle te esse oportet et nequam et malum,
		hominem peregrinum atque aduenam qui irrideas.
	MIL	at hercle te hominem et sycophantam et subdolum,
		qui huc aduenisti nos captatum, migdilix,
		bisulci lingua quasi proserpens bestia.
1035	AGO	maledicta hinc aufer, linguam compescas face.
		male dicere huic tu temperabis, si sapis.
		meis consanguineis nolo te iniuste loqui.
		Carthagini ego sum gnatus, ut tu sis sciens.
	HAN	o mi popularis, salue!
	AGO	et tu edepol, quisquis es.
1040		et si quid opus est, quaeso, dic atque impera
		popularitatis causa.
	HAN	habeo gratiam.
		[uerum ego hic hospitium habeo: Antidamae filium
		quaero—commonstra si nouisti—Agorastoclem.]
		sed ecquem adulescentem tu hic nouisti Agorastoclem?

1036 tu *om.* A   1042–43 *del. Seyffert*
1042 ego hic Ω, *transp. Ritschl*

128

MIL   He wants you to be informed so that you won't think he's taken anything in secret and by stealth.

HAN   *Mu phonnim si corathi.*

MIL   (*to Agorastocles*) Oh! Please don't do what he asks you.

AGO   What does he say or what does he ask? Tell me.

MIL   That you should have him put under a wicker basket and 1025
have many stones placed on top in order to kill him.

HAN   *Gune bal samem ierasan.*

AGO   Tell me, what is it? What does he say?

MIL   Now I really don't know anything.

HAN   (*to Milphio*) But so as to make you know, I'll speak Latin
from now on. You must be a bad and useless slave since 1030
you mock a stranger and a newcomer at that.

MIL   But you must be a swindler and a trickster since you've
come here in order to catch us out, you double-tongued
creature,[58] with a forked tongue like a creeping beast.

AGO   (*to Milphio*) Stop your insults and do control your tongue. 1035
You'd better refrain from insulting this man. I don't want
you to speak rudely to my kinsmen. (*to Hanno*) Just so
that you know, I was born in Carthage.

HAN   O my compatriot, my greetings!

AGO   And mine to you, whoever you are. And if you need 1040
anything, please say so and command me, for the sake of
our shared nationality.

HAN   Thank you. [But I have hospitality here; I'm looking for
the son of Antidamas, Agorastocles—show him to me if
you know him.] But do you know any young man called
Agorastocles here?

---

[58] *Migdilix* is of uncertain meaning. I have translated it as "double-tongued creature" because it is possibly derived from Greek *migda*, "in a mixed way," and Latin *–lix*, "tongue."

1045	AGO	siquidem Antidamai quaeris adoptaticium,
		ego sum ipsus quem tu quaeris.
	HAN	hem! quid ego audio?
	AGO	Antidamae gnatum me esse.
	HAN	si ita est, tesseram
		conferre si uis hospitalem, eccam attuli.
	AGO	agedum huc ostende. est par probe. nam habeo domi.
1050	HAN	o mi hospes, salue multum! nam mi tuos pater
		patritus hercle hospes Antidamas fuit.
		haec mi hospitalis tessera cum illo fuit.
	AGO	ergo hic apud me hospitium tibi praebebitur.
		nam hau repudio hospitium nec Carthaginem.
1055		ind' sum oriundus.
	HAN	di dent tibi omnes quae uelis!
		quid ais? qui potuit fieri uti Carthagini
		gnatus sis? hic autem habuisti Aetolum patrem.
	AGO	surruptus sum illim. hic me Antidamas hospes tuos
		emit et is me sibi adoptauit filium.
1060	HAN	Demarcho item ipse fuit adoptaticius.
		sed mitto de illoc, ad te redeo. dic mihi,
		ecquid meministi tuom parentum nomina,
		patris atque matris?
	AGO	memini.
	HAN	memoradum mihi,
		si noui forte aut si sunt cognati mihi.
1065	AGO	Ampsigura mater mihi fuit, Iahon pater.
	HAN	patrem atque matrem uiuerent uellem tibi.
	AGO	an mortui sunt?

1049 nam Ω, quam *Seyffert*   1051 ergo *P*, hercle *Maurach*
1053 tibi *om. A*   1058 illinc Ω, *quod seruare possis si cum*
Mueller Antidama *scribas*

AGO If you're looking for the adopted son of Antidamas, I am 1045
the very man you're looking for.

HAN Oh! What do I hear?

AGO That I'm the son of Antidamas.

HAN If this is the case and if you want to compare your
shard of hospitality, look, I've brought mine along. (*produces it*)

AGO Go on, show it to me. (*inspecting it*) It's the proper counterpart: I have mine at home.

HAN O my guest-friend, many greetings! Your father Anti- 1050
damas was my father's guest-friend. I had this shard of
hospitality with him.

AGO Then you'll receive hospitality here at my place: I do not
reject either the hospitality or Carthage. That's where 1055
I'm from.

HAN May all the gods give you what you wish! What do you
say? How could it happen that you were born in Carthage? But here you had an Aetolian father.

AGO I was kidnapped from there. Here Antidamas, your
guest-friend, bought me and adopted me as his son.

HAN He himself was likewise the adopted son of Demarchus. 1060
But I'll stop about him, I'm returning to you. Tell me, do
you remember the names of your parents, of your father
and your mother?

AGO I do.

HAN Tell me, if by chance I know them or if they're my relatives.

AGO My mother was Ampsigura and my father Iahon. 1065

HAN I wish your father and mother were alive.

AGO Have they died?

HAN	factum, quod ⟨ego⟩ aegre tuli.
	nam mihi sobrina Ampsigura tua mater fuit;
	pater tuos, is erat frater patruelis meus,
1070	et is me heredem fecit quom suom obiit diem,
	quo me priuatum aegre patior mortuo.
	sed si ita est, ut tu sis Iahonis filius
	signum esse oportet in manu laeua tibi,
	ludenti puero quod memordit simia.
1075	ostende: inspiciam. aperi, si audes; atque adest.
AGO	mi patrue, salue.
HAN	et tu salue, Agorastocles.
	iterum mihi gnatus uideor quom te repperi.
MIL	pol istam rem uobis bene euenisse gaudeo.
	sed te moneri num neuis?
HAN	sane uolo.
1080 MIL	paterna oportet filio reddi bona.
	aequom est habere hunc bona quae possedit pater.
HAN	hau postulo aliter: restituentur omnia;
	suam sibi rem saluam sistam, si illo aduenerit.
MIL	facito sis reddas, etsi hic habitabit, tamen.
1085 HAN	quin mea quoque iste habebit, si quid me fuat.
MIL	festiuom facinus uenit mi in mentem modo.
HAN	quid id est?
MIL	tua est opus opera.
HAN	dic mihi, quid lubet?
	profecto uteris, ut uoles, operam meam.
	quid est negoti?
MIL	potin tu fieri subdolus?
1090 HAN	inimico possum, amico est insipientia.

1067 ego *add. Lambinus*   1075 audi *P*, si audes *Goetz et*
Loewe   ades *P*, adest *Muretus*   1087 est opus *CD*, opus est *B*

HAN Yes, which was hard for me: your mother, Ampsigura, was my second cousin; your father, he was my first cousin, and he made me his heir when he passed away; 1070 it's hard for me to be deprived of him through his death. But if it's true that you are Iahon's son, you should have a mark on your left hand, which a monkey made by biting you when you were playing. Show it: I'll inspect it. (*Agorastocles shows his hand*) Open up, please; and here it 1075 is.

AGO My uncle, greetings.

HAN And mine to you, Agorastocles. I feel born again now that I've found you.

MIL I'm happy that that has turned out well for you two. (*to Hanno*) But you don't mind getting advice, do you?

HAN I don't mind at all.

MIL His father's goods ought to be restored to the son. It's 1080 only fair that he should have the goods his father possessed.

HAN I don't disagree; they will all be restored. I'll give him his belongings safe and sound if he comes there.

MIL Please do make sure that you return them, even if he continues to live here.

HAN Yes, and he'll also have mine if anything happens to me. 1085

MIL A pleasant course of action has just occurred to me.

HAN What's that?

MIL Your assistance is needed.

HAN Tell me, what would you like? You'll have my assistance the way you want it. What business is it?

MIL Can you become wily?

HAN Toward an enemy I can, toward a friend it's stupidity. 1090

1090 insipientia est *P, transp. Pylades*

MIL	inimicus hercle est huius.
HAN	male faxim lubens.
MIL	amat ab lenone hic.
HAN	facere sapienter puto.
MIL	leno hic habitat uicinus.
HAN	male faxim lubens.
MIL	ei duae puellae sunt meretrices seruolae

1095 sorores: earum hic alteram efflictim perit
neque eam incestauit umquam.

HAN   acerba amatio est.
MIL hunc leno ludificatur.
HAN   suom quaestum colit.
MIL hic illi malam rem dare uolt.
HAN   frugi est si id facit.
MIL nunc hoc consilium capio et hanc fabricam apparo,
1100 ut te allegemus, filias dicas tuas
surruptasque esse paruolas Carthagine,
manu liberali causa ambas asseras
quasi filiae tuae sint ambae. intellegis?
HAN intellego hercle. nam mi item gnatae duae
1105 cum nutrice una surruptae sunt paruolae.
MIL lepide hercle assimulas. iam in principio id mi placet.
HAN pol magis quam uellem.
MIL   eu hercle mortalem catum,
malum crudumque et callidum et subdolum!
ut afflet, quo illud gestu faciat facilius!
1110 me quoque dolis iam superat architectonem.
HAN sed earum nutrix qua sit facie mi expedi.

1103 ambe *P*, iamne *Leo*
1105 surreptas uni *P*, (sunt s)urruptae *A*
1108 est ollidum *P*, et callidum *Pylades*, estolidum *Leo*

MIL	It's this chap's enemy.
HAN	I'd do him a bad turn with pleasure.
MIL	He's in love with a girl from a pimp.
HAN	I believe that he's doing a smart thing.
MIL	The pimp lives here as his neighbor.
HAN	I'd do him a bad turn with pleasure.

MIL He has two slave girls, prostitutes and sisters: this chap 1095
is madly in love with one of them and has never had sex
with her.

HAN That's a bitter love.

MIL The pimp is tricking him.

HAN He's doing his job.

MIL This chap wants to give him trouble.

HAN He's sensible if he does so.

MIL Now I'm hatching this plan and preparing this trick: we 1100
are to send you, and you are to say they're your daugh-
ters and were kidnapped from Carthage when they were
little, and you are to assert their freedom, as if they were
your daughters. You understand?

HAN Yes, I do indeed: my two daughters were kidnapped in 1105
the same way together with their nurse when they were
little.

MIL You're pretending in a delightful way. Already in the
beginning I like it.

HAN Well, more than I'd wish. (*starts to cry*)

MIL (*half aside*) Goodness, a tricky mortal, bad and unfeeling
and clever and wily! The way he's accompanying it with
tears so as to make it easier to carry out! Me too, the 1110
master builder, he already surpasses with his guiles.

HAN But tell me what their nurse looks like.

MIL	statura hau magna, corpore aquilo est.	
HAN		ipsa ea est.
MIL	specie uenusta, ore atque oculis pernigris.	
HAN	formam quidem hercle uerbis depinxti probe.	
1115 MIL	uin eam uidere?	
HAN		filias malo meas.

       sed i, [atque] euoca illam; si eae meae sunt filiae,
       si illarum est nutrix, me continuo nouerit.

MIL   heus, ecquis hic est? nuntiate ut prodeat
       foras Giddeneni. est qui illam conuentam esse uolt.

V. iii: GIDDENIS. MILPHIO. HANNO.
AGORASTOCLES. PVER

1120 GID	quis pultat?	
MIL		qui te proxumust.
GID		quid uis?
MIL		eho,

       nouistin tu illunc tunicatum hominem qui siet?

GID   nam quem ego aspicio? pro supreme Iuppiter!
       erus meus hicquidem est, mearum alumnarum pater,
       Hanno Carthaginiensis.

MIL   ecce autem mala!

1125   praestrigiator hic quidem Poenus probust,
       perduxit omnis ad suam sententiam.

GID   o mi ere, salue, Hanno insperatissume
       mihi tuisque filiis, salue atque—eho,
       mirari noli nec me contemplarier.

1130   cognoscin Giddenenem ancillam tuam?

HAN noui. sed ubi sunt meae gnatae? id scire expeto.

1112 aquilost *Gellius*, aquilo Ω, aquilino *Nonius*
1116 atque *del. Pareus*

MIL   She's not of great height, and has darkish skin.

HAN   It's her very self.

MIL   She's of pretty appearance, with a very swarthy face and eyes.

HAN   You've painted her looks properly with your words.

MIL   Do you want to see her? 1115

HAN   I'd prefer to see my daughters. But go, call her out; if they're my daughters and if she's their nurse, she'll recognize me instantly.

MIL   (*knocking at the pimp's door*) Hey, is anyone here? Tell Giddenis to come out. There's someone who wants to meet her.

Enter GIDDENIS *from the pimp's house.*

GID   Who is knocking? 1120

MIL   The man who's next to you.

GID   What do you want?

MIL   Hey, do you know who that chap in a tunic is?

GID   Who do I see? Jupiter above! This is my master, the father of my nurslings, Hanno from Carthage.

MIL   (*half aside*) Just look at the sly woman! This Carthaginian 1125 is a clever trickster, he's brought everyone over to his opinion.

GID   O my master, greetings, Hanno most unhoped for by me and your daughters, greetings and—hey, don't be surprised or look me over. Don't you recognize your slave 1130 girl Giddenis?

HAN   I do. But where are my daughters? That's what I'm keen to know.

	GID	apud aedem Veneris.
	HAN	quid ibi faciunt? dic mihi.
	GID	Aphrodisia hodie Veneris est festus dies:
		oratum ierunt deam ut sibi esset propitia.
1135	MIL	pol satis scio, impetrarunt, quando hic hic adest.
	AGO	eho an huius sunt illae filiae?
	GID	ita ut praedicas.
		tua pietas nobis plane auxilio fuit,
		quom huc aduenisti hodie in ipso tempore;
		namque hodie earum mutarentur nomina
1140		facerentque indignum genere quaestum corpore.
	PVER	hau amma si lli.
	GID	hauo bane si lli mustine
		mepsi etenes te dum et alamma cestimim.
	AGO	quid illi locuti sunt inter se? dic mihi.
	HAN	matrem hic salutat suam, haec autem hunc filium.
1145		tace atque parce muliebri supellectili.
	AGO	quae ea est supellex?
	HAN	clarus clamor.
	AGO	sine modo.
	HAN	tu abduc hosce intro et una nutricem simul
		iube hanc abire hinc ad te.
	AGO	fac quod imperat.
	MIL	sed quis illas tibi monstrabit?
	AGO	ego doctissume.
1150	MIL	abeo igitur.
	AGO	facias modo quam memores mauelim.
		patruo aduenienti cena curetur uolo.
	MIL	lachanna uos, quos ego iam detrudam ad molas,

---

[59] From chaste girls to prostitutes.

138

GID	At the temple of Venus.
HAN	What are they doing there? Tell me.
GID	Today it's the Aphrodisia, the feast day of Venus; they've gone to pray to the goddess that she may be well disposed toward them.
MIL	I know well enough that they've succeeded since this chap is here. 1135
AGO	(*to Giddenis*) Hey, are they his daughters?
GID	(*to Agorastocles*) Just as you say. (*to Hanno*) Your piety has clearly helped us, since you've come here today in the nick of time; today their names would have been changed[59] and they'd be earning a living with their bodies in a manner unworthy of their family. 1140
BOY	(*to Giddenis*) *Hau amma si lli.*
GID	(*to the boy*) *Hauo bane si lli mustine mepsi etenes te dum et alamma cestimim.*
AGO	(*to Hanno*) What have they said to each other? Tell me.
HAN	(*to Agorastocles*) He's greeting his mother, and she on the other hand this son of hers. (*to Giddenis*) Be quiet and spare us the female furniture. 1145
AGO	What furniture is that?
HAN	Loud shouting.
AGO	Just let her be.
HAN	(*to Milphio*) You, take these people inside and at the same time have this nurse go over to you.
AGO	(*to Milphio*) Do what he tells you to.
MIL	(*to Hanno*) But who will show the women to you?
AGO	I myself, most skillfully.
MIL	Then I'm going away. 1150
AGO	I'd rather you just did so than said so. I want a dinner prepared for my uncle on his arrival.
MIL	(*to the servants*) *Lachanna*, folks, whom I'll push down

139

      ind' porro ad puteum atque ad robustum codicem.
      ego faxo hospitium hoc leniter laudabitis.
1155 AGO audin tu, patrue? dico, ne dictum neges:
      tuam mihi maiorem filiam despondeas.
    HAN pactam rem habeto.
    AGO   spondesne igitur?
    HAN   spondeo.
    AGO mi patrue, salue. nam nunc es plane meus.
      nunc demum ego cum illa fabulabor libere.
1160   nunc, patrue, si uis tuas uidere filias,
      me sequere.
    HAN   iamdudum equidem cupio et te sequor.
    AGO quid si eamus illis obuiam?
    HAN   at ne interuias
      praeterbitamus metuo. magne Iuppiter,
      restitue certas mi ex incertis nunc opes.
1165 AGO ego quidem amores meos mecum confido fore.
      sed eccas uideo ipsas.
    HAN   haecin meae sunt filiae?
      quantae e quantillis iam sunt factae!
    AGO   scin quid est?
      tragicae sunt: in calones sustolli solent.
 [MIL opino hercle hodie, quod ego dixi per iocum,
1170   id euenturum esse et seuerum et serium,
      ut haec inueniantur hodie esse huius filiae.

    1160–61 *uersus secl. Maurach*
    1165 meos amores *Loeb, transp. Pylades*
    1168 thraecae sunt in celonem *A*, thraece sunt caelum ne *P*, tragi-
cae sunt: in calones *Leo*   1169–73 *del. Ussing*

---

[60] Comic actors wore flat shoes, while tragic ones had high boots.

to the mills this instant, and from there further to the pit and to the solid block. I'll make sure that you'll praise this hospitality in moderation.

Exeunt MILPHIO, GIDDENIS, *and the porters into the house of Agorastocles.*

AGO   Can you hear me, uncle? I'm telling you, so don't say you 1155
haven't been told: you should betroth your older daughter to me.

HAN   Consider it settled.

AGO   Do you betroth her then?

HAN   Yes, I do.

AGO   Greetings, my dear uncle: now you're really mine. Now
at last I'll talk with her freely. If you want to see your 1160
daughters now, uncle, follow me.

HAN   I've been keen on seeing them for a long time now and I'm following you.

AGO   How about going to meet them?

HAN   But I'm afraid that we might walk past them on the way.
Great Jupiter, turn what's mine from uncertain to certain now.

AGO   I for one trust that my sweetheart will be with me. But 1165
look, I can see them in person.

HAN   Are these my daughters? They used to be so small, and now they're so big!

AGO   Do you know what it is? They're tragic actresses: they're normally placed on heels.[60]

[MIL   I do believe that what I said in jest will happen seriously 1170
and earnestly today, that they will be discovered to be this man's daughters.

PLAUTUS

AGO   pol istuc quidem iam certum est. tu istos, Milphio,
      abduce intro. nos hasce hic praestolabimur.]

V. iv: ADELPHASIVM. ANTERASTILIS.
HANNO. AGORASTOCLES

ADE   fuit hodie operae pretium quoiuis qui amabilitati ani-
      mum adiceret
1175 oculis epulas dare, delubrum qui hodie ornatum eo
      uisere uenit.
1176 deamaui ecastor illi [ego] hodie
1176ᵃ lepidissuma munera meretricum,
1177 digna diua uenustissuma Venere,
1177ᵃ nec contempsi eius opes hodie.
      tanta ibi copia uenustatum aderat, in suo quique loco
      sita munde.
1179 aras tus, myrrhinus, omnis odor
1179ᵃ complebat. hau sordere uisust
1180 festus dies, Venus, nec tuom fanum:
1180ᵃ tantus ibi clientarum erat numerus
1181 quae ad Calydoniam uenerant Venerem.
1181ᵃ ANTE certo enim, quod quidem ad nos duas
1182 attinuit, praepotentes pulchre
1182ᵃ pacisque potentes, soror, fuimus,
1183 neque ab iuuentute inibi irridiculo
1183ᵃ habitae, quod pol,
1183ᵇ soror, ceteris omnibus factum est.
ADE   malim istuc aliis uideatur quam uti tu te, soror, col-
      laudes.
1185 ANTE spero equidem.
ADE   et pol ego, quom ingeniis quibus sumus
                              atque aliae gnosco;
      eo sumus gnatae genere ut deceat nos esse a culpa
      castas.

142

AGO   That's certain now. You, Milphio, take them inside. We
will wait for the girls here.]

Enter ADELPHASIUM *and* ANTERASTILIS *from the left without
noticing anyone.*

ADE   It was worthwhile today for anyone who pays attention
to beauty to give food to his eyes, for anyone who came   1175
there today to see the decorated shrine. I was delighted
there today with the really pleasing gifts of prostitutes,
worthy of the most charming goddess Venus, and I didn't
despise her powers today; such a great amount of lovely
things was there, all put neatly in their place. Incense
and the odor of myrrh and everything filled the altars.
The feast day didn't seem mean, Venus, and neither did   1180
your shrine: such a great number of female devotees was
there, who had come to the Venus of Calydon.

ANTE Yes, certainly, as far as the two of us were concerned,
we had the upper hand beautifully and achieved peace,
my sister, and we weren't ridiculed by the youth there,
which, my sister, happened to all the others.

ADE   I'd rather others had that impression than that you
praised yourself, my sister.

ANTE I for one hope they do!   1185

ADE   So do I, when I realize what our talents and those of
others are. We were born in such a family that we ought
to be pure from guilt.

1176 illic ego *P*, illic eo *A*, illi *Weise*
1179 arabius *P*, ara(bus) *A*, aras tus *Leo*

	HAN	Iuppiter, qui genus colis alisque hominum, per quem uiuimus uitalem aeuom,
		quem penes spes, uitae sunt hominum omnium, da diem hunc sospitem, quaeso,
		[rebus meis agundis,] ut quibus annos multos carui quasque e patria perdidi paruas—
1190		redde is libertatem, inuictae praemium ut esse sciam pietati.
1191	AGO	omnia faciet Iuppiter faxo,
1191ᵃ		nam mi est obnoxius et me
1191ᵇ		metuit.
	HAN	tace quaeso.
1192	AGO	ne lacruma, patrue.
1192ᵃ	ANTE	ut uolup est homini, mea soror, si quod agit cluet uictoria;
		sicut nos hodie inter alias praestitimus pulchritudine.
	ADE	stulta, soror, magis es quam uolo. an tu eo pulchra uidere, opsecro,
1195		si tibi illi non os oblitum est fuligine?
1196	AGO	o patrue, o patrue mi!
	HAN	quid est,
1196ᵃ		fratris mei gnate, gnate quid uis? expedi.
1197	AGO	at enim hoc uolo agas.
	HAN	at enim ago istuc.
1197ᵃ	AGO	⟨o⟩ patrue mi patruissume.
1198	HAN	quid est?
	AGO	est lepida et lauta. ut sapit!
1198ᵃ	HAN	ingenium patris habet quod sapit.
	AGO	quae res? iam diu edepol sapientiam tuam haec quidem abusa est.
1200		nunc hinc sapit, hinc sentit quicquid sapit, ex meo amore.

HAN   (*quietly, with tears*) Jupiter, you who protect and nurture mankind, through whom we live our span of life, in whom the hopes and lives of all men lie, please give me this day as one of deliverance [for doing my things], so that the girls whom I was without for many years and whom I lost from my country when they were small—restore their freedom to them, so that I may know that there is a reward for unconquerable piety.   1190

AGO   (*quietly*) I'll make sure Jupiter will do everything: he's answerable to me and fears me.

HAN   (*quietly*) Please be quiet.

AGO   (*quietly*) Stop crying, uncle.

ANTE   (*to Adelphasium*) How pleased is man, my dear sister, if what he does is renowned for victory; just as we stood out in beauty among the others today.

ADE   My sister, you're more stupid than I'd wish. Please, do you consider yourself beautiful just because your face   1195 wasn't besmirched with ash there?

AGO   (*still quietly*) O my uncle, o my dear uncle!

HAN   What is it, nephew, nephew mine, what do you want? Tell me.

AGO   Well, I want you to pay attention.

HAN   Well, I am paying attention.

AGO   O my uncliest uncle!

HAN   What is it?

AGO   She's charming and neat. How clever she is!

HAN   As for the fact that she's clever, she has her father's nature.

AGO   What? She used up your cleverness already long ago. Now   1200 she's clever and has sense on my account, in anything she's clever at, because of my love.

1189 rebus meis agundis *del. Leo*   1197[a] o *add. Leo*

ADE   non eo genere sumus prognatae, tam etsi sumus ser-
       uae, soror,

       ut deceat nos facere quicquam quod homo quisquam
         irrideat.

       multa sunt mulierum uitia, sed hoc e multis maxumum
         est,

       quom sibi nimis placent minusque addunt operam uti
         placeant uiris.

1205   ANTE   nimiae uoluptati est quod in extis nostris portentum
       est, soror,

       quod[que] haruspex de ambabus dixit—

AGO   uelim de me aliquid dixerit.

ANTE   —nos fore inuito domino nostro diebus paucis liberas.

       id ego, nisi quid di aut parentes faxint, qui sperem hau
         scio.

AGO   mea fiducia hercle haruspex, patrue, his promisit, scio,

1210   libertatem, quia me amare hanc scit.

ADE   soror, sequere hac.

ANTE   sequor.

HAN   prius quam abitis, uos uolo ambas. nisi piget, consistite.

ADE   quis reuocat?

AGO   qui bene uolt uobis facere.

ADE   facere occasio est.

       sed quis homo est?

AGO   amicus uobis.

ADE   quiquidem inimicus non siet.

AGO   bonus est hic homo, mea uoluptas.

ADE   pol istum malim quam malum.

1215   AGO   siquidem amicitia est habenda, cum hoc habenda est.

ADE   hau precor.

1206 quod[que] *Bothe*

146

ADE   (*to Anterastilis*) Even though we're slaves, my sister, we weren't born in such a family that we ought to do anything anyone would laugh at. Women's vices are many, but this is the greatest out of the many, that they like themselves too much and make too little effort to be liked by men.

ANTE What was shown in the entrails of our sacrifice, my sister,   1205 gives me enormous joy, and also what the soothsayer said about both of us—

AGO   (*quietly*) I wish he'd said something about me.

ANTE —that we'd be free against our master's will within a few days. Unless the gods or our parents do something, I don't know how I can hope for that.

AGO   (*quietly*) My uncle, I know the soothsayer promised them freedom relying on me, because he knows I love   1210 this girl.

ADE   My sister, follow me this way.

ANTE Yes.

HAN   (*approaching the girls*) Before you leave, I want to speak to you both. If it's no trouble, stand still.

ADE   Who is calling us back?

AGO   Someone who wants to do you a good turn.

ADE   There's an opportunity to do so. But who is the man?

AGO   A friend of yours.

ADE   So long as he's not an enemy.[61]

AGO   He's a good man, my darling.

ADE   I'd rather have a good man than a bad one.

AGO   If you want to have friendship, you must have it with   1215 him.

ADE   I'm not asking for it.

---

[61] I.e., not being an enemy already counts as being a friend.

AGO	multa bona uolt uobis facere.
ADE	bonus bonis bene feceris.
HAN	gaudio ero uobis—
ADE	at edepol nos uoluptati tibi.
HAN	—libertatique.
ADE	istoc pretio tuas nos facile feceris.
AGO	patrue mi, ita me di amabunt, ut ego, si sim Iuppiter,

1220 iam hercle ego illam uxorem ducam et Iunonem extru-
dam foras.
ut pudice uerba fecit, cogitate et commode,
ut modeste orationem praebuit!

| HAN | certo haec mea est. |

sed ut astu sum aggressus ad eas!

AGO	lepide hercle atque commode.
HAN	pergo etiam temptare?
AGO	in pauca confer: sitiunt qui sedent.

1225 HAN quid istic? quod faciundum est quor non agimus? in ius
uos uolo.

AGO	nunc, patrue, tu frugi bonae es. tene. uin ego hanc ap- prendam?
ADE	an patruos est, Agorastocles, tuos hic?
AGO	iam faxo scibis.

nunc pol ego te ulciscar probe, nam faxo . . . mea eris
sponsa.

| HAN | ite in ius, ne moramini. antestare me atque duce. |

1217–18 *uersus del. Langrehr*   1224 perge *P*, pergo *Acidalius*
(*quia* p. etiam temptare *Hannoni dat B*)
    1226 nunc patrue tu frugi bonae es uin hanc ego adprehendam tene
(*cum spatio ante* tene) *A*, nunc tene pa. tu fr. si bonae es uin ego hanc
adpraedam tene (*cum spatio ante* uin *BD, omisso altero* tene *CD*) *P*,
corr. Leo

AGO He wants to do you many good turns.

ADE (*to Hanno*) As a good man you'll do a good turn to good people.

HAN I'll bring you joy—

ADE (*interrupting*) But we'll bring you pleasure.

HAN —and freedom.

ADE For that price you'll easily make us yours.

AGO (*quietly*) My uncle, as truly as the gods will love me, if I were Jupiter, I'd marry that girl at once and throw Juno[62]   1220 out. How chastely, thoughtfully, and pleasantly she's spoken, how modestly she's made her speech!

HAN (*quietly*) She's certainly mine. But how cleverly I approached them!

AGO (*quietly*) Charmingly and pleasantly indeed.

HAN (*quietly*) Am I to continue to test them?

AGO (*quietly*) Keep it short: (*pointing to the audience*) those who are sitting are thirsty.

HAN (*to the girls*) Well then? Why aren't we doing what must   1225 be done? I want you in court.

AGO Now, my uncle, you're decent. (*pointing to Anterastilis*) Hold her. Do you want me to grab this one?

ADE Is this your uncle, Agorastocles?

AGO I'll let you know in a moment. Now I'll take revenge on you properly: I'll make sure that . . . you'll be my betrothed.

HAN Go to court, you two, stop wasting my time. (*to Agorastocles*) Take me as witness and take them along.

---

[62] Wife of Jupiter, the king of gods.

| 1230 | AGO | ego te antestabor, postea . . . hanc amabo atque amplexabor. |

1230 AGO ego te antestabor, postea . . . hanc amabo atque amplexabor.
sed illud quidem uolui dicere—immo [hercle] dixi quod uolebam.

HAN moramini. in ius uos uoco, nisi honestiust prehendi.

ADE quid in ius uocas nos? quid tibi debemus?

AGO   dicet illi.

ADE etiam me meae latrant canes?

AGO   at tu hercle alludiato:

1235 dato mihi pro offa sauium, pro osse linguam obicito.
ita hanc canem faciam tibi oleo tranquilliorem.

HAN it' si itis.

ADE   quid nos fecimus tibi?

HAN   fures estis ambae.

ADE nosn' tibi?

HAN   uos inquam.

AGO   atque ego scio.

ADE   quid id furti est?

AGO   hunc rogato.

HAN quia annos multos filias meas celauistis clam me

1240 atque equidem ingenuas liberas summoque genere gnatas.

ADE numquam mecastor reperies tu istuc probrum penes nos.

AGO da pignus, ni nunc perieres, in sauium, uter utri det.

ADE nil tecum ago, apscede opsecro.

AGO   atque hercle mecum agendum est.
nam hic patruos meus est, pro hoc mihi patronus sim necesse est;

1245 et praedicabo quo modo [uos] furta faciatis multa

1231 hercle *del. Bentley*
1245 uos *del. Becker*

AGO I'll take you as witness, then . . . I'll love and embrace 1230
this girl. (*touches Hanno's ear to make him a witness*) But
I wanted to say that thing—no, I said what I wanted.

HAN (*to the girls*) You're wasting my time. I'm summoning
you to court, unless it's more honorable to be seized.

ADE Why are you summoning us to court? What do we owe
you?

AGO He'll tell you there.

ADE Are even my own dogs barking at me?

AGO Well then, make merry with me: give me a kiss instead 1235
of a dumpling, offer me your tongue instead of a bone.
In that way I'll make this dog more placid for you than
olive oil.

HAN (*to the girls*) Go if you're going.

ADE What have we done to you?

HAN You've both robbed me.

ADE We you?

HAN Yes, you.

AGO I know it, too.

ADE (*to Agorastocles*) What robbery is that?

AGO Ask him.

HAN Because you've concealed my daughters from me for
many years, freeborn, free girls born in a great family to 1240
boot.

ADE You'll never find that crime with us.

AGO Make a bet if you aren't committing perjury now, for a
kiss, which one gives it to which.

ADE I'm not having any dealings with you, please go away.

AGO But you have to deal with me: this is my uncle, I must be
his representative.[63] (*to both*) And I'll tell you in what 1245

[63] Foreigners need a legal representative if they are involved in
court proceedings.

151

       quoque modo ⟨uos⟩ huius filias apud uos habeatis ser-
          uas,

       quas uos ex patria liberas surruptas esse scitis.

ADE ubi sunt eae? aut quas, opsecro—

AGO   satis iam sunt maceratae.

HAN quid si eloquamur?

AGO   censeo hercle, patrue.

ADE   misera timeo

1250   quid hoc sit negoti, mea soror; ita stupida sine animo
          asto.

HAN aduortite animum, mulieres. primum, si id fieri possit,
       ne indigna indignis di darent, id ego euenisset uellem;
       nunc quod boni mihi di danunt, uobis uostraeque ma-
          tri,

       eas dis est aequom gratias nos agere sempiternas,

1255   quom nostram pietatem approbant decorantque di im-
          mortales.

       uos meae estis ambae filiae et hic est cognatus uoster,
       huiusce fratris filius, Agorastocles.

ADE   amabo,
       num hi falso oblectant gaudio nos?

AGO   at ita me di seruent
       ut hic pater est uoster. date manus.

ADE   salue, insperate nobis

1260   pater, te complecti nos sine.

ANTE   cupite atque exspectate
       pater, salue.

ADE   ambae filiae sumus.

ANTE   amplectamur ambae.

AGO quis me amplectetur postea?

1246 uos *add. Lindsay ex priore uersu*

way you're committing many thefts and in what way you keep his daughters with you as slaves, who you know were kidnapped from their country where they were free.

ADE Where are they? Or which ones, please—

AGO (*interrupting*) They've been tormented enough now.

HAN What if we tell them?

AGO I do think so, uncle.

ADE Poor me, I'm afraid what business this is, my dear sister; so stupefied am I standing here and out of my mind. 1250

HAN Pay attention, women. First, if it were possible that the gods should never inflict undeserved things on those who don't deserve them, I would like that to have happened; but as things are, it's right for us, me, you, and your mother, to give eternal thanks to the gods for the good things they're giving us, since the immortal gods 1255 approve of our piety and crown it. You're both my daughters and this is your relative, the son of (*points to himself*) this man's brother, Agorastocles.

ADE (*to Anterastilis*) Please, are they delighting us with false joy?

AGO (*to the girls*) No, as truly as the gods may preserve me, this is your father. Give him your hands.

ADE Greetings, our unhoped-for father, let us embrace you! 1260

ANTE Our desired and long-awaited father, greetings!

ADE We're both your daughters.

ANTE Let's both embrace you. (*they do so*)

AGO Who will embrace me afterward?

1252 euenisset *A*, euenire *P*   1257 huiusce Ω, Iahonis *Guyet*
1258 me ita Ω, *transp. Geppert*   1261 *post* salue *nulla nota
personae, sed spatium in B*   sunt *P*, su* *A*, sumus ς

PLAUTUS

HAN   nunc ego sum fortunatus,
        multorum annorum miserias nunc hac uoluptate sedo.
ADE uix hoc uidemur credere.
HAN   magis qui credatis dicam.
1265   nam uostra nutrix prima me cognouit.
ADE   ubi ea, amabo, est?
HAN apud hunc est.
AGO   quaeso, qui lubet tam diu tenere collum?
        omitte saltem tu altera. nolo ego istunc enicari
        prius quam te mi desponderit.
ADE   mitto.
ANTE   sperate, salue.
HAN condamus alter alteram ergo in neruom bracchialem.
1270   quibus nunc in terra melius est?
AGO   eueniunt digna dignis.
HAN tandem huic cupitum contigit.
AGO   o Apelle, o Zeuxis pictor,
        quor estis numero mortui, hoc exemplo ut pingeretis?
        nam alios pictores nil moror huius modi tractare exem-
          pla.
HAN di deaeque omnes, uobis habeo merito magnas gratias
1275   quom hac me laetitia affecistis tanta et tantis gaudiis
        ut meae gnatae ad me redirent in potestatem meam.
[ADE mi pater, tua pietas plane nobis auxilio fuit.

1265 primum Ω, prima *Bentley*   1267 enicari *T*, istuc enicam
BCD, enicasme *A ut uidetur*, istunc enicari *Lindsay*
    1268 te mihi *P*, tibi *A*   *si A sequimur*, enicas me *prioris uersus
et* prius quam tibi desponderit *Adelphasio tribuere debemus*
    1269 alterum Ω, alteram *Geppert*
    1272 numero estis Ω *Festus, transp. Reiz*
    1276 in *P*, et *A*   1277–79 *del. Geppert*

154

HAN Now I'm fortunate, with this joy I'm now calming the wretched experiences of many years.

ADE It's hard for us to believe this.

HAN I'll tell you how you can believe it more easily: your nurse 1265 was the first to recognize me.

ADE Where is she, please?

HAN She's with him. (*points to Agorastocles*)

AGO Please, why do you wish to have your arms around his neck for so long? (*to Adelphasium*) At least you second one let go. I don't want him to be suffocated before he's betrothed you to me.

ADE I'm letting go.

ANTE My hoped-for father, greetings.

HAN Then let's put each other into a prison of arms. (*embraces Anterastilis again*) What people now are better off on 1270 earth?

AGO Deserved things happen to those who deserve them.

HAN At last this man (*points to himself*) has got what he wished for.

AGO O Apelles! O painter Zeuxis![64] Why did you die too early to paint this scene? Yes, I don't care for other painters dealing with such scenes.

HAN All gods and goddesses, I give you great thanks deservedly for imbuing me with this great happiness and 1275 these great joys, that my daughters have returned to me into my authority.

[ADE My father, your piety has clearly helped us.

---

[64] Famous Greek painters of the fourth and fifth centuries.

AGO   patrue, facito in memoria habeas tuam maiorem filiam
      mihi te despondisse—

HAN   memini.

AGO   —et dotis quid promiseris.]

V. v: ANTAMYNIDES. ADELPHASIVM.
ANTERASTILIS. HANNO. AGORASTOCLES

1280 ANTA si ego minam non ultus fuero probe quam lenoni dedi,
      tum profecto me sibi habento scurrae ludificatui.
      is etiam me ad prandium ad se abduxit ignauissumus,
      ipse abiit foras, me reliquit pro atriensi in aedibus.
      ubi nec leno neque illae redeunt nec quod edim quic-
        quam datur,

1285   pro maiore parte prandi pignus cepi, abii foras;
      sic dedero: aere militari tetigero lenunculum.
      nanctus est hominem mina quem argenti circumduc-
        eret.
      sed mea amica nunc mihi irato obuiam ueniat uelim:
      iam pol ego illam pugnis totam faciam uti sit merulea,

1290   ita ‹eam› repplebo atritate, atrior multo ut siet
      quam Aegyptini, qui cortinam ludis per circum ferunt.

ANTE tene sis me arte, mea uoluptas; male ego metuo mi-
      luos—
      mala illa bestia est—ne forte me auferat pullum tuom.

ADE   ut nequeo te satis complecti, mi pater!

ANTA   ego me moror.

1295   propemodum hoc opsonare prandium potero mihi.
      sed quid hoc est? quid est? quid hoc est? quid ego
        uideo? quo modo?
      quid hoc est conduplicationis? quae haec est congemi-
        natio?

    1290 eam *add. Bentley*   atrior *P,* atritior *A*

156

AGO Uncle, make sure you remember that you've betrothed
your older daughter to me—

HAN (*interrupting*) Yes, I remember.

AGO —and what dowry you've promised.]

Enter ANTAMYNIDES *from the pimp's house.*

ANTA (*to the audience*) If I don't take revenge properly for the   1280
mina I gave to the pimp, then the men about town can
indeed poke fun at me. He even invited me in for lunch,
the big crook, went out himself, and left me as major-
domo in the house. When neither pimp nor girls re-
turned and I wasn't given anything to eat, I took security   1285
for the larger part of the lunch and left. That's how I'll
do it: I'll make the little pimp pay his army tax. He's
found the right man to cheat out of a silver mina! But
now that I'm angry I'd like my girlfriend to meet me:
with my fists I'll make sure that she's black as a blackbird
this instant, I'll fill her with blackness to such an extent   1290
that she's much blacker than the Egyptians who carry the
cauldron[65] round the circus during the games.

ANTE (*to Hanno*) Please hold me tight, my darling; I'm terribly
afraid that the kite—that bad beast—might by chance
snatch me, your chicken, away from you.

ADE How I can't embrace you enough, my dear father!

ANTA (*to the audience*) I'm wasting my time. I'll practically be   1295
able to buy myself a lunch with this. (*shows what he has
taken from the pimp's house*) But what's this? What is it?
What's this? What do I see? How? What doubling is this?
What twinning is this? Who is this chap with long tunics

---

65 With water, for cooling racehorses.

quis hic homo est cum tunicis longis quasi puer caupo-
    nius?
satin ego oculis cerno? estne illaec mea amica Anteras-
    tilis?
1300 et ea est certo. iam pridem ego me sensi nihili pendier.
non pudet puellam amplexari baiolum in media uia?
iam hercle ego illunc excruciandum totum carnufici
    dabo.
sane genus hoc mulierosum est tunicis demissiciis.
sed adire certum est hanc amatricem Africam.
1305 heus tu, tibi dico, mulier, ecquid te pudet?
quid tibi negoti est autem cum istac? dic mihi.
HAN   adulescens, salue.
ANTA   nolo, nihil ad te attinet.
quid tibi hanc digito tactio est?
HAN   quia mi lubet.
ANTA lubet?
HAN   ita dico.
ANTA   ligula, i in malam crucem!
1310 tune hic amator audes esse, hallex uiri,
aut contrectare quod mares homines amant?
deglupta maena, sarrapis, sementium,
manstruca, halagora, sampsa, tum autem plenior
ali ulpicique quam Romani remiges.

1309 ligula *CD*, legula *B*, *fortasse* lingula *legendum est*

[66] He is called a baggage carrier as a general insult to his status and
because both girls cling to him like pieces of luggage.
[67] *Ligula* is intended as an insult, but its precise meaning is unclear;
normally the word means "spoon" or "shoelace" (in the latter case
mostly spelled *lingula*).

like a tavern boy? Do I see clearly enough with my eyes? Isn't that my girlfriend Anterastilis? Yes, it's certainly 1300 her. For a while now I've felt that I'm considered worthless. Isn't the girl ashamed of embracing a baggage carrier[66] in the middle of the street? Now I'll hand that chap over to the hangman to be tortured totally. This kind with their tunics hanging down is definitely addicted to women. But I'm resolved to approach my African lover-girl. *(to Anterastilis)* Hey you, I'm talking to you, woman, 1305 don't you have any shame? *(to Hanno)* And what business do you have with that woman? Tell me.

HAN   Greetings, young man.

ANTA No, it's none of your business. Why do you touch this girl even with a finger?

HAN   Because I want to.

ANTA You want to?

HAN   That's what I say.

ANTA You shoelace,[67] go and be hanged! Do you dare to be a 1310 lover here, you dregs[68] of a man, or to touch what men love? You skinned[69] sprat, Persian tunic, mantle,[70] sheepskin coat, salt market, crushed olive, and more stuffed with common and Phoenician garlic[71] than Roman rowers!

[68] *Hallex* is the sediment in *garum*, a fermented fish sauce.

[69] An insult based on Hanno's presumable circumcision, a custom common among Semitic peoples.   [70] The meaning of *sementium* is unclear. Hanno is being insulted by being referred to as if he were one of the products Carthaginian tradesmen sell; since *sementium* stands in between two items of clothing, I have translated it as "mantle."

[71] *Ulpicum*, "Phoenician garlic," is a larger variety of garlic (Colum. 11. 3. 20).

1315   AGO   num tibi, adulescens, malae aut dentes pruriunt,
               qui huic es molestus, an malam rem quaeritas?
     ANTA   quin adhibuisti, dum istaec loquere, tympanum?
               nam te cinaedum esse arbitror magis quam uirum.
     AGO   scin quam cinaedus sum? ite istinc, serui, foras
1320   efferte fustis.
     ANTA   heus tu, si quid per iocum
               dixi, nolito in serium conuortere.
     ANTE   quid tibi lubido est, opsecro, Antamynides,
               loqui inclementer nostro cognato et patri?
               nam hic noster pater est; hic nos cognouit modo
1325   et hunc sui fratris filium.
     ANTA   ita me Iuppiter
               bene amet, bene factum! gaudeo et uolup est mihi
               siquidem quid lenoni optigit magni mali
               quomque e uirtute uobis fortuna optigit.
     ANTE   credibile ecastor dicit. crede huic, mi pater.
1330   HAN   credo.
     AGO   et ego credo. sed eccum lenonem optume.
     [HAN   credo.
     AGO   et ego credo. edepol hic uenit commodus.]
               bonum uirum eccum uideo, se recipit domum.
     [HAN   quis hic est?
     AGO   utrumuis est, uel leno uel Lycus.
               in seruitute hic filias habuit tuas
1335   et mi auri fur est.
     HAN   bellum hominem, quem noueris!]

       1317 quor non Ω, quin *Geppert*
       1327 siquid *A*, siquidem *P*, siquidem quid *Camerarius*
       1330 optume *A*, Lycum *P*   1331 *non fertur in P*
       1333–35 *uersus om. A*

AGO   Young man, are your jaws or teeth itching, since you're   1315
annoying him, or are you looking for trouble?

ANTA Why didn't you use a tambourine[72] while saying that? I
believe you're more of a catamite than a man.

AGO   Do you know what sort of catamite I am? (*into his house*)
Come outside, slaves, and bring clubs!   1320

ANTA (*suddenly afraid*) Hey you, if I said anything in jest, don't
turn it into earnest.

ANTE Please, Antamynides, why do you wish to insult our rela-
tive and father? Yes, this is our father; he's just recog-
nized us and this nephew of his.   1325

ANTA So love me Jupiter, excellent! I'm happy and pleased if
the pimp has got into some major trouble, and because
you attained this success in accordance with your vir-
tue.

ANTE What he says is believable. Believe him, my dear fa-
ther.

HAN   Yes, I do.   1330

AGO   And so do I. But look, the pimp, perfect.

[HAN (*to the soldier*) I believe you.

AGO   (*also to the soldier*) And so do I. (*seeing Lycus*) Really,
he's coming in the nick of time.] Look, I can see the good
man, he's returning home.

[HAN Who is this?

AGO   Whichever you wish, a pimp or a Lycus. He kept your
daughters in slavery and robbed me of my gold.   1335

HAN   A delightful chap for you to know!]

---

[72] The *tympanum* is a percussion instrument used in the rites of
Cybele, whose most radical male followers castrated themselves and
assumed female personalities.

AGO rapiamus in ius.
HAN   minime.
AGO   quapropter?
HAN   quia
       iniuriarum multo induci satius est.

V. vi: LYCVS. AGORASTOCLES. HANNO. ANTAMYNIDES

LYC decipitur nemo, mea quidem sententia,
       qui suis amicis narrat recte res suas;
1340   nam omnibus amicis meis idem unum conuenit,
       ut me suspendam, ne addicar Agorastocli.
AGO leno, eamus in ius.
LYC   opsecro te, Agorastocles,
       suspendere ut me liceat.
HAN   in ius te uoco.
LYC quid tibi mecum autem?
HAN   quia ⟨enim⟩ hasce aio liberas
1345   ingenuasque esse filias ambas meas;
       eae sunt surruptae cum nutrice paruolae.
LYC iam pridem equidem istuc sciui, et miratus fui
       neminem uenire qui istas assereret manu.
       meae quidem profecto non sunt.
ANTA   leno, in ius eas.
1350 LYC de prandio tu dicis. debetur, dabo.
AGO duplum pro furto mi opus est.
LYC   sume hinc quid lubet.
HAN et mihi suppliciis multis.
LYC   sume hinc quid lubet.
ANTA et mihi quidem mina argenti.

       1337 iniuriarum Ω, in ius bonum uirum *Leo*   induci *P*, indici
A
       1344 enim *add. Bothe*

AGO Let's drag him to court.

HAN Not at all.

AGO Why?

HAN Because it's much better for him to be brought in as defendant for his injustices.[73]

Enter LYCUS *from the right.*

LYC (*to himself*) Nobody is deceived, in my opinion at least, who tells his friends his affairs openly: all my friends 1340 agree on this one point, that I should hang myself so as not to become the bond slave of Agorastocles.

AGO Pimp, let's go to court.

LYC I beg you, Agorastocles, to let me hang myself.

HAN I'm summoning you to court.

LYC But what do I have to do with you?

HAN Because I claim that these girls are both my free and 1345 freeborn daughters; they were kidnapped with their nurse when they were little.

LYC I've known that for a long time, and I was surprised that nobody came to lay his hand on them. Indeed, they don't belong to me.

ANTA Pimp, go to court.

LYC You are talking about the lunch. You're owed one, I'll 1350 give you one.

AGO I require double payment for the theft.

LYC Take from me what you wish.

HAN And I require substantial reparations.

LYC Take from me what you wish.

ANTA And I require a silver mina.

[73] The line is not very clear syntactically and semantically. Hanno seems to prefer a more cautious way of dealing with the pimp.

LYC   sume hinc quid lubet.
        collo rem soluam iam omnibus quasi baiolus.

                       [EXITVS SPVRIVS

1355 AGO numquid recusas contra me?
     LYC   hau uerbum quidem.
     AGO ite igitur intro, mulieres. sed, patrue mi,
           tuam, ut dixisti, mihi desponde filiam.
     HAN haud aliter ausim.
     ANTA   bene uale.
     AGO   et tu bene uale.
     ANTA leno, arrabonem hoc pro mina mecum fero.
1360 LYC perii hercle!
     AGO   immo hau multo post si in ius ueneris.
     LYC quin egomet tibi me addico. quid praetore opust?
           uerum opsecro te ut liceat simplum soluere,
           trecentos Philippos; credo corradi potest:
           cras auctionem faciam.
     AGO   tantisper quidem
1365   ut sis apud me lignea in custodia.
     LYC fiat.
     AGO   sequere intro, patrue mi, ut [hunc] festum diem
           habeamus hilare, huius malo et nostro bono.
           multum ualete. multa uerba fecimus;

1355–71 *del.* Leo
1366 hunc *om.* A

---

[74] A porter serves people by carrying things on his neck, while Lycus wants to put a noose around his.

LYC Take from me what you wish. Now I'll pay everybody with my neck like a porter.[74]

[*The following passage is a post-Plautine ending of the play, presumably created to shorten it somewhat.*]

AGO Do you object to my procedure?   1355
LYC Not a word.
AGO Then go inside, women.

Exeunt ADELPHASIUM *and* ANTERASTILIS *into the house of Agorastocles.*

AGO But, my dear uncle, betroth your daughter to me, as you said.
HAN I wouldn't dare to act differently.
ANTA Goodbye.
AGO And goodbye to you.
ANTA (*showing what he has taken from the pimp's house*) Pimp, I'm carrying this with me as deposit for the mina.
LYC I'm dead!   1360
AGO No, you shall be, not much later, when you come to court.
LYC No, I'm making myself your bond slave. What do you need the praetor for? But I beg you to let me pay the simple sum, three hundred Philippics. I believe it can be scraped together: tomorrow I'll hold an auction.
AGO In the meantime you should be at my place in wooden   1365 stocks.
LYC Yes.
AGO Follow me in, my dear uncle, so that we can enjoy the feast day, with his misfortune and our good fortune. (*to the audience*) Fare very well. We've made a lot of words;

malum postremo omne ad lenonem reccidit.
1370 nunc, quod postremum est condimentum fabulae,
si placuit, plausum postulat comoedia.]

V. vii: AGORASTOCLES. LYCVS. ANTAMYNIDES.
HANNO. ADELPHASIVM. ANTERASTILIS
[PARS ALTERIVS EXITVS SPVRII

AGO quam rem agis, miles? qui lubet patruo meo
loqui inclementer? ne mirere mulieres
quod eum sequontur: modo cognouit filias
1375 suas esse hasce ambas.
LYC   hem, quod uerbum auris meas
tetigit? nunc perii!
ANTA   unde haec perierunt domo?
AGO Carthaginienses sunt.
LYC   at ego sum perditus.
illuc ego metui semper ne cognosceret
eas aliquis, quod nunc factum est. uae misero mihi!
1380 periere, opinor, duodeuiginti minae,
qui hasce emi.
AGO   et tute ipse periisti, Lyce.
HAN quis hic est?
AGO   utrumuis est, uel leno uel Lycus.
in seruitute hic filias habuit tuas,
et mi auri fur est.
HAN   bellum hominem, quem noueris!
1385 ANTA leno, rapacem te esse semper credidi,
uerum etiam furacem ⟨aiunt⟩ qui norunt magis.
LYC accedam. per ego [te] tua te genua opsecro
et hunc, cognatum quem tuom esse intellego:
quando boni estis, ut bonos facere addecet
1390 facite ut ⟨uos⟩ uostro subueniatis supplici.

in the end all trouble fell back onto the pimp. Now if you 1370
enjoyed the comedy, it demands the final seasoning of a
play, applause.]

[*The following passage is part of another post-Plautine ending.*

AGO What are you doing, soldier? Why do you wish to insult
my uncle? Don't be surprised that the women are fol-
lowing him; he's just recognized that they're both his 1375
daughters.

LYC (*aside*) Oh! What word has touched my ears? Now I'm
dead!

ANTA From where were they lost?

AGO They're Carthaginians.

LYC (*aside*) But I am ruined. I was always afraid that someone
would recognize them, which has happened now. Poor,
wretched me! I think the eighteen minas for which I 1380
bought them have perished.

AGO (*overhearing him*) And you've perished yourself, Lycus.

HAN Who is this?

AGO Whichever you like, a pimp or a Lycus. He kept your
daughters in slavery, and he robbed me of my gold.

HAN A delightful chap for you to know!

ANTA Pimp, I've always believed you to be greedy, but those 1385
who know you better say that you're also thieving.

LYC I'll approach. (*clasping the knees of Agorastocles*) I en-
treat you by your knees, and him, who I realize is your
relative; since you're good, act the way good people
ought to act: come to the aid of your suppliant. I've 1390

1372–97 *del. Camerarius*
1386 aiunt *add. Brix*   1387 te *del. Kaempf*
1390 facite et Ω, facite ut ‹uos› *Hasper*, faciatis *Leo*

iam pridem equidem istas esse sciui liberas
et exspectabam si qui eas assereret manu.
nam meae ⟨eae⟩ prorsum non sunt. tum autem aurum
    tuom
reddam quod apud me est et ius iurandum dabo
1395   me malitiose nil fecisse, Agorastocles.
AGO   quid mihi par facere sit cum me egomet consulam.
omitte genua.
LYC   mitto, si ita sententia est.]

EXITVS PLAVTINVS

ANTA heus tu, leno!
LYC   quid lenonem uis inter negotium?
ANTA ut minam mi argenti reddas prius quam in neruom ab-
    ducere.
1400 LYC di meliora faxint!
ANTA   sic est: hodie cenabis foris.
aurum, argentum, collum, leno, tris res nunc debes
    simul.
HAN quid med hac re facere deceat egomet mecum cogito.
si uolo hunc ulcisci, litis sequar in alieno oppido,
quantum audiui ingenium et mores eius quo pacto
    sient.
1405 ADE mi pater, ne quid tibi cum istoc rei sit, fac missum
    opsecro.
ANTE ausculta sorori. abi, diiunge inimicitias cum improbo.
HAN hoc age sis, leno. quamquam ego te meruisse ut pereas
    scio,
non experiar tecum.

1391 sciui esse P, *transp. Bothe*   1393 eae *add. Geppert*
1400 estu ideo P, est hodie *Hasper*, esto ideo *Lindsay*

168

known for a long time that they're free and I was waiting
to see if anyone would assert their freedom: they don't
belong to me at all. Then again, I'll give you your gold
back, which is with me, and I'll swear an oath that I didn't   1395
do anything out of ill will, Agorastocles.

AGO I'll think about what I ought to do. Let go of my knees.

LYC (*doing so*) Yes, if that's your decree.]

This last passage seems to be the genuinely Plautine one.

ANTA Hey you, pimp!

LYC What do you want the pimp for in the middle of busi-
ness?

ANTA You must return my silver mina before you're taken to
prison.

LYC May the gods forbid!   1400

ANTA That's the situation: today you'll dine out. You owe three
things at the same time now, pimp: gold, silver, and your
neck.

HAN (*to his family*) I'm thinking about what I should do in this
situation. If I want to take revenge on him, I'll be pursu-
ing a case in a foreign town, to judge from what I've
heard his nature and character are like.

ADE My dear father, don't have anything to do with that man,   1405
please let it go.

ANTE (*also to Hanno*) Listen to my sister. Go away, drop your
enmity with that crook.

HAN Do pay attention, pimp. Even though I know you've de-
served to perish, I won't go to court with you.

1405 siet *P*, sit *Bothe*   acmassum *P*, fac missum *Pradel*

AGO   neque ego; si aurum mihi reddes meum,
      leno, quando ex neruo emissu's . . . compingare in car-
        cerem.
1410 LYC iamne autem ut soles?
      ANTA   ego, Poene, tibi me purgatum uolo.
      si quid dixi iratus aduorsum animi tui sententiam,
      id uti ignoscas quaeso; et quom istas inuenisti filias,
      ita me di ament, mi uoluptati est.
      HAN   ignosco et credo tibi.
      ANTA leno, tu autem amicam mihi des facito aut [auri] mihi
        reddas minam.
1415 LYC uin tibicinam meam habere?
      ANTA   nil moror tibicinam;
      nescias utrum ei maiores buccaene an mammae sient.
      LYC dabo quae placeat.
      ANTA   cura.
      LYC   aurum cras ad te referam tuom.
      AGO facito in memoria habeas.
      LYC   miles, sequere me.
      ANTA   ego uero sequor.
      AGO quid ais, patrue? quando hinc ire cogitas Carthaginem?
1420   nam tecum mi una ire certum est.
      HAN   ubi primum potero, ilico.
      AGO dum auctionem facio, hic opus est aliquot ut maneas
        dies.
      HAN faciam ita ut uis.
      AGO   age sis, eamus, nos curemus.
      GREX   plaudite.

1414 auri *del. Seyffert*

AGO Neither will I; if you give me back my gold, pimp, when you've been let out of the fetters . . . you'll be put into prison.

LYC Your usual ways now?   1410

ANTA Carthaginian, I want to apologize to you. If I said anything against your wishes in my anger, I ask you to forgive me for it; and as truly as the gods may love me, I'm pleased that you found those girls to be your daughters.

HAN I forgive and believe you.

ANTA Pimp, you, on the other hand, must make sure to give me a girlfriend or to return my mina to me.

LYC Do you want to have my flute girl?   1415

ANTA I don't care for a flute girl; you wouldn't know whether her cheeks or her breasts are bigger.

LYC I'll give you one you'll like.

ANTA Take care of it.

LYC (*to Agorastocles*) I'll return your gold to you tomorrow.

AGO Make sure you remember.

LYC Soldier, follow me.

ANTA Yes indeed.

Exeunt LYCUS *and* ANTAMYNIDES *into the former's house.*

AGO What do you say, uncle? When do you plan to go to Carthage? I'm resolved to go with you.   1420

HAN As soon as I can, at once.

AGO You need to stay here for some days while I'm holding an auction.

HAN I'll do as you wish.

AGO Go on please, let's go and give ourselves a good time.

TROUPE Give us your applause!

THE PUNIC PASSAGES
IN THE *POENULUS*

In several Plautine comedies Greek words and phrases occur, and although even early Latin already had a plethora of nativized Greek loans, many of the Greek words and phrases in comedy are clearly to be considered foreign. Nevertheless, the majority of people in the audience will have understood such Greek elements without difficulty, which allows Plautus to create his own Greek puns. Knowledge of other foreign languages could not be presupposed, which explains why Plautus generally does not employ them in his plays, even for comic effect.[1] The exception is the *Poenulus*, where a large amount of Punic is spoken, mostly by Hanno, but to a lesser extent also by other characters. There are two large texts in ll. 930–39 and ll. 940–49, both spoken by Hanno, and there are fifteen very short pieces between l. 994 and l. 1152.

Apart perhaps from some sailors and merchants, who may have had a basic command of the language, few people in the

---

[1] An exception occurs in the *Caecus uel Praedones* fr. 10, where a man says *mu* in answer to a question and is immediately identified as an *Afer*. *Afer* can refer to any African, but it also specifically indicates a Carthaginian. If Plautus has not simply made up the word in order to make fun of the foreigner, it could be the Punic question word *mu*, "what" (see my comments on l. 1010).

audience will have understood these Punic passages. This is why I have left them untranslated in the English version of the play. But since the Punic in the *Poenulus* is real Punic and not gibberish invented in order to make the audience laugh, the passages deserve comment and translation. However, two caveats have to be made from the outset. First, even though Punic is a language that is understood reasonably well, there remain certain gaps in our knowledge, partly concerning morphosyntax and partly concerning the lexicon. Second, the text transmitted in the manuscripts is corrupt. Naturally, mistakes occur when texts are copied, and such mistakes increase greatly in number when the copyists do not understand the language. But while correcting mistakes in a Latin text is often relatively straightforward, the situation is more complicated when the language concerned is not fully understood and, to make matters worse, cannot be rendered satisfactorily in the Latin alphabet. Because of this, I will from time to time juxtapose different solutions in my commentary or forgo a translation altogether. In fact, I believe that apart from making the Punic passages accessible to those who are not specialists in Semitic, my main contribution here is to draw a distinction between what is certain, what is plausible but not proven, and what cannot be explained at all.

INTRODUCTION

Punic in Its Semitic Context

Just as Latin is an Indo-European language, Punic belongs to the Semitic language family; this was already recognized at the end of the sixteenth century, when Joseph Justus Scaliger stated that the speech of the Carthaginian Hanno differs little from Hebrew. Nowadays the Semitic language family is typically subdivided into two major groups:[2] on the one hand there is East Semitic, comprising Akkadian and Eblaite, and on the other hand there is West Semitic, comprising all other Semitic languages. West Semitic is in turn divided into South Semitic, with languages like Ge'ez, the language of Ethiopian liturgy, and Central Semitic.[3] Central Semitic comprises Arabic on the one hand and Northwest Semitic on the other. Northwest Semitic contains three major branches: Ugaritic, Aramaic, and Canaanite. The Canaanite languages are all very closely related; they are Hebrew, Phoenician, Moabite, Edomite, Ammonite, and the language of the letters of El Amarna (Akkadian with strong Canaanite influence). Punic is a later form of Phoenician. Since Hebrew is the language of the Canaanite group that is best understood, scholars trying to explain obscure elements of Punic normally have recourse to Hebrew.

The Phoenician homeland is the coastal area of southern Syria and northern Palestine. The oldest Phoenician texts date from around 1100 BC, the latest from the first century BC. Phoenician is mainly known from inscriptions; nothing of the rich Phoenician literature mentioned by Greek and Roman writers has come down to us. Although several thousand inscriptions have been found, our knowledge of the language is still limited because many of the texts are formulaic or contain

[2] For details see Faber (1997). Traditional subgrouping relied heavily on the accidents of geography and culture, but modern subgrouping is based on linguistic, especially morphological, innovations.

[3] Central Semitic is not universally recognized as a subgroup, even though the arguments in its favor are convincing. The existence of a Central Semitic subgroup was first postulated by Robert Hetzron (for a brief discussion see Versteegh 1997: 14–18).

mostly onomastic material; for instance, funerary inscriptions typically follow the same patterns and inscriptions indicating ownership require little more than the owners' names.

The Phoenicians were a seafaring nation and founded colonies throughout the Mediterranean. Linguistically the most important of these new foundations was Carthage, a city in what is now Tunisia. The dialect of Carthage, at first difficult to distinguish from other forms of Phoenician because of the conservative nature of orthography and writing conventions in general, developed in its own way and is referred to as Punic. Punic continued to be spoken in North Africa long after the language of the homeland had died out and even after Carthage was destroyed in 146 BC. Saint Augustine (AD 354–430) mentioned that it was still spoken by a large number of people in his day (*epist.* 17. 2).

Script and Sound System, Writing Conventions, and Problems of Rendering Punic in the Latin Alphabet

The Phoenician script[4] only marks sounds that can stand at the beginning of a word or a syllable; since in Phoenician words and syllables cannot begin with vowels, the Phoenician script contains only consonants. In this respect it is no different from the old Hebrew and Aramaic scripts. Phoenician has twenty-two consonant signs, and these seem to correspond closely to the consonantal phonemes of the language:[5]

[4] For recent introductions see Jongeling and Kerr (2005) or Jongeling (2008).

[5] In what follows, I use the standard transliteration system for the Phoenician alphabet rather than the symbols of the International Phonetic Association. Lowercase letters are used to transliterate the Phoe-

stops: p, b, t, d, ṭ, k, g, ḳ/q, ʾ
nasals: m, n
fricatives: s, z, ṣ, š, ḥ, ʿ, h
liquids: r, l
glides: w, y

At a relatively early stage, the Greeks took over the Phoenician alphabet. Several Phoenician consonant sounds had no equivalent in Greek, which allowed the Greeks to use the signs for these sounds in a different function, as vowel signs. A West Greek variety of the alphabet was subsequently adopted by the Etruscans, who passed it on to the Romans.

Much later, vocalism began to be indicated in biblical Hebrew. The vocalism of Phoenician (and Punic) can be reconstructed partly through comparison with Hebrew and other Semitic languages which marked vowels in their scripts, partly through the study of later developments within Phoenician and Punic, and partly through the analysis of borrowings and information arising through language contact. Nevertheless, a number of uncertainties remain.

Among the stops, ṭ and ḳ are called "emphatic." Like their nonemphatic counterparts *t* and *k* they were voiceless, and their emphatic quality was probably a pharyngeal secondary articulation; phoneticians would write the nonemphatic stops as [t] and [k] and the emphatic ones as [tˤ] and [kˤ]. This secondary articulation resulted in a retraction of the tongue root and thus, in the case of ḳ, in a uvular rather than a velar closure (hence the symbol *q*). ʾ is a glottal stop [ʔ] as in the London

---

nician alphabet to indicate sounds. The corresponding uppercase letters represent the letters of the Phoenician alphabet.

Cockney pronunciation of *better* as [beʔə] or in Arabic '. In Hebrew the voiced and voiceless stops had fricative variants. Whether this was also the case for Phoenician and Punic is uncertain. Many scholars believe that no such variants existed, but assume that p turned into f in all instances. The Plautine text provides conflicting evidence. On the one hand there are spellings with *ph* and f; the former could stand for an aspirated stop, p^h, or a fricative, f,[6] while the latter has to be a fricative unless a copyist unfamiliar with Punic routinely changed the spelling *ph* to f. But on the other hand, Milphio's misunderstandings of Punic *palu* (l. 1017) and *phonnim* (l. 1023) as *palas*, "spades," and *supponi/imponi*, "place under/place on," indicate that Plautus had a plosive pronunciation in mind, that is, p or p^h for both spellings p and *ph*.

Among the fricatives, $\d{s}$ is emphatic (phonetic symbol [sˤ]) and $\check{s}$ is palato-alveolar, like the first sound in English *shine*. There are two pharyngeal fricatives with no counterpart in English: $\d{h}$ is voiceless (phonetic symbol [ħ]) and ' is voiced (phonetic symbol [ʕ]). Close equivalents can be found in Arabic.

Languages change, and Punic is no exception. At least some varieties of Punic gradually merged the emphatic stops with their nonemphatic counterparts. Similarly, the various sibilants are often confused in late Punic epigraphy, indicating a partial or complete merger of s, z, $\d{s}$, and $\check{s}$. Late inscriptions in the Phoenician alphabet also show confusion between the letters originally indicating laryngeal and pharyngeal sounds, for instance ' and '; this points to further mergers or loss of these

---

[6] In Plautus' time the graphemic sequence *ph* would have been pronounced as a stop, but not all Punic in the *Poenulus* was written by Plautus and belongs to his period.

sounds. In addition, the glides y and w were not preserved in a number of environments.

In some cases the loss of such consonants led to compensatory lengthening of preceding vowels. Similar changes happened in Hebrew, where such consonant signs could from then on be used to mark long vowels as well as consonants. Consonantal signs used in vocalic function are called *matres lectionis* ("reading aides"). Like Hebrew, Punic makes use of them, albeit in a more limited way; for instance, Punic inscriptions often use ' at the end of a word to indicate a long vowel, which in Phoenician remained unmarked.[7]

A number of Punic inscriptions in the Greek and Latin alphabets exist. These inscriptions are not always easy to understand, because the Greek and Latin alphabets are so different from their original Phoenician source that they cannot render the Punic consonantal phonemes adequately. Furthermore, even where these two daughter alphabets can render Punic sounds well, because Punic has, for instance, merged k and q, the more phonetic spellings are not always useful, because a more conservative orthography in the Punic script can help us to identify lexemes more easily by comparing them with their equivalents in older Phoenician texts. On the other hand, such inscriptions in the Greek and Latin alphabets help us to understand the Punic vowel system. However, even though the Greek and Latin alphabets can render vowels more clearly than the late Punic system of *matres lectionis*, they are not nearly as helpful as the Phoenician consonant alphabet is for understanding the consonantal phonemes of the language.

Since Phoenician and older Punic are better understood

---

[7] The system of *matres lectionis* in Punic is described in more detail in Jongeling and Kerr (2005: 7–8).

than late Punic, partly because they are still closer to the other Canaanite languages, the best way to deal with the late inscriptional evidence in the Greek and Latin alphabets is to transpose them into the Phoenician script or a Romanized version thereof with special characters; then the consonants are more clearly differentiated. Editors have to make the difficult decision whether, for instance, a Latin *t* corresponds to a Phoenician *t* or *ṭ*, but such a procedure enables us to see better what words we are dealing with, even if it is also somewhat anachronistic because of the mergers of sounds and the subsequent orthographic confusions mentioned above. When it comes to interpreting these late texts, the contribution of the vowels is less important, however significant it is linguistically.

Scholars working on the Punic attested in Plautus use essentially the same procedure as for Punic inscriptions in the Latin alphabet. However, not all Punic texts in Plautus follow the same Latin conventions of orthography. The first Punic text in the *Poenulus* is Hanno's entrance monologue. There are two versions of it, commonly called Text 1 (ll. 930–39) and Text 2 (ll. 940–49); of this monologue, a Latin equivalent exists (ll. 950–60, without the spurious l. 954[8]), which is of great help in understanding the Punic.

Text 1 is transmitted only in the Palatine manuscripts. It frequently contains the letter *y* and the digraphs *ph*, *th*, and *ch*. The letter *y* corresponds to the Punic vowel sound *u* (and sometimes *i*), and the digraphs correspond to the nonemphatic stops *p*, *t*, and *k*. The letter *y* and the digraphs were not needed for purely Latin words and occurred in transliterations of

---

[8] The verse was deleted by Lindemann because it does not fit syntactically. It has no equivalent in the Punic versions either. This means that Text 1, Text 2, and the Latin version are each ten lines long.

Greek only after Plautus, who presumably used u, p, t, and c instead. All Plautine manuscripts use y and the digraphs in Greek words, which shows that the Plautus text was modernized orthographically, presumably in the first century BC or later. While we could in theory regard Text 1 as an old text which was orthographically updated, in practice this is highly unlikely. The reason is that Text 2, which is transmitted in the Ambrosian palimpsest as well as the Palatine manuscripts, follows more archaic spelling conventions and has not been updated orthographically, except in the first line (l. 940), where we find y and the digraph *th*.[9]

Text 2 therefore seems to be the original text inserted by Plautus.[10] Whether he took it from the Greek original of the play or commissioned a Latin-Punic bilingual to compose it for him remains unclear. As will be seen below, Text 2 is by and large unintelligible. Insofar as we can tell today, it does not correspond very closely to the Latin version. If Text 2 suffered substantial corruption already shortly after Plautus' lifetime, as is quite likely because the copyists will not have understood it, this corruption may well be the reason for the creation of Text 1. On this assumption, Text 1 and possibly the Latin translation, which seems to correspond closely to Text 1, could be the work of a scholar of the Varronian era or later, when the new orthography was the norm. Text 1 would have been created as a substitute for the barely intelligible Text 2.

[9] For more details, see Gratwick (1971).

[10] The same conclusion is reached by Gratwick (1971) and also by Gray (1923), the latter, however, for different reasons; Gray argues that Text 1 is less idiomatic Semitic and must have been written later. Interestingly, Sznycer (1967: 131–32) comes to the opposite conclusion by looking at the Punic from a linguistic angle. Clearly, in a less well-known language it is best to rely on external criteria like orthography.

The archetype that all our manuscripts go back to presumably contained both Punic texts and the Latin translation. However, when two versions of a passage occur side by side in a manuscript, one is often left out in the process of copying the text. The Palatine manuscripts have preserved both Punic texts with the Latin translation, but the Ambrosian palimpsest lacks Text 1, the scholar's version of the Punic passage.

Interestingly, the minor Punic passages that are scattered over ll. 942–1142 are in the modern orthography in all manuscripts, which indicates that they were adapted at the same time that Text 1 was written. Incidentally, the fact that the palimpsest also employs the modern orthography here is another indication that its archetype contained the modernized Text 1.

Neither the old Latin orthography nor the new is good at indicating pharyngeal and glottal sounds. This means that ', h, ', and even h, for which Latin did have a letter, are by and large not written at all. It is unclear whether this indicates that h was lost in Punic pronunciation, perhaps together with the other three sounds, or whether it was not written because it was not a sound familiar to many Romans. All of these pharyngeal and glottal sounds were or at least had been highly frequent phonemes; as a consequence, the signs for them are highly frequent letters in old inscriptions. Thus it becomes quite difficult to identify the Punic words in Latin script with lexemes in earlier and better understood inscriptions. A problem of similar magnitude concerns the sibilants. The Punic texts in the Latin alphabet do not distinguish between the signs for original s, z, $ṣ$, $š$, rendering all of them as s. The modern orthography did at least have the letter z, but it does not occur in the Punic passages, probably because the phoneme was rare in Punic to begin with. Finally, there are no special letters for the emphatic stops *ṭ* and *q*. Here, however, the texts in the new orthography do make a distinction that Text 2 did not make. Text 2 uses the letter *t* for both *t* and *ṭ*, and *c* for both *k* and *q*. The modern texts, on the other hand, quite consistently use *th* and *ch* for the nonemphatic stops and *t* and *c* for the emphatic ones.

Another major difficulty is word division. Punic inscriptions sometimes, but not always, contain word dividers. The Punic texts in the Ambrosian palimpsest have no indications of word division, just like the Latin ones. In the Palatine manuscripts, where Latin words are separated by spaces, the Punic text also contains spaces, but these were introduced late and are unreliable as indications of word division. This means that we can separate words reliably only when we recognize letter sequences through our knowledge of Phoenician and Punic.

Gratwick (1969), in an overly harsh review of Sznycer (1967), argues that several types of words ought to be distinguished in our Punic passages:

(a) Strings of letters occurring more than once in the Punic and having the same translational equivalent in the Latin; these words are certain, especially if they recur in Punic inscriptions in the Greek or Latin alphabet.

(b) Strings of letters which have no translational equivalents in the Latin (like *anech*, "I") but which are attested in inscriptions in the Greek or Latin alphabet; such words can often be explained plausibly.

(c) Everything else; here the interpretation depends on often arbitrary word division of the Punic text in Plautus and on identification of the resulting chunks with Punic and other Semitic roots.

Gratwick considers all words in category (c) as doubtful. I do not take such an *a priori* negative view. For Text 1 we have a Latin translation, so word division and identification of the resulting elements with Punic roots is not a doomed undertaking, even though some uncertainties remain. In principle, the Latin translation should also help us with Text 2, but this text is too corrupt to allow much analysis. With regard to the short Punic pieces later in the play, I by and large share Gratwick's skepticism for words in category (c).

Punic Morphology and Syntax

The morphology and syntax of the Canaanite languages differ from Latin and Indo-European in many respects. Here is not the place to discuss Punic grammar in detail. Readers interested in the subject should consult Harris (1936) as basic introduction, Segert (1976) as more advanced reading, and Friedrich, Röllig, Amadasi Guzzo, and Mayer (1999) as reference work. Krahmalkov (2001) is also to be recommended, even though his analyses of the Punic passages in the *Poenulus* are idiosyncratic in several respects (see Krahmalkov 1970 and 1988); far more reliable in his analysis of our passages is Sznycer (1967). As a dictionary of Phoenician and Punic, Krahmalkov (2000) is useful; for lexical parallels in Hebrew, the most convenient work is Koehler and Baumgartner (2004). My aim here is more modest: I shall merely mention those grammatical features the reader will encounter in the Punic texts of the *Poenulus*.

Punic nouns inflect for number and gender. The numbers Punic nouns can have are singular and plural, and to a very limited extent dual, but the dual is not attested in our passages. The plural and dual are marked by suffixes and to some extent vowel alternations; sometimes feminine singular nouns also show special suffixes. There are only two genders, masculine and feminine. The masculine plural ends in *-im* and the feminine plural in *-ut*. Just as in other languages, not all nouns have stable gender. Thus the noun YM, "day," is masculine and mostly has the masculine plural ending, but, as in Hebrew, the feminine plural ending occurs here as well (see l. 934).

Possessive relations are expressed in a way that is fundamentally different from English. In the English phrase *John's house*, for example, the possessor is marked by a suffix and the possessum remains unchanged. In *the house of John*, the word order is different, but it is still the possessor, *John*, that is marked, this time with a preposition. In Punic the possessum regularly precedes the possessor and the latter remains unmarked. The possessum, by contrast, undergoes vowel weakening and sometimes takes a special suffix; in Semitic grammars one speaks of the possessum being in the "construct state." An example occurs in l. 1027 (*gune bal samem*). The first noun, G'N, "majesty," normally has a plural G'NM, but here the plural is in the construct state, *gune*; B'L, "lord," is also in the construct state, though here no change can be seen; and ŠMM, "heavens," is unmarked. The whole phrase then means "the majesty of the lord of the heavens."

Punic also has a definite article, H-, "the." Its use, however, is not obligatory if a noun is definite, and in our text it rarely occurs.

Not much needs to be said about word formation here. Punic can form nouns from verb roots by attaching a prefix *m-* (as in l. 933) or *t-* (as perhaps in l. 939). The *m*-nouns mostly indicate actions described by the verb root. The *t*-nouns have similar functions but are much rarer.

Punic, like Hebrew, has both free and suffixed pronouns. Subject pronouns and demonstrative pronouns in all syntactic functions are free. By contrast, object pronouns are expressed as verbal suffixes and possessive pronouns as nominal ones; prepositions are also mostly combined with suffixed rather than free pronouns.

The Semitic verb system is highly complex. At its heart lie verb roots which typically, though not always, have three consonants. Verb roots that maintain three consonants throughout all stems are said to belong to the "strong" verbs, whereas verb roots that only have two consonants or lose one or two consonants when prefixes or suffixes are added belong to the "weak" verbs.

From most verb roots different stems can be formed by adding prefixes, geminating consonants, or modifying the vocalism. Different stems are used for active, passive, causative, reflexive, and so on. The basic active stem is called qal in Hebrew (*qal* = "light"), and Phoenician grammars typically adopt this term as well; since its third-person singular masculine has no affixes and, like the other forms of the basic stem, no geminate consonants, it is often used as the base form in dictionaries. Other stems are traditionally named after the third-person masculine singular forms of the verb P'L, "do, make." Thus there is a stem pi'el, which ought to have a geminate second consonant (but ' cannot be geminated); its meaning is causative ("make someone do something"), intensive ("do something intensely/repeatedly"), or factitive ("bring about a state"). In l. 938 we have the form *bynny*, which seems to be the pi'el of the weak root BYN, "notice"; the meaning is causative: "make notice" = "show." Another stem is called pu'al (see the form *tumam* in l. 941); it is the passive equivalent of the pi'el. In *ysthyal* of l. 931 the (mostly reflexive) stem yitpaʻel is attested. The verb in question has the root Š'L, "request," to which a prefix *yit* (here *'it* because it is first-person singular) is added; but if the first root consonant is a sibilant, there is metathesis, hence the form *ysthyal* rather than **ythsyal*.

The morphology of the Punic verb is complex. From each stem two "tenses" can be formed, the perfect (where the persons are marked by suffixes) and the imperfect (where the persons are marked by prefixes and sometimes also suffixes). These "tenses" have temporal, aspectual, and other functions. Thus the perfect is used for past reference, but also for performative speech acts ("I hereby do *x*") or wishes. The imperfect is used for present and future reference but can also occur in commands.

Punic verbs have both finite and nonfinite forms. The former inflect for person, number, and, differently from Latin, gender. Nonfinite verbs are participles and infinitives. Like Hebrew, Punic distinguishes between the absolute infinitive and the construct infinitive. These infinitives have different morphology and different syntactic and semantic roles. The former can, for instance, be combined with free personal pronouns and function as a narrative verb form, whereas the latter can, for example, be combined with the preposition L and function as a purpose clause.

Semitic grammar distinguishes between verbal and nominal clauses. Verbal clauses describe actions or events and contain a finite verb, typically at the beginning of the clause, though Punic is not very strict in this respect. Nominal clauses are more unusual from a Latin perspective. They describe states or situations and do not contain finite verbs. The predicate can consist of, for example, an adjective or a noun. Thus the second relative clause in l. 930 contains no verb at all and the predicate is a locative expression ("who this place" = "who are in this place").

Proto-Semitic still had a three-case system, but these cases no longer exist in Punic. The subject is left unmarked. The direct object can also be unmarked, but often it is preceded by the preposition 'T (written *yth* in the *Poenulus*), whose only function is to indicate that the following constituent is the direct object.[11] Other syntactic roles are mostly marked by a number of different prepositions.

Relative clauses in Latin are always introduced by relative pronouns indicating the gender and number of their head nouns as well as the syntactic functions they have in the subordinate clauses. English relative pronouns are similar: in *the man whom I saw*, the pronoun *whom* shows that the head noun, *man,* is human and has object function in the subordinate clause. However, English can also introduce relative clauses with the subordinator *that*, a subordinator which leaves all this information unspecified. Punic follows the second strategy; its relative particle 'Š only indicates that a relative clause begins, but leaves gender, number, and semantic function of the head noun in the relative clause unclear.

Not much else needs to be said about Punic syntax here, except that Hanno's entrance monologue may well be influenced by Latin structures to some extent. In l. 958, for instance, we find the Latin phrase *hospitalem . . . tesseram,* "guest's shard," and Hanno's phrase *chirs aelichot,* "shard of hospitality" (l. 937), seems to be an imitation of this phrase.

---

[11] The Latin of the Bu Njem ostraca, which shows clear signs of language contact with Punic, marks direct objects with the preposition *ad*, in imitation of Punic 'T; for details see Adams (1994).

The Metrical Structure of the Punic Passages

Plautine comedy is entirely in verse, and the short passages in Punic are metrically integrated into the iambic senarii in which they are embedded. It is therefore understandable that scholars have tried to analyze Text 1 and Text 2 as poetry as well. What structures native Punic poetry had is unknown, but if Hebrew poetry is anything to go by, it was not metrical and had no rhymes. In Hebrew poetry, for instance the Psalms or some passages in the Book of Job, the formal element consists in the repetition of a thought in slightly modified form in the next line (*parallelismus membrorum*). It will become obvious from my analysis of the two long texts that this is not how they are structured. Instead, it makes more sense to check whether the lines scan as Roman meters. This approach was already taken by Sisenna in the first century BC, as the fifth-century grammarian Rufinus (*gramm.* 6.560.28–561.2) tells us; Sisenna analyzed the longer Punic passages as iambics, presumably as iambic senarii. However, this is possible only if one ignores Punic vowel quantities as well as Roman rules of scansion. L. 930, for instance, contains *macom* as the penultimate word, followed by a monosyllable beginning with a consonant. In order to scan the line as an iambic senarius, one would have to treat *macom* as ending in a short vowel; but it ends in a consonant,[12] and the comparative evidence shows that both its vowels are long. Glück and Maurach (1971–1972) also attempt to scan the text,

---

[12] To be more precise, *macom* ends in a consonant in Punic pronunciation, but in Latin final *–m* was not normally pronounced as a consonant; it rendered the preceding vowel long and nasalized. To what extent a genuine Punic pronunciation was aimed at in the performances of the *Poenulus* is unknown.

but not entirely in senarii; they assume a structure that consists of varying iambic meters like the senarius, the septenarius, and so on. While this attempt is more successful, it still requires violating Latin scansion rules and ignoring what little we know of Punic syllable structure; in addition, if the passage were in mixed iambics, it would presumably be a Plautine song, which seems rather unlikely. Thus it seems best to treat Text 1 and Text 2 as prose. Glück and Maurach are of course right in saying that prose in a Plautine comedy is an anomaly, but so is the insertion of a lengthy passage in a foreign language.

TEXT 1

General Remarks

Text 1 (ll. 930–39) corresponds very closely to the Latin version (ll. 950–60, without l. 954). This makes it relatively easy to understand the Punic: where the meaning is uncertain, we know what words to look for and how to reconstitute the original Punic text. The spelling conventions going back to the Varronian era or later also help with this to some extent.

Text 1 is found only in the Palatine manuscripts. As *B* is generally the most reliable Palatine manuscript, I have by and large adopted its readings, except that I do not follow the haphazard word separation there. Important textual variants, but not for instance variations between *y*, *i*, and *u*, are listed immediately underneath each line; the readings of the Codex Turnebi (see Lindsay 1898) are indicated only where substantially different. This is followed by a Romanized version of what the text in the Punic script would have looked like; the words, with grammatical analysis and translation, are all listed in the glossary at the end of this section.[13] Underneath each transcription I have added a literal translation of the Punic text, followed in turn by the Latin line with English translation. Where there are major problems in the text, they are discussed underneath the translations.

Text and Analysis

l. 930

yth alonim u alonuth si corathi sy macom syth

Variants: ythalonim *B*, nythalonim *CD*, ythalonium *T* | corathi *P*, carothi *edd.*

'T 'LNM W 'LNT 'Š QR'TY 'Š MQM ST

"the gods and goddesses whom I invoke, who (are in) this place"

Latin l. 950: deos deasque ueneror qui hanc urbem colunt

"I pray to the gods and goddesses who inhabit this city"

Discussion: The expected vocalism in the verb is *carothi* rather than *corathi*. Some editors change the text here, but the verb is transmitted in the same form in ll. 940 and 1023 as well.

---

[13] Unless indicated otherwise, the words are found in (Phoenician or) Punic inscriptions; attestations are easy to check with the help of Krahmalkov (2000). For Hebrew parallels one can consult Koehler and Baumgartner (2004).

l. 931

chy mlachthi in ythmum ysthyalm ych ibarcu mysehi

Variants: mlachchun *BD*, mlahchun *C*, mlachthun *Gildemeister*, mlachthi in *Sznycer* | ycth (yer *T*) *P*, ych *edd.* | ibarui *P*, ibarcu *Gildemeister*

K ML'KT-Y HN 'TMM 'ŠT'L-M W K YBRK' MṢ-Y

"I ask them that I may complete my work here and that they may bless my travel"

Latin l. 951: ut quod de mea re huc ueni rite uenerim

"that as for the thing I came here for, I've come righteously"

Discussion: ych probably also shows the common confusion between *y* and *u*; the conjunction "and" is normally rendered *u* and not *y*. The form *ibarcu* is a pi'el with intensive rather than causative function.

l. 932

li pho caneth yth bynuthi iad aed in byn ui

Variants: aedin *CD*, edyn *B* | bynui *B*, bynuii *T*, binuthii *CD*

L PH QNYTY 'T BNWT-Y YḤD 'D HN BN 'Ḥ-Y

"may I get my daughters here, at the same time also my brother's son"

Latin l. 952 and beginning of l. 953: measque hic ut gnatas et mei fratris filium reperire me siritis

"and that you let me find my daughters here and my brother's son"

Discussion: 'D HN, "up to here, still, also," occurs in Hebrew in the contracted form 'DN.

l. 933

by marob sy llohom alonim uy by mysyrthoho‹m›

Variants: bymarob *B*, birnarob *CD* | syllohom alonim *BCD*, hamolomim *T* | by *BC*, ubi *D* | mysyrthoho‹m› *Sznycer*

B MʿRB ʾŠ L-KM ʾLNM W B MṢRT-KM

"in the care which you, gods, have, and in your protection"

Latin second half of l. 953: di uostram fidem!

"Gods, your protection!"

Discussion: Literally the Punic means "in the care which (is) for you, gods, and in your protection." The double *l* in *sy llohom* is unexplained but can perhaps reflect a geminate pronunciation of the sound following the relative subordinator (in Hebrew the consonant following the definite article is also geminated). Sznycer, who restores *mysyrthoho‹m›*, believes that the suffix marks the third-person masculine plural (-HM). However, the old -*hum* is only preserved in Byblian, while Punic generally has -*om* (or a new -*nom*), so that the preservation of the ending –*hum*/-*hom* in the *Poenulus* would be highly unusual; moreover, in the Punic in Plautus the Punic letter H is not normally rendered by Latin *h* but left out entirely. A third objection against Sznycer's interpretation is that the Latin version has the second-person plural. The second-person masculine plural suffix is -KM. This should be written –*chom* in Text 1. –*hom* either represents a velar fricative

193

pronunciation in this suffix or is simply a misspelling. I tend toward this second interpretation because K is consistently written *ch*, regardless of phonological environment.

l. 934

byth lymmoth ynnochoth uulech antidamas chon

Variants: ynnoctoth *P*, ynnochoth *Ewald* (*cf.* innocho 936)

B ʿT L YMT HN-KHT H-HLK Antidamas KWN

"in times past Antidamas was the guest-friend here"

Latin l. 955: sed hic mihi antehac hospes Antidamas fuit

"but here I had Antidamas as my guest-friend before"

Discussion: The preposition L here seems to be used to express a genitival relation ("in the time of the days" = "in the time of the past"); this usage can be paralleled in both Punic and Hebrew, even though the regular sequence of construct state and prepositionless absolute state is more common. However, since *l* and *i* are often confused in minuscule manuscripts, we can perhaps read *iymmoth*, "days," in which case we would have the regular possessive construction.

l. 935

ys si dobrim chy fel yth chil ys chon chen liful

Variants: yssid dobrim *BCD*, yssiderbrum *T* | thyfel *P*, chy fel *Sznycer* | chem *B*, them *CD*, chen *Gildemeister*

ʾŠ ʾŠ DBRM K PʿL ʾT KL ʾŠ KWN KN L- PʿL

"a man of whom they say that he has done all that he needed to do like this"

Latin l. 956: eum fecisse aiunt sibi quod faciundum fuit

"they say he did what he had to do"

Discussion: Literally the Punic means "a man of whom (they) say that he has done all that was for doing like this."

l. 936

yth binim ys dybur ch innochoth u agorastocles

Variants: thinnochot nu *B*, thinno chut nu *CD*, ch innochoth u *Krahmalkov* (*cf. etiam* hu 946)

'T BN-M 'Š DBR K HN-KHT H' Agorastocles

"as for his son, one says that he (is) here, Agorastocles"

Latin l. 957: eius filium esse hic praedicant Agorastoclem

"people claim that his son Agorastocles lives here"

Discussion: The construction of the Punic seems to be a Latinism. The Punic begins with a direct object in imitation of the Latin accusative and infinitive but later has the subordinator K. The Punic impersonal construction contains the noun "man" in combination with the singular participle, while the Latin text has the impersonal third-person plural.

l. 937

ythem anechi hy chirs aelichot sith naso‹t›

Variants: anethi *P*, anechi *Krahmalkov* (*cf.* anec 947) | aeli-
chot *B*, lychot *CD*, elycothi *T* | naso *P*, nasot *Benary*
(*cf. 947*)

ʾT-M ʾNKY Hʾ ḤRŠ H-HLKT ST NŠʾTY

"look, to him I have brought this shard of hospitality"

Latin l. 958: ad eum hospitalem hanc tesseram mecum fero

"to him I am bringing along this shard of hospitality with me"

Discussion: The presentative particle *hy* (normally "there is,"
here rendered as "look") is odd in the middle of the sen-
tence and has no equivalent in the Latin. Perhaps it is a
dittography because of the preceding *anethi/anechi* and
should be deleted. The correction of *naso* to *nasot* by Be-
nary is based on the corresponding form in l. 947; in the
orthography of Text 1, this should actually be *nasothi*.

l. 938

bynny id li chi ily gubulim lasibitthim

Variants: chil liichily *B*, chil liihily *CD*, chid lithyly *T*, li chi ily
Sznycer

BYNʾ YD L-Y K ʾL GBLM L-ŠBT-M

"they have shown me by hand that he lives in this area (lit. that
these regions (are) for his living)"

Latin l. 959: is in hisce habitare monstratust regionibus

"he was shown to live in this area"

Discussion: The interpretation I am adopting for *bynny id* ("they have shown by hand") is that of Sznycer. I do so hesitatingly. *Bynny*, "they have shown," is relatively unproblematic, but *yd*, "hand," has no Latin equivalent and does not fit in well syntactically; one would expect it to be combined with a preposition, and even then the phrase is unparalleled. Gray renders the phrase as BNW 'WD, "to us there is testimony." BNW is the preposition B with a first-person plural suffix. 'WD, only attested in Hebrew, can stand for a witness as well as his testimony. The main problem with Gray's analysis is that Hanno consistently refers to himself in the first-person singular, not the first-person plural. Krahmalkov's interpretation is equally problematic. To begin with, it involves two emendations: instead of *bynny id*, one has to read *hynny yyd*. The first word would be the deictic particle HN; here the only problem is that Plautine Punic does not normally render H. The second word would belong to the verbal root 'WD, "give witness" (only attested in Hebrew); here we would be dealing with the third-person masculine singular hoph'al, a stem which has passive meaning, so this would roughly correspond to Latin *monstratust*, "he was shown." Perhaps the solution is to accept Sznycer's *bynny* and to emend *id li* to *ili*, "they"; in that case the first part of the line simply means "they have shown that."

l. 939

bodi aly thera ynnynny yslym mon choth iusim

Variants: ynnynnu *B*, ynnynu *CD*, ynnynny *Sznycer* | lusim *BCD*, iufim *T*

B ʿD-Y L TWR HN-NY ʾŠʾL-M MN KHT YṢʾM

"while I am on watch, look at me, I shall ask them, the ones coming out from here"

Latin l. 960: hos percontabor qui hinc egrediuntur foras

"I'll ask these people who are coming out"

Discussion: The first half of the line has no equivalent in the Latin, which makes it more difficult to handle. The noun ʿD, "duration" (Hebrew ʿWD), can have adverbial functions, especially when preceded by the preposition B. Here the noun is combined with a suffixed pronoun, a construction that is rather common in Hebrew. *Aly thera* is problematic. Sznycer thinks of the preposition ʿLY, "on," which in Hebrew is the poetic equivalent of ʿL. However, Punic only has ʿL and ʿLT. It is possible that we are dealing with haplography and that *alyth thera* became *aly thera* in the process of copying. *Thera* is difficult to explain. Hebrew has a verb RʾH, "see," which is not attested in Punic. Sznycer assumes that *thera* is a *t*-derivative of this verb, but no such derivative is attested in Punic or in Hebrew, which actually has an *m*-derivative. Consequently, this interpretation has to be discarded. A connection with the Hebrew noun TRʾ, "appearance," seems equally unlikely. Krahmalkov's explanation does not convince me in the form he states it. He divides *a lyther* and takes *a* as an abbreviation of *anech*, "I," while *lyther* is the preposition L with the construct infinitive TWR, "watch." While the second part of his explanation can be defended, it is hard to believe in the existence of abbreviations in this text, since Roman actors would not have known what they stood for. I have hesitatingly accepted Krahmalkov's L-TWR ("while I am for watching" = "while I am about to watch"), but I cannot explain vowels before and after this phrase. HN is vocalized *hinnē* in Hebrew, so ynny is a close match.

Glossary

This glossary lists the words in a Romanized version of the Punic script. It also follows the regular order of the Roman alphabet. ' and ' come before A, and letters with diacritics come after their counterparts without diacritics.

'H	brother
'L	these (*masculine / feminine plural pronoun*)
'LNM	gods (*-M = masculine plural marker*)
'LNT	goddesses (*-T = feminine plural marker*)
'NK(Y)	I
'Š[1]	*relative particle*
'Š[2]	man
'Š'L (*root* Š'L)	ask (*1st sg. impf. qal*)
'ŠT'L (*root* Š'L)	request (*1st sg. impf. hitpaʻel*)
'T[1]	*direct object marker*
'T[2]	toward
'TMM (*root* TMM)	complete (*1st sg. impf. qal*)
ʻD[1]	up to
ʻD[2]	duration (*in combination with the preposition B used as an adverbial*)
ʻT	time
B	in

BN	son
BNT	daughters (-T = *feminine plural marker*)
BYN'	show (*3rd pl. perfect pi'el of* BYN, "notice"; *root not attested in inscriptions but common in Hebrew*)
DBR	say (*masc. sg. participle qal*)
DBRM	say (*masc. pl. participle qal*)
GBLM	area (-M = *masc. pl. marker; in the singular the meaning* "border" *is more common*)
H-	*definite article*
H'[1]	*third-person masculine singular pronoun*
H'[2]	*presentative particle*
HLK	guest-friend (*masculine singular participle of* HLK, "travel")
HLKT	travel, hospitality (*noun is not inscriptional, but the verbal basis* HLK, "travel," *is*)
HN	here; look (*deictic and presentative particle, independent or combined with* KHT *or pronominal suffixes*)
ḤRŠ	pottery (*here:* piece of pottery, shard)
K	*subordinator*
KHT	here
KL	all

200

-KM	*enclitic 2nd pl. masc. pronoun*
KN	thus
KWN	be (*3rd sg. perf. qal*)
L¹	for, to, in
L²	*wish particle*
-M¹	*enclitic 3rd sg. masc. pronoun*
-M²	*enclitic 3rd pl. masc. pronoun*
M'RB (*noun is not inscriptional, but the verbal basis* 'RB, "care," *is*)	care
ML'KT	work
MN	from
MQM	place
MṢ'	travel, journey
MṢRT (*noun is not inscriptional, but the verbal basis* NṢR, "protect," *is*)	protection
NŠ'TY (*root* NŠ')	bring (*1st sg. perf. qal*)
-NY	*enclitic 1st sg. pronoun in object function*
P'L	do, make (*3rd sg. masc. perf. qal / infinitivus constructus qal*)
PH (*not inscriptional but attested in Hebrew*)	here
QNYTY (*root* QNY)	acquire (*1st sg. perf. qal*)
QR'TY (*root* QR')	invoke (*1st sg. perf. qal*)
ST	this
ŠBT	live (*infinitivus constructus qal, root* YŠB)
TWR	watch (*infinitivus constructus qal*)

W	and
-Y	*enclitic 1st sg. pronoun in possessive function*
YBRK' (*root* BRK)	bless (*3rd pl. masc. impf. pi'el*)
YD	hand
YḤD (*not inscriptional but attested in Hebrew*)	together, at the same time
YMT	days (*-T = feminine plural marker, here with a masculine noun*)
YṢ'M (*root* YṢ')	come out (*-M = masc. pl. marker; participle qal*)

TEXT 2

General Remarks

Text 2 (ll. 940–49) is found in the Ambrosian palimpsest as well as in the Palatine manuscripts. It is corrupt in all branches of the transmission, but especially so in the Palatine manuscripts, where the passage has been compressed into eight lines and in addition heavily Latinized. Latinization can, for example, be seen in l. 941, where the Palatine manuscripts contain the Latin word *concubitum* instead of a phonetically similar Punic word, or in l. 946, where they have the Latin *at enim*. For this reason I have mainly relied on the palimpsest, listing the variants in the Palatine manuscripts underneath. As much of the text remains obscure, I have not attempted to translate everything. Instead, I discuss underneath each line what can and what cannot be understood.

Text and Analysis

l. 940

yth alonim u alonuth si corathi is thymchy macom syth

Variants: ythalonim *A*, exanolim *BD*, xanolim *C* | ualoniuth *A*, uolanus *P* | sicorathi *A*, succurati *P* | isthymhimihy *A*, mistimalti *P*, is thymchy *Sznycer* | syth *A*, esse *P*

Discussion: The line is almost identical with l. 930. The only differences are the occurrence of a full form of the relative pronoun (*is* instead of *si*) and the presence of another word, *thymchy*. The latter is Sznycer's correction of the apparently dittographic reading in the Ambrosian palimpsest, while the Palatine manuscripts do not contain anything that can be understood as it is or with minor corrections. In Sznycer's interpretation, *thymchy* stands for TMKY, the construct state masculine plural of the participle of TMK, "hold, grasp." The verb is attested in both Punic and Hebrew. If this interpretation is correct, the line means "the gods and goddesses whom I invoke, who hold/own this place."

l. 941

combaepumamitalmetlotiambeat

Variants: sic A, concubitum abellocutim beat (beant *D*) *P*

Discussion: The line cannot be understood as a whole. Sznycer divides *co mbae tumam* (*pumam* in *A*, but Studemund indicates that the first letter could also be a *t* or a *c*). This he analyzes as K MB'-Y YTMM. K is supposed to be the common subordinator, but this is normally vocalized as *chi* rather than *co*. MB' is a Punic noun meaning "entrance," here combined with an enclitic first-person singular pronoun. YTMM is the third-person masculine singular imperfect pu'al of TMM, "be good," with the initial vowel lost by scribal error or merged with the preceding word. If Sznycer is correct, this part means "that my entrance (into this city) will be made perfect." This corresponds well with the Latin text. The rest of the line defies analysis.

l. 942

iulecantheconaalonimbalumbar dechor

Variants: sic A, lula canti (cant *CD*) chona *P*

Discussion: Not much in this line is clear. The word *alonim*, "gods," can be isolated, and *canthe* corresponds to *caneth* in l. 932, which in combination with the wish particle L at the beginning of the line (*lu* in *P*) means "may I acquire." Sznycer analyzes *cona/chona* as KH, "here," together with the adhortative particle N'. This is possible, but by no means certain.

l. 943

bats****hunesobinesubicsillimbalim

Variants: sic A, enuses hui ec silic (silihc *CD*) panasse (pan esse *CD*) *P*

Discussion: The line is incomprehensible. *Bat* at the beginning could be BT, "daughter," but the plural *banoth* would be expected here. *Silli* could be the relative particle 'Š followed by the preposition L, "for," with an enclitic first-person singular pronoun ("which (is) for me"); but as the rest of the line is unclear, this too has to remain uncertain.

l. 944

esseantidamossonalemuedubertefet

Variants: sic A, at idmascon (athidmascon *CD*) alem uiduberte (uedeberte *C*) felono *P*

Discussion: The only word that is absolutely certain in this line is Antidamas (*antidamos* in *A*). Sznycer interprets *esse* as 'Š, "man," followed by the relative particle 'Š. In *duber* we probably have a form of the common verb DBR, "say," perhaps a masculine singular participle (Hebrew *dōbēr*). If Friedrich, Röllig, Amadasi Guzzo, and Mayer are right in saying that 'Š, "man," + participle can also be used impersonally ("one does"), *esse . . . duber* could simply mean "one says" ('Š DBR). *Alem* could conceivably be ʿLM, "young man," a noun attested in Hebrew but not in Punic, which, however, has the derivative ʿLMT, "young woman," which presupposes the existence of ʿLM in Punic as well. Alternatively, *alem* could be the preposition ʿL, "above, about," with the enclitic third-person masculine singular pronoun -M; in that case, however, the word order would be somewhat strange. Thus we can translate: "one says young Antidamas . . ." or "one says Antidamas . . . about him . . ." The rest defies interpretation.

l. 945

donobun*huneccilthumucommucroluful

Variants: sic A, butune (buthune *CD*) celtumco mucro luful
  (mucro luful *T*, mucrolueui *BC*, muerolueui *D*) *P*

Discussion: In the Latin version and in Text 1 we are told in
  this line that Antidamas has died. Both versions use the eu-
  phemism of doing what one has to do. This is in fact the
  only part that is clear in this line. The last part, *luful*, cor-
  responds to *liful* in l. 935, which can be analyzed as L- P'L,
  "to do" (preposition L, "for," + construct infinitive P'L,
  "do").

l. 946

altanimauosduberithemhuarcharistolem

Variants: sic A, at enim auoso uber henthra (hent hya *CD*)
  charistoclem *P*

Discussion: The last word, despite textual corruption in all
  manuscripts, clearly renders Agaristoclem (accusative). Be-
  fore that we seem to have *hu*, which is H', "he." The string
  uos duber has a corresponding element in l. 936 ("one
  says"). Since this line seems to correspond to l. 936 quite
  well, one would expect a statement to the effect that
  Agorastocles is "his [i.e., Antidamas'] son"; perhaps the se-
  quence *tanim* should be emended to *banim* (BN-M), "his
  son."

l. 947

sittesedanecnasotersahelicot

Variants: sic A, ette seanec (seanehc *CD*) nasoctelia helicos
  (elicos *D*) *P*

Discussion: This line contains several elements that we already saw in l. 937. *Anec* is the first-person singular pronoun 'NK(Y), "I." The form *nasot*, which enabled us to correct *naso* from l. 937, is the first-person singular perfect NŠ'TY, from the root NŠ', "bring." *Ers ahelicot* also corresponds to a phrase from l. 937, ḤRŠ H-ḤLKT, "shard of hospitality." The beginning of the line is less clear. The Ambrosian palimpsest has *sittesed*, while the Palatine manuscripts have *ette se*. If we take *ette* as the correct reading, it could be 'T-' and mean "to him" (preposition with enclitic third-person masculine singular pronoun). *Sed* or *se* remains difficult. A relative particle, 'Š, makes little syntactic sense here, and the demonstrative ST, which in l. 937 modifies the shard of hospitality, can hardly be separated from this noun phrase. The elements which are reasonably clear can be translated thus: "to him I have brought the shard of hospitality."

l. 948

alemusdubertimurmucopsuistiti

Variants: sic A, alemus dubertermi compsuestipti (compsuespti *CD*) *P*

Discussion: This line is essentially unclear. *Alem* could be 'LM, "young man," as in l. 944, if one accepts the word there, or "about him," which is the alternative interpretation in l. 944. We can then divide *us duberti* or *us duber*. In the first case *us* could be the relative particle 'Š and *duberti* the first-person singular perfect piʿel of DBR, "speak," DBRTY, yielding the meaning "the young man of whom I have spoken." In the second case we would have

'Š, "man," and the masculine singular participle qal of DBR, "speak," which yields the translation "the young man, one says, . . ." or "about him one says."

l. 949

aocca anec lictor bode si ussilim limmim co ius⟨im⟩

Variants: aocca *A*, aode *B*, aoda *CD* | anec *ABD*, enehc *C* | iussilim *A*, iussum *P* | limmim *A*, limnim *BD*, limum *C* | lus Ω, iusim *Sznycer* (*cf.* 939)

Discussion: Another problematic line. The second half, *ussilim limmim co iusim*, is clear and corresponds well with the second half of l. 939. It means "I shall ask them, the ones coming out." The only differences are that instead of MN from l. 939 we have the well-attested double preposition L-MN, and that instead of KHT, "here," we have the equally well-attested byform KH. In the first half of the line, *anec* means "I" and *lictor* seems to be a Latinization of what in l. 939 was (*a*)*lyther*(*a*), "about to watch."[14] *Aocca* can be analysed as 'ḤKH, the first-person singular imperfect piʻel of ḤKH, a verb attested in Hebrew but not in Punic; the meaning is "I shall wait." If *bode* corresponds to B ʻD-Y, "while I," from l. 939, the syntax makes little sense: one would expect a nonverbal predicate to follow, but what follows is a whole clause, possibly introduced by the relative particle *si* ('Š).

---

[14] A lictor is a Roman official.

THE PUNIC PASSAGES IN THE *POENULUS*

THE SHORT PASSAGES

General

The short passages after Hanno's entrance monologue are transmitted in all manuscripts. Some of them are "translated" by Milphio, who obviously knows no more than one or two words of Punic and simply uses Latin words that sound similar to the Punic ones. Nevertheless, in some cases the context helps us to understand what is being said. However, in the absence of a Latin translation as we had it for Text 1, much of the meaning remains uncertain. I list textual variants underneath each short passage and discuss the meaning in some detail, without trying to translate everything.

Text and Discussion

l. 994: auo.

Discussion: Agorastocles has asked his slave Milphio to approach and address Hanno in Punic. *Auo* is the only Punic word Milphio manages. It is a greeting from the verbal root ḤWY, "live." The masculine singular imperative *ḥauē*, "live," was borrowed into Latin as the greeting *aue*, from which a Latin plural form, *auete*, could be formed. Here the vocalism shows that we cannot be dealing with the imperative. Presumably *auo* is the third-person masculine singular perfect qal used as a wish, "may he live." If so, Hanno is addressed in the third person, which is not unusual.

209

PLAUTUS

l. 995: anno byn mytthymbal carthadati anech.

Variants: annobyn *A*, annon *P* | myttkymbal *A*, muthumbal *P* | leudradait *A*, le bechaedre *P*, carthadati *Schröder* | anech *P*, anneck *A*

Discussion: Milphio has asked Hanno and his servants where they are from and this is the reply he receives. Most of it is straightforward. The last word, *anech*, is the subject pronoun 'NK, "I." The rest of the sentence forms the verbless predicate. The first word in the line is the speaker's name, Hanno (ḤN'), a common name. This is followed by the speaker's filiation, expressed by *byn* (BN), "son," followed by his father's name, which was Mytthymbal or rather, with a more probable vocalization, Matanbaal (MTNB'L, meaning "gift of Baal," the most important Phoenician god). What comes next in the manuscripts makes no sense. Since Milphio tells Agorastocles that the man they have encountered is "Hanno from Carthage, the son of the Carthaginian Mytthymbal," and since the pieces that are clear from the Punic correspond well to Milphio's translation, we can assume that Hanno also states where he is from, especially since his statement is a reply to this particular question. Schröder emended the manuscript readings in a rather drastic way to *carthadati*, QRTḤDTY, "Carthaginian." This is the adjective to the place-name QRT ḤDŠT, Carthage, which means "New City" (QRT means "city," and ḤDŠT is the feminine form of the adjective ḤDŠ, "new"). One would expect the form QRTḤDŠTY, with Š, but this would cause metrical difficulties and the form without Š is attested on Cyprus, where a city of the same name existed.

210

The whole sentence means "I am Hanno, son of the Carthaginian Matanbaal."

l. 998: auo . . . donni.

Discussion: Hanno is greeting Agorastocles. Milphio correctly interprets *auo* as greeting, but because he does not know any Punic, he regards *donni* as equivalent to Latin *doni*, "gift, present" (genitive singular). However, *donni* stands for 'DN-Y; the first element means "lord, master" and the second is the enclitic first-person singular possessive pronoun, hence "my lord" as a polite way of referring to Agorastocles. One can compare biblical Hebrew *'adonai*, "my lord" (formally a plural). Hanno thus says, "May my lord live."

l. 1001: auo donni.

Variants: donnim *A*, nonni *B*, nonne *CD*

Discussion: Milphio, when told by Agorastocles to greet Hanno, simply repeats his words from l. 998.

l. 1002: mechar bocca.

Variants: me har *P*, mepkar *A* | bocca *P*, bua *A*

Discussion: In the Palatine manuscripts the spelling *h* in the first word probably stands for *ch* (Punic letter K), either because of a fricative pronunciation or because of textual corruption; the Latin rendition of Punic very rarely uses *h* on its own. The confusion between the letters *H* and *K* is very common in the Ambrosian palimpsest, as it is in many

211

majuscule texts, which points to an earlier reading, *mephar*; but as no root MPR is attested in Punic or Hebrew, we should probably follow what the Palatine manuscripts point to and read *mechar*. In the second word, the reading of the Palatine manuscripts is to be preferred because Milphio misinterprets Hanno's sentence as containing Latin *bucca*, "cheek." The interpretation of the sentence remains doubtful. The second word is slightly clearer. It could consist of the preposition B, "for," and the enclitic second-person singular masculine personal pronoun -K (as the comparative evidence shows, probably vocalized -*kā*), in which case it would mean "for you." *Mechar*, if the form is restored correctly, is more difficult. Sznycer tentatively suggests MKR, "merchandise," a word attested in Hebrew but not in Punic. The fact that this noun is not attested in Punic is not really problematic because MKR, "sell," and its participle MKR, "salesman," are found in inscriptions. But the interpretation is probably to be rejected because Hanno has not come to sell things. Perhaps Sznycer's second suggestion is to be preferred; he compares Hebrew MKR, "acquaintance," an *m*-noun from the verb NKR, "get to know." However, neither the noun nor the verb is attested in Punic. With this caveat in mind, we can interpret the sentence as being addressed to Agorastocles, whom Hanno asks about Milphio: "Is he an acquaintance of yours?"

l. 1006: rufe ynny cho is tam.

Variants: ynnycckoissam *A*, en nuco istam *B*, n nuco istam *CD*

Discussion: Milphio has said that Hanno probably thinks that they are medical doctors. Agorastocles has told Milphio to tell Hanno that they are not. Milphio has just tried to get Hanno's attention when Hanno gives this reply. The first word is certain. It is a present participle of the root RP', "heal." Both the verb and its participle, meaning "doctor, physician," are attested in Punic. The rest of the line is doubtful. Sznycer treats *ynny* as if it were Hebrew 'YN-NW; 'YN is a Hebrew noun functioning as negation for declarative clauses, here followed by an enclitic first-person plural pronoun. If he is correct, the phrase means "for us there is no physician" or "we do not have a physician." However, in Punic inscriptions this negation is not attested, and others are used instead. *Cho* corresponds straightforwardly to the well-attested KH, "here." *Is* could be 'Š, "man," and *tam* could conceivably belong to the root TM, "perfect, good," which is attested in Hebrew but not in Punic. If one accepts the somewhat doubtful interpretations of *ynny* and *tam*, the sentence means "we do not have a doctor here, good man." The address as "good man" is ironic, just as its Latin equivalent, *bone uir*, would be—by now Hanno has realized that Milphio is an incompetent good-for-nothing.

l. 1010: mu phursa . . . mi uulech ianna.

Variants: muphursa *P*, mupkursa *A* | miuulec hi an na *B*, mui-alech ianna *CD*, miu*** *A*

Discussion: Agorastocles tells Milphio to ask Hanno why he has come; Milphio does ask, but in a rude way. Hanno's reply, *mu phursa*, can possibly be translated as "what is the meaning (of your speech)," indicating that he is upset at being spoken to rudely. Question words are not attested in Punic inscriptions, but Hebrew has MH, "what." The verbal root PRŠ, "explain," is attested in both Punic and Hebrew, and the noun PRŠH, "meaning," occurs in Hebrew. After Hanno's words, Agorastocles asks Milphio what was meant, and Hanno says *mi uulech ianna*. *Mi* probably corresponds to Hebrew MY, "who," and we already saw *uulech* above (l. 934); it stands for H-HLK, "the guest-friend, stranger" (article + noun). *Ianna* could belong to the root 'NH, "ask," in which case it is the third-person singular masculine imperfect qal Y'NH. The whole sentence then means: "Who will reply to the stranger?"

l. 1013: lech lachannani limini chot.

Variants: leck *A*, laech *B*, ia lehc *C*, la lehc *D* | lackannani *A*, lach ananim *B*, lahcananim *CD* | limini chot *P*, limniickto *A*

Discussion: The first word is certain, the rest less so. Milphio's interpretation is simply based on what sounds similar in Latin and does not help us any further. *Lech* is the masculine singular imperative of the well-attested verb HLK, "go." *Lachanna(ni)* recurs in l. 1152 and from its use there could possibly be an insult; Schröder interprets it as the preposition L, "to," and a noun KNN, "cross," from the Hebrew root KNN, "set up." This would correspond to the common Latin phrase *i in crucem*, "go to the cross." But neither the noun nor the verb is attested in Punic, and Hebrew has the verb but not the noun. So this has to remain highly dubious. An alternative, perhaps more likely inter-

pretation is as a repeated imperative *lech* with the adhorta-
tive particle N', which occurs in Hebrew after imperatives.
Limini could be the double preposition L-MN, "from,"
which is attested in inscriptions. *Chot* means "here" and is
related to the common KH in the same meaning. Thus
Hanno says to Milphio, with whom he is annoyed, "go away
from here!" He seems to add an insult or to double the im-
perative, but this is uncertain.

l. 1016: assam.

Variants: assam *A*, issam *P*

Discussion: Agorastocles has just said that he believes Hanno
to be a merchant. In Hanno's reply, the reading *assam*
rather than *issam* has to be adopted because of Milphio's
reply, *aruinam quidem*, "yes, lard"; Milphio interprets
Hanno's word as a Latin one, and the only one which fits
the context is *assam*, "roasted." What the Punic stands for
is not certain; most scholars interpret the word as *ʾāšam*,
the third-person singular masculine perfect qal of 'ŠM, "be
guilty," a verb which is frequent in Hebrew but not actually
attested in Punic. On this interpretation, Hanno says to Ag-
orastocles: "he [i.e., Milphio] has become guilty."

l. 1017: palu umer gad etha.

Variants: palumirgadetka *A*, palum erga detha *B*, palum erga
dectha *CD*

Discussion: Milphio has been misinterpreting Hanno's speech
for some time when the latter says this. The Ambrosian pa-

215

limpsest and the Palatine manuscripts by and large have
the same text, which receives further confirmation from
Milphio's interpretation based on Latin words that sound
similar: *palas*, "spades," and *mergas*, "reaping boards." The
interpretation of the Punic is relatively certain. It consists
of two nominal clauses. The first has *umer* as its subject,
which corresponds to 'MR, "word, speech," attested in in-
scriptions. The predicate *palu* is a noun which does not oc-
cur in inscriptions but corresponds to Hebrew PL', "won-
der, marvel." Hanno is thus mocking Milphio's attempts at
translating, saying that his speech is wonderful or strange.
The second sentence has *etha* as subject, which occurs as
'T in inscriptions and is the second-person masculine sin-
gular pronoun "you." *Gad* is less certain. Gray takes it as
the form GD' found in inscriptions, which means "goat,"
and interprets the sentence as an insult: "you are a goat,"
i.e., "you are an idiot."

l. 1023: mu phonnim si corathi[m].

Variants: miphonnium *P*, mufonnim *A* | siccoratim *A*, sucora-
him *BC*, sicoraphim *D*

Discussion: Spelling and pronunciation of Hanno's words are
secured by Milphio's nonsensical but phonologically help-
ful Latin interpretation. Milphio's *supponi*, "place under,"
and *imponi*, "place on," correspond to the Punic *phonnim*,
and *sub cratim*, "underneath a wickerwork basket," fit well
with *si corathi* or *si corathim*; since final -*m* in Latin had
lost its consonantal value in most contexts and was only
rendered as nasalization of the preceding vowel, not too
much should be made of the final -*m* of *corathim* transmit-

ted in all manuscripts, because there are good reasons for deleting it. The interpretation of the line is not unproblematic. Sznycer points out that *si corathi* had already occurred in l. 930 and interprets it in the same way as there, as "whom I invoke/call on." He regards *muphonnim* as a verb form of PNN, "turn," a root not actually attested in Punic but corresponding to the Hebrew root PNH with the same meaning. Krahmalkov's interpretation is completely different. He wants the sentence to mean "do you remember any Punic?," corresponding to what Milphio asks Agorastocles in l. 985; why this should be the case is unclear. For Krahmalkov, *mu* is the question word "what," already seen in l. 1010, but he interprets it as introducing a yes-or-no question, for which there are neither Punic nor Hebrew parallels. He takes *phonnim* to mean "Punic." Formally *phonnim* is a masculine plural ("Phoenicians"), but Krahmalkov points out that the masculine plural is attested as a language name elsewhere (KRSYM, "the Corsic language"). *Sicorathim* is then taken as a form of ZKR, "remember," a root attested in both Punic and Hebrew. However, since there is no reason why Hanno should just utter a translation of Milphio's earlier words, a different interpretation seems more likely. I think Sznycer is right in taking *si corathi* as "whom I am calling on" again. I would prefer to interpret *phonnim* as "Phoenicians" rather than as a language name. As for the question word *mu*, I would like to take it as negative particle; this of course has no parallels in Punic, where question words are not attested in inscriptions, but the equivalent Hebrew question word MH, "what," has negative meaning from time to time, a meaning it acquired when a negative answer was expected. If my interpretation is correct, the sentence means "the ones I am calling on are not Phoenicians." Hanno has realized that his interlocutors are not Phoenicians (and hence know no Punic).

l. 1027: gune bal samem ierasan.

Variants: gunebbalsamem *A*, gunebel balsamen *P* | i erasan *P*, lyryla *A*

Discussion: Two words in this sentence are clear beyond doubt. *Bal samem*, attested also as *Baalsamen* in Augustine (*Quaest. Hept.* 7.16), is the name of the highest Punic deity, B'L ŠMM, or "lord of the heavens." ŠMM, "heavens," is a noun attested only in the plural in both Punic and Hebrew. The beginning of the line is more difficult. If one accepts the reading of the palimpsest, *gune* could be the construct state plural of G'N, "majesty," a noun not attested in Punic but common in Hebrew, especially in combination with divine names. The last word has to remain obscure. The Palatine manuscripts deviate markedly from the Ambrosian palimpsest here. Schröder treats *ierasan* as 'ḤRŠNY (or, perhaps better, 'ḤRŠNW), the first-person singular perfect jif'il of ḤRŠ, "be silent." The root is attested only in Hebrew, not in Punic, but in Hebrew the causative meaning of this stem is securely attested. If correct, the perfect is used either as a wish or as a performative speech act. The sentence would then mean: "O majesty of the lord of the heavens, I'm silencing him!" However, certainty for the second half of the sentence cannot be reached.

l. 1141, first part: hau amma si lli.

Variants: auamma illi *A*, haudones illi *P*

Discussion: Hanno comments that one of his slave boys is
greeting his mother, Giddenis, whom he has just recog-
nized. *Amma* is Punic 'M', "mother," a well-attested word.
We have already come across the greeting *auo*, which was
analyzed as third-person masculine singular perfect qal of
ḤWY, "live." Here we expect a feminine form, not a short-
ened *au*, but it is possible that the final vowel was merged
with the following word or that we are dealing with a
scribal error. The spelling of the word with *h* in the Pala-
tine manuscripts in all likelihood does not reflect the Punic
fricative at the beginning of the word but is the result of a
confusion with Latin *hau(d)*, "not." *Si lli* is the relative par-
ticle 'Š followed by the preposition L, "for," with an enclitic
first-person singular pronoun; gemination of a consonant
after the relative particle could also be observed in l. 933.
The sentence then means "may the mother who is mine
live" or, more prosaically, "greetings to my mother."

l. 1141, second part -1142: hauo[n] bane si lli mustine

mepsi etenes te dum et alamma cestimim.

Variants: hauon *P*, kauon *A* | bane *A*, bene *P* | siilli *P*, sill* *A* |
mustine *AC*, inustine *BD* | *uersum alterum sic habet P*, mip
staetemest*sdumetalan****stimim *A*

Discussion: Hanno's comment on the passage is that Giddenis
is greeting her son. Unfortunately, he is not more precise

than that. The first words are clear because they corre-
spond closely to what the son had said to his mother. We
find the wish *auo*, "may he live," and the relative clause
"who is mine." *Bane* (*bene* looks like a Latinization, since
in Latin *bene* means "well") is probably BN-Y, the word for
"son" with an enclitic first-person singular pronoun. The
whole phrase means "may my son, who is mine, live," in
other words, "greetings to my son." The rest is incompre-
hensible. Krahmalkov believes that we are dealing with a
Punic translation of a passage from the *Aulularia* and ren-
ders it as "let us drink wine; let us drink the blood of the
vine!—No! I shall drink water!" This is rather far-fetched.

l. 1152: lachanna.

Variants: lachanna *A*, lachanam *P*

Discussion: Milphio repeats a word that was said to him
   above in l. 1013. He is clearly frustrated and feels deflated
   after his attempts at Punic have been shown to be useless.
   Now he has to take Hanno's Punic servants into the house
   and says *lachanna* to them, which is either an insult or the
   imperative of HLK, "go," with the adhortative particle N'.
   If it is the latter, Milphio clearly does not understand the
   grammar: *lech* is the imperative masculine singular, but he
   is addressing several people.

REFERENCES

Adams, J. N. (1994), "Latin and Punic in Contact? The Case of
   the Bu Njem Ostraca," in *Journal of Roman Studies* 84: 87–
   112.

Faber, A. (1997), "Genetic Subgrouping of the Semitic Languages," in R. Hetzron (ed.), *The Semitic Languages* (London), pp. 3–15.

Friedrich, J., Röllig, W., Amadasi Guzzo, M. G., and Mayer, W. R. (1999), *Phönizisch-punische Grammatik*, 3rd ed. (Rome).

Glück, J. J. and Maurach, G. (1971–1972), "Punisch in Plautinischer Metrik," in *Semitics* 2: 93–126.

Gratwick, A. S. (1969), "*Isti orationi Oedipo opust coniectore*," review of Sznycer (1967), in *Classical Review* NS 19: 53–55.

——— (1971), "Hanno's Punic Speech in the *Poenulus* of Plautus," in *Hermes* 99: 25–45.

Gray, L. H. (1923), "The Punic Passages in the 'Poenulus' of Plautus," in *American Journal of Semitic Languages and Literatures* 39: 73–88.

Harris, Z. S. (1936), *A Grammar of the Phoenician Language* (New Haven).

Jongeling, K. (2008), *Handbook of Neo-Punic Inscriptions* (Tübingen).

Jongeling, K., and Kerr, R. M. (2005), *Late Punic Epigraphy: An Introduction to the Study of Neo-Punic and Latino-Punic Inscriptions* (Tübingen).

Koehler, L., and Baumgartner, W. (2004), *Hebräisches und aramäisches Lexikon zum Alten Testament*, 2 vols. (Leiden).

Krahmalkov, C. R. (1970), "The Punic Speech of Hanno," in *Orientalia* 39: 52–74.

——— (1988), "Observations on the Punic Monologues of Hanno in the *Poenulus*," in *Orientalia* 57: 55–66.

——— (2000), *Phoenician-Punic Dictionary* (Louvain).

——— (2001), *A Phoenician-Punic Grammar* (Leiden).

221

Lindsay, W. M. (1898), "The Carthaginian Passages in the 'Poenulus' of Plautus," in *Classical Review* 12: 361–64.

Segert, S. (1976), *A Grammar of Phoenician and Punic* (Munich).

Sznycer, M. (1967), *Les passages puniques en transcription latine dans le "Poenulus" de Plaute* (Paris).

Versteegh, K. (1997), *The Arabic Language* (Edinburgh).

PSEUDOLUS

INTRODUCTORY NOTE

Although we do not know who wrote the Greek original of the *Pseudolus* or what it was called, we know with certainty when the Plautine play was first performed. The Ambrosian palimpsest has preserved a production notice that informs us that the comedy was staged at the Megalesian Games when Marcus Junius, the son of Marcus, was city praetor. This was in 191, toward the end of Plautus' career. A decade earlier, in 204, when the Second Punic War was gradually coming to an end, the Romans, on the advice of the Delphic oracle, brought a sacred stone to Rome, a stone which, according to the inhabitants of Pessinus in Phrygia, was the manifestation of Cybele, the Great Mother or *Megale Meter*. The games in her honor, newly introduced and held every April, were called the Megalesia. Particularly impressive games were held in April 191, when her temple was finally finished, and it is on this occasion that the *Pseudolus* was first performed. The play is generally acknowledged as one of Plautus' masterpieces and was still popular in the time of Cicero, who saw Roscius playing the pimp Ballio (*Rosc. com.* 7. 20).

Our manuscripts preserve the remains of a prologue (ll. 1–2), which in all likelihood was not written by Plautus himself; for although Plautus does occasionally refer to himself in the prologues, the term *Plautina . . . fabula*, "Plautine play" (l. 2), seems to be a phrase used by later generations to refer to our author's comedies, as in the prologue to the *Casina* (l. 12), which was clearly written after the death of Plautus.

The plot of the *Pseudolus* shows striking similarities to both the *Curculio* and the *Bacchides*. If the most widely accepted attempts at dating the latter two plays are accepted, Plautus has reused some of the material in the *Curculio* for the *Pseudolus*, whereas the *Bacchides* depends on the *Curculio* or the *Pseudolus*, or both. Like the *Curculio*, the first scene of the *Pseudolus* (ll. 3–132) begins with a young man who is in tears because his girlfriend, who belongs to a pimp, is going to be taken away from him. The young, impecunious man in the *Pseudolus* is called Calidorus, and Pseudolus, the eponymous hero of our play, is the clever slave who will help him. Calidorus' girlfriend, Phoenicium, belongs to the pimp Ballio, who has promised her to the Macedonian soldier Polymachaeroplagides. The soldier has reached an agreement with Ballio: the girl's price is twenty minas, and of these he has already paid fifteen; should either the soldier himself or one of his servants come with the remaining five minas and the soldier's seal, Ballio is to give the girl to him. The deadline for payment is the day of our play.

This first scene is essentially Greek in content. In the Roman law of Plautus' day the practice of giving a part payment did not exist. In Rome there would have been an oral contract between the pimp and the soldier, and this contract would have been binding. By contrast, in Greece nothing, except for the part payment, could prevent the pimp from selling the girl to Calidorus if he brought twenty minas; and even after receiving a part payment from the soldier the pimp could sell the girl to Calidorus, his only obligation toward the soldier being the repayment of the fifteen minas. However, this first scene does contain one oral contract, and this is a contract between Calidorus and Pseudolus, who promises his young master twenty minas. Legally Pseudolus, being a slave, cannot make a real contract, but the agreement between him and Calidorus has the form of a contract that is binding according to Roman law. This promise now obliges Pseudolus to produce the money, which leads to a greater emphasis on the slave's cunning, a typical Plautine adaptation.

We first encounter Ballio in the second scene (ll. 133–229), a long passage of song in which he says that it is his birthday and threatens and mistreats his slaves and prostitutes, among them Phoenicium (ll. 225–29). The passage seems far more Plautine than Greek, and the treatment of Phoenicium certainly is due to Plautus: Ballio threatens to prostitute her to the common people, completely disregarding his agreement with the soldier, for the sole purpose of displaying his brutality.

There are remarkable discrepancies between the first scene and the third (ll. 230–393), and these are explained most easily if we assume that the third scene is by and large a Plautine invention. The discrepancies were undoubtedly less noticeable onstage, where the lengthy sung passage between the first and the third scene will to some extent have obscured the contradictions. In the third scene we learn that there was a contract between Ballio and Calidorus but that Calidorus was unable to pay. Such a contract would have been too important for a Greek playwright to pass over in the first scene, which points to a

Plautine invention; a further indication that this contract does not come from the Greek original is the fact that Calidorus did not make the typical part payment. An even more important consideration is that the two contracts can hardly coexist. In the first half of the third scene, Calidorus speaks to Ballio in a subservient way, feeling guilty for not paying; he does not seem to know at all that there is a contract between Ballio and the soldier, for if he knew, he would certainly be incensed and feel cheated rather than being subdued and submissive. In the third scene, Calidorus and Pseudolus also entreat Ballio to extend their deadline, completely ignoring the fact that it is not their deadline that matters, but the deadline the soldier has, which is the day of the play. In conclusion, in the first scene Calidorus appears not to know about his own contract with the pimp, whereas in the third he cannot know about the soldier's contract with the pimp. Such a state of affairs would be highly unusual in a Greek play but is quite normal in Plautus, who puts emphasis on the comedy of individual scenes rather than on a coherent plot. But why did Plautus feel the need to introduce a second contract at all? Without a second contract, the pimp's behavior, at least according to Roman law, would be entirely acceptable and there would be no reason for the audience to despise and hate Ballio so intensely. Now that the audience has a good reason to dislike Ballio, Plautus comes up with a very Roman *flagitatio* (ll. 357–70), in which Calidorus and Pseudolus keep insulting the pimp in order to make him feel guilty or upset and to make him change his mind. Needless to say, the callous pimp takes it all in his stride.

The result of the third scene is that Calidorus and Pseudolus now have two tasks to accomplish: they have to prevent the sale of the girl to the soldier, and they have to get hold of twenty minas to buy her themselves. Preventing the purchase by the soldier comes first in time and importance; bringing twenty minas to the pimp will not save Calidorus if the soldier comes with the remainder of his payment. Pseudolus sends Calidorus away to find a reliable friend so as to accomplish the first task together with him.

In the fourth scene (ll. 394–414) Pseudolus delivers a soliloquy and expresses his worries. He feels uncertain that he can manage the first and especially the second task. He is soon interrupted by the arrival of Calidorus' father, Simo, and his neighbor Callipho. In this fifth scene, Simo complains bitterly about his son's profligate lifestyle and his being corrupted by Pseudolus. Callipho, a mild old gentleman, advises him to stay calm and not to be too strict. Pseudolus now sees his chance to sort out the second task, the procurement of the money. In Roman comedy, stingy fathers are the typical source of money, and in our play, too, Pseudolus wants to swindle Simo out of it. He announces his intention openly, which makes Simo even angrier, whereas Callipho is impressed rather than angered. The great achievement of Pseudolus in this scene is that he manages to connect the two tasks: he persuades Simo to promise him twenty minas if he can get Phoenicium away from Ballio. Callipho is asked to stay in town as a witness and to make sure that Simo will pay in the end if Pseudolus can keep his promise to abduct Phoenicium from Ballio.

Several scholars have found fault with the fourth and fifth scenes, but most of the oddities are minor and can be explained without problems. Thus Pseudolus is very con-

PLAUTUS

fident in the third and fifth scenes when he speaks to
Calidorus and Simo, respectively, but in the fourth scene,
when he delivers his soliloquy, he appears timid and ner-
vous. The great plan announced to his two masters simply
does not exist in the fourth scene. Yet this is hardly surpris-
ing: it is only natural that Pseudolus should reassure Cali-
dorus and bluff in front of Simo, while being honest
with the audience. Similarly, in the first scene Pseudo-
lus does not even know about the love between Calidorus
and Phoenicium, whereas in the fifth scene he says to
Simo that he has known about it for a long time, and in
the fourth scene, the soliloquy, he even states that he at-
tempted to defraud Simo but was prevented from doing
so. What Pseudolus says to Simo in the fifth scene could
conceivably be regarded as bluffing, but the discrepancy
between the first and fourth scenes remains. If, as argued
above, the first scene by and large goes back to the Greek
original, where Pseudolus does not know about his young
master's love at first, the incoherent statement in the
fourth act presumably goes back to Plautus, who invented
the contract between Calidorus and the pimp and subse-
quently made Pseudolus attempt to steal money from the
old man at a time before our play on account of this second
contract.

What is the second act in modern editions begins with
a song by Pseudolus in which he claims to have a plan, a
plan which is later abandoned. The fact that we have a
song here and a plan that is completely irrelevant for the
course of the action means that this passage is probably a
Plautine invention. This is important because after l. 573[a],
the end of the first act, the stage is empty; Pseudolus
leaves, saying that the flute player will entertain the audi-

ence in the meantime. Thus at first sight it looks as if, coinciding with the modern act break, we had a Greek act break here, with an empty stage and a choral interlude, but since the first scene of the second act is probably entirely Plautine, it is more likely that the act break in the Greek original came elsewhere, perhaps between the third and fifth scenes of what is now the first act.

After Pseudolus' song we meet Harpax, the soldier's servant, who brings the soldier's seal and the remaining five minas with him. Pseudolus, claiming to be Ballio's slave, tells Harpax that Ballio is away and manages to persuade Harpax to give him the sealed letter. Harpax then goes to an inn, where he wants to stay till summoned by Pseudolus, who promises to fetch him as soon as Ballio arrives so that he can pay and take Phoenicium away. After Harpax has left, Calidorus arrives with his friend Charinus, who will lend Pseudolus five minas and his clever slave Simia; Simia has to dress as a soldier's servant, deliver the letter with the five minas, and take the girl away. Pseudolus, Calidorus, and Charinus go to the forum to get Simia ready, and an unnamed slave boy belonging to Ballio comes onstage to entertain the audience with his lament about the hardships of being a pimp's slave.

Not much later, Ballio comes back with a boastful cook who is supposed to cook his birthday meal. There is a lengthy argument between the disgruntled Ballio and the pompous, overpriced cook. As soon as the cook and his assistants are in Ballio's house, Simia comes, claims to be Harpax, hands over the seal and the money, and takes Phoenicium away.

Ballio is overjoyed because he believes that Pseudolus cannot trick him any longer. He tells Simo that Phoenicium is already on her way to the soldier, and when Simo remains skeptical, he promises him twenty minas and the girl in addition if this is not the case. Naturally, the pimp's downfall is not far away. The real Harpax comes, angry that Pseudolus did not fetch him, and meets Ballio and Simo. The two ridicule him, believing him to be a con man hired by Pseudolus. When they finally realize that they are dealing with the real Harpax, Ballio is in despair because he now has to repay fifteen minas to Harpax, give up Phoenicium, and pay twenty minas to Simo. Ballio does not reappear in our play. What happened to his birthday meal is unclear; he probably decided to cancel it.

What is the fifth act in modern editions consists of two scenes. First, Pseudolus returns, probably from the house of Charinus, and sings a song about the joys of the party he has had with Calidorus, Phoenicium, and Charinus (ll. 1246–84). This song, accompanied by dancing and interspersed with mild obscenities, is probably an expansion of a much shorter Greek passage.

The last scene of our play requires a more detailed discussion. In the first place it needs to be said that ll. 1238–45, immediately before the fifth act, are probably purely Plautine. Just as Plautus expanded the role of the clever slave, he is likely to have inserted himself this scene of Simo's praise of Pseudolus, a scene which borders on hero worship. In the last scene of the play, Simo is subject to remarkable mood swings. In 1291–91[a] he decides to be gentle to Pseudolus, just as in the last scene of the fourth act; in 1294–1304 he attacks him verbally and physically; and in 1313–32 there is a role reversal, with Simo entreating Pseudolus for some of the money he has to hand over and with Pseudolus playing the master. To some extent, these mood swings can be explained on psychological grounds; first, Simo decides to be gentle, then, when confronted with his drunken and rude slave, he changes his mind, and finally, when there is an opportunity to get some of the money back by being polite, he is submissive and even willing to go drinking with his slave. However, it cannot go unnoticed that it is rather odd that Callipho, who was supposed to remain present, does not reappear at all. Of course there are occasionally characters in comedy that appear and do not reappear, but these normally merely serve to entertain, to introduce someone else, or to present background information. This is clearly not the case here. It is perhaps possible that in the Greek original Simo was consistently angry in the last scene until Callipho managed to calm him down and persuade him to pay as agreed. If so, the initial politeness of Simo and the final bizarre role reversal would be Plautine, and this fits precisely with what we know of Plautus' predilection for the clever slave-hero.

However much or little of the last scene is purely Plautine, Simo does not really lose any money. Ballio has promised Simo twenty minas, and the girl in addition. Pseudolus has taken the girl away from Ballio, but after Ballio's promise he will not have to pay. If Simo now gives Pseudolus twenty minas, he does not suffer any true loss. Pseudolus is free to offer Simo half or even more of the twenty minas. If the role reversal with the promise of money to Simo at the end of the play goes back to Plautus, as is likely, it is also possible that the pimp's exuberant promise (l. 1075) to let go of the girl and not just the twenty minas is Plautine too. In the Greek original we would then have had Ballio paying twenty minas to Simo, Simo passing the sum

233

PLAUTUS

on to Pseudolus, Pseudolus to Calidorus, and Calidorus giving it back to Ballio, as payment for Phoenicium. Ballio would not be completely ruined and, more important, Pseudolus would not have spare money to promise to Simo in exchange for taking part in the drinking bout that ends the play.

SELECT BIBLIOGRAPHY

Editions and Commentaries

Auden, H. W. (1896), *The Pseudolus of Plautus: Edited with Introduction and Notes* (Cambridge).

Sturtevant, E. H., with F. E. Brown, F. W. Schaefer, and J. P. Showerman (1932), *T. Macci Plauti Pseudolus: Edited with an Introduction and Notes* (New Haven).

Willcock, M. M. (1987), *Plautus: Pseudolus* (Bristol).

Criticism

Forehand, W. E. (1972), "*Pseudolus* 868–872: Ut Medea Peliam concoxit," in *Classical Journal* 67: 293–98.

Görler, W. (1983), "Plautinisches im Pseudolus," in *Würzburger Jahrbücher für die Altertumswissenschaft* NS 9: 89–107.

Holmes, N. (2002), "Foot Notes," in *Hermes* 130: 237–38.

Jocelyn, H. D. (1987), "Studies in the Indirect Tradition of Plautus' *Pseudolus* I: Rufinus, Pliny, Varro," in *Filologia e forme letterarie: Studi offerti a Francesco della Corte*, vol. 2 (Urbino), 57–72.

——— (1988), "Studies in the Indirect Tradition of Plautus' *Pseudolus* III: The 'Archaising Movement,' Republican Comedy and Aulus Gellius' *Noctes Atticae*," in N. Horsfall (ed.), *Vir bonus discendi peritus: Studies in Celebration of Otto Skutsch's Eightieth Birthday* (London), 57–72.

———— (1991), "Studies in the Indirect Tradition of Plautus' *Pseudolus* II: Verrius Flaccus' *De significatu uerborum*," in *Studi di filologia classica in onore di G. Monaco*, vol. 2 (Palermo), 569–80.

———— (2000), "The Unpretty Boy of Plautus' *Pseudolus* (767–789)," in E. Stärk and G. Vogt-Spira (eds.), *Dramatische Wäldchen: Festschrift für Eckard Lefèvre zum 65. Geburtstag* (Zurich), 431–60.

Lefèvre, E. (1997), *Plautus'* Pseudolus (Tübingen).

Paratore, E. (1963), "La structure du Pseudolus," in *Revue des études latines* 41: 123–64.

Questa, C. (1965), "Per un'edizione dello *Pseudolus*," in *Studi italiani di filologia classica* NS 37: 3–40.

Skutsch, O. (1942), "Notes on the *Pseudolus* of Plautus," in *Classical Review* 56: 66–68.

Williams, G. (1956), "Some Problems in the Construction of Plautus' Pseudolus," in *Hermes* 84: 424–55.

PSEVDOLVS

DIDASCALIA

M. IVNIO. M. FIL. PR. VRB. AC. ME.
(= Marco Iunio Marci filio praetore urbano acta Megalesiis)

ARGVMENTVM I

Praesentis numerat quindecim miles minas,
Simul consignat symbolum, ut Phoenicium
Ei det leno qui eum cum relicuo afferat.
Venientem caculam interuortit symbolo
5 **D**icens Syrum se Ballionis Pseudolus
Opemque erili ita tulit; nam Simiae
Leno mulierem, quem is supposuit, tradidit.
Venit Harpax uerus: res palam cognoscitur
Senexque argentum quod erat pactus reddidit.

ARGVMENTVM II

Calidorus iuuenis m‹eretricem Phoenicium›
efflictim deperibat, nummorum indigus;
eandem miles, qui uiginti mulierem

arg. 2, 1 m‹eretricem Phoenicium› *Leo*

236

PSEUDOLUS

STAGE RECORD

Acted at the Megalesian games when Marcus Junius, son of Marcus, was city praetor.

PLOT SUMMARY 1

A soldier pays fifteen minutes cash down, and at the same time affixes his seal to a token, so that the pimp will give Phoenicium to the man who brought its equivalent with the rest of the money. Pseudolus cheats the soldier's servant out of the token 5 when he arrives, claiming to be Ballio's Syrus, and in this way he brings help to his master's son; for the pimp hands the woman over to Simia, whom Pseudolus palms off on him. The real Harpax comes; the matter comes out into the open, and the old man pays the money he had agreed on.

PLOT SUMMARY 2

Young Calidorus was madly in love with the prostitute Phoenicium, but lacked money. A soldier was also in love with her;

minis mercatus abiit, soluit quindecim.
5 scortum reliquit ad lenonem ac symbolum
ut qui attulisset signum simile cetero
cum pretio secum aueheret emptam mulierem.
mox missus ut prehendat scortum a milite
uenit calator militaris. hunc dolo
10 aggreditur adulescentis seruos Pseudolus
tamquam lenonis atriensis: symbolum
aufert minas⟨que⟩ quinque acceptas mutuas
dat subditicio caculae cum symbolo;
lenonem fallit sycophanta[cie] cacula.
15 scorto Calidorus potitur, uino Pseudolus.

arg. 2, 8 adpraehendit *A*, ut prehendat *Bugge*
arg. 2, 12 que *add. Ritschl*
arg. 2, 14 secophantacie *A*, sycophanta *Ritschl*

having bought the woman for twenty minas, he paid fifteen and
left. He left the prostitute and a token at the pimp's place, so 5
that the person who brought a similar seal with the rest of the
price would take the purchased woman with him. Soon after,
the soldier's servant came, sent by the soldier to fetch the pros-
titute. The young man's slave, Pseudolus, assails him with trick- 10
ery, pretending to be the pimp's majordomo. He takes away the
token and gives five borrowed minas together with the token
to a counterfeit servant. The trickster servant deceives the
pimp. Calidorus gets the prostitute and Pseudolus wine. 15

PLAUTUS

PERSONAE

PSEVDOLVS seruos
CALIDORVS adulescens
BALLIO leno
SIMO senex
CALLIPHO senex
HARPAX cacula
CHARINVS adulescens
SERVI
MERETRICES
PVER
COQVOS
SIMIA sycophanta

SCAENA

Athenis

PSEUDOLUS

CHARACTERS

PSEUDOLUS a slave; belongs to Simo and his son Calidorus

CALIDORUS a young man; in love with Phoenicium, a girl
   owned by Ballio

BALLIO a pimp; greedy and heartless

SIMO an old man; concerned about his son Calidorus and
   suspicious of Pseudolus

CALLIPHO an old man; Simo's neighbor and friend

HARPAX a soldier's servant; comes to take Phoenicium to his
   master

CHARINUS a young man; friend of Calidorus

SLAVES belong to Ballio

PROSTITUTES also belong to Ballio

SLAVE BOY servant of Ballio

COOK hired by Ballio

SIMIA an impostor; helps Pseudolus

STAGING

The stage represents a street in Athens. On the street there are
three houses; the one on our left belongs to Callipho, the one
in the middle to Simo, and the one on the right to Ballio. To
our left the street leads to the harbor and to our right to the
city center.

PROLOGVS

exporgi meliust lumbos atque exsurgier:
Plautina longa fabula in scaenam uenit.

ACTVS I

I. i: PSEVDOLVS. CALIDORVS

PSEV si ex te tacente fieri possem certior,
ere, quae miseriae te tam misere macerant,
5 duorum labori ego hominum parsissem lubens,
mei te rogandi et tis respondendi mihi;
nunc quoniam id fieri non potest, necessitas
me subigit ut te rogitem. responde mihi:
quid est quod tu exanimatus iam hos multos dies
10 gestas tabellas tecum, eas lacrumis lauis
nec tui participem consili quemquam facis?
eloquere, ut quod ego nescio id tecum sciam.
CALI misere miser sum, Pseudole.
PSEV   id te Iuppiter
prohibessit!
CALI   nihil hoc Iouis ad iudicium attinet:
15 sub Veneris regno uapulo, non sub Iouis.

6 et tui tis *Gellius*, et tui *Nonius*, etui *A*, et te *P*

242

PROLOGUE

Enter the SPEAKER OF THE PROLOGUE *from the right.*

It's better to stretch your loins and get to your feet: a long play by Plautus is about to come onstage.

Exit the SPEAKER OF THE PROLOGUE *to the right.*

ACT ONE

Enter PSEUDOLUS *and* CALIDORUS *from Simo's house, the latter carrying writing tablets and crying silently.*

PSEU Master, if while you're silent I could get the information
out of you as to what misery is vexing you so miserably, 5
I'd have been happy to spare two people from trouble,
me from asking you and you from answering me. Now
since this cannot happen, necessity forces me to ask you.
Answer me: why is it that you've been carrying tablets
around with you for several days already, half dead, and 10
that you wash them with your tears and don't take anyone
into your confidence? Tell me so that I may know to-
gether with you what at present I don't know.
CALI I'm feeling really miserable, Pseudolus.
PSEU Jupiter forbid!
CALI This has nothing to do with Jupiter's jurisdiction; I'm 15
getting a thrashing under the rule of Venus, not that of
Jupiter.

243

PLAUTUS

PSEV licet me id scire quid sit? nam tu me antidhac
supremum habuisti comitem consiliis tuis.
CALI idem animus nunc est.
PSEV   face me certum quid tibi est;
aut re iuuabo aut opera aut consilio bono.
20 CALI cape has tabellas, tute hinc narrato tibi
quae me miseria et cura contabefacit.
PSEV mos tibi geretur. sed quid hoc, quaeso?
CALI   quid est?
PSEV ut opinor, quaerunt litterae hae sibi liberos:
alia aliam scandit.
CALI   ludis iam ludo tuo?
25 PSEV has quidem pol credo nisi Sibylla legerit,
interpretari alium posse neminem.
CALI quor inclementer dicis lepidis litteris
lepidis tabellis lepida conscriptis manu?
PSEV an, opsecro hercle, habent quas gallinae manus?
30   nam has quidem gallina scripsit.
CALI   odiosus mihi es.
lege uel tabellas redde.
PSEV   immo enim pellegam.
aduortito animum.
CALI   non adest.
PSEV   at tu cita.
CALI immo ego tacebo, tu istinc ex cera cita.
nam istic meus animus nunc est, non in pectore.
35 PSEV tuam amicam uideo, Calidore.
CALI   ubi ea est, opsecro?

19 iuuabo aut re Ω, *transp. Bothe*

244

PSEU May I know what's the matter? Previously you had me as chief associate in your counsels.

CALI I have the same intention now.

PSEU Inform me what's wrong with you. I'll support you with money or help or good advice.

CALI Take these tablets and tell yourself from them what misery and worry is consuming me. 20

PSEU I'll obey you. *(takes and examines them)* But what's this, please?

CALI What is it?

PSEU I think these letters are trying to have babies; they're climbing all over each other.

CALI Are you cracking your usual jokes now?

PSEU I do believe that unless the Sibyl[1] reads this letter, no one 25 else can interpret it.

CALI Why are you insulting a charming letter written on charming tablets by a charming hand?

PSEU Really, I ask you, have chickens got hands? Surely a 30 chicken wrote this one.

CALI You're getting on my nerves. Read or return the tablets.

PSEU No, I'll read them through. Give me your sole attention.

CALI My soul isn't here.

PSEU Then summon it.

CALI No, *I* shall be quiet, *you* summon it from there from the wax: that's where my soul is now, not in my breast.

PSEU I can see your girlfriend, Calidorus. 35

CALI Where is she, please?

---

[1] A prophetess.

PSEV	eccam in tabellis porrectam: in cera cubat.
CALI	at te di deaeque quantum est—
PSEV	seruassint quidem!
CALI	quasi solstitialis herba paulisper fui:
	repente exortus sum, repentino occidi.
40 PSEV	tace, dum tabellas pellego.
CALI	ergo quin legis?
PSEV	"Phoenicium Calidoro amatori suo
	per ceram et lignum litterasque interpretes
	salutem impertit et salutem ex te expetit
	lacrumans titubanti animo, corde et pectore."
45 CALI	perii! salutem nusquam inuenio, Pseudole,
	quam illi remittam.
PSEV	quam salutem?
CALI	argenteam.
PSEV	pro lignean salute uis argenteam
	remittere illi? uide sis quam tu rem geras.
CALI	recita modo: ex tabellis iam faxo scies
50	quam subito argento mi usus inuento siet.
PSEV	"leno me peregre militi Macedonio
	minis uiginti uendidit, uoluptas mea;
	et prius quam hinc abiit quindecim miles minas
	dederat; nunc unae quinque remorantur minae.
55	ea causa miles hic reliquit symbolum,
	expressam in cera ex anulo suam imaginem,
	ut qui huc afferret eius similem symbolum

42 lignum *Ausonius*, linum Ω
44 titubanti⟨que⟩ *Ritschl*

---

[2] Lit. "salvation"; Latin has the same word, *salus*, for "greetings"

PSEU Look here, stretched out on the tablets: she's lying in the wax.

CALI (*angrily*) But you, may all the gods and goddesses, as many as there are—

PSEU (*interrupting*) Preserve me!

CALI Like the grass of midsummer, I lived for a short time: in an instant I sprang up, in an instant I withered away.

PSEU Be quiet while I'm reading through the tablets.   40

CALI Then why aren't you reading?

PSEU "Phoenicium sends her dearest wishes to Calidorus, her lover, through the medium of wax and wood and letters, and seeks her dearest wish[2] from you, weeping, with wavering spirits, heart, and breast."

CALI I'm dead! I can't find her dearest wish anywhere to send   45
back to her, Pseudolus.

PSEU What dearest wish?

CALI One made of silver.

PSEU For dearest wishes made of wood you want to send her back wishes made of silver? Please watch what you're doing.

CALI Just read it out; I'll make sure that in a second you'll know from the tablets how immediately I need to find   50
money.

PSEU "The pimp has sold me abroad to a Macedonian soldier for twenty minas, my darling; and the soldier gave him fifteen minas before he left. Now only five minas are delaying him. For this reason the soldier has left a token   55
here, his picture pressed into wax from his ring, so that the pimp would send me away together with the man

and "salvation," and I have tried to reproduce the pun with "dearest wishes" (= "greetings") and "dearest wish" (= "salvation").

cum eo simul me mitteret. ei rei dies
haec praestituta est, proxuma Dionysia."

60   CALI   cras ea quidem sunt: prope adest exitium mihi,
           nisi quid mihi in te est auxili.

      PSEV   sine pellegam.

      CALI   sino, nam mi uideor cum ea fabularier;
           lege: dulce amarumque una nunc misces mihi.

      PSEV   "nunc nostri amores, mores, consuetudines,
65   iocus, ludus, sermo, suauisauiatio,
           compressiones artae amantum corporum,
67   teneris labellis molles morsiunculae,
67[a]   nostr[or]um orgiorum ⟨osculat⟩iunculae,
68   papillarum horridularum oppressiunculae,
           harunc uoluptatum mi omnium atque itidem tibi
70   distractio, discidium, uastities uenit,
           nisi quae mihi in te est aut tibi est in me salus.
           haec quae ego sciui ut scires curaui omnia;
           nunc ego te experiar quid ames, quid simules. uale."

      CALI   est misere scriptum, Pseudole.

      PSEV   oh! miserrume.

75   CALI   quin fles?

      PSEV   pumiceos oculos habeo: non queo
           lacrumam exorare ut exspuant unam modo.

      CALI   quid ita?

      PSEV   genus nostrum semper siccoculum fuit.

      CALI   nilne adiuuare me audes?

      PSEV   quid faciam tibi?

   67[a] *non fertur in P*   nostr[or]um *Lorenz*   ⟨osculat⟩iunculae
Loewe
   69 ibidem Ω, itidem ς

who brought here a token similar to that one. For this business this day was fixed, the day preceding the Dionysia."[3]

CALI That's tomorrow; my end is close by, unless I have some help in you. 60

PSEU Let me read it through.

CALI Yes: I seem to be talking to her. Read: now you're mixing sweet and bitter together for me.

PSEU "Now as for our passions, ways, and habits, jest, play, 65 chat, and sweet kisses, the tight squeezing of loving bodies, the tender little bites with gentle lips, the little kisses of our secret meetings, the little pinchings of firm little breasts, a disseverance, disunion, and desolation of all these pleasures is coming to me and in the same way 70 to you, unless I have some help in you or you in me. I've taken care that you'd know all that I have come to know. Now I'll find out to what extent you love me and to what extent you are only pretending. Farewell!" (*returns the tablets*)

CALI It's written woefully, Pseudolus.

PSEU Oh! Very woefully!

CALI Why aren't you crying? 75

PSEU I have eyes as dry as flint; I can't persuade them to spit out a single tear.

CALI How come?

PSEU Our family has always been dry-eyed.

CALI Don't you want to support me at all?

PSEU What should I do for you?

---

[3] Greek festival in honor of Dionysus, god of vegetation and wine; it was regularly held in March and during it there were theater performances.

CALI	eheu!
PSEV	"eheu"? id quidem hercle ne parsis: dabo.
80 CALI	miser sum, argentum nusquam inuenio mutuom.
PSEV	eheu!
CALI	neque intus nummus ullus est.
PSEV	eheu!
CALI	ille abducturus est mulierem cras.
PSEV	eheu!
CALI	istocin pacto me adiuuas?
PSEV	do id quod mihi est;
	nam is mihi thesaurus iugis in nostra domo est.
85 CALI	actum est de me hodie. sed potes tu mutuam
	drachumam dare unam mihi quam cras reddam tibi?
PSEV	uix hercle, opinor, [est] si me opponam pignori.
	sed quid ea drachuma facere uis?
CALI	restim uolo
	mihi emere.
PSEV	quam ob rem?
CALI	qui me faciam pensilem.
90	certum est mihi ante tenebras tenebras persequi.
PSEV	quis mi igitur drachumam reddet, si dedero tibi?
	an tu te ea causa uis sciens suspendere
	ut me defrudes, drachumam si dederim tibi?
CALI	profecto nullo pacto possum uiuere
95	si illa a me abalienatur atque abducitur.
PSEV	quid fles, cucule? uiues.
CALI	quid ego ni fleam,
	quoi nec paratus nummus argenti siet
	nec libellai spes sit usquam gentium?

82 abducturus est *P*, abducturust *A*
84 domost *A*, est domo *P*

250

CALI Dear me!

PSEU "Dear me"? Don't spare that: I'll give it to you.

CALI I'm wretched, I can't find money on loan anywhere. 80

PSEU Dear me!

CALI And inside I don't have a single coin.

PSEU Dear me!

CALI He's going to take her away tomorrow.

PSEU Dear me!

CALI Is that how you're supporting me?

PSEU I'm giving you what I have: I have a never-ending store of it at home.

CALI I'm finished today. But can you lend me one drachma 85
which I'll return to you tomorrow?

PSEU Hardly, I think, even if I pawn myself. But what do you want to do with that drachma?

CALI I want to buy myself a rope.

PSEU What for?

CALI To set myself swinging. I've decided to enter the realms 90
of dark before darkness falls.

PSEU Then who will return the drachma to me, if I give you one? Do you want to hang yourself knowingly in order to cheat me, if I give you a drachma?

CALI Indeed I can't survive in any way if she's removed and 95
taken away from me.

PSEU Why are you crying, you cuckoo? You'll survive.

CALI Why shouldn't I cry? I don't have a single silver coin available and I don't have hope for a farthing anywhere on earth.

---

87 est *del. plerique edd.*   opino[r] etsi *Ritschl*

PSEV ut litterarum ego harum sermonem audio,
100   nisi tu illi lacrumis fleueris argenteis,
        quod tu istis lacrumis te probare postulas,
        non pluris refert quam si imbrim in cribrum geras.
        uerum ego te amantem, ne paue, non deseram.
        spero alicunde hodie me bona opera aut hac mea
105   tibi inuenturum esse auxilium argentarium.
        atque id futurum undeunde dicam nescio,
        nisi quia futurum est: ita supercilium salit.
CALI utinam quae dicis dictis facta suppetant!
PSEV scis tu quidem hercle, mea si commoui sacra,
110   quo pacto et quantas soleam turbellas dare.
CALI in te nunc omnes spes sunt aetati meae.
PSEV satin est si hanc hodie mulierem efficio tibi
        tua ut sit aut si tibi do uiginti minas?
CALI satis, si futurum est.
PSEV   roga me uiginti minas,
115   ut me effecturum tibi quod promisi scias.
        roga, opsecro hercle. gestio promittere.
CALI dabisne argenti mi hodie uiginti minas?
PSEV dabo. molestus nunciam ne sis mihi.
        atque hoc, ne dictum tibi neges, dico prius:
120   si neminem alium potero, tuom tangam patrem.
CALI di te mihi semper seruent! uerum, si potest,
        pietatis causa . . . uel etiam matrem quoque.

100 drachmis Ω, lacrumis *Bothe*
102 geras *P*, legas *A*, ingeras *Salmasius*

---

[4] Which is what the Danaids did as punishment in the Under-world.

PSEU As I hear the speech of this letter, unless you cry silver   100
tears for her, your wish to ingratiate yourself with her by
those tears is of no more use than pouring water into a
sieve.[4] But I won't desert you, lover that you are, stop
being afraid. I expect to find financial help for you from   105
somewhere today, either through my good effort or (*lifting up his left hand, used for stealing*) this one of mine.
And I don't know where I should say it'll come from,
except that come it will: that's how my eyebrow is twitching.[5]

CALI If only your deeds support the words you speak!

PSEU You know what fine little uproars I usually cause and how   110
I do so, if I get ready for the sacrifice.[6]

CALI All hopes for my life lie in you now.

PSEU Is it enough if I bring it about that this woman is yours
today, or if I give you twenty minas?

CALI Yes, if it's going to happen.

PSEU Ask me for twenty minas so that you know that I'm going   115
to do what I promised you. Ask me, please do. I'm keen
to promise it.

CALI Will you give me twenty silver minas today?

PSEU I will give them.[7] Now don't be a nuisance to me. And
I'm telling you in advance, so don't deny that you've been
told: if I can't cheat anyone else, I'll cheat your father.   120

CALI May the gods always keep you safe for me! But if possible, for the sake of filial duty . . . you can even cheat my
mother as well.

[5] A good omen.   [6] *Sacra commouere* is a religious technical
term referring to preparations for a sacrifice (Serv. *Aen.* 4. 301).

[7] Formula of the *stipulatio*, an oral but binding contract in Roman
law.

PSEV de istac re in oculum utrumuis conquiescito.
CALI oculum? anne in aurem?
PSEV   at hoc peruolgatum est minus.
125   nunc, ne quis dictum sibi neget, dico omnibus,
           pube praesenti in contione; omni poplo,
           omnibus amicis notisque edico meis,
           in hunc diem a me ut caueant, ne credant mihi.
CALI st!
130   tace opsecro hercle.
PSEV   quid negoti est?
CALI   ostium
           lenonis crepuit.
PSEV   crura mauellem modo.
CALI atque ipse egreditur penitus, periuri caput.

I. ii: BALLIO. SERVI. MERETRICES.
PSEVDOLVS. CALIDORVS

BAL exite, agite exite, ignaui, male habiti et male conciliati,
       quorum numquam quicquam quoiquam uenit in
           mentem ut recte faciant,
135   quibus, nisi ad hoc exemplum experior, non potest
           usura usurpari.
       neque ego homines magis asinos numquam uidi, ita
           plagis costae callent:
       quos quom ferias, tibi plus noceas. eo enim ingenio hi
           sunt flagritribae,

124 oculum utrum *P*, utrum *A*, oculum *Bentley*
132 penitus Ω, intus *Acidalius*

---

[8] "To sleep on whichever ear one likes" was proverbial for having
no worries (cf. Ter. *Haut.* 342).

PSEU As far as that issue is concerned, you can sleep on which-
ever eye you like.

CALI Eye? Or on whichever ear?[8]

PSEU But my phrase is less trite. (*to the audience*) Now, so that   125
no one can deny having been told, I'm telling everybody,
while the adult male population is present in this pub-
lic meeting; I'm announcing to the whole people, to all
my friends and acquaintances, that they should be on
their guard against me today and that they shouldn't
trust me.

CALI Hush! Please be quiet.   130

PSEU What's the matter?

CALI The pimp's door has creaked.

PSEU I only wish it was his shins.[9]

CALI And he's coming out himself from deep within, that
fount of perjury. (*they withdraw a little*)

Enter BALLIO *from his house, carrying a whip and attended by
a slave boy with a wallet around his neck. They are followed by
six* SLAVES, *one of whom has a bucket and one an ax.*

BAL Come out, will you? Come out, you good-for-nothings,
whom I am a fool to keep and was a fool to buy! It never
occurs to any of you to do anything right; no possible use   135
can be made of you, unless I treat you in this fashion!
(*beats them*) I've never seen human beings who were
such asses, to judge from how their ribs have grown hard
from blows. When you hit them, you hurt yourself more.
That's the nature of these whip-spoilers, who have these

---

[9] Breaking the shins was a punishment for slaves who had run
away.

qui haec habent consilia, ubi data occasio est, rape,
    clepe, tene,
harpaga, bibe, es, fuge: hoc est
eorum officium, ut mauelis lupos apud ouis quam hos
    domi
linquere custodes.
at faciem quom aspicias eorum, hau mali uidentur:
    opera fallunt.
nunc adeo hanc edictionem nisi animum aduortetis
    omnes,
nisi somnum socordiamque ex pectore oculisque
    emouetis,
ita ego uostra latera loris faciam ut ualide uaria sint,
ut ne peristromata quidem aeque picta sint Campanica
neque Alexandrina beluata tonsilia tappetia.
atque heri iam edixeram omnibus dederamque eas pro-
    uincias,
uerum ita uos estis praediti callenti ingenio improbi,
officium uostrum ut uos malo cogatis commonerier;
nempe ita animati estis uos: uincitis duritia hoc atque
    me.
hoc sis uide, ut alias res agunt! hoc agite, hoc animum
    aduortite,
huc adhibete auris quae ego loquor, plagigera genera
    hominum.
numquam edepol uostrum durius tergum erit quam
    terginum hoc meum.
quid nunc? doletne? em sic datur, si quis erum seruos
    spernit.
assistite omnes contra me et quae loquor aduortite ani-
    mum.

plans: when they're given an opportunity, it's rob, filch, grab, steal, drink, eat, flee. This is their appointed task, 140 so that you'd prefer leaving wolves with sheep to leaving these to watch over your house. But when you look at their faces, they don't seem bad; it's in their work that they fail you. Now unless you all pay attention to this edict and unless you remove sleep and laziness from your hearts and eyes, I'll make sure that your sides are so 145 dreadfully discolored from the whip that not even Campanian coverlets or smooth Alexandrian carpets adorned with animal figures are equally colorful.[10] And I'd already told you all yesterday and given you your tasks, but you crooks have such callous brains that you have to be 150 reminded of your duty with a thrashing. That's what your attitude is like: with your hardness you get the better of this here (*cracks his whip*) and of myself. Just look at how they don't pay attention! Pay attention to this, mind this, apply your ears here to what I'm saying, you stripe-bearing specimens of humanity! Your hides will never be tougher than this rawhide whip of mine. (*beats* 155 *them again*) Well then? Does it hurt? There, that's how I like it if any slave despises his master. All of you, stand opposite me and pay attention to what I'm saying.

[10] Campania, a region in southern Italy, and Alexandria, a city in Egypt, produced high-quality textiles.

---

140 officium *A*, opus *P*   149 neglegentes *P*, (ne)glenti *A*, callenti *Leo*   improbi *A*, improbo *P*   153 loquor *A*, loquar *P*   156 loquor *P*, loquar *A*

tu qui urnam habes aquam ingere, face plenum ahe-
    num sit coquo.
te cum securi caudicali praeficio prouinciae.

SER at haec retunsa est.

BAL   sine siet; itidem uos [quoque estis] plagis omnes:
160 numqui minus ea gratia tamen omnium opera utor?
tibi hoc praecipio ut niteant aedes. habes quod facias:
    propera, abi intro.
tu esto lectisterniator. tu argentum eluito, idem ex-
    struito.
haec, quom ego a foro reuortar, facite ut offendam
    parata,
uorsa, sparsa, tersa, strata, lautaque unctaque omnia uti
    sint.
165 nam mi hodie natalis dies est, decet eum omnis uos
    concelebrare.
pernam, callum, glandium, sumen facito in aqua
    iaceant. satin audis?
magnufice uolo me uiros summos accipere, ut mi rem
    esse reantur.
intro abite atque haec cito celera, ne mora quae sit, co-
    quos quom ueniat;
ego eo in macellum, ut piscium quicquid ibi est pretio
    praestinem.
170 i, puere, prae. ne quisquam pertundat cruminam cau-
    tio est.
uel opperire, est quod domi dicere paene fui oblitus.

---

159 quoque estis *del. Lindsay*   163 foro reuortor *CD*, forore
uertor *B*, foro reuortar *Ritschl*   164 unctaque *Seruius*, coc-
taque *P*   167 summos uiros *P, transp. Bothe*   168 caelebrate
P, cele(b)ra *Lindsay, qui* abite *singularem esse putat*

258

(*to the slave with a bucket*) You there, you have a bucket, put water into it, make sure the cook's boiler is full. (*as this slave goes in, to the one with the ax*) You with the ax I make head of the wood-cutting department.

SLAVE But it's blunt.

BAL So what? You folks are just as blunt from thrashings: do   160
I make any less use of your work for that reason? (*as the slave goes in, to another*) Your job is to make the house shine. You have something to do: hurry, go in. (*as the slave goes in, to another*) You shall be the couch arranger.[11] (*as the slave goes in, to another*) You must clean the silverware and set it out. (*as the slave goes in, into the house*) Make sure that when I return from the market I find that all this is ready, swept, sprinkled, wiped clean, set in order, washed, and given a shine: today is my birth-   165
day and you all ought to celebrate it. (*to the last slave*) Let the ham, pork rind, sweetbread, and sow's udder soak in water. Can you hear me? I want to have a magnificent reception for distinguished men so that they think I have money. Go in and hurry up with these things quickly, so that there won't be a delay when the cook comes. (*as the slave goes in, into the house*) I'm going to the market to buy up any fish that's there for cash. (*to the   170
boy with the purse*) Go in front, boy. I need to watch out that nobody drills a hole into my wallet. Or wait, there's something I almost forgot to say at home. (*into the house*)

[11] The *lectisternium* or "arrangement of couches" was part of the Megalesian Festival; couches were laid out for the gods and food was presented to them.

169 est *P*, ibist *Ritschl*

auditin? uobis, mulieres, hanc habeo edictionem.
uos quae in munditiis, mollitiis, deliciisque aetatulam
   agitis,
uiris cum summis, inclutae amicae, nunc ego scibo
   atque hodie experiar
quae capiti, quae uentri operam det, quaeq' suae rei,
   quae somno studeat;
quam libertam fore mi credam et quam uenalem hodie
   experiar.
facite hodie ut mi munera multa huc ab amatoribus
   conueniant.
nam nisi mihi penus annuos hodie conuenit, cras poplo
   prostituam uos.
natalem scitis mi esse diem hunc: ubi isti sunt quibus
   uos oculi estis,
quibus uitae, quibus deliciae estis, quibus sauia, mam-
   mia, mellillae?
maniplatim mi munerigeruli facite ante aedis iam hic
   assint.
quor ego uestem, aurum atque ea quibus est uobis
   usus, praebeo? [aut] quid mi
domi nisi malum uostra opera est hodie? improbae uini
   modo cupidae estis:
eo uos uostrosque adeo pantices madefactatis, quom
   ego sim hic siccus.
nunc adeo hoc factu est optumum ut nomine quemque
   appellem suo,
ne dictum esse actutum sibi quaepiam uostrarum mi
   neget:
aduortite animum cunctae.
principio, Hedylium, tecum ago, quae amica es fru-
   mentariis,

Can you hear me? I'm making this pronouncement for you, my women.

Enter four PROSTITUTES *from Ballio's house.*

BAL You who spend your lives in neatness, comfort, and pleasure together with distinguished men, you famous girlfriends, now I'll know and today I'll find out which of 175 you is striving for a free head and which for a full belly, and which is seeking profit and which sleep; I'll find out which I should believe will become my freedwoman and which need to be sold. Make sure that many presents come here to me from your lovers today: unless a year's provisions come in to me today, I'll prostitute you to the common people tomorrow. You know that this is my birthday. Where are the men the apples of whose eyes you are, whose life and whose pleasure you are, whose 180 kisses, lovely breasts, and honey cakes? Make sure that present-bearers are here in front of the house in troops right now. Why do I provide you with clothing, jewelry, and the things you need? What return have you shown me today except for trouble? You crooks are only keen on wine; with that you irrigate yourselves and also your bellies, while I am dry here. Now the best thing for me 185 to do is to address each of you by name, so that none of you can claim instantly she hasn't been told. All of you, pay attention! (*singling out one*) First, Hedylium, I'm dealing with you, you who are the girlfriend of the

---

180 mammia *A*, mamilla *P*   182 aut *om. P*
183 uino *P Nonius*, uini *Beroaldus*
184 uestrosque adeo pantices *Nonius*, uestros panticesque adeo Ω

		quibus cunctis montes maxumi frumenti [acerui] sunt
		⟨structi⟩ domi:
190		fac sis sit delatum huc mihi frumentum, hunc annum
		quod satis,
		mi et familiae omni sit meae, atque adeo ut frumento
		afluam,
		ut ciuitas nomen mihi commutet meque ut praedicet
		lenone ex Ballione regem Iasonem.
194	CALI	audin furcifer quae loquitur?
194ᵃ		satin magnuficus tibi uidetur?
195	PSEV	pol iste atque etiam maleficus.
195ᵃ		sed tace atque hanc rem gere.
	BAL	Aeschrodora, tu quae amicos tibi habes lenonum ae-
		mulos
		lanios, qui item ut nos iurando iure malo male
		quaerunt rem, audi:
		nisi carnaria tria grauida tegoribus onere uberi hodie
		mihi erunt, cras te, quasi Dircam olim ut memorant
		duo gnati Iouis
200		deuinxere ad taurum, item ego te distringam ad car-
		narium; id
		tibi profecto taurus fiet.
	CALI	nimis sermone huius ira incendor.
202	PSEV	huncine hic hominem pati
202ᵃ		colere iuuentutem Atticam?
203		ubi sunt, ubi latent quibus aetas
203ᵃ		integra est, qui amant a lenone?
204		quin conueniunt? quin una omnes

---

189 acerui *del. Acidalius*, structi *add. Ritschl*

corn merchants, who all have huge mountains of corn piled up at home. Do have corn brought to me here, an amount sufficient for myself and all my household for this year, and so much that I overflow with corn, so that the city changes my name and calls me King Jason[12] instead of pimp Ballio. 190

CALI   *(to Pseudolus)* Can you hear what the criminal is saying? Doesn't he seem boastful to you?

PSEU   Yes, and nasty to boot. But be quiet and pay attention. 195

BAL   *(to another girl)* Aeschrodora, you who have the butchers, the pimps' rivals, as boyfriends, who just like us acquire money in a nasty way through perjury,[13] listen: unless I have three meat racks heavy with carcasses of large size today, I'll tie you to a meat rack tomorrow, the way they say the two sons of Jupiter once bound Dirce onto a bull.[14] This will become the bull for you. 200

CALI   *(to Pseudolus)* I'm getting really angry about his speech.

PSEU   To think that the youth of Attica put up with this man living here! Where are the men, where are they hiding, who are young in years and who love girls from the pimp? Why don't they get together? Why don't they all

---

[12] King Jason, tyrant of Pherae around 380, or perhaps Iasion, son of Zeus and Electra, beloved of Demeter, the goddess of grain, and father of Plutos ("Wealth").

[13] Pun on the two meanings of *ius malum*, impossible to reproduce: it means "bad/false oath" and "bad broth." The butchers referred to had eating establishments attached to their shops.

[14] Antiope, having given birth to Zeus' sons Amphion and Zethos, was repudiated by her husband, who subsequently married Dirce. When Dirce treated Antiope cruelly, Antiope's sons tied her to the horns of a bull.

204ᵃ   peste hac populum hunc liberant?
205   sed uah!
205ᵃ   nimium stultus, nimium fui
205ᵇ   indoctus: illine audeant
205ᶜ   id facere quibus ut seruiant
206–   suos amor cogit? [simul prohibet faciant aduorsum eos
7   quod nolint.]

     CALI   uah! tace.
     PSEV   quid est?
208   CALI   male morigeru's [male facis] mi quom sermoni huius
             opsonas.
     PSEV   taceo.
     CALI   at taceas malo multo quam tacere dicas.
     BAL   tu autem,
210   Xytilis, fac ut animum aduortas, quoius amatores oliui
      δύναμιν domi habent maxumam.
      si mihi non iam huc culleis
      oleum deportatum erit,
      te ipsam culleo ego cras faciam ut deportere . . . in per-
          gulam;
215   ibi tibi adeo lectus dabitur ubi tu hau somnum capias,
          sed ubi
      usque ad languorem—tenes
      quo se haec tendant quae loquor.
      ain, excetra tu? quae tibi amicos tot habes tam probe
          oleo onustos,
      num quoipiam est hodie tua tuorum opera conseruo-
          rum
220   nitidiusculum caput? aut num ipse ego pulmento utor
          magis
      unctiusculo? sed scio, tu oleum hau magni pendis, uino
      te deungis. sine modo,

free the people from this pest together? But bah! I've   205
been too stupid, too unsophisticated; would they dare to
do this to men to whom their love forces them to be
subservient? [At the same time it prevents them from
doing anything they don't want against them.]

CALI Bah! Be quiet.

PSEU What's the matter?

CALI You obey me badly by drowning out his speech.

PSEU I'm quiet.

CALI But I'd much prefer you to *be* quiet rather than just *say*
that you're quiet.

BAL (*to another girl*) But you, Xytilis, whose lovers have an   210
enormous amount of olive oil at home, mind you pay
attention. Unless oil is brought to me here in leather
bags this instant, I'll make sure that you yourself will be
carried in a leather bag . . . to the common brothel.[15]   215
And there you'll get a bed, not where you can sleep,
but where, till you're worn out—you get the drift of my
words. Do you say so, you snake? Even though you have
so many boyfriends so well laden with oil, does any of
your fellow slaves have a head that is a little glossier on   220
account of you today? Or do I myself have any savory
dish that's the least bit richer? But I know, you don't care
much for oil, you rub yourself down with wine. Never

[15] An unexpected joke. It was parricides who were put in leather
bags and thrown into the Tiber.

205ª nimius stultus nimis *A*, nimis sum stultus nimium *P, corr. Bothe*   206–7 simul . . . nolint *del. Ritschl*   208 male morigerus *P, om. A*   male facis *del. Ritschl*   sermone Ω, sermoni *Ritschl*   huius *A*, huic *P*   222 deuincis Ω, deungis *Acidalius*

reprehendam ego cuncta hercle una opera, nisi quidem
    hodie tu omnia
facis effecta quae loquor.
225   tu autem quae pro capite argentum mihi iam iamque
    semper numeras,
ea pacisci modo scis, sed quod pacta es non scis solu-
    ere,
Phoenicium, tibi ego haec loquor, deliciae summatum
    uirum:
nisi hodie mi ex fundis tuorum amicorum omne huc
    penus affertur,
cras Phoenicium poeniceo corio inuises pergulam.

I. iii: CALIDORVS. PSEVDOLVS. BALLIO

230 CALI Pseudole, non audis quae hic loquitur?
     PSEV   audio, ere, equidem atque animum aduorto.
     CALI quid mi es auctor huic ut mittam, ne amicam hic meam
          prostituat?
     PSEV nil curassis. liquido es animo: ego pro me et pro te
          curabo.
          iam diu ego huic bene et hic mi uolumus et amicitia est
          antiqua:
          mittam hodie huic suo die natali malam rem magnam
          et maturam.
235 CALI quid opust?
     PSEV   potin aliam rem ut cures?
     CALI   at—
     PSEV   bat!
     CALI   crucior.
     PSEV   cor dura.

mind, I'll make you pay for all this at the same time, unless you sort out everything today that I'm telling you to do. (*to the last girl*) And as for you, who are always on 225 the point of paying out money for your freedom, you only know how to make these arrangements, but you don't know how to pay what you've arranged; Phoenicium, I'm talking to you, you darling of the men of highest rank! Unless I'm brought your whole keep here today from the estates of your boyfriends, Phoenicium, you'll go to the common brothel tomorrow, with a hide that's Phoenician purple.

Exeunt the PROSTITUTES *into Ballio's house.*

CALI Pseudolus, can't you hear what he's saying?   230
PSEU Yes, master, I can and I'm paying attention.
CALI What do you advise me to send him so that he won't prostitute my girlfriend here?
PSEU Don't worry at all. Be calm. I'll take care of myself and you. For a long time now Ballio and I have been each other's well-wishers and our friendship is old. Today on his birthday I'll send him a big and full-grown thrashing.
CALI (*downcast*) What's the use?   235
PSEU Can't you worry about something else?
CALI But—
PSEU (*interrupting*) Tut!
CALI I'm being tortured.
PSEU Steel your heart.

---

223 hodie tu omnia *P*, tu haec omnia *A*

CALI	non possum.	
PSEV		fac possis.
CALI		quonam pacto possim?
PSEV		uince animum.

in rem quod sit praeuortaris quam in re aduorsa animo
    auscultes.

CALI nugae istaec sunt: non iucundum est nisi amans facit
    stulte.

PSEV   pergin?

239 CALI o Pseudole mi, sine sim nihili,

239ᵃ   mitt' me sis.

PSEV   sino, modo ego abeam.

240 CALI mane, mane, iam ut uoles med esse ita ero.

PSEV   nunc tu sapis.

240ᵃ BAL it dies: ego mihi cesso:

241   i prae, puere.

CALI   heus, abit. quin reuocas?

241ᵃ PSEV quid properas? placide.

CALI   at prius quam abeat.

242 BAL quid [hoc], malum, tam placide is, puere?

PSEV hodie nate, heus, hodie nate, tibi ego dico, heus, hodie
    nate,

redi et respice ad nos. tametsi occupatu's,

245 moramur. mane, em colloqui qui uolunt te.

BAL quid hoc est? quis est qui moram mi occupato
    molestam optulit?

PSEV   qui tibi sospitalis
    fuit.

BAL   mortuost qui fuit: qui sit usust.

PSEV nimis superbe.

236 uincere animum *P*, uince animum *Leo (qui haec uerba Pseudolo
dat)*   239ᵃ sino *W*, sine *cett. Palatini*

CALI I can't.

PSEU Make sure that you can.

CALI How could I?

PSEU Conquer your feelings. Attend to what may be to your advantage instead of listening to your feelings when there's a crisis.

CALI That's nonsense: there's no fun in it unless a lover behaves stupidly.

PSEU Are you carrying on?

CALI O Pseudolus dear, let me be useless, please let me go.

PSEU I'll let you go, if only I can go away myself. (*turns away*)

CALI Wait, wait, now I'll be the way you want me.   240

PSEU Now you're being smart.

BAL (*to the boy*) The day is passing; I'm wasting my time. Walk in front, boy.

CALI (*to Pseudolus*) Hey, he's leaving. Why don't you call him back?

PSEU Why are you rushing? Easy.

CALI But before he leaves.

BAL Why the deuce are you walking so slowly, boy?

PSEU (*to Ballio*) Birthday boy! Hey, birthday boy! I'm talking to you! Hey, birthday boy! Come back and look at us. Even if you're busy we're going to delay you. Wait! Here   245 are the ones who want to speak to you.

BAL (*without looking back*) What's the matter? Who is it who has brought me tedious delay, even though I'm busy?

PSEU A man who has been your salvation.

BAL The man who has been my salvation is dead; I need one who is my salvation now.

PSEU Too proud!

---

242 quod hoc *P*, quid *Ritschl*

	BAL	nimis molestu's.
	CALI	reprehende hominem, assequere.
	BAL	i puere.
250	PSEV	occedamus hac obuiam.
	BAL	Iuppiter te
		perdat, quisquis es.
	PSEV	te uolo.
	BAL	at uos ego ambos.
		uorte hac te, puere.
	PSEV	non licet colloqui te?
	BAL	at mi non lubet.
	PSEV	sin tuam est quippiam in rem?
	BAL	licetne, opsecro, bitere an non licet?
	PSEV	uah!
255		manta.
	BAL	omitte.
	CALI	Ballio, audi. surdu's [sum]?
	BAL	profecto inanilogistae.
	CALI	dedi dum fuit.
	BAL	non peto quod dedisti.
	CALI	dabo quando erit.
	BAL	ducito quando habebis.
	CALI	eheu, quam ego malis perdidi modis
		quod tibi detuli et quod dedi!
	BAL	mortua
260		uerba re nunc facis; stultus es, rem actam agis.
	PSEV	nosce saltem hunc quis est.
	BAL	iam diu scio
		qui fuit: nunc qui sit ipsus sciat.
		ambula tu.

251 at *P*, hau *Lindsay*

270

BAL	You're too tedious.
CALI	(*to Pseudolus*) Hold him back, follow him!
BAL	Go, boy.
PSEU	(*to Calidorus*) Let's go this way to meet him.
BAL	May Jupiter ruin you!
PSEU	No, you . . . I want to speak to.
BAL	(*not listening to the first part*) But I want you both ruined. Turn this way, boy.
PSEU	Can't we speak to you?
BAL	But I don't want to.
PSEU	What if it's something in your interest?
BAL	Please, can I go or not?
PSEU	Bah! Wait. (*grabs him*)
BAL	Let go!
CALI	Ballio, listen. Are you deaf?
BAL	Yes, to a gabbler.
CALI	I gave you money as long as I had some.
BAL	I'm not asking for what you gave.
CALI	I'll give you money when I have some.
BAL	You can take her when you have some.
CALI	Poor me! How wretchedly I lost what I brought to you and gave you!
BAL	Now that your money is finished, you bring words. You're being stupid, you're doing business that's already been done.
PSEU	At least look who this is. (*points to Calidorus*)
BAL	I've known for a long time already who he was; let him know for himself who he is now. (*to his boy*) You, go.

250

255

260

252 te puere P, transp. Müller
255 BAL surdus sum P, surdu's [sum] BAL Jachmann
262 sit A, estis P

	PSEV	potin ut semel modo,
		Ballio, huc cum lucro respicias?
265	BAL	respiciam istoc pretio; nam si sacruficem summo Ioui
		atque in manibus exta teneam ut poriciam, interea loci
		si lucri quid detur, potius rem diuinam deseram.
		non potest pietati opsisti huic, utut res sunt ceterae.
	PSEV	deos quidem quos maxume aequom est metuere, eos
		minimi facit.
270	BAL	compellabo. salue multum, serue Athenis pessume.
	PSEV	di te deaeque ament uel huius arbitratu uel meo,
		uel, si dignu's alio pacto, neque ament nec faciant
		bene.
	BAL	quid agitur, Calidore?
	CALI	amatur atque egetur acriter.
	BAL	misereat, si familiam alere possim misericordia.
275	PSEV	heia! scimus nos quidem te qualis sis; ne praedices.
		sed scin quid nos uolumus?
	BAL	pol ego propemodum: ut male sit mihi.
	PSEV	et id et hoc quod te reuocamus. quaeso animum
		aduorte.
	BAL	audio.
		atque in pauca, ut occupatus nunc sum, confer quid
		uelis.
	PSEV	hunc pudet, quod tibi promisit quaque id promisit die,
280		quia tibi minas uiginti pro amica etiam non dedit.
	BAL	nimio id quod pudet facilius fertur quam illud quod
		piget.

272

PSEU Can't you look back here just this once, Ballio, since there's profit in it?

BAL (*finally turning round*) I'll look back on that consider- 265
ation; yes, if I were sacrificing to Jupiter above and hold-
ing the inward parts in my hands so as to offer them, and
if in the meantime some profit were offered to me, I'd
rather leave the sacrifice. One can't stand in the way of
this sacred duty, be everything else as it may.

PSEU (*aside*) He cares absolutely nothing for the gods, whom
one ought to fear absolutely.

BAL (*aside*) I'll address him. (*to Pseudolus*) My warmest 270
greetings, worst slave in Athens.

PSEU May the gods and goddesses love you according to my
master's wish or mine, or if you deserve otherwise, may
they not love you and not do you any good turns.

BAL What are you up to, Calidorus?

CALI I'm in love and a dire financial situation.

BAL I'd have pity on you if I could feed my household on
pity.

PSEU Very funny! We know what you're like; you needn't tell 275
us. But do you know what we want?

BAL Pretty much: that I should have a bad time.

PSEU Yes, that, and in addition the thing which we called you
back for. Please pay attention.

BAL I'm listening. And since I'm busy now, keep what you
want short.

PSEU This chap here is embarrassed about his promise to you,
and the date by which he said he'd fulfill it, because 280
he still hasn't given you the twenty minas for his girl-
friend.

BAL Embarrassment is much easier to handle than regret. *He*

non dedisse istunc pudet: me quia non accepi piget.

PSEV at dabit, parabit: aliquot hos dies manta modo.

nam id hic metuit ne illam uendas ob simultatem suam.

285 BAL fuit occasio, si uellet, iam pridem argentum ut daret.

CALI quid si non habui?

BAL   si amabas, inuenires mutuom,

ad danistam deuenires, adderes faenusculum,

surruperes patri.

PSEV   surruperet hic patri, audacissume?

non periclum est ne quid recte monstres.

BAL   non lenonium est.

290 CALI egon patri surrupere possim quicquam, tam cauto
      seni?

atque adeo, si facere possim, pietas prohibet.

BAL   audio.

pietatem ergo istam amplexator noctu pro Phoenicio.

sed quom pietatem ⟨te⟩ amori uideo tuo praeuortere,

omnes ⟨homines⟩ tibi patres sunt? nullus est tibi quem
      roges

295   mutuom argentum?

CALI   quin nomen quoque iam interiit "mutuom."

PSEV heus tu, postquam hercle isti a mensa surgunt satis poti
      uiri,

qui suom repetunt, alienum reddunt nato nemini,

postilla omnes cautiores sunt ne credant alteri.

283 aliquod Ω, aliquot *Acidalius*, aliquos *Mueller*
291 possim *C*, possem *BD*
293 pietate *P*, pietatem te *Mueller*
294 homines *add. Bentley*

is embarrassed that he hasn't given me anything; *I* regret that I haven't received anything.

PSEU But he will pay, he will obtain it; just wait these few days. Well, he's afraid that you might sell the girl because of your quarrel with him.

BAL He had the opportunity to give me the money long ago 285 if he'd wanted to.

CALI What if I didn't have any?

BAL If you'd been in love, you should have got the money on loan, you should have gone to the moneylender, added a little interest, or stolen it from your father.

PSEU He should have stolen it from his father, you absolutely shameless creature? There's no danger that you could give any proper advice.

BAL That's not something that pimps do.

CALI Could I steal anything from my father, such a cautious 290 old man? And what's more, even if I could, my filial piety prevents me.

BAL I understand. Then embrace that filial piety of yours at night instead of Phoenicium. But since I can see that you prefer filial piety to your love, are all men your fathers? Don't you have anyone you could ask for money 295 on loan?

CALI Indeed, the very word "loan" doesn't exist now.

PSEU (*to Ballio*) Hey you, since those men rose from the table after having enough to drink,[16] those who demand their own money back but don't pay out to a single soul what belongs to him, everyone is more careful not to lend to anyone.

[16] Of wine or lucre. Possibly the statement as a whole refers to the prosecution of moneylenders in 192 BC; the reference remains somewhat obscure, and the text may be corrupt or incomplete.

CALI nimis miser sum, nummum nusquam reperire argenti
          queo;
300   ita miser et amore pereo et inopia argentaria.
BAL   eme die caeca hercle oliuom, id uendito oculata die:
          iam hercle uel ducentae fieri possunt praesentes mi-
              nae.
CALI perii! annorum lex me perdit quinauicenaria.
          metuont credere omnes.
BAL   eadem est mihi lex: metuo credere.
305 PSEV credere autem! eho an paenitet te quanto hic fuerit
              usui?
BAL   non est iustus quisquam amator nisi qui perpetuat data.
          det, det usque: quando nil sit, simul amare desinat.
CALI nilne te miseret?
BAL   inanis cedis, dicta non sonant.
          atque ego te uiuom saluomque uellem.
PSEV   eho an iam mortuost?
310 BAL   utut est, mihi quidem profecto cum istis dictis mortu-
              ost:
          ilico uixit amator, ubi lenoni supplicat.
          semper tu ad me cum argentata accedito querimonia;
          nam istuc quod nunc lamentare, non esse argentum
              tibi,
          apud nouercam querere.
PSEV   eho an umquam tu huius nupsisti patri?
315 BAL   di meliora faxint!
PSEV   face quod te rogamus, Ballio,
          mea fide, si isti formidas credere. ego in hoc triduo
          aut terra aut mari, alicunde euoluam id argentum tibi.

---

[17] A somewhat obscure line. My interpretation is based on Paul.
Fest. p. 189. 2–3 Lindsay (*oculatum pro praesenti,* "*oculatum* means
'for cash'").

CALI I'm terribly wretched, I can't find a silver coin anywhere;   300
that's how I'm perishing from love and lack of funds,
poor me.

BAL Buy olive oil on credit and sell it for cash:[17] you can in-
stantly come by even two hundred minas in cash.

CALI I'm dead! The twenty-five-year law[18] is ruining me. Ev-
erybody is afraid to give me credit.

BAL The same law binds me: I'm afraid to give you credit.

PSEU How do you mean, "give credit"? Hey there, aren't you   305
satisfied with all the use you've made of him?

BAL No one is a proper lover unless he keeps giving. He
should always give and give; when he has nothing, he
should stop loving at the same time.

CALI Don't you have any pity at all?

BAL You're walking along empty-handed, your words don't
ring the bell. And yet I'd like you to be alive and well.

PSEU What! Is he dead already?

BAL Whatever he is, with those words of his he's dead as far   310
as I'm concerned. A lover's life is over immediately when
he appeals to a pimp. Always come to me with a com-
plaint that's adorned with silver: as for what you're wail-
ing about now, that you don't have money, you're practi-
cally complaining to your stepmother.[19]

PSEU What! Have you ever married his father?

BAL May the gods forbid it!   315

PSEU Do what we're asking you for, Ballio, on my credit if
you're afraid to trust him. Within three days from now
I'll wrench out this money for you from either land or
sea, from somewhere.

[18] The *lex Plaetoria*, a law which made financial transactions with
minors under twenty-five illegal.

[19] The prototype of a pitiless person.

	BAL	tibi ego credam?
	PSEV	quor non?
	BAL	quia pol qua opera credam tibi una opera alligem fugitiuam canem agninis lactibus.
320	CALI	sicin mi aps te bene merenti male refertur gratia?
	BAL	quid nunc uis?
	CALI	ut opperiare hos sex dies aliquos modo, ne illam uendas neu me perdas hominem amantem.
	BAL	animo bono es. uel sex menses opperibor.
	CALI	eugae, homo lepidissume!
	BAL	immo uin etiam te faciam ex laeto laetantem magis?
325	CALI	quid iam?
	BAL	quia enim non uenalem iam habeo Phoenicium.
	CALI	non habes?
	BAL	non hercle uero.
	CALI	Pseudole, i accerse hostias, uictumas, lanios, ut ego huic sacruficem summo Ioui; nam hic mihi nunc est multo potior Iuppiter quam Iuppiter.
	BAL	nolo uictumas: agninis me extis placari uolo.
330	CALI	propera, quid stas? i accerse agnos. audin quid ait Iuppiter?
	PSEV	iam hic ero; uerum extra portam mi etiam currendum est prius.
	CALI	quid eo?
	PSEV	lanios inde accersam duo cum tintinnabulis, eadem duo greges uirgarum inde ulmearum adegero, ut hodie ad litationem huic suppetat satias Ioui.

---

20 The Esquiline Gate, outside of which executioners stayed, who wore bells to warn people of their approach.

BAL I should trust you?

PSEU Why not?

BAL Because I'd as soon tie up a runaway dog with lambs' intestines as trust you.

CALI Am I, who deserved so well of you, to receive such a poor   320
return?

BAL What do you want now?

CALI That you should wait for six days or so, and that you shouldn't sell her or ruin me, her lover.

BAL Take heart. I'll even wait for six months.

CALI Hurray, most charming man!

BAL That's nothing; do you want me to turn you from joyful to even more joyful?

CALI How so?   325

BAL Because I don't intend to sell Phoenicium anymore.

CALI You don't?

BAL No, I don't.

CALI Pseudolus, go and bring small and big animals for sacrifice and butchers, so that I may sacrifice to this man as Jupiter on high; he's a far mightier Jupiter to me now than Jupiter himself.

BAL I don't want big animals for sacrifice. I want to be placated with lambs' intestines.

CALI (to Pseudolus) Hurry! Why are you standing around? Go   330
and bring lambs! Can't you hear what Jupiter is saying?

PSEU I'll be back soon. But first I need to run outside the Gate.[20]

CALI Why there?

PSEU I'll bring two butchers with bells from there, and at the same time I'll get two flocks of elm rods from there, so that there will be a sufficient supply to obtain a favorable omen from this Jupiter today.

335 BAL   i in malam crucem!

PSEV   istuc ibit Iuppiter lenonius.

BAL   ex tua re est ut ego emoriar.

PSEV   quidum?

BAL   ego dicam tibi:

    quia edepol, dum ego uiuos uiuam, numquam eris
      frugi bonae.

    ex tua re non est ut ego emoriar.

PSEV   quidum?

BAL   sic, quia

    si ego emortuos sim, Athenis te sit nemo nequior.

340 CALI   dic mihi, opsecro hercle, uerum serio hoc quod te
      rogo.

    non habes uenalem amicam tu meam Phoenicium?

BAL   non edepol habeo profecto, nam iam pridem uendidi.

CALI   quo modo?

BAL   sine ornamentis, cum intestinis omnibus.

CALI   meam tu amicam uendidisti?

BAL   ualide, uiginti minis.

345 CALI   uiginti minis?

BAL   utrum uis, uel quater quinis minis,

    militi Macedonio, et iam quindecim habeo minas.

CALI   quid ego ex te audio?

BAL   amicam tuam esse factam argenteam.

CALI   quor id ausu's facere?

BAL   lubuit, mea fuit.

CALI   eho, Pseudole,

    i gladium affer.

PSEV   quid opus gladio?

CALI   qui hunc occidam . . . atque me.

350 PSEV   quin tu ted occidis potius? nam hunc fames iam oc-
      ciderit.

BAL	Go and be hanged!	335
PSEU	That's where the pimpish Jupiter will go.	
BAL	It's to your advantage that I should die.	
PSEU	How so?	
BAL	I'll tell you: because as long as I live my life you'll never be any good. (*after a pause*) It's not to your advantage that I should die.	
PSEU	How so?	
BAL	Because if I'm dead, you are the worst man in Athens.	
CALI	Please earnestly tell me the truth about what I ask you. You don't intend to sell my girlfriend Phoenicium?	340
BAL	Indeed I don't: I sold her long ago.	
CALI	How?	
BAL	Without her decorations, but with all her fixtures and fittings.	
CALI	You've sold my girlfriend?	
BAL	Very much so, for twenty minas.	
CALI	For twenty minas?	345
BAL	Or for four times five minas, take your pick; I sold her to a Macedonian soldier, and I already have fifteen minas.	
CALI	What do I hear from you?	
BAL	That your girlfriend's been converted to cash.	
CALI	Why did you dare to do this?	
BAL	I felt like it and she belonged to me.	
CALI	Hey, Pseudolus, go and bring a sword.	
PSEU	What do you need a sword for?	
CALI	To kill him . . . and myself.	
PSEU	Why don't you kill yourself instead? Hunger will kill this chap instantly.[21]	350

[21] Because he will lose his customer.

CALI quid ais, quantum terram tetigit hominum periuris-
     sume?
     iurauistin te illam nulli uenditurum nisi mihi?
BAL fateor.
CALI   nemp' conceptis uerbis?
BAL   etiam consutis quoque.
CALI periurauisti, sceleste.
BAL   at argentum intro condidi.
355 ego scelestus nunc argentum promere possum domo:
     tu qui piu's, istoc es genere gnatus, nummum non
     habes.
CALI Pseudole, assiste altrim secus atque onera hunc male-
     dictis.
PSEV   licet.
     numquam ad praetorem aeque cursim curram, ut emit-
     tar manu.
CALI ingere mala multa.
PSEV   iam ego te differam dictis meis.
360 impudice.
BAL   ita est.
CALI   sceleste.
BAL   dicis uera.
PSEV   uerbero.
BAL quippini?
CALI   bustirape.
BAL   certo.
PSEV   furcifer.
BAL   factum optume.
CALI sociofraude.
BAL   sunt mea istaec.

351 terra Ω, terram *Geppert*

CALI   *(to Ballio)* What do you say, you greatest perjurer of all men that have touched the earth? Didn't you swear that you wouldn't sell her to anyone other than me?

BAL   I admit it.

CALI   In formal, fitting words?

BAL   In fitting words and also tailored ones.

CALI   You've perjured yourself, you criminal.

BAL   But I've put the money away inside. I, the criminal, can 355 now draw cash from home. You are a paragon of virtue and are born in such a great family, and yet you don't have a single coin.

CALI   Pseudolus, stand on the other side and pile heaps of abuse onto him.

PSEU   All right. I'd never run to the praetor[22] equally quickly in order to be set free.

CALI   Throw a lot of abuse at him.

PSEU   I'll tear him to pieces with my words right now. *(to Bal-* 360 *lio)* You shameless creature!

BAL   Indeed.

CALI   You criminal!

BAL   You speak the truth.

PSEU   You whipping stock!

BAL   Why not?

CALI   You grave robber!

BAL   Certainly.

PSEU   You thug!

BAL   Perfect.

CALI   You cheat!

BAL   Those are my qualities.

[22] Roman official with mainly legal functions, among them manumissions.

PSEV   parricida.

BAL   perge tu.

CALI sacrilege.

BAL   fateor.

PSEV   periure.

BAL   uetera uaticinamini.

CALI legerupa.

BAL   ualide.

PSEV   permities adulescentum.

365   BAL   acerrume.

CALI fur.

BAL   babae!

PSEV   fugitiue.

BAL   bombax!

CALI   fraus populi.

BAL   planissume.

PSEV fraudulente.

CALI   impure.

PSEV   leno.

CALI   caenum.

BAL   cantores probos!

CALI uerberauisti patrem atque matrem.

BAL   atque occidi quoque
        potius quam cibum praehiberem: num peccaui quip-
          piam?

PSEV in pertusum ingerimus dicta dolium, operam ludimus.

370   BAL numquid aliud etiam uoltis dicere?

CALI   ecquid te pudet?

BAL ten amatorem esse inuentum inanem quasi cassam
        nucem!
        uerum quamquam multa malaque [in me] dicta dixistis
        mihi,

PSEU You parricide!

BAL   (*to Calidorus*) You, continue!

CALI You temple robber!

BAL   I admit it.

PSEU You perjurer!

BAL   That's old news.

CALI You lawbreaker!

BAL   Absolutely.

PSEU You ruin of the young men!

BAL   Very biting.

CALI You thief!   365

BAL   Goodness!

PSEU You runaway!

BAL   Wow!

CALI You deception of the people!

BAL   Plain as can be.

PSEU You trickster!

CALI (*also to Ballio*) You piece of dirt!

PSEU (*also to Ballio*) You pimp!

CALI (*still to Ballio*) You piece of filth!

BAL   What a charming chorus!

CALI You beat your father and mother!

BAL   What's more, I killed them, to avoid having to feed them.
      Did I do anything wrong?

PSEU (*to Calidorus*) We're pouring our words into a jar with
      holes in it, we're wasting our effort.

BAL   Do you two wish to say anything else?   370

CALI Don't you feel any shame?

BAL   To think that you should have been revealed to be a lover
      as empty as a hollow nut! But even though you two have
      uttered a lot of abuse against me, if the soldier doesn't

---

372 in me *del. Ritschl*

nisi mihi hodie attulerit miles quinque quas debet mi-
nas,

sicut haec est praestituta summa ei argento dies,

375   si id non affert, posse opinor facere me officium
meum.

CALI quid id est?

BAL   si tu argentum attuleris, cum illo perdidero fidem:

hoc meum est officium. ego, operae si sit, plus tecum
loquar;

sed sine argento frustra es qui me tui misereri postulas.

haec mea est sententia, ut tu hinc porro quid agas con-
sulas.

380 CALI iamne abis?

BAL   negoti nunc sum plenus.

PSEV   paulo post magis.

illic homo meus est, nisi omnes di me atque homines
deserunt.

exossabo ego illum simulter itidem ut murenam co-
quos.

nunc, Calidore, te mihi operam dare uolo.

CALI   ecquid imperas?

PSEV hoc ego oppidum ammoenire ut hodie capiatur uolo;

385   ad eam rem usust homine astuto, docto, cauto, et cal-
lido,

qui imperata effecta reddat, non qui uigilans dormiat.

CALI cedo mihi, quid es facturus?

PSEV   temperi ego faxo scies.

nolo bis iterari, sat sic longae fiunt fabulae.

CALI optumum atque aequissumum oras.

PSEV   propera, adduc hominem cito.

385 hominem astutum doctum Ω, homine astuto docto
Ritschl   cauto et callido *A*, scitum et callidum *P*

bring me the five minas today which he owes me, since
this day was set as the deadline for this money, if he   375
doesn't bring it, I think I can do my duty.

CALI What's that?

BAL If you bring me the money, I'll break my agreement with
him: this is my duty. If I had time, I'd talk to you some
more. But without money you're deceiving yourself if
you expect me to have pity on you. This is my decision,
so that you can take it from here and come up with a plan
of what to do.

CALI Are you leaving already?   380

BAL I have a lot on my hands at the moment.

Exeunt BALLIO and his slave boy to the right.

PSEU (*aside*) A little later you'll have more on your hands. (*to
Calidorus*) That chap is mine, unless all the gods and
men leave me in the lurch. I'll remove the bones from
him the same way a cook removes them from a lamprey.
Now, Calidorus, I want you to assist me.

CALI (*keenly*) Are you giving me any orders?

PSEU I want to lay siege to this town so that it can be captured
today. For this purpose I need a smart, clever, cautious,   385
and tricky man, someone who turns commands into re-
sults and not someone who is asleep while he's awake.

CALI Tell me, what are you going to do?

PSEU I'll let you know in good time. I don't want it to be re-
peated twice over, our plays are quite long enough as
it is.

CALI What you ask is perfectly good and fair.

PSEU Hurry, bring him to me quickly.

390	CALI	pauci ex multis sunt amici, homini qui certi sient.
	PSEV	ego scio istuc. ergo utrumque, tibi nunc dilectum para
		ex multis, atque exquire illinc unum qui certus siet.
	CALI	iam hic faxo aderit.
	PSEV	potin ut abeas? tibi moram dictis creas.

I. iv: PSEVDOLVS

PSEV postquam illic hinc abiit, tu astas solus, Pseudole.
395   quid nunc acturu's, postquam erili filio
    largitu's dictis dapsilis? ubi sunt ea?
    quoi nec parata est gutta certi consili,
    [neque adeo argenti, nec nunc quid faciam scio.]
    neque exordiri primum unde occipias habes
400   neque ad detexundam telam certos terminos.
    sed quasi poeta, tabulas quom cepit sibi,
    quaerit quod nusquam est gentium, reperit tamen,
    facit illud ueri simile quod mendacium est,
    nunc ego poeta fiam: uiginti minas,
405   quae nusquam nunc sunt gentium, inueniam tamen.
    atque ego me iam pridem huic daturum dixeram
    et uolui inicere tragulam in nostrum senem;
    uerum is nescioquo pacto praesensit prius.
    sed comprimunda uox mihi atque oratio est:
410   erum eccum uideo huc Simonem una simul
    cum suo uicino Calliphone incedere.
    ex hoc sepulcro uetere uiginti minas
    effodiam ego hodie quas dem erili filio.
    nunc huc concedam unde horum sermonem legam.

390 qui certi *P*, certe qui *A*   392 exquire illis unum qui certus
siet *P*, atque exquire ex illis paucis unum qui certust cedo *A*, atque
exquire illinc unum qui certus siet *Leo*
    398 *uersum del. Ussing*

CALI Out of so many there are few friends that a man can   390
     count on.

PSEU I know that. So do both: make a selection out of the many
     now and find the one who you can count on from that
     lot.

CALI I'll have him here in a second.

PSEU Can't you leave? You're wasting your time with your
     words.

Exit CALIDORUS *to the right.*

PSEU Now that he's left, you stand alone here, Pseudolus.   395
     What are you going to do now after being so generous
     with promises to master's son? Where are they? Not a
     drop of certain counsel is ready for you, [or indeed of
     money. And I don't know what I should do now.] You
     have neither a starting point for beginning your web nor   400
     fixed limits for finishing it. Yet just as a poet, when he
     takes writing tablets, looks for something that doesn't
     exist anywhere, but finds it nonetheless and makes likely
     what is a lie, I shall now become a poet: even though the
     twenty minas don't exist anywhere, I'll find them none-   405
     theless. And I'd said to him long ago that I'd give it to
     him and I wanted to harpoon our old man; yet somehow
     he got wind of it before. But I need to keep my voice and
     speech in check: look, I can see my master Simo coming   410
     here together with his neighbor Callipho. I'll dig twenty
     minas out of this old tomb today so that I can give it to
     master's son. Now I'll walk over here, where I can listen
     to their conversation. (*steps aside*)

I. V: SIMO. PSEVDOLVS. CALLIPHO

415 SIMO   si de damnosis aut si de amatoribus
          dictator fiat nunc Athenis Atticis,
          nemo anteueniat filio, credo, meo:
          ita nunc per urbem solus sermoni omnibust,
          eum uelle amicam liberare et quaerere
420   argentum ad eam rem. hoc alii mihi renuntiant;
          atque id iam pridem sensi et subolebat mihi,
          sed dissimulabam.

PSEV   iam illi foetet filius.
          occisa est haec res, haeret hoc negotium.
          quo in commeatum uolui . . . argentarium
425   proficisci, ibi nunc oppido opsaepta est uia.
          praesensit: nihil est praedae praedatoribus.

CALL   homines qui gestant quique auscultant crimina
          si meo arbitratu liceat, omnes pendeant,
          gestores linguis, auditores auribus.
430   nam istaec quae tibi renuntiantur, filium
          te uelle amantem argento circumducere,
          fors fuat an istaec dicta sint mendacia;
          sed si sint ea uera, ut nunc mos est, maxume,
          quid mirum fecit? quid nouom, adulescens homo
435   si amat, si amicam liberat?

PSEV   lepidum senem!
SIMO   uetus nolo faciat.

CALL   at enim nequiquam neuis;
          uel tu ne faceres tale in adulescentia.
          probum patrem esse oportet qui gnatum suom
          esse probiorem quam ipsus fuerit postulet.
440   nam tu quod damni et quod fecisti flagiti

---

422 *uersus non fertur in Palatinis*   felat *A*, foetet *Loewe*

Enter SIMO *and* CALLIPHO *from the latter's house without noticing Pseudolus.*

SIMO If a dictator[23] were to be chosen from among the profli- 415
gates or the lovers in Attic Athens now, I believe there
would be no stronger candidate than my son, given how
he alone is the topic of conversation throughout the city
now. They say he wants to free his girlfriend and is look-
ing for the money for it. Other people report this to me; 420
and I've felt it for a long time already and got a whiff of
it, but pretended otherwise.

PSEU *(aside)* He can smell his son now. This matter is dead,
this business is stuck. Where I wanted to go foraging . . . 425
for money, my way is completely sealed off now. He's had
a premonition; there's no pillage for the pillagers.

CALL People who spread and listen to accusations would all be
hanged, if I could have my way, the spreaders by their
tongues and the listeners by their ears. Well, as for those 430
reports you get, that your lovesick son wants to swindle
you out of your money, perhaps those words are lies. But
even if they are true, what extraordinary thing has he
done by today's standards? What novelty is it if a young
man is in love and if he sets his girlfriend free? 435

PSEU *(aside)* A charming old man!

SIMO I don't want him to act out an old story.

CALL But it's in vain that you don't want it; or you shouldn't
have done such a thing in your own youth. Someone who
expects his son to be more decent than he was himself
must be a decent father. Well, the damage and disgrace 440

---

[23] A Roman magistrate with plenary powers, chosen in times of crisis.

populo uiritim potuit dispertirier.
idn' tu mirare, si patrissat filius?

PSEV ὦ Ζεῦ, quam pauci estis homines commodi! em,
illic est pater patrem esse ut aequom est filio.

445 SIMO quis hic loquitur? meus hic est quidem seruos
Pseudolus.
hic mihi corrumpit filium, scelerum caput;
hic dux, hic illi est paedagogus, hunc ego
cupio excruciari.

CALL   iam istaec insipientia est,
iram in propromptu gerere. quanto satius est
450   adire blandis uerbis atque exquirere
sintne illa necne sint quae tibi renuntiant!
bonus animus in mala re dimidium est mali.

SIMO tibi auscultabo.

PSEV   itur ad te, Pseudole.
orationem tibi para aduorsum senem.
455   erum saluto primum, ut aequom est; postea
si quid superfit uicinos impertio.

SIMO salue. quid agitur?

PSEV   statur hic ad hunc modum.

SIMO statum uide hominis, Callipho, quam basilicum!

CALL bene confidenterque astitisse intellego.

460 PSEV decet innocentem qui sit atque innoxium
seruom superbum esse apud erum potissumum.

CALL sunt quae te uolumus percontari, quae quasi
per nebulam nosmet scimus atque audiuimus.

---

449 *ro**om**u A, promptu P, propromptu *Lindsay*

you committed could have been distributed to the people and each man would have got a share.[24] Are you surprised if the son takes after his father?

PSEU (*still aside*) O Zeus, how few you accommodating people are! There, that is a father the way a father ought to be toward his son.

SIMO (*to Callipho*) Who is talking here? (*finally spotting Pseudolus*) This is my slave Pseudolus. He is spoiling my son, the fount of iniquity; he is the leader, he is his tutor, him I wish to be tortured.

445

CALL That now is stupidity, to carry your anger on your sleeve. How much better it is to approach him with flattering words and to inquire if what people report to you is the case or not! A calm mind in a bad situation makes it only half as bad.

450

SIMO I'll listen to you.

PSEU (*aside*) You're being approached, Pseudolus. Prepare your speech against the old man. (*loudly*) I'm greeting my master first, as is appropriate; then I give any surplus greeting to the neighbors.

455

SIMO My greetings. What are you up to?

PSEU I'm standing here like this.

SIMO Look at the chap's posture, Callipho, how pompous!

CALL I realize that he's taken a good and confident posture.

PSEU A slave who is without guilt and without fault ought to be proud, especially in front of his master.

460

CALL There are things we'd like to ask you about, things we know and have heard about as if through a fog.

---

[24] Callipho talks as if Simo's misdeeds were a public dinner provided by some benefactor.

	SIMO	conficiet iam te hic uerbis ut tu censeas
465		non Pseudolum, sed Socratem tecum loqui.
	PSEV	ita est, iam pridem tu me spernis, sentio.

SIMO   conficiet iam te hic uerbis ut tu censeas
465   non Pseudolum, sed Socratem tecum loqui.
PSEV   ita est, iam pridem tu me spernis, sentio.
      paruam esse apud te mihi fidem ipse intellego.
      cupis me esse nequam: tamen ero frugi bonae.
SIMO   fac sis uociuas, Pseudole, aedis aurium,
470   mea ut migrare dicta possint quo uolo.
PSEV   age loquere quiduis, tam etsi tibi suscenseo.
SIMO   min domino seruos tu suscenses?
PSEV   tam tibi
      mirum id uidetur?
SIMO   hercle qui, ut tu praedicas,
      cauendum est mi aps te irato, atque alio tu modo
475   me uerberare atque ego te soleo cogitas.
      quid censes?
CALL   edepol merito esse iratum arbitror
      quom apud te parua est ei fides.
SIMO   iam sic sino.
      iratus sit: ego ne quid noceat cauero.
      sed quid ais? quid hoc quod te rogo?
PSEV   siquid uis roga.
480   quod scibo Delphis tibi responsum dicito.
SIMO   aduorte ergo animum et fac sis promissi memor.
      quid ais? ecquam scis filium tibicinam
      meum amare?
PSEV   ναὶ γάρ.
SIMO   liberare quam uelit?

     467 paruam *P*, parum *A*, paruom *Lindsay*
     477 parumste *P*, paruast ei *Ritschl*

SIMO Now he'll knock you out with his words so that you'll think that it's not Pseudolus but Socrates[25] talking to you. 465

PSEU Quite so, you've been looking down on me for a long time now, I can feel it. I understand myself that you have little faith in me. You wish me to be useless; still, I'll be useful.

SIMO Please open the portals of your ears, Pseudolus, so that my words can go where I want them to. 470

PSEU Go on, say anything you like, even if I'm angry with you.

SIMO You, a slave, are angry with me, your master?

PSEU Does that seem so strange to you?

SIMO Heavens, the way you say it I need to be on my guard against you in your anger; and you're planning to beat 475 me in another way than the one I usually employ with you. (to Callipho) What do you think?

CALL I think he's right to be angry because you have so little faith in him.

SIMO All right now. Let him be angry: I'll be on my guard that he won't do any harm. (to Pseudolus) But what do you say? What about what I'm asking you?

PSEU If you want anything, ask. What I know you shall say has 480 been given to you as a reply from Delphi.[26]

SIMO Then pay attention and mind you remember your promise. What do you say? Do you know that my son is in love with some flute girl?

PSEU Yes indeed.

SIMO One he wants to set free?

---

[25] Most famous Greek philosopher (469–399). [26] Greek city with a famous oracle; Pseudolus accordingly replies in Greek.

PSEV καὶ τοῦτο ναὶ γάρ.

SIMO   ecquas uiginti minas

485   per sycophantiam atque per doctos dolos

       paritas ut a me auferas?

PSEV   aps ted ego auferam?

SIMO ita, quas meo gnato des, qui amicam liberet?

       fatere, dic "καὶ τοῦτο ναί."

PSEV   καὶ τοῦτο ναί.

CALL fatetur.

SIMO   dixin, Callipho, dudum tibi?

490 CALL memini.

SIMO   quor haec, tu ubi resciuisti ilico,

       celata me sunt? quor non resciui?

PSEV   eloquar.

       quia nolebam ex me morem progigni malum,

       erum ut ⟨suos⟩ seruos criminaret apud erum.

SIMO iuberes hunc praecipitem in pistrinum trahi.

495 CALL numquid peccatum est, Simo?

SIMO   immo maxume.

PSEV desiste, recte ego meam rem sapio, Callipho;

       peccata mea sunt. animum aduorte nunciam

       quapropter nati amoris te expertem habuerim:

       pistrinum in mundo scibam, si dixem, mihi.

500 SIMO non a me scibas pistrinum in mundo tibi,

       quom ea mussitabas?

PSEV   scibam.

SIMO   quin dictum est mihi?

493 suos *add. Mueller*
495 peccatum est Simo *P*, Simo peccatum est *Bothe*
498 te expertem amoris nati *P, transp. Bothe*
499 id faxem *P*, dixem *Ritschl*

PSEU Yes indeed again.

SIMO Are you preparing to take away twenty minas from me   485
      through trickery and clever guiles?

PSEU I should take it away from you?

SIMO Yes, in order to give them to my son, so that he can set
      his girlfriend free with it? Admit it, say "yes" again.

PSEU Yes again.

CALL (*to Simo*) He admits it.

SIMO Didn't I tell you so a while ago, Callipho?

CALL I remember.   490

SIMO (*to Pseudolus*) Why was this concealed from me as soon
      as you got to know of it? Why didn't I find out?

PSEU I'll tell you. Because I didn't want to be the origin of the
      evil custom of a slave accusing his own master in front of
      his other master.

SIMO (*to Callipho*) You'd order him to be dragged headlong to
      the mill.

CALL No wrong has been done, has it, Simo?   495

SIMO Yes, an enormous wrong.

PSEU (*to Callipho*) Stop it, I know my business all right, Cal-
      lipho. The wrongdoings are mine. (*to Simo*) Now pay
      attention to why I kept you in the dark about your son's
      love affair: I knew that the mill would be waiting for me
      if I'd told you.

SIMO Didn't you know that the mill was waiting for you from   500
      me when you kept quiet about it?

PSEU I did.

SIMO So why wasn't I told?

297

PSEV quia illud malum aderat, istuc aberat longius;
      illud erat praesens, huic erant dieculae.

SIMO quid nunc agetis? nam hinc quidem a me non potest

505   argentum auferri, qui praesertim senserim.
      ne quisquam credat nummum iam edicam omnibus.

PSEV numquam edepol quoiquam supplicabo, dum quidem
      tu uiues. tu mihi hercle argentum dabis,
      aps te equidem sumam.

SIMO   tu a me sumes?

PSEV   strenue.

510 SIMO excludito mi hercle oculum, si dedero.

PSEV   dabis.
      iam dico ut a me caueas.

CALL   certe edepol scio,
      si apstuleris, mirum et magnum facinus feceris.

PSEV faciam.

SIMO   si non apstuleris?

PSEV   uirgis caedito.
      sed quid si apstulero?

SIMO   do Iouem testem tibi

515   te aetatem impune habiturum.

PSEV   facito ut memineris.

SIMO egon ut cauere nequeam, quoi praedicitur?

PSEV praedico ut caueas. dico, inquam, ut caueas. caue.
      em istis mi tu hodie manibus argentum dabis.

CALL edepol mortalem graphicum, si seruat fidem!

520 PSEV seruitum tibi me abducito, ni fecero.

SIMO bene atque amice dicis. nam nunc non meu's.

PSEU Because that trouble was at hand, yours was still some way off; that one was present, for this one there was a delay of a few days.

SIMO What will you two do now? From me the money can't be taken away, since I've got wind of it. Now I'll announce to all and sundry that no one should lend you a coin. 505

PSEU I'll never implore anyone else while you are alive. You will give me the money, I'll take it from you.

SIMO You'll take it from me?

PSEU With gusto.

SIMO Knock out my eye, if I give it to you. 510

PSEU You will. Now I'm telling you to be on your guard against me.

CALL I know for sure, if you take it away, you'll have accomplished a great and amazing deed.

PSEU I'll do so.

SIMO What if you don't take it away?

PSEU Beat me with rods. But what if I do take it away?

SIMO I give you Jupiter as my witness that you won't be punished for the rest of your life. 515

PSEU Mind you remember.

SIMO Shouldn't I be able to look out for myself, now that I've been warned?

PSEU I'm telling you in advance that you should be on your guard. I'm telling you, I insist, that you should be on your guard. Be on your guard! There, with those hands you'll give me the money.

CALL A marvelous mortal, if he keeps his word!

PSEU (*to Simo*) Take me away as your slave if I don't. 520

SIMO (*with irony*) That's kind and friendly of you. After all, now you don't belong to me.

PSEV uin etiam dicam quod uos magis miremini?
523 CALL studeo hercle audire, nam ted ausculto lubens.
523ª [SIMO agedum, nam satis lubenter te ausculto loqui.]
PSEV prius quam istam pugnam pugnabo, ego etiam prius
525 dabo aliam pugnam claram et commemorabilem.
SIMO quam pugnam?
PSEV em ab hoc lenone uicino tuo
per sycophantiam atque per doctos dolos
tibicinam illam tuos quam gnatus deperit,
ea circumducam lepide lenonem.
SIMO quid est?
530 PSEV effectum hoc hodie reddam utrumque ad uesperum.
SIMO siquidem istaec opera, ut praedicas, perfeceris,
uirtute regi Agathocli antecesseris.
sed si non faxis, numquid causae est ilico
quin te in pistrinum condam?
PSEV non unum diem,
535 uerum hercle in omnis quantum est; sed si effecero,
dabin mi argentum quod dem lenoni ilico
tua uoluntate?
CALL ius bonum orat Pseudolus;
"dabo" inque.
SIMO at enim scin quid mihi in mentem uenit?
quid si hisce inter se consenserunt, Callipho,
540 aut de compecto faciunt consutis dolis,
qui me argento interuortant?
PSEV quis me audacior
sit, si istuc facinus audeam? immo sic, Simo:
si sumus compecti seu consilium umquam iniimus

523ª *uersum secl. Bergk*
541 circumuertant *P*, interuortant *Fleckeisen*

300

PSEU Do you want me to say something that you'll be even more surprised about?

CALL I'm keen to hear it: I enjoy listening to you.

[SIMO *(also to Pseudolus)* Go on: I quite enjoy listening to you.]

PSEU Before fighting this fight, I'll also put up some other   525
impressive and memorable fight.

SIMO What fight?

PSEU Here you go: this neighbor of yours, the pimp, I'll wittily swindle him out of that flute girl your son loves through trickery and clever guiles.

SIMO What's that?

PSEU I'll bring both things about today by the evening.   530

SIMO If you succeed in these works as you announce, you'll surpass King Agathocles[27] in derring-do. But if you don't, do you have any objection to me putting you into the mill at once?

PSEU Not for a single day, but for all eternity; but if I succeed,   535
will you give me the money to give to the pimp at once and out of your own volition?

CALL *(to Simo)* What Pseudolus asks is only fair; say "I shall give it."

SIMO But do you know what occurs to me? What if they've come to an arrangement with each other, Callipho, or are   540
acting on a previous agreement with their patched-up tricks so as to trick me out of the money?

PSEU Who'd be bolder than me if I dared do such a deed? No, listen to me, Simo: if we've ever made an agreement or

---

[27] Agathocles (361–289) was originally a potter but later became tyrant of Syracuse and king of Sicily.

544		aut si de istac re umquam inter nos conuenimus,
544[a]		quasi in libro [quom] scribuntur calamo litterae,
545		stilis me totum usque ulmeis conscribito.
	SIMO	indice ludos nunciam, quando lubet.
	PSEV	da in hunc diem operam, Callipho, quaeso mihi
		ne quo te ad aliud occupes negotium.
	CALL	quin rus ut irem iam heri constitueram.
550	PSEV	at nunc disturba quas statuisti machinas.
	CALL	nunc non abire certum est istac gratia;
		lubido est ludos tuos spectare, Pseudole.
		et si hunc uidebo non dare argentum tibi
		quod dixit, potius quam id non fiat ego dabo.
555	SIMO	non demutabo.
	PSEV	namque edepol, si non dabis,
		clamore magno et multum flagitabere.
		agite amolimini hinc uos intro nunciam
		ac meis uicissim date locum fallaciis.
	CALL	fiat, geratur mos tibi.
	PSEV	sed te uolo
560		domi usque adesse.
	CALL	quin tibi hanc operam dico.
	SIMO	at ego ad forum ibo. iam hic ero.
	PSEV	actutum redi.
		suspicio est mi nunc uos suspicarier,

544[a] quom *del. Weise*

hatched a plan, or if we've ever come together concern-
ing this matter, then just as letters are written in a book
with a pen, so you can scribble all over me with writing 545
instruments of elm.

SIMO Let the games begin now as soon as you please.

PSEU For this day, Callipho, please be at my disposal, so that
you won't busy yourself with any other undertaking.

CALL But I'd already decided yesterday to go to my country
estate.

PSEU Well then, rearrange the positions of your siege engines 550
now.

CALL Now I've decided not to go away because of what you
say; I'm keen to watch your games, Pseudolus. And if I
see that he doesn't give you the money he said he would,
I'll give it to you myself rather than that it shouldn't hap-
pen at all.

SIMO I won't go back on my word. 555

PSEU Yes, if you don't give it, you'll be dunned with a loud
outcry for a long time. (*to both*) Go on, remove your-
selves inside now and give me in turn room for my
tricks.

CALL Yes, you'll be obeyed.

PSEU (*to Callipho*) But I want you to be at home throughout. 560

CALL Yes, I grant you my assistance.

Exit CALLIPHO into his house.

SIMO I'm going to the forum. I'll be back soon.

Exit SIMO to the right.

PSEU (*calling after him*) Return at once! (*to the audience*) It's
my suspicion now that you suspect that I'm promising

	me idcirco haec tanta facinora promittere,
	quo uos oblectem, hanc fabulam dum transigam,
565	nec sim facturus quod facturum dixeram.
	non demutabo. atque etiam certum, quod sciam,
	quo id sim facturus pacto nil etiam scio,
	nisi quia futurum est. nam qui in scaenam prouenit
	nouo modo nouom aliquid inuentum afferre addecet.
570	si id facere nequeat, det locum illi qui queat.
	concedere aliquantisper hinc mi intro lubet,
	dum concenturio in corde sycophantias.
573	⟨sed mox⟩ exibo, non ero uobis morae;
573ᵃ	tibicen uos interibi hic delectauerit.

ACTVS II

II. i: PSEVDOLVS

PSEV	pro Iuppiter, ut mihi quicquid ago lepide omnia pros-	
	pereque eueniunt:	
575	nec quod dubitem nec quod timeam meo in pectore	
	conditum est consilium.	
	nam ea stultitia est, facinus magnum timido cordi	
	credere; nam omnes	
	res perinde sunt	
	ut agas, ut eas magni facias; nam ego in meo pectore	
	prius ⟨omnes⟩	
	ita paraui copias,	
580	duplicis, triplicis dolos, perfidias, ut, ubiquomque ho-	
	stibus congrediar	
581–	—maiorum meum fretus uirtute dicam, mea industria	
82	et malitia fraudulenta—	
	facile ut uincam, facile ut spoliem meos perduellis meis	
	perfidiis.	

such great deeds in order to entertain you while I'm
bringing this play to an end, and that I'm not going to do   565
what I'd said I would. I won't go back on my word. And
as far as I know, I don't know anything certain yet about
how I'll do this, except that it will happen: a man who
comes onstage ought to bring something newfound in a
new way. If he can't do this, he should give place to the   570
one who can. I wish to withdraw inside for a short time
while I marshal my tricks in my heart. But I'll soon come
out, I won't waste your time. The flute player will enter-
tain you here in the meantime.

Exit PSEUDOLUS *into Simo's house.*

ACT TWO

Enter PSEUDOLUS *from Simo's house.*

PSEU O Jupiter! How delightfully and successfully everything
I do is turning out for me: a plan that I don't need to have   575
doubts or fears about is placed in my heart. It's stupidity
to entrust a big undertaking to a timid heart: all things
are exactly the way you perform them, the way you attach
importance to them; I prepared all troops in my breast
beforehand, double and triple tricks and deceptions, so   580
that whenever I meet the enemy—I'll say so relying on
the bravery of my ancestors and my own treacherous
effort and wickedness—so that I'll win easily and despoil

---

564 quo *A*, quin *P*, qui *ς*
573 *uersus non fertur in P*   sed mox *add. Leo*
578 omnes *add. Leo*

		nunc inimicum ego hunc communem meum atque uostrorum omnium
585		Ballionem exballistabo lepide: date operam modo;
585ᵃ		hoc ego oppidum ammoenire ut hodie capiatur uolo.
586		atque huc meas legiones adducam; si hoc expugno— facilem hanc rem
586ᵃ		meis ciuibus faciam—
587		post\<id\> ad oppidum hoc uetus continuo meum exercitum protinus obducam:

ind' me et simul participes omnis meos praeda onerabo atque opplebo,

metum et fugam perduellibus meis me ut sciant natum.

590   eo sum genere gnatus: magna me facinora decet efficere

quae post mihi clara et diu clueant.

sed hunc quem uideo, quis hic est qui oculis meis obuiam ignobilis obicitur?

lubet scire quid hic uelit cum machaera et huic quam rem agat hinc dabo insidias.

II. ii: HARPAX. PSEVDOLVS

594–95   HAR   hi loci sunt atque hae regiones quae mi ab ero sunt demonstratae,

ut ego oculis rationem capio quam mi ita dixit erus meus miles,

septumas esse aedis a porta ubi ille habitet leno quoi iussit

symbolum me ferre et hoc argentum. nimis uelim certum qui id mi faciat

Ballio leno ubi hic habitat.

600   PSEV   st! tace, tace, meus hic est homo,

my opponents through my guiles easily. Now I'll can- 585
nonball Ballio wittily, this common enemy of mine and
of you all. Just pay attention: I want to lay siege to this
town so that it may be captured today. And I'll bring my
troops here. (*points to Ballio's house*) If I conquer it—I'll
make this easy for my fellow citizens—then I'll instantly
lead my army against this old town. (*points to Simo's
house*) From there I'll load and fill myself and also all my
comrades with booty, so that they may know that I was
born to instill fear and flight in my enemies. Such is the 590
stock from which I was born, I ought to do great deeds
that bring me great and long renown afterward. But who
is this unknown person whom I see, who is thrown in the
way of my eyes? I wish to know what he wants here with
his sword and I'll ambush his plans from here. (*steps
aside*)

Enter HARPAX *from the harbor, with cloak, hat, and sword and
a wallet around his neck.*

HAR (*to himself*) These are the places and these the regions 595
that I was shown by my master, that's how I draw the
conclusion with my eyes from what my master told me;
he said it was the seventh house from the gate where that
pimp lives to whom he told me to bring the token and
this money. I'd very much like someone to tell me for
certain whereabouts here the pimp Ballio lives.

PSEU (*aside*) Hush! Be quiet, be quiet, this chap is mine, un- 600

584 uostrum Ω, uostrorum *Guyet*
587 post‹id› *Lindsay*
593 uelit *P*, ueniat *A*

600ᵃ		ni omnes di atque homines deserunt.
601		nouo consilio nunc mihi opus est,
601ᵃ		noua res subito mi haec obiecta est:
602		hoc praeuortar principio;
602ᵃ		illa omnia missa habeo
602ᵇ		quae ante agere occepi.
603		iam pol ego hunc stratioticum
603ᵃ		nuntium aduenientem
603ᵇ		probe percutiam.
	HAR	ostium pultabo atque intus euocabo aliquem foras.
605	PSEV	quisquis es, compendium ego te facere pultandi uolo;
		nam ego precator et patronus foribus processi foras.
	HAR	tune es Ballio?
	PSEV	immo uero ego eius sum Subballio.
	HAR	quid istuc uerbi est?
	PSEV	condus, promus sum, procurator peni.
	HAR	quasi te dicas atriensem.
	PSEV	immo atriensi ego impero.
610	HAR	quid tu, seruosne es an liber?
	PSEV	nunc quidem etiam seruio.
	HAR	ita uidere, et non uidere dignus qui liber sies.
	PSEV	non soles respicere te, quom dicis iniuste alteri?
	HAR	hunc hominem malum esse oportet.
	PSEV	di me seruant atque amant,
		nam haec mihi incus est: procudam ego hodie hinc
		multos dolos.
615	HAR	quid illic solus secum loquitur?
	PSEV	quid ais tu, adulescens?
	HAR	quid est?
	PSEV	esne tu an non es ab illo militi Macedonio,

601ᵃ subito mihi haec *P*, haec subito mihi *A*

308

less all gods and men leave me in the lurch. Now I need a new plan; this new situation has been thrown my way suddenly. I'll give my first attention to this; I'll say good-bye to all those things that I began to do earlier. Now I'll knock this military envoy down properly on his arrival.

HAR (*to himself*) I'll knock at the door and call someone out.

PSEU (*approaching him*) Whoever you are, I want you to dis-   605
pense with knocking: I've come forward as intercessor and patron for the door.

HAR Are you Ballio?

PSEU No, rather I am his Under-Ballio.

HAR What sort of word is that?

PSEU I'm the getter-in and giver-out, the superintendent of supplies.

HAR As if you were calling yourself the majordomo.

PSEU No, I give commands to the majordomo.

HAR What about you, are you a slave or a free man?   610

PSEU For the time being I'm a slave.

HAR That's what you look like and you don't look as if you deserve to be free.

PSEU Don't you normally look at yourself when you insult someone else?

HAR (*aside*) This chap must be a bad one.

PSEU (*aside*) The gods save and love me; this is my anvil: I'll hammer out many guiles from here today.

HAR (*aside*) What is he talking to himself about?   615

PSEU What do you say, young man?

HAR What is it?

PSEU Are you or aren't you the slave of that Macedonian sol-

seruos eius qui hinc a nobis est mercatus mulierem,
qui argenti meo ero lenoni quindecim dederat minas,
quinque debet?

HAR   sum. sed ubi tu me nouisti gentium

620   aut uidisti aut collocutu's? nam equidem Athenas antid-
hac

numquam adueni nec te uidi ante hunc diem umquam
oculis meis.

PSEV quia uidere inde esse; nam olim quom abiit, argento
haec dies

praestituta est, quoad referret nobis, nec dum rettulit.

624– HAR immo adest.
25 PSEV   tun attulisti?

HAR   egomet.

PSEV   quid dubitas dare?

HAR tibi ego dem?

PSEV   mihi hercle uero, qui res rationesque eri
Ballionis curo, argentum accepto [expenso] et quoi de-
bet dato.

HAR si quidem hercle etiam supremi promptas thesauros
Iouis,

tibi libellam argenti numquam credam.

PSEV   dum tu sternuas,

630   res erit soluta.

HAR   uinctam potius sic seruauero.

PSEV uae tibi! tu inuentu's uero meam qui furcilles fidem.
quasi mi non sescenta tanta soli soleant credier.

HAR potest ut alii ita arbitrentur et ego ut ne credam tibi.

PSEV quasi tu dicas me te uelle argento circumducere.

627 expenso *del.* Bothe

dier who bought a woman from us here and who gave
my master, the pimp, fifteen minas and owes him five?

HAR Yes, I am. But where on earth did you get to know me   620
or see me or speak to me? I've never come to Athens
before and I've never set eyes on you before this day.

PSEU Because you seem to be from there: some time ago,
when he left, this day was established for when he should
pay us the money, and he hasn't paid it yet.

HAR No, it's here.   625

PSEU Have you brought it?

HAR Yes.

PSEU Why are you hesitating to give it to me?

HAR I should give it to *you*?

PSEU Yes, to me: I take care of my master Ballio's finances and
accounts, I receive money and pay it to the man whom
he owes.

HAR Even if you're the steward of the treasures of Jupiter
above, I'd never entrust a farthing[28] to you.

PSEU In the time it would take you to sneeze the matter will   630
be resolved.

HAR No thanks; I'd rather keep it unresolved like this.

PSEU Curse you! You've turned up to shake my credit. As if six
hundred times as much wasn't regularly entrusted to
me!

HAR It's possible that others hold that opinion and that I don't
trust you.

PSEU As if you were saying that I wanted to cheat you out of
the money.

---

[28] Lit. a "silver libella"; a libella is worth only one-tenth of a den-
arius.

635	HAR	immo uero quasi tu dicas quasique ego autem id sus- picer.
		sed quid est tibi nomen?
	PSEV	seruos est huic lenoni Syrus,
		eum esse me dicam. Syrus sum.
	HAR	Syrus?
	PSEV	id est nomen mihi.
	HAR	uerba multa facimus. erus si tuos domi est, quin prouo- cas,
		ut id agam quod missus huc sum?
	PSEV	quicquid est nomen tibi,
640		si intus esset, euocarem. uerum si dare uis mihi,
		magis erit solutum quasi ipsi dederis.
	HAR	at enim scin quid est?
		reddere hoc, non perdere erus me misit. nam certo scio
		hoc, febrim tibi esse, quia non licet huc inicere ungu- las.
		ego nisi ipsi Ballioni nummum credam nemini.
645	PSEV	at illic nunc negotiosust: res agitur apud iudicem.
	HAR	di bene uortant! at ego quando eum esse censebo domi,
		rediero. tu epistulam hanc a me accipe atque illi dato.
		nam istic symbolust inter erum meum et tuom de mu- liere.
	PSEV	scio equidem: ut qui argentum afferret atque expres- sam imaginem
650		huc suam ad nos, cum eo aiebat uelle mitti mulierem.
		nam hic quoque exemplum reliquit eius.
	HAR	omnem rem tenes.
	PSEV	quid ego ni teneam?
	HAR	dato istunc symbolum ergo illi.

312

HAR	No, as if you were saying it and as if I were suspecting it. 635
	But what's your name?
PSEU	(*aside*) The pimp has a slave called Syrus, I'll say that I'm
	him. (*aloud*) I'm Syrus.
HAR	Syrus?
PSEU	That's my name.
HAR	We're making a lot of words. If your master's at home,
	why don't you call him out so that I can do what I was
	sent for?
PSEU	Whatever your name is, if he were inside, I'd call him 640
	out. But if you want to give it to me, it'll be paid more
	surely than if you'd given it to himself.
HAR	But you know what? My master sent me to pay this, not
	to lose it. I know for sure that you have a fever because
	you can't dig your claws into it. I won't entrust a single
	coin to anyone other than Ballio himself.
PSEU	But he's busy now; he has a case on before the judge. 645
HAR	May the gods let it turn out well! But when I believe he's
	at home, I'll return. You, take this letter from me and
	give it to him: the token between my master and yours
	about the woman is there. (*hands over a letter*)
PSEU	I know: he said he wanted the woman to be sent with the
	man who brought the money and his stamped image 650
	here to us. He left a copy of it here too.
HAR	You've got the whole business.
PSEU	Why shouldn't I have got it?
HAR	Then give him that token.

---

639 quicquid est nomen tibi *Harpagi dat Acidalius*
642 misit *P*, iussit *uel* misit *A*
649 ut *del. Ritschl*
650 suam huc Ω, huc suam *Bothe*

PSEV   licet.
          sed quid est tibi nomen?
HAR   Harpax.
PSEV   apage te, Harpax, hau places;
          huc quidem hercle haud ibis intro, ne quid ἅρπαξ
            feceris.
655 HAR hostis uiuos rapere soleo ex acie: eo hoc nomen mihi
            est.
PSEV pol te multo magis opinor uasa ahena ex aedibus.
HAR non ita est. sed scin quid te oro, Syre?
PSEV   sciam si dixeris.
HAR ego deuortor extra portam huc in tabernam tertiam
          apud anum illam doliarem, claudam, crassam,
            Chrysidem.
660 PSEV quid nunc uis?
HAR   inde ut me arcessas, erus tuos ubi uenerit.
PSEV tuo arbitratu, maxume.
HAR   nam ut lassus ueni de uia,
          me uolo curare.
PSEV   sane sapis et consilium placet.
          sed uide sis ne in quaestione sis quando arcessam mihi.
HAR quin ubi prandero, dabo operam somno.
PSEV   sane censeo.
665 HAR numquid uis?
PSEV   dormitum ut abeas.
HAR   abeo.
PSEV   atque audin, Harpage?
          iube sis te operiri: beatus eris, si consudaueris.

PSEU Okay. But what's your name?

HAR Harpax.

PSEU Away with you, Harpax, I don't like the look of you; here you won't go in, don't play the harpy.

HAR I normally snatch enemies alive from the battle line; that's why I have this name. 655

PSEU I think it much more likely that you snatch brass pots from houses.

HAR No, it's not like that. But do you know what I ask of you, Syrus?

PSEU I'll know it when you tell me.

HAR I'm stopping by outside the gate here in the third inn, at the place of that old woman shaped like a wine jar, limping, and fat, Chrysis.

PSEU What do you want now? 660

HAR That you fetch me from there when your master comes.

PSEU As you like it, with the greatest pleasure.

HAR Well, since I've come exhausted from traveling, I want to look after myself.

PSEU That's very wise of you and I like your plan. But do make sure that you don't need to be searched for when I fetch you.

HAR No, when I've had lunch, I'll turn my attention to a nap.

PSEU Quite right.

HAR Do you want anything? 665

PSEU Only that you go off and sleep.

HAR I'm off. (*turns to go*)

PSEU And can you hear me, Harpax? Get yourself well covered; you'll be refreshed if you sweat.

Exit HARPAX *to the left.*

315

II. iii: PSEVDOLVS

PSEV di immortales, conseruauit me illic homo aduentu suo.
suo uiatico redduxit me usque ex errore in uiam.
namque ipsa Opportunitas non potuit mi opportunius
670 aduenire quam haec allata est mi opportune epistula.
nam haec allata cornu copiae est, ubi inest quicquid
    uolo:
hic doli, hic fallaciae omnes, hic sunt sycophantiae,
hic argentum, hic amica amanti erili filio.
atque ego nunc me ut gloriosum faciam et copi pec-
    tore,
675 quo modo quicque agerem, ut lenoni surruperem mu-
    lierculam,
iam instituta, ornata cuncta in ordine, animo ut uol-
    ueram,
certa, deformata habebam; sed profecto hoc sic erit:
centum doctum hominum consilia sola haec deuincit
    dea,
Fortuna. atque hoc uerum est: proinde ut quisque For-
    tuna utitur,
680 ita praecellet atque exinde sapere eum omnes dicimus.
bene ubi quoi scimus consilium accidisse, hominem ca-
    tum
eum esse declaramus, stultum autem illum quoi uortit
    male.
stulti hau scimus frustra ut simus, quom quid cupienter
    dari
petimus nobis, quasi quid in rem sit possimus noscere.
685 certa mittimus dum incerta petimus; atque hoc euenit
in labore atque in dolore, ut mors obrepat interim.
sed iam satis est philosophatum. nimis diu et longum
    loquor.

PSEU Immortal gods, that man has saved me by his arrival.
With what he carried on his journey he's brought me
from my uncertain course back onto the right road: Op-
portunity herself couldn't have come more opportunely   670
than the opportuneness of the arrival of this letter. Yes,
it was brought to me as a cornucopia which has every-
thing I want inside. Here there are tricks, here there are
all devices, here there are deceptions, here there's gold,
here the girlfriend for master's lovesick son. And so as to
show my prowess and how fertile in invention my breast
is: how to carry out each point in order to abduct the   675
woman from the pimp was already completely set up and
prepared step for step, as I wanted it in my heart, and I
had it in definite form and completely shaped. But in-
deed it's like this: this goddess alone, Fortune, conquers
the plans of a hundred clever men. Yes indeed, that's
true: in proportion as each one has Fortune, he excels   680
and we all say that he's wise. When we know that some-
one's plan was successful, we declare him a smart man,
but stupid the one whose plan was unsuccessful. In our
stupidity we don't know how we deceive ourselves when
we keenly demand to get something, as if we could know
what was going to be to our advantage. We let go of   685
certainties while chasing after uncertainties; and in the
midst of toil and pain it so happens that death creeps
up on us in the meantime. But enough of this philoso-
phizing now. I've been talking at great length. Immortal

---

681 quid discimus *P*, quod discimus *A*, quoi scimus *Acidalius*
683 quod Ω, quid *Lipsius*

di immortales! aurichalco contra non carum fuit
meum mendacium, hic modo quod subito commentus
    fui,

690   quia lenonis me esse dixi. nunc ego hac epistula
tris deludam, erum et lenonem et qui hanc dedit mi
    epistulam.

eugae! par pari aliud autem quod cupiebam contigit:
uenit eccum Calidorus, ducit nescioquem secum simul.

II. iv: CALIDORVS. CHARINVS. PSEVDOLVS

CALI dulcia atque amara apud te sum elocutus omnia:
695   scis amorem, scis laborem, scis egestatem meam.
696 CHAR commemini omnia: id tu modo, me quid uis facere, fac
    sciam.
696ᵃ [CALI quom haec tibi alia sum elocutus, uix rem scis de sym-
    bolo.
696ᵇ CHAR omnia, inquam. tu modo quid me facere uis fac ut
    sciam.]

CALI Pseudolus mi ita imperauit, ut aliquem hominem stren-
    uom,
beneuolentem adducerem ad se.

CHAR   seruas imperium probe.
nam et amicum et beneuolentem ducis. sed istic
    Pseudolus
700   nouos mihi est.

CALI   nimium est mortalis graphicus, εὑρετής mihi est.
is mihi haec sese effecturum dixit quae dixi tibi.

696ᵃ–96ᵇ *uersus non feruntur in A, secl. Ritschl*
696ᵃ *uis scires si scis P, uix rem scis Leo*

---

[29] Greek *oreikhalkos* refers to a form of brass. The first element,

gods! It wasn't dear at its weight in mountain copper,[29] my lie which I came up with here so suddenly, when I   690 said I belong to the pimp. With this letter I'll now deceive three people, my master and the pimp and the man who gave me this letter. (*looking around*) Hurray! Another thing I wished for, just like the other, has come to pass: look, Calidorus is coming, he's bringing someone with him.

Enter CALIDORUS *and* CHARINUS *from the right, without noticing Pseudolus.*

CALI   I've told you all my sweet and bitter experiences; you   695 know my love, you know my distress, you know my poverty.

CHAR   I remember everything. Just let me know what you want me to do.

[CALI   While I told you these other things, you hardly know the issue about the token.

CHAR   Everything, I say. Just let me know what you want me to do.]

CALI   Pseudolus commanded me to bring him some energetic chap well disposed to me.

CHAR   You follow your command well: you're bringing both a friend and someone who is well disposed to you. But that Pseudolus is new to me.   700

CALI   He's a terribly smart mortal, he's my very own inventor. He said he'd bring about what I told you.

meaning "mountain," was poorly understood and associated with a monophthongized pronunciation of *aurum*, "gold"; in Plautus the word refers to a fictitious metal of great value.

	PSEV	magnufice hominem compellabo.
	CALI	quoia uox resonat?
	PSEV	io!

PSEV   io te, te, tyranne, te, te ego, qui imperitas Pseudolo,
quaero quoi ter trina triplicia, tribus modis tria gaudia,
705   artibus tribus tris demeritas dem laetitias, de tribus
705ᵃ   fraude partas per malitiam, per dolum et fallacias;
in libello hoc opsignato ad te attuli pauxillulo.

CALI   illic homo est.

CHAR   ut paratragoedat carnufex!

PSEV   confer gradum
contra pariter, porge audacter ad salutem bracchium.

CALI   dic utrum Spemne an Salutem te salutem, Pseudole?

710 PSEV   immo utrumque.

CHAR   Vtrumque, salue. sed quid actum est?

PSEV   quid times?

CALI   attuli hunc.

PSEV   quid, attulisti?

CALI   "adduxi" uolui dicere.

PSEV   quis istic est?

CALI   Charinus.

PSEV   eugae! iam χάριν τούτῳ ποιῶ.

CHAR   quin tu si quid opust, mi audacter imperas?

PSEV   tam gratia est.
bene sit tibi, Charine. nolo tibi molestos esse nos.

703 te rogo *P*, t***go *A*, te te ego *Leo*
713 gratia *A*, graciam *P*, gratiast *Pareus*

---

30 In the Latin, Calidorus uses *afferre*, "bring," which can have a
person as object, even though it also means "carry." He then expresses

PSEU (*aside*) I'll address him pompously.

CALI Whose voice is resounding?

PSEU (*approaching them*) Io! Io! You, you, ruler, you, you, who
      command Pseudolus, you I seek in order to give you
      thrice three times three joys, triple in three ways, three   705
      delights acquired by three devices, won by fraud from
      three victims. In this tiny, sealed dispatch I've brought
      them to you. (*produces the letter*)

CALI (*to Charinus*) That's him.

CHAR How the crook out-tragedies tragedy!

PSEU (*to Calidorus*) Match your step to face me, boldly stretch
      out your arm to greet me.

CALI (*shaking his hand*) Tell me whether I should greet you
      as Hope or Salvation, Pseudolus.

PSEU As both.   710

CHAR Mister Both, my greetings. But what's been done?

PSEU Why are you afraid?

CALI I've conveyed this man with me. (*points to Charinus*)

PSEU What, you've conveyed him?

CALI "I've brought him," I meant to say.[30]

PSEU Who is that?

CALI Charinus.

PSEU Hurray! Now thank you just the same.[31]

CHAR Why don't you command me boldly if you need any-
      thing?

PSEU Thanks, but no thanks. Be well, Charinus. I don't want
      us to be a nuisance to you.

himself unambiguously by using *adducere*, which does not have this
second meaning.   [31] Pseudolus answers in unidiomatic Greek,
with a pun on *charin*, "thanks," and *Charinus*; the Greek makes sense
only when translated back into Latin.

715 CHAR uos molestos? nil molestum est mihi quidem.
 PSEV   tum igitur mane.
 CALI quid istuc est?
 PSEV   epistulam hanc modo intercepi et symbolum.
 CALI symbolum? quem symbolum?
 PSEV   qui a milite allatust modo.
   eius seruos qui hunc ferebat cum quinque argenti
    minis,
   tuam qui amicam hinc arcessebat, ei os subleui modo.
720 CALI quo modo?
 PSEV   horum causa haec agitur spectatorum fabula:
   hi sciunt qui hic affuerunt; uobis post narrauero.
 CALI quid nunc agimus?
 PSEV   liberam hodie tuam amicam amplexabere.
 CALI egone?
 PSEV   tu istic ipsus, inquam, si quidem hoc uiuet caput;
   si modo mihi hominem inuenietis propere.
 CHAR   qua facie?
 PSEV   malum,
725   callidum, doctum, qui quando principium prehenderit,
   porro sua uirtute teneat quid se facere oporteat;
   atque qui hic non uisitatus saepe sit.
 CHAR   si seruos est,
   numquid refert?
 PSEV   immo multo mauolo quam liberum.
 CHAR posse opinor me dare hominem tibi malum et doctum,
    modo
730   qui a patre aduenit Carysto necdum exit ex aedibus

---

715 nihil molestumst mihi *A*, mihi molestum est *P*, mihi molestum
est id *Pius*   716 hanc *A*, modo hanc *P*, hanc modo *Guyet*
   718 cum . . . minis *A*, et . . . minas *P*

322

CHAR You a nuisance? It's no nuisance to me at all. 715
PSEU Well then, wait. (*shows the letter again*)
CALI What's that?
PSEU I just intercepted this letter and token.
CALI Token? What token?
PSEU The one that was brought from the soldier just now. I just fooled his slave, who was carrying it with five silver minas and who was trying to fetch your girlfriend from here.
CALI How? 720
PSEU This play is being staged for the sake of the spectators. Those who were present already know; I'll tell you two later.
CALI What are we doing now?
PSEU You'll embrace your girlfriend as a free woman today.
CALI I?
PSEU You there yourself, I tell you, if this head of mine lives; if only you find me someone quickly.
CHAR Like what?
PSEU Someone bad, clever, smart, who, when he's understood 725 the beginning, knows by himself what he needs to do further; and someone who hasn't been often seen about here.
CHAR Does it matter if it's a slave?
PSEU No, I much prefer a slave to a free man.
CHAR I think I can give you a bad and smart chap, someone who just came from my father from Carystus[32] and hasn't 730

---

[32] City in Euboea, a Greek island.

---

729 modo *P*, domo *A*

quoquam neque Athenas aduenit umquam ante hester-
num diem.

PSEV bene iuuas. sed quinque inuentis opus est argenti minis
mutuis quas hodie reddam: nam huius mihi debet
pater.

CHAR ego dabo, ne quaere aliunde.

PSEV   o hominem opportunum mihi!

735   etiam opust chlamyde et machaera et petaso.

CHAR   possum a me dare.

PSEV di immortales! non Charinus mi hic quidem, sed Copia
est.

     sed istic seruos ex Carysto qui hic adest ecquid sapit?

CHAR hircum ab alis.

PSEV   manuleatam tunicam habere hominem addecet.

     ecquid is homo habet aceti in pectore?

CHAR   atque acidissumi.

740 PSEV quid, si opus sit ut dulce promat indidem, ecquid ha-
bet?

CHAR   rogas?

     murrinam, passum, defrutum, mellam, mel quoiuis
modi;

     quin in corde instruere quondam coepit pantopolium.

PSEV eugepae! lepide, Charine, meo me ludo lamberas.

     sed quid nomen esse dicam ego isti seruo?

CHAR   Simiae.

745 PSEV scitne in re aduorsa uorsari?

CHAR   turbo non aeque citust.

PSEV ecquid argutust?

CHAR   malorum facinorum saepissume.

737 isti (iste D^l) P, iste A, istic *Merula*
739 acidissumi P, acidissumum A

been out of the house anywhere yet and never came to Athens before yesterday.

PSEU You're a great help. But I need to find five silver minas on loan, which I'll be able to repay today because (*pointing to Calidorus*) his father owes me.

CHAR I'll give it to you, stop looking elsewhere.

PSEU O what a convenient chap you are for me! I also need a   735
cloak, a sword, and a hat.

CHAR I can supply them.

PSEU Immortal gods! He isn't Charinus for me, but a charitable institution.[33] But does that slave from Carystus who is here have any sense?

CHAR Scents? There's a goat in his armpits.

PSEU He ought to have a tunic with long sleeves. Does he have any vinegar[34] in his breast?

CHAR Yes, and what's more, it's very biting.

PSEU What if he needs to bring out something sweet from the   740
same place, does he have anything?

CHAR You ask? Spiced wine, raisin wine, liqueur, honeyed wine, honey of any type; indeed he once had the idea of setting up a general store inside himself.

PSEU Well done! Charinus, you wittily beat me at my own game. But what should I say is that slave's name?

CHAR Simia.

PSEU Does he know how to turn in a critical situation?   745

CHAR A spinning top isn't as fast.

PSEU Has he lots of judgment?

CHAR Judgments, yes, any amount, and for heinous crimes, too.

---

[33] Lit. "Abundance." In the Latin, *Copia* and *Charinus* alliterate.
[34] Metaphor for sharp wit and cleverness.

PSEV	quid quom manufesto tenetur?
CHAR	anguilla est, elabitur.
PSEV	ecquid is homo scitust?
CHAR	plebi scitum non est scitius.
PSEV	probus homo est, ut praedicare te audio.
CHAR	immo si scias,

750 ubi te aspexerit, narrabit ultro quid sese uelis.
sed quid es acturus?

PSEV	dicam. ubi hominem exornauero,

subditiuom fieri ego illum militis seruom uolo;
symbolum hunc ferat lenoni cum quinque argenti
   minis,
mulierem ab lenone abducat: em tibi omnem fabulam!
755 ceterum quo quicque pacto faciat ipsi dixero.

CALI	quid nunc igitur stamus?
PSEV	hominem cum ornamentis omnibus

exornatum adducite ad me iam ad tarpezitam Aeschi-
   num.
sed properate.

CALI	prius illi erimus quam tu.
PSEV	abite ergo ocius.

quicquid incerti mi in animo prius aut ambiguom fuit,
760 nunc liquet, nunc defaecatum est cor mihi; nunc per-
   uium est:
omnis ordine his sub signis ducam legiones meas
aui sinistra, auspicio liquido atque ex <mea> sententia;
confidentia est inimicos meos me posse perdere.
nunc ibo ad forum atque onerabo meis praeceptis
   Simiam,

760 peruiast *P*, peruiumst ς   761 ordines *P*, ordine his *Mueller*
762 ex sententia *P Nonius*, ex mea sententia *Bothe*

326

PSEU What if he's caught in the act?

CHAR He's an eel, he slips away.

PSEU Is he a man of decision?

CHAR A decision of the people is no more decisive.

PSEU He's a decent chap, the way I hear you describe him.

CHAR No, if you knew, the moment he spots you he'll tell you 750
of his own accord what you want of him. But what are
you going to do?

PSEU I'll tell you. When I've fitted him out, I want him to
become a counterfeit slave of the soldier. He must bring
this token with the five minas to the pimp and take the
woman away from the pimp: there, that's the whole story
for you! As for the rest, how he should do everything, I'll 755
tell him in person.

CALI Then why are we standing around now?

PSEU Bring him to me now, to the banker Aeschinus, fitted out
with all the paraphernalia. But hurry up!

CALI We'll be there before you.

Exeunt CALIDORUS *and* CHARINUS *to the right.*

PSEU (*calling after them*) Then go quickly. (*to the audience*)
Whatever was uncertain or unclear in my heart before 760
is clear now, my heart is freed from the dregs now; the
passage is easy now: I'll lead all my troops in order under
these standards, with the bird to the left, with positive
auspices, and according to my own wish. I have confi-
dence that I can annihilate my enemies. Now I'll go to
the forum and heap my instructions onto Simia, what he 765

765   quid agat, ne quid titubet, docte ut hanc ferat falla-
             ciam.
        iam ego hoc ipsum oppidum expugnatum faxo erit le-
             nonium.

ACTVS III

III. i: PVER

PVER quoi seruitutem di danunt lenoniam
        puero, atque eidem si addunt turpitudinem,
        ne illi, quantum ego nunc corde conspicio meo,
770   malam rem magnam multasque aerumnas danunt.
        uelut haec mi euenit seruitus, ubi ego omnibus
        paruis magnisque miseriis praefulcior:
        neque ego amatorem mi inuenire ullum queo
        qui amet me, ut curer tandem nitidiuscule.
775   nunc huic lenoni hodie est natalis dies:
        interminatus est a minimo ad maxumum,
        si quis non hodie munus misisset sibi,
        eum cras cruciatu maxumo perbitere.
        nunc nescio hercle rebus quid faciam meis;
780   neque ego illud possum quod illi qui possunt solent.
        nunc, nisi lenoni munus hodie misero,
        cras mihi potandus fructus est fullonius.
        eheu, quam illae rei ego etiam nunc sum paruolus!
        atque edepol ut nunc male malum metuo miser,
785   si quispiam det qui manus grauior siet,
        quamquam illud aiunt magno gemitu fieri,
        comprimere dentes uideor posse aliquo modo.

776 interminatust *P*, interminatus est ς

should do so as not to waver, so that he may carry this trick off cleverly. I'll make sure that this pimp town itself will be conquered instantly.

Exit PSEUDOLUS *to the right.*

ACT THREE

Enter a SLAVE BOY *from Ballio's house.*

BOY   If the gods make a boy slave to a pimp, and if they give him ugliness to boot, then truly, as far as I can now see in my heart, they allot a big thrashing and many toils to 770 him. For instance, this slavery has come upon me where I'm used as a prop for all small and big miseries; and I can't find myself any lover to make love to me, so that I'd be treated a little bit more neatly at last. Now it's this 775 pimp's birthday today: he's threatened anyone, from the youngest to the oldest, that if anyone doesn't send him a present today, he'll perish under greatest torture tomorrow. Now I really don't know what to do in a fix like mine; 780 nor can I do what those who can normally do.[35] Now unless I send the pimp a present today, I have to drink the fuller's produce[36] tomorrow. Dear me, how small I am for that sort of thing even now! And yet, as terribly afraid as I am of a beating now, poor me, if any- 785 one were to give me something whereby my hand may be heavier,[37] I think I'll be able to grit my teeth, even

---

[35] *Posse*, "be able," typically refers to the active part in intercourse.   [36] The acid used to clean woolens was often urine; the boy would thus have to provide oral intercourse.   [37] I.e., money.

sed comprimenda est mihi uox atque oratio:
erus eccum recipit se domum et ducit coquom.

III. ii: BALLIO. COQVOS. PVER

790 BAL forum coquinum qui uocant stulte uocant,
nam non coquinum est, uerum furinum est forum.
nam ego si iuratus peiorem hominem quaererem
coquom, non potui quam hunc quem duco ducere,
multiloquom, gloriosum, insulsum, inutilem.
795 quin ob eam rem Orcus recipere ad se hunc noluit,
ut esset hic qui mortuis cenam coquat;
nam hic solus illis coquere quod placeat potest.

CO si me arbitrabare isto pacto ut praedicas,
quor conducebas?

BAL inopia: alius non erat.
800 sed quor sedebas in foro, si eras coquos,
tu solus praeter alios?

CO ego dicam tibi:
hominum ego auaritia factus sum improbior coquos,
non meopte ingenio.

BAL qua istuc ratione?

CO eloquar.
quia enim, quom extemplo ueniunt conductum
coquom,
805 nemo illum quaerit qui optumus et carissumust:
illum conducunt potius qui uilissumust.
hoc ego fui hodie solus opsessor fori.

---

802 auaritia ego sum factus *P, transp. Ritschl*

---

[38] Reference to anal intercourse.
[39] The god of the Underworld.

though they say that that thing elicits loud cries of pain.[38]
But I need to restrain my voice and speech: look, my
master's returning home and bringing a cook.

Exit SLAVE BOY *into Ballio's house.*
Enter BALLIO *with his slave boy from the right, followed by*
a COOK *with his* SLAVE BOY *and some servants carrying the*
shopping.

BAL   People who talk of a cook market talk rubbish: it's not a   790
cook market but a crook market. Well, if I'd sworn to
look for a worse man to be my cook, I couldn't have
brought one worse than the one I'm bringing, a waffling,
pompous, witless, useless git. Indeed, Orcus[39] has re-   795
fused to take him into his place so that there would be
someone here to cook dinner for the dead:[40] he alone
can cook something they like.

CO   If you thought that I was the way you state, why did you
hire me?

BAL   Dearth: there was no one else. But why were you sitting   800
in the market, if you were a cook, you alone beyond the
others?

CO   I'll tell you: through people's greed I've become a less
desirable cook, not through my own nature.

BAL   How so?

CO   I'll tell you. Because the moment people come to hire a
cook, nobody looks for the one who is best and most   805
expensive; they prefer to hire the cheapest one. That's
why I was the only occupant of the market today. Those

40 Every February a banquet was provided for the departed.

illi drachumissent miseri: me nemo potest
minoris quisquam nummo ut surgam subigere.
810 non ego item cenam condio ut alii coqui,
qui mihi condita prata in patinis proferunt,
boues qui conuiuas faciunt herbasque oggerunt,
813 eas herbas herbis aliis porro condiunt:
815 apponunt rumicem, brassicam, betam, blitum,
814 indunt coriandrum, feniculum, alium, atrum holus,
816 eo laserpici libram pondo diluont,
teritur sinapis scelera, quae illis qui terunt
prius quam triuerunt oculi ut exstillent facit.
ei homines cenas ubi coquont, quom condiunt,
820 non condimentis condiunt, sed strigibus,
uiuis conuiuis intestina quae exedint.
hoc hic quidem homines tam breuem uitam colunt,
quom hasce herbas huius modi in suom aluom con-
gerunt,
formidolosas dictu, non esu modo.
825 quas herbas pecudes non edunt, homines edunt.
BAL quid tu? diuinis condimentis utere,
qui prorogare uitam possis hominibus,
qui ea culpes condimenta?
CO audacter dicito;
nam uel ducenos annos poterunt uiuere
830 meas qui esitabunt escas quas condiuero.
nam ego cocilendrum quando in patinas indidi
aut cepolendrum aut maccidem aut saucaptidem,
eaepse sese [patinae] feruefaciunt ilico.
haec ad Neptuni pecudes condimenta sunt:

815 *ante* 814 *posuit Sauppe*   833 eaepse se patinae *A*, eae
ipsae sese patinae *P*, eaepse sese *Leo*

wretches may be one-drachma men; as for me, no one
can force me to get out of bed for less than two drachmas. 810
I don't season dinner the same way as other cooks, who
serve up seasoned meadows in their pans, who turn the
guests into oxen and present them with herbs and then
continue to season those herbs with other herbs: they 815
add sorrel, cabbage, beet, spinach; they put in coriander,
fennel, garlic, horse parsley; they pour in a pound of
silphium;[41] and they grate wretched mustard, which
makes the eyes of those who grate it cry before they've
grated it. When these people cook dinners and season
them, they don't season them with seasonings but with 820
screech owls,[42] to eat up the guests' intestines while
they're still alive. That's why people live such short lives
here, because they stuff herbs of this type into their bel-
lies, frightening to mention, let alone to eat. Humans eat 825
herbs which farm animals don't eat.

BAL What about you? Do you use divine seasonings with
which you can prolong people's lives, since you find fault
with those seasonings?

CO You can say so boldly; people who eat the dainties I
season can live for even two hundred years each. Yes, 830
when I put cocilendrum[43] into the pans, or cepolendrum
or maccis or saucaptis, the pans instantly bring them-
selves to a boil. These are the seasonings for Neptune's

[41] Juice of the silphium plant, a now extinct species that grew
around Cyrene, was a highly valued spice.

[42] Screech owls were thought to drink blood and eat the heart and
intestines of children and the dead.

[43] A made-up spice, like the ones that follow.

835		terrestris pecudes cicimandro condio aut
		hapalopside aut cataractria.
	BAL	at te Iuppiter
		dique omnes perdant cum condimentis tuis
		cumque tuis istis omnibus mendaciis!
	CO	sine sis loqui me.
	BAL	loquere atque i in malam crucem.
840	CO	ubi omnes patinae feruont, omnis aperio;
841		is odos dimissis manibus in caelum uolat.
843	BAL	odos dimissis manibus?
	CO	peccaui insciens.
844	BAL	quidum?
	CO	quia "manibus pedibus" uolui dicere.
842		eum odorem cenat Iuppiter cottidie.
845	BAL	si nusquam is coctum, quidnam cenat Iuppiter?
	CO	it incenatus cubitum.
	BAL	i in malam crucem.
		istacin causa tibi hodie nummum dabo?
	CO	fateor equidem esse me coquom carissumum;
		uerum pro pretio facio ut opera appareat
850		mea quo conductus uenio.
	BAL	ad furandum quidem.
	CO	an tu inuenire postulas quemquam coquom
		nisi miluinis aut aquilinis ungulis?
	BAL	an tu coquinatum te ire quoquam postulas
		quin ibi constrictis ungulis cenam coquas?
855		nunc adeo tu, qui meus es, iam edico tibi

841 manibus *A*, pedibus *P*   843 manibus *A*, pedibus *P*
844 dimissis pedibus *A*, quia (quiam *B*) demissis (di- *D*) manibus
P, quia manibus pedibus *Holmes*   842 *post* 844 *posuit Acidalius*
845 is coctis (coctum *D*²) *P*, coctum is *A*

334

cattle.[44] Land animals I season with cicimandrum or 835
hapalopsis or cataractria.

BAL   May Jupiter and all the gods ruin you with your season-
ings and with all those lies of yours!

CO   Please let me speak.

BAL   Speak and go hang yourself.

CO   When all the pans are boiling, I open them all. That scent 840
flies to heaven with arms stretched out.[45]

BAL   The scent with arms stretched out?

CO   That was a slip of the tongue.

BAL   How so?

CO   Because I meant to say "with hands and feet."[46] Jupiter
has that scent for dinner every day.

BAL   If you don't go anywhere to cook, what does Jupiter have 845
for dinner?

CO   Then he goes to bed without having dinner.

BAL   Go and be hanged. Am I going to give you a didrachma
for the sake of that?

CO   I do admit that I'm a very expensive cook; but I take care
that I give value for money in the house to which I've 850
come as cook.

BAL   Yes, as regards stealing.

CO   Do you expect to find any cook except one with the claws
of a kite or an eagle?

BAL   Do *you* expect to go anywhere to cook unless you cook
dinner there with your claws tied up? (*to his boy*) No, 855
I'm announcing to you, who are mine, that you must

44 Neptune is the god of the sea; Neptune's cattle are fish.

45 I.e. like a runner, with one in front and one behind.

46 I.e. with full exertion. The cook is using an even less appropriate
metaphor.

ut nostra properes amoliri omnia,
tum ut huius oculos in oculis habeas tuis:
quoquo hic spectabit, eo tu spectato simul;
si quo hic gradietur, pariter progredimino;
860   manum si protollet, pariter proferto manum:
suom si quid sumet, id tu sinito sumere;
si nostrum sumet, tu teneto altrinsecus.
si iste ibit, ito, stabit, astato simul;
si conquiniscet istic, conquiniscito.
865   item his discipulis priuos custodes dabo.

CO   habe modo bonum animum.

BAL   quaeso qui possum doce
bonum animum habere qui te ad me adducam do-
mum?

CO   quia sorbitione faciam ego hodie te mea,
item ut Medea Peliam concoxit senem,
870   quem medicamento et suis uenenis dicitur
fecisse rursus ex sene adulescentulum,
item ego te faciam.

BAL   eho, an etiam es ueneficus?

CO   immo edepol uero hominum seruator [magis].

BAL   ehem!

874–   quanti istuc unum me coquinare perdoces?
75   CO   quid?

BAL   ut te seruem ne quid surrupias mihi.

864 conquiniscito *A*, conquiniscito simul *P*, ceueto simul *Nonius*
873 magis *om. A*

---

[47] Medea rejuvenated Aeson by cutting him to pieces and boiling
him but was responsible for the death of Pelias, since his daughters did

hurry to remove all our things and then that you must keep his eyes in yours: wherever he looks, you must look at the same time; if he walks anywhere, you must walk there equally; if he stretches out his hand, you must 860 stretch out your hand equally; if he takes anything of his own stuff, you must let him take it; if he takes anything of ours, you must hold on to it from the other side. If he walks, you must walk, if he stands, you must stand at the same time. If he squats down there, you must squat down. In the same way I'll give separate guards to each 865 of his disciples.

CO (*to Ballio*) Take heart.

BAL Please instruct me, how can I take heart when I'm taking you home to me?

CO Because with my broth I'll treat you the same way today as Medea cooked up old Pelias, whom she's said to have 870 turned from an old man into a young one again with her medicine and potions;[47] I'll treat you in the same way.

BAL Tell me, are you also a sorcerer?

CO No, but the savior of mankind.

BAL Hm! At what price will you teach me this one cooking 875 lesson?

CO Which one?

BAL To watch over you so that you won't steal anything from me.

not follow the procedure properly. The cook is probably making fun of Ballio. The myth is too well known for Plautus to get it wrong, and it seems arbitrary to claim that alternative versions might have existed (Cic. *Cato* 83, where the boiling of Pelias in order to rejuvenate him is mentioned, does not actually indicate a happy outcome).

CO   si credis, nummo; si non, ne mina quidem.
      sed utrum tu amicis hodie an inimicis tuis
      daturu's cenam?
BAL   pol ego amicis scilicet.
880 CO quin tu illo inimicos potius quam amicos uocas?
      nam ego ita conuiuis cenam conditam dabo
      hodie atque ita suaui suauitate condiam:
      ut quisque quicque conditum gustauerit,
      ipsus sibi faciam ut digitos praerodat suos.
885 BAL quaeso hercle, prius quam quoiquam conuiuae dabis,
      gustato tute prius et discipulis dato,
      ut praerodatis uostras furtificas manus.
CO   fortasse haec tu nunc mihi non credis quae loquor.
BAL molestus ne sis; nimium iam tinnis; tace.
890   em illic ego habito. intro abi et cenam coque.
      propera.
PVER   quin tu is accubitum? et conuiuas cedo.
      corrumpitur iam cena.
BAL   em, subolem sis uide!
      iam hic quoque scelestus est coqui sublingulo.
      profecto quid nunc primum caueam nescio,
895   ita in aedibus sunt fures, praedo in proxumo est.
      nam mi hic uicinus apud forum paulo prius
      pater Calidori opere edixit maxumo
      ut mihi cauerem a Pseudolo seruo suo
      ne fidem ei haberem. nam eum circum ire in hunc
        diem,
900   ut me, si posset, muliere interuorteret;
      eum promisisse firmiter dixit sibi
      sese abducturum a me dolis Phoenicium.

    901 firmiter *P*, fortiter *A*

CO   If you trust me, for a didrachma; if not, not even for a
     mina. But are you giving a dinner to your friends today
     or to your enemies?

BAL To my friends of course.

CO   Why don't you invite your enemies rather than your   880
     friends to it? Because I'll give the guests a dinner sea-
     soned in such a way and with such great sweetness that
     whenever anyone tastes anything seasoned by me, I'll
     have him chewing off his own fingers.

BAL Please taste it yourself and give it to your disciples before 885
     giving it to any guest, so that you chew off your own
     thieving hands.

CO   Perhaps you don't believe what I'm saying now.

BAL Don't be a nuisance. You're chattering frightfully; shut
     up. Look, I live there. Go in and cook dinner. Hurry   890
     up!

BOY Why don't you go and recline at table? And produce the
     guests. The dinner's already going bad.

Exeunt the COOK, *his* SLAVE BOY, *and the servants into Ballio's
house.*

BAL There, do look at the young imp! This under-dish-licker
     of the cook is also a crook already. In fact, I don't know
     what I should be on my guard against first: in my house   895
     there are thieves, next door there's a robber. Well, my
     neighbor, the father of Calidorus, told me in the forum
     a little earlier that I should be on my guard against
     Pseudolus, his slave, and that I shouldn't trust him; that
     he was prowling around today so as to trick me out of the 900
     woman if he could; he said he'd promised him firmly that
     he'd take Phoenicium away from me with his guiles. Now

339

nunc ibo intro atque edicam familiaribus
profecto ne quis quicquam credat Pseudolo.

ACTVS IV

IV. i: PSEVDOLVS. SIMIA

905	PSEV	si umquam quemquam di immortales
905ᵃ		uoluere esse auxilio adiutum,
906		tum me et Calidorum seruatum
906ᵃ		uolunt esse et lenonem exstinctum,
907		quom te adiutorem genuerunt
907ᵃ		mihi tam doctum hominem atque astutum.
908		sed ubi illic est? sumne ego homo insipiens,
908ᵃ		qui haec mecum egomet loquar solus?
909		dedit uerba mihi hercle, ut opinor:
909ᵃ		malus cum malo stulte caui.
910		tum pol ego interii, homo si ille abiit, neque hoc opus
		quod uolui hodie efficiam.
		sed eccum uideo uerberceam statuam: ut it, ut magnu-
		fice infert sese!
		ehem, te hercle ego circumspectabam, nimis metue-
		bam male ne abiisses.
913	SIMI	fuit meum officium ut facerem, fateor.
913ᵃ	PSEV	ubi restiteras?
	SIMI	ubi mi lubitum est.
	PSEV	istuc ego satis scio.
	SIMI	quor ergo quod scis me rogas?
915	PSEV	at hoc uolo monere te.
	SIMI	monendu's ne me moneas.

I'll go in and tell my household members that absolutely no one should trust Pseudolus in anything.

Exeunt BALLIO *and his slave boy into their house.*

ACT FOUR

Enter PSEUDOLUS *from the right, followed at some distance by* SIMIA; *the latter is wearing a military cloak, a hat, and a sword. In the course of the scene they walk to the left of the stage, the harbor entrance.*

PSEU   If the immortal gods ever wanted anyone supported with   905
help, they want me and Calidorus saved and the pimp
exterminated, since they produced you as my supporter,
such a clever and smart fellow. (*looking around*) But
where is he? Aren't I an idiot since I'm talking about this
to myself alone? He's tricked me, I think; crook that I
am, I failed to be on my guard against the crook. I'm   910
dead if he's gone, and I won't succeed in the work I
wanted today. But look, I can see the statue made from
beatings: how he's strutting along, how he's giving him-
self airs! (*to Simia*) Hey, I was looking around for you; I
was very much afraid that you might have given me the
slip.

SIMI   It would have been my duty to do so, I admit it.

PSEU   Where did you stop?

SIMI   Where I wanted to.

PSEU   I know that well enough.

SIMI   Then why do you ask me what you know?

PSEU   But I want to advise you about this.   915

SIMI   You're to be advised not to give me advice.

	PSEV	nimis tandem ego aps te contemnor.

PSEV nimis tandem ego aps te contemnor.

SIMI quippe ego te ni contemnam,
stratioticus homo qui cluear?

919 PSEV iam hoc uolo quod occeptum est agi.

919ᵃ SIMI numquid agere aliud me uides?

920 PSEV ambula ergo cito.

SIMI   immo otiose uolo.

PSEV haec ea occasio est: dum ille dormit, uolo
tu prior ut occupes adire.

923 SIMI quid properas? placide, ne time.

923ᵃ   ita ille faxit Iuppiter,

924   ut ille palam ibidem assiet,

924ᵃ   quisquis ille est qui adest a milite.

925   numquam edepol erit ille potior

925ᵃ   Harpax quam ego. habe animum bonum:
pulchre ego hanc explicatam tibi rem dabo.
sic ego illum dolis atque mendaciis
in timorem dabo militarem aduenam,
ipsus sese ut neget esse eum qui siet

930 meque ut esse autumet qui ipsus est.

PSEV   qui potest?

931 SIMI occidis me quom istuc rogitas.

931ᵃ PSEV o hominem lepidum!

SIMI te quoque etiam dolis atque mendaciis,
qui magister mihi es, antidibo, ut scias.

PSEV Iuppiter te mihi seruet!

SIMI   immo mihi.

935 sed uide, ornatus hic me satin condecet?

935ᵃ PSEV optume habet.

SIMI   esto.

PSEV tantum tibi boni di immortales duint quantum tu tibi
optes;

PSEU I'm really being despised by you.

SIMI Why shouldn't I despise you, I who am a famous military man?

PSEU Now I want what was begun to be done.

SIMI Can you see me doing anything else?

PSEU Then walk quickly.   920

SIMI No, I want to do so at a leisurely pace.

PSEU This is our chance: while that chap's asleep, I want you to be the first to approach him.

SIMI Why are you in a hurry? Slowly, stop being afraid. May great Jupiter bring it about that he's openly present in the same place, whoever it is who's present from the soldier. He'll never be a better Harpax than me. Take   925 heart: I'll set the matter straight for you beautifully. With my tricks and lies I'll put that military arrival in such fear that he himself will deny being the one he is and that   930 he'll claim that I am the one he himself is.

PSEU How is that possible?

SIMI You're killing me by asking that.

PSEU What a charming chap!

SIMI You too, who are my teacher, I'll surpass with my tricks and lies, just so that you know.

PSEU May Jupiter preserve you for myself!

SIMI No, for myself. But look, does this get-up suit me well   935 enough?

PSEU It fits perfectly.

SIMI Excellent.

PSEU May the immortal gods give you as much good as you

		nam si exoptem quantum dignu's tantum dent, minus nihilo sit.
938		neque ego hoc hominem quemquam uidi magis malum et maleficum.
938ᵃ	SIMI	tun id mi?
	PSEV	taceo.
939		sed ego quae tibi bona dabo et faciam,
939ᵃ		si hanc sobrie rem accurassis!
940	SIMI	potin ut taceas? memorem immemorem facit qui mo-net quod memor meminit.

teneo omnia, in pectore condita sunt, meditati sunt
mihi doli docte.

PSEV probus est hic homo.
SIMI neque hic est neque ego.
PSEV at uide ne titubes.
SIMI potin ut taceas?
PSEV ita me di ament—
SIMI ita non facient: mera iam mendacia fundes.
PSEV —ut ego ob tuam, Simia, perfidiam te amo et metuo et
magni facio.
945 SIMI ego istuc aliis dare condidici: mi optrudere non potes
palpum.
PSEV ut ego accipiam te hodie lepide, ubi effeceris hoc opus.
SIMI hahahae!
PSEV lepido uictu, uino, unguentis, et inter pocula
pulpamentis;
ibidem una aderit mulier lepida tibi sauia super sauia
quae det.
SIMI lepide accipis me.
PSEV immo si efficis, tum faxo magis dicas.

943 fundes *P*, fundis *A*

344

wish for yourself: if I were to wish that they should give you as much as you deserve, it would be less than nothing. I've never seen anyone worse and more wicked.

SIMI Are *you* saying that to me?

PSEU I'm quiet. But what good things I'll give you and do for you if you sort this out soberly!

SIMI Can't you be quiet? A man who reminds another about   940
what that man remembers well makes the man remembering it forgetful. I've got it all, it's stored in my breast, my schemes have been thought over cleverly.

PSEU (*indicating Simia*) This is a decent fellow.

SIMI (*pointing back at Pseudolus*) He isn't, nor am I.

PSEU But make sure you don't stumble.

SIMI Can't you be quiet?

PSEU As truly as the gods may love me—

SIMI (*interrupting*) Truly, they won't do so: you're now pouring out pure lies.

PSEU —as I love you for your perfidy, Simia, and respect and honor you.

SIMI I've learned to give that sort of flattery to others: you   945
can't pat me on the head.

PSEU What a charming reception I'll give you today when you've accomplished this business!

SIMI Hahaha!

PSEU With lovely food, wine, and perfumes, and with tidbits between the cups; and in the same place there will be a charming lady with you, who'll give you kisses upon kisses.

SIMI You're giving me a charming reception.

PSEU No, if you accomplish it, then I'll make sure you'll say so even more.

950	SIMI	nisi effecero, cruciabiliter
950ᵃ		carnufex me accipito.
951		sed propera mi monstrare ubi sit os lenonis aedium.
	PSEV	tertium hoc est.
	SIMI	st! tace, aedes hiscunt.
	PSEV	credo, animo male est
		aedibus.
	SIMI	quid iam?
	PSEV	quia edepol ipsum lenonem euomunt.
	SIMI	illicine est?
	PSEV	illic est.
	SIMI	mala merx est, ‹Pseudole›. illuc sis uide,
955		ut transuorsus, non prouorsus cedit, quasi cancer solet.

IV. ii: BALLIO. PSEVDOLVS. SIMIA

	BAL	minus malum hunc hominem esse opinor quam esse
		censebam coquom,
		nam nil etiam dum harpagauit praeter cyathum et can-
		tharum.
	PSEV	heus tu, nunc occasio est et tempus.
	SIMI	tecum sentio.
	PSEV	ingredere in uiam dolose: ego hic in insidiis ero.
960	SIMI	habui numerum sedulo: hoc est sextum a porta proxu-
		mum
		angiportum, in id angiportum me deuorti iusserat;
		quotumas aedis dixerit, id ego admodum incerto scio.
	BAL	quis hic homo chlamydatus est aut unde est aut quem
		quaeritat?
		peregrina facies uidetur hominis atque ignobilis.

954 mercist *P*, merx est *Pius*   Pseudole *add. Bothe*
962 incerto *P*, incerte *A*

346

SIMI Unless I accomplish it, the hangman can give me a re- 950
ception with torture. But make haste to show me where
the mouth of the pimp's house is.

PSEU The third one here.

SIMI Hush! Be quiet, the house is gaping.

PSEU I believe the house is feeling sick.

SIMI How so?

PSEU Because it's vomiting out the pimp himself. (*the door
opens and Ballio appears, keeping an eye on what is go-
ing on inside*)

SIMI Is that him?

PSEU Yes, it is.

SIMI He's a bad piece, Pseudolus. Do look at that, how he 955
walks sideways, not forward, like a crab. (*they go away a
little so that the pimp will not see them*)

Enter BALLIO from his house.

BAL I think that this cook is not such a bad man as I thought:
he hasn't stolen anything yet apart from a ladle and a
tankard.

PSEU (*to Simia*) Hey you, now is the chance and time.

SIMI I agree with you.

PSEU Enter the street with guile; I'll stay here out of sight.

SIMI (*apparently to himself while coming forward*) I've kept 960
count of the number diligently: this is the sixth alley from
the gate, and into this alley he told me to turn; but I'm
not entirely sure what number he said the house was.

BAL (*aside*) Who is that man in a cloak, or where is he from,
or who is he looking for? The man's face seems foreign
and unknown.

965	SIMI	sed eccum qui ex incerto faciet mihi quod quaero certius.
	BAL	ad me adit recta. unde ego hominem hunc esse dicam gentium?
	SIMI	heus tu qui cum hirquina barba stas, responde quod rogo.
	BAL	eho, an non prius salutas?
	SIMI	nulla est mihi salus dataria.
969–70	BAL	nam pol hinc tantundem accipies.
	PSEV	iam inde a principio probe.
	SIMI	ecquem in angiporto hoc hominem tu nouisti? te rogo.
	BAL	egomet me.
	SIMI	pauci istuc faciunt homines quod tu praedicas, nam in foro uix decumus quisque est qui ipsus sese nouerit.
	PSEV	saluos sum, iam philosophatur.
	SIMI	hominem ego hic quaero malum,
975		legerupam, impurum, periurum atque impium.
	BAL	me quaeritat, nam illa mea sunt cognomenta; nomen si memoret modo. quid est ei homini nomen?
	SIMI	leno Ballio.
	BAL	sciuin ego? ipse ego is sum, adulescens, quem tu quaeris.
	SIMI	tun es Ballio?
979–80	BAL	ego enim uero is sum.
	SIMI	ut uestitu's, es perfossor parietum.
	BAL	credo, in tenebris, conspicatus si sis me, apstineas manum.

975 impurum . . . impium A, impium . . . improbum P
978 quaeris A, quaeritas P

348

SIMI (*spotting Ballio*) But look, someone who can make what   965
      I'm looking for more certain from less certain.

BAL   (*aside*) He's coming straight to me. Where on earth
      should I say he's from?

SIMI Hey, you, the one standing around with a goat's beard,
      answer my question.

BAL   Oho! Aren't you greeting me first?

SIMI I have no greeting to give away.

BAL   You'll get the same back from me.   970

PSEU (*aside*) Proper right from the start!

SIMI Do you know anyone in this alley? I'm asking you.

BAL   I know myself.

SIMI Few people do what you say: in the forum there's hardly
      one in ten who knows himself.

PSEU (*aside*) I'm safe, he's already philosophizing.

SIMI I'm looking for a bad chap here, a lawbreaker, a filthy,   975
      perjured, and godless creature.

BAL   (*aside*) He's looking for me: those are my epithets; if only
      he were to say my name. (*aloud*) What's the name of that
      chap?

SIMI Pimp Ballio.

BAL   (*aside*) Didn't I know it? (*aloud*) I myself am the chap
      you're looking for, young man.

SIMI Are you Ballio?

BAL   Yes, I am indeed.   980

SIMI The way you're dressed, you're a burglar.

BAL   No doubt you'd keep your hands off me if you saw me in
      the dark.[48]

---

[48] For Greeks the two main categories of criminals were house-
breakers (*toikhorukhoi*) and muggers (*lopodutai*). Simia accuses Ballio
of being one of the former, and Ballio retorts that Simia is one of the
latter.

SIMI   erus meus tibi me salutem multam uoluit dicere.

         hanc epistulam accipe a me, hanc me tibi iussit dare.

BAL   quis is homo est qui iussit?

PSEV   perii! nunc homo in medio luto est;

985   nomen nescit, haeret haec res.

BAL   quem hanc misisse ad me autumas?

SIMI   nosce imaginem: tute eius nomen memorato mihi,

         ut sciam te Ballionem esse ipsum.

BAL   cedo mi epistulam.

SIMI   accipe et cognosce signum.

BAL   oh! Polymachaeroplagides

         purus putus est ipsus. noui. heus! Polymachaeroplagidi

990   nomen est.

SIMI   scio iam me recte tibi dedisse epistulam,

         postquam Polymachaeroplagidem elocutus nomen es.

BAL   quid agit is?

SIMI   quod homo edepol fortis atque bellator probus.

         sed propera hanc pellegere quaeso epistulam—ita ne-

            gotium est—

         atque accipere argentum actutum mulieremque emit-

            tere.

995   nam hodie Sicyoni necesse est me esse aut cras mor-

            tem exsequi,

         ita erus meus est imperiosus.

BAL   noui, notis praedicas.

SIMI   propera pellegere epistulam ergo.

BAL   id ago, si taceas modo.

---

991 Polymachaeroplagidem *AB*, Polymachaeroplagidae *CD*

995 necesse est hodie Sicyoni Ω, *transp. Ritschl*

997 pellegere epistulam ergo Ω, legere ep. ergo *Guyet*, pell. ergo
ep. *Bothe*

SIMI   My master wanted me to give you his warm greetings. (*producing the letter*) Take this letter from me, he told me to give it to you.

BAL   Who is the man who told you to do so?

PSEU   (*aside*) I'm dead! Now he's deep in the mud; he doesn't 985
know the name, our business is stuck.

BAL   Who do you say sent this to me?

SIMI   See if you know the picture; you yourself must tell me his name so that I may know that you are Ballio in person.

BAL   Give me the letter.

SIMI   Take it and see if you know the seal. (*hands it over*)

BAL   (*half aside*) Oh! It's Polymachaeroplagides himself, pure and simple. I know him. (*to Simia*) Hey! Polymachaeroplagides is his name. 990

SIMI   Now I know that it was right to give you the letter, now that you've said the name Polymachaeroplagides.

BAL   What is he up to?

SIMI   The deeds of a brave man and noble warrior. But please be quick to read through this letter—I'm in a hurry—and to receive the money instantly and to send out the girl: I need to be in Sicyon today[49] or die tomorrow, that's 995
how domineering my master is.

BAL   I know, you're telling those who are well informed.

SIMI   Then be quick to read through the letter.

BAL   That's what I'm doing, if only you were quiet. "The sol-

---

[49] This is hardly possible, as it is seventy miles from Athens to Sicyon. The real Harpax says in l. 1174 that the journey took him one and a half days.

"miles lenoni Ballioni epistulam
conscriptam mittit Polymachaeroplagides,
1000 imagine opsignatam quae inter nos duo
conuenit olim."
SIMI   symbolust in epistula.
BAL uideo et cognosco signum. sed in epistula
nullam salutem mittere scriptam solet?
SIMI ita militaris disciplina est, Ballio:
1005 manu salutem mittunt bene uolentibus;
eadem malam rem mittunt male uolentibus.
sed ut occepisti, perge opera experirier
quid epistula ista narret.
BAL   ausculta modo.
"Harpax calator meus est, ad te qui uenit—"
1010 tun es is Harpax?
SIMI   ego sum atque ipse ἅρπαξ quidem.
BAL "—qui epistulam istam fert; ab eo argentum accipe;
cum eo simitu mulierem mitti uolo.
salutem scriptam dignum est dignis mittere:
te si arbitrarem dignum, misissem tibi."
1015 SIMI quid nunc?
BAL   argentum des, abducas mulierem.
SIMI uter remoratur?
BAL   quin sequere ergo intro.
SIMI   sequor.

IV. iii: PSEVDOLVS

PSEV peiorem ego hominem magisque uorsute malum
numquam edepol quemquam uidi quam hic est Simia;
nimisque ego illum hominem metuo et formido male
1020 ne malus item erga me sit ut erga illum fuit,
ne in re secunda nunc mi obuortat cornua,

352

dier Polymachaeroplagides is sending this written letter
to the pimp Ballio, sealed with the picture that was once   1000
agreed upon among the two of us."

SIMI   The token is on the letter.

BAL   I can see the token and recognize it. But does he have
the habit of not sending any written wish for well-being
in his letters?

SIMI   That's the custom in the army, Ballio: with their hands   1005
they give well-being to those who wish them well; with
the same hands they give a thrashing to those who wish
them ill. But as you've begun, continue to make an effort
to find out what that letter tells you.

BAL   Just listen. "Harpax is my batman who has come to
you—" Are you that Harpax?   1010

SIMI   I am, and a very harpy indeed.

BAL   "—and who's brought you that letter. Take the money
from him; I want the woman to be sent together with
him. It's right to send good wishes in writing to those who
deserve them; if I thought you deserved them, I'd have
sent them to you."

SIMI   Well then?   1015

BAL   Give me the money and take the woman away.

SIMI   Which of us is delaying?

BAL   Then follow me in.

SIMI   Yes.

Exeunt BALLIO *and* SIMIA *into the former's house.*

PSEU   I've never seen a worse man and bad in a more wicked
way than this Simia is; and I'm terribly afraid and scared   1020
that he could be bad to me in the same way he was bad
to that chap, and that he might turn his horns against me

si occasionem capsit qui ⟨sic⟩ sit malus;
atque edepol equidem nolo, nam illi bene uolo.

1024–
25

nunc in metu sum maxumo triplici modo:
primum omnium iam hunc comparem metuo meum
ne deserat me atque ad hostis transeat;
metuo autem ne erus redeat etiam dum a foro,
ne capta praeda capti praedones fuant.

1030

quom haec metuo, metuo ne ille huc Harpax aduenat
prius quam hinc hic Harpax abierit cum muliere.
perii hercle! nimium tarde egrediuntur foras.
cor colligatis uasis exspectat meum,

1034–
35

si non educat mulierem secum simul,
ut exulatum ex pectore aufugiat meo.
uictor sum, uici cautos custodes meos.

IV. iv: SIMIA. PSEVDOLVS

SIMI ne plora, nescis ut res sit, Phoenicium,
uerum hau multo post faxo scibis accubans.

1040

non ego te ad illum duco dentatum uirum
Macedoniensem, qui te nunc flentem facit:
quoiam esse te uis maxume, ad eum ducere:
Calidorum hau multo post faxo amplexabere.

PSEV quid tu intus quaeso desedisti tam diu?

1045

mihi cor retunsum est oppugnando pectore.

SIMI occasionem repperisti, uerbero,
ubi perconteris me, insidiis hostilibus?
quin hinc metimur gradibus militariis?

1022 ceperit capsti *P*, capsit *Camerarius*   sic *add. Karsten*

now in his success, if he gets an opportunity to be bad
like this. And I for one don't want it, as I'm well disposed
to him. Now I'm in greatest fear in a threefold way: first   1025
of all I'm afraid now that this comrade of mine could
desert me and go over to the enemy; but I'm also afraid
that my master might return from the forum now and
that the robbers will themselves be caught after catching
their booty. And while I fear this, I fear that the real   1030
Harpax might come here before my Harpax has left with
the woman. I'm dead! They're coming out far too slowly.
My heart is waiting with its baggage tied up so that if he   1035
doesn't take the woman out with him at the same time,
it may flee out of my chest into exile. (*as the door opens*)
I'm the winner! I've won over my wary warders!

Enter SIMIA *from the pimp's house, followed by Phoenicium.*

SIMI Stop crying, you don't know what the situation is, Phoe-
nicium; but I'll make sure you'll find out soon while re-
clining at table. I'm not taking you to that saber-toothed   1040
Macedonian who is now making you cry; you're being
brought to the man to whom you most want to belong.
I'll make sure you'll embrace Calidorus in a little while.
PSEU Please, why did you sit inside for so long, doing nothing?   1045
My heart is bruised from battering at my ribs.
SIMIA You whipping stock, did you find an opportunity to ques-
tion me while we're surrounded by the enemy? Why
don't we get away at the quick march?

1042 duco te *P*, ducere *Ussing*
1044 quam *P*, tam *Acidalius*

1049–50 PSEV   atque edepol, quamquam nequam homo es, recte
        mones.
        ite hac triumphi ad cantharum recta uia.

IV. v: BALLIO

BAL   hahae! nunc demum mi animus in tuto loco est
        postquam iste hinc abiit atque abduxit mulierem.
        iube nunc uenire Pseudolum, scelerum caput,
1055   et abducere a me mulierem fallaciis.
        conceptis hercle uerbis, satis certo scio,
        ego periurare me mauellem miliens
        quam mi illum uerba per deridiculum dare.
        nunc deridebo hercle hominem, si conuenero;
1060   uerum in pistrino credo, ut conuenit, fore.
        nunc ego Simonem mi obuiam ueniat uelim,
        ut mea laetitia laetus promiscam siet.

IV. vi: SIMO. BALLIO

SIMO   uiso quid rerum meus Vlixes egerit,
        iamne habeat signum ex arce Ballionia.
1065 BAL   o fortunate, cedo fortunatam manum,
        [Simo].
SIMO   quid est?
BAL   iam—
SIMO   quid iam?
BAL   nihil est quod metuas.
SIMO   quid est?
        uenitne homo ad te?
BAL   non.
SIMO   quid est igitur boni?
BAL   minae uiginti sanae et saluae sunt tibi,
        hodie quas aps te est instipulatus Pseudolus.

1051 triumphi *P*, triumphe *A*   1066 Simo *del. Bentley*

PSEU Yes, even though you're a rascal, you give sound advice. 1050
      You two, go directly this way to the celebratory drink.

Exeunt PSEUDOLUS, SIMIA, *and Phoenicium to the right.*
Enter BALLIO *from his house.*

BAL   Haha! Now at last I can relax since that chap has left and
      taken the woman away. Now let Pseudolus come, the
      fount of iniquity, and take her away from me with his 1055
      tricks. I know quite for sure, I'd rather perjure myself
      with solemn words a thousand times over than let him
      make a laughingstock of me. Now I'll make fun of him if
      I meet him; but I believe he'll be in the mill, as was 1060
      agreed. Now I'd like Simo to come my way so that he
      may be equally joyful on account of my joy.

Enter SIMO *from the right.*

SIMO I'm checking what my Ulysses has been up to, whether
      he already has the image from the Ballionian citadel.[50]
BAL   O lucky man, give me your lucky hand.   1065
SIMO What's the matter?
BAL   Now—
SIMO (*interrupting*) What now?
BAL   There's nothing for you to be afraid of.
SIMO What's that? Has he come to you?
BAL   No.
SIMO Then what good news do you have?
BAL   The twenty minas of yours which Pseudolus undertook
      to get from you today are safe and sound.

[50] Ulysses, together with Palamedes, stole the Palladium from Troy,
an image of Pallas Athene that kept the city safe.

1070	SIMO	uelim quidem hercle.
	BAL	roga me uiginti minas,
		si illic hodie illa sit potitus muliere
		siue eam tuo gnato hodie, ut promisit, dabit.
		roga, opsecro hercle; gestio promittere,
		omnibus modis tibi esse rem ut saluam scias;
1075		atque etiam habeto mulierem dono tibi.
	SIMO	nullum est periclum, quod sciam, stipularier,
		ut concepisti uerba: uiginti minas
		dabin?
	BAL	dabuntur.
	SIMO	hoc quidem actum est hau male.
		sed conuenistin hominem?
	BAL	immo ambo simul.
1080	SIMO	quid ait? quid narrat? quaeso, quid dicit tibi?
	BAL	nugas theatri, uerba quae in comoediis
		solent lenoni dici, quae pueri sciunt:
		malum et scelestum et periurum aibat esse me.
	SIMO	pol hau mentitust.
	BAL	ergo haud iratus fui:
1085		nam quanti refert te ei nec recte dicere
		qui nihili faciat quique infitias non eat?
	SIMO	quid est? quid non metuam ab eo? id audire expeto.
	BAL	quia numquam abducet mulierem iam, nec potest,
		a me. meministin tibi me dudum dicere
1090		eam ueniisse militi Macedonio?
	SIMO	memini.
	BAL	em illius seruos huc ad me argentum attulit
		et opsignatum symbolum—

1071 ille Ω, illic *Lindsay in apparatu*

SIMO I hope so.   1070

BAL   Ask for twenty minas from me in case he's got hold of
      that woman today or in case he'll give her to your son
      today as he promised.[51] Please ask for them; I'm keen
      to promise, so that you may know absolutely that your
      money is safe; and you can also have the woman as a   1075
      present.

SIMO As far as I know there's no risk in making a stipula-
      tion the way that you've set the words. Will you give me
      twenty minas?

BAL   Yes, they will be given.

SIMO That's all okay. But have you met him?

BAL   Yes, in fact both at the same time.

SIMO What does he say? What's his story? Please, what did he   1080
      tell you?

BAL   Stage rubbish, the words which are normally said to a
      pimp in comedies and which even children know: he said
      that I'm a crook and a criminal and a perjurer.

SIMO He didn't lie.

BAL   That's why I wasn't angry: well, what advantage is there 1085
      in speaking abusively to a man who thinks nothing of it
      and doesn't deny the charge?

SIMO Well then? Why shouldn't I be afraid of him? That's what
      I'm keen to hear.

BAL   Because he'll never take the woman away from me now,
      and he can't. Do you remember me telling you a while
      ago that she'd been sold to a Macedonian soldier?   1090

SIMO Yes.

BAL   Well, his slave brought the money here to me, and the
      sealed token—

---

[51] Another *stipulatio*.

SIMO   quid postea?

BAL   —qui inter me atque illum militem conuenerat:
      is secum abduxit mulierem hau multo prius.

1095 SIMO bonan fide istuc dicis?

BAL   unde ea sit mihi?

SIMO uide modo ne illic sit contechinatus quippiam.

BAL   epistula atque imago me certum facit;
      quin illam [quidem iam] in Sicyonem ex urbe abduxit
         modo.

SIMO bene hercle factum! quid ego cesso Pseudolum
1100   facere ut det nomen ad Molas coloniam?
     sed quis hic homo est chlamydatus?

BAL   non edepol scio,
      nisi ut opseruemus quo eat aut quam rem gerat.

IV. vii: HARPAX. BALLIO. SIMO

HAR malus et nequam est homo qui nihili eri imperium sui
         seruos facit,
     nihili est autem suom qui officium facere immemor est
         nisi est ammonitus.
1105   nam qui liberos [esse] ilico se arbitrantur,
     ex conspectu eri si sui se abdiderunt,
     luxantur, lustrantur, comedunt quod habent, i nomen
         diu
     seruitutis ferunt.
     nec boni ingeni quicquam in is inest,
1110   nisi ut improbis se artibus teneant.
     cum his mihi nec locus nec sermo
     conuenit neque is umquam nobilis fui.
     ego, ut mi imperatum est, etsi abest, hic adesse erum
         arbitror.
     nunc ego illum metuo, quom hic non adest,

PSEUDOLUS

SIMO (*interrupting*) What then?

BAL —which had been agreed on between me and that sol-
dier; he took the woman away with him not long ago.

SIMO Are you saying that in good faith? 1095

BAL Where should I have that from?

SIMO Just check that he hasn't plotted something.

BAL The letter and picture give me certainty; what's more,
he's already taken her out of the city to Sicyon.

SIMO Excellent! Why am I hesitating to make Pseudolus give 1100
in his name for joining the colony "the Mills"? (*looks
around*) But who is that chap with a cloak?

BAL I really don't know, but let's watch where he's going or
what he's up to.

Enter HARPAX *from the left.*

HAR (*to the audience*) A slave who thinks nothing of his mas-
ter's command is bad and useless, but someone who is
forgetful in doing his duty unless he's reminded is worth-
less. Yes, those who immediately consider themselves 1105
free if they've removed themselves from their master's
eyes, and revel, go wenching, and eat up what they have,
those carry the name of slavery for long. They don't have
a fragment of honest disposition in them, unless it be the 1110
disposition of supporting themselves by shameless de-
vices. I don't approve of consorting or conversing with
them and I've never been known to them. When I'm
given an order, I consider my master to be present, even
if he's away. Now I'm afraid of him, while he's not here,

1098 quidem iam *del. Leo*   adduxit *P*, abduxit ç
1105 esse *del. Guyet*   1112 umquam *del. Lindsay*

361

1115	ne quom assit metuam. ei rei operam dabo.
	nam in taberna usque adhuc, si ueniret Syrus,
	quoi dedi symbolum, mansi, uti iusserat:
	leno ubi esset domi, me aibat arcessere;
	uerum ubi is non uenit nec uocat,
1120	uenio huc ultro, ut sciam quid rei sit,
1120ᵃ	ne illic homo me ludificetur.
1121	nec quicquam est melius quam ut hoc pul—
1121ᵃ	tem atque aliquem euocem hinc intus. le—
1122	no argentum hoc uo—
1123	lo a me accipiat atque amittat
1123ᵃ	mulierem mecum simul.

BAL heus tu!

SIMO   quid uis?

BAL   hic homo meus est.

SIMO   quidum?

BAL   quia praeda haec mea est:

1125   scortum quaerit, habet argentum. iam ammordere
      hunc mi lubet.

SIMO iamne illum comesurus es?

BAL   dum recens est,
  [dum] dator, dum calet, deuorari decet iam.
  boni me uiri pauperant, improbi augent;
  populo strenui, mi improbi usui sunt.

1130 SIMO malum quod tibi di dabunt; sic scelestu's.

1131 HAR me nunc commoror, quom has fores non ferio, ut sciam
1131ᵃ   sitne Ballio domi.

1132 BAL Venus mi haec bona dat, quom hos huc adigit
1133   lucrifugas, damnicupidos, qui
1133ᵃ   se suamque aetatem bene curant,

1117 ut *P*, uti *Bentley*

362

so that I won't be afraid of him while he is here. I'll at- 1115
tend to this. Well, as Syrus, to whom I gave the token,
had told me to, I've waited in the inn up until now for
him to come. He said he'd fetch me when the pimp was
at home. But since he's neither coming nor calling me,
I'm taking the initiative in coming here in order to find 1120
out what's the matter, so that that chap won't make a fool
of me. There's no better plan than to knock here and call
someone out. I want the pimp to receive this money from
me and to send the woman off together with me.

BAL (*to Simo*) Hey you!

SIMO What do you want?

BAL This chap belongs to me.

SIMO How so?

BAL Because this is my booty; he's looking for a prostitute and 1125
has money. Now I'd like to get my teeth into him.

SIMO Will you eat him up at once?

BAL He must be served up while he's fresh, while he's warm
he ought to be swallowed instantly. Good men make me
poorer, bad men make me richer. Energetic men are
valuable for the people, but bad men are valuable for
me.

SIMO The gods will give you some trouble, you're such a crim- 1130
inal.

HAR (*to himself*) Now I'm wasting my time by not knocking
at this door in order to find out if Ballio is at home.

BAL (*still to Simo*) Venus is giving me these good things when
she's driving these people here who shun profit and seek
loss, who look well after themselves and their youthful

1127 dum datur dum calet *P*, dum calet dum datur *A*, dator dum
calet *Leo*   1132 dat quum *A*, dat atquom *B*, dat at cum *CD*

1134		edunt, bibunt, scortantur: illi
1134ª		sunt alio ingenio atque tu,
1135		qui nec tibi bene esse patere et illis quibus est inuides.
	HAR	heus ubi estis uos?
	BAL	hic quidem ad me recta habet rectam uiam.
	HAR	heus ubi estis uos?
	BAL	heus adulescens, quid istic debetur tibi?
		bene ego ab hoc praedatus ibo; noui, bona scaeua est mihi.
	HAR	ecquis hoc aperit?
	BAL	heus chlamydate, quid istic debetur tibi?
1140	HAR	aedium dominum lenonem Ballionem quaerito.
	BAL	quisquis es, adulescens, operam fac compendi quaerere.
	HAR	quid iam?
	BAL	quia tute ipsus ipsum praesens praesentem uides.
	HAR	tun is es?
	SIMO	chlamydate, caue sis tibi a curuo infortunio
		atque in hunc intende digitum: hic leno est.
	BAL	at hic est uir bonus.
1145		sed tu, bone uir, flagitare saepe clamore in foro,
		quom libella nusquam est, nisi quid leno hic subuenit tibi.
	HAR	quin tu mecum fabulare?
	BAL	fabulor. quid uis tibi?
	HAR	argentum accipias.
	BAL	iamdudum, si des, porrexi manum.
	HAR	accipe: hic sunt quinque argenti lectae numeratae minae.
1150		hoc tibi erus me iussit ferre Polymachaeroplagides,
		quod deberet, atque ut mecum mitteres Phoenicium.

1142 ipsum *A*, coram *P*   1144 bonus *A*, probus *P*

desires, who eat, drink, and wench. Those have a different character from you; you can't bear having a good 1135
time yourself and are jealous of those who do.

HAR (*knocking at the door*) Hey, where are you folks?

BAL (*to Simo*) He's coming directly to my place.

HAR (*still knocking*) Hey, where are you folks?

BAL Hey, young man! What are you owed in that place?
(*aside*) I'll go away from him well supplied with booty. I
know it, I have a good omen.

HAR (*still knocking*) Won't anyone open this door?

BAL Hey, you there with a cloak, what are you owed there?

HAR I'm looking for the master of the house, pimp Ballio. 1140

BAL Whoever you are, young man, spare yourself the trouble
of looking.

HAR Why?

BAL Because you can see him face-to-face.

HAR (*to Simo*) Are you him?

SIMO You there with a cloak, do watch out for curved trouble
(*lifts up his crooked stick*) and point the finger at him: he
is the pimp.

BAL (*also to Harpax*) But he is the good man. (*to Simo*) But 1145
you, good man, often get dunned loudly in the forum,
when you don't have a farthing anywhere, unless this
pimp comes to your assistance.

HAR (*to Ballio*) Why aren't you talking with me?

BAL I am. What do you want now?

HAR Take the money. (*produces the wallet*)

BAL I've been holding my hand out for a long time, waiting
if you give it to me.

HAR Take it. (*hands it over*) Here there are five picked and
counted silver minas. My master Polymachaeroplagides 1150
told me to bring you this, his debt, and you were to send
Phoenicium with me.

BAL	erus tuos?
HAR	ita dico.
BAL	miles?
HAR	ita loquor.
BAL	Macedonius?
HAR	admodum, inquam.
BAL	te ad me misit Polymachaeroplagides?
HAR	uera memoras.
BAL	hoc argentum ut mihi dares?
HAR	si tu quidem es

1155   leno Ballio.

BAL	atque ut a me mulierem tu abduceres?
HAR	ita.
BAL	Phoenicium esse dixit?
HAR	recte meministi.
BAL	mane:

iam redeo ad te.

HAR	at maturate propera, nam propero: uides

iam diem multum esse?

BAL	uideo: hunc aduocare etiam uolo;

mane modo istic, iam reuortar ad te. quid nunc fit,
    Simo?

1160   quid agimus? manufesto hunc hominem teneo qui ar-
    gentum attulit.

SIMO	quidum?
BAL	an nescis quae sit haec res?
SIMO	iuxta cum ignarissumis.
BAL	Pseudolus tuos allegauit hunc, quasi a Macedonio

milite esset.

SIMO	haben argentum ab homine?
BAL	rogitas quod uides?

BAL   Your master?

HAR   That's what I'm saying.

BAL   The soldier?

HAR   That's what I'm stating.

BAL   From Macedonia?

HAR   Yes, I say.

BAL   Polymachaeroplagides has sent you to me?

HAR   You speak the truth.

BAL   So that you would give me this money?

HAR   If indeed you are pimp Ballio.   1155

BAL   And so that you would take the woman away from me?

HAR   Yes.

BAL   He said it's Phoenicium?

HAR   You remember it correctly.

BAL   Wait; I'll return to you in a second.

HAR   But hurry fast, as I'm in a hurry: can you see that it's already late in the day?

BAL   Yes. I still want to call this chap in as a counselor. Just wait there, I'll get back to you in a second. (*to Simo*) What's happening now, Simo? What are we to do? I've   1160 caught the chap who's brought the money red-handed.

SIMO   How so?

BAL   Don't you know what this is?

SIMO   Those who are absolutely in the dark know as much about it as I do.

BAL   Your Pseudolus has commissioned him to pretend to be from the Macedonian soldier.

SIMO   Do you have the money from the chap?

BAL   You ask what you can see?

1159 fiet *P*, fit *Bentley*

SIMO   heus, memento ergo dimidium istinc mihi de praeda
        dare:

1165   commune istuc esse oportet.

BAL   quid, malum? id totum tuom est.

HAR   quam mox mi operam das?

BAL   tibi do equidem. quid nunc mi es auctor, Simo?

SIMO   exploratorem hunc faciamus ludos suppositicium
        adeo donicum ipsus sese ludos fieri senserit.

BAL   sequere. quid ais? nemp' tu illius seruos es?

HAR   planissume.

1170 BAL   quanti te emit?

HAR   suarum in pugna uirium uictoria.
        nam ego eram domi imperator summus in patria mea.

BAL   an etiam umquam ille expugnauit carcerem, patriam
        tuam?

HAR   contumeliam si dices, audies.

BAL   quotumo die
        ex Sicyone huc peruenisti?

HAR   altero ad meridiem.

1175 BAL   strenue mehercle iisti.

SIMO   quam uis pernix hic est homo:
        ubi suram aspicias, scias posse eum . . . gerere crassas
          compedis.

BAL   quid ais? tune etiam cubitare solitu's in cunis puer?

SIMO   scilicet.

BAL   etiamne facere solitus es—scin quid loquar?

SIMO   scilicet solitum esse.

HAR   sanin estis?

    1172 umquam ille *P*, ille umquam *A*
    1175 quam uis pernix hic est homo *P*, quam uelis pernix homo
est *A*

SIMO   Hey, then remember to give me half of the booty; it   1165
ought to be shared.

BAL   What, damn it? It belongs entirely to you.

HAR   (*calling Ballio back*) How long before you give me your
attention?

BAL   (*to Harpax*) I for one am already giving it to you. (*to
Simo*) What do you advise me to do now, Simo?

SIMO   Let's make fun of this pretend spy till he himself realizes
he's being made fun of.

BAL   (*to Simo*) Follow me. (*to Harpax*) What do you say?
You're his slave, aren't you?

HAR   Obviously.

BAL   How much did he buy you for?   1170

HAR   For the victory of his armed forces in battle: I was the
top commander at home in my country.

BAL   He also conquered prison, your own country, did he?

HAR   If you utter an insult, you'll hear one.

BAL   After how many days did you arrive here from Sicyon?

HAR   On the second day at midday.

BAL   You really walked energetically.   1175

SIMO   He's as speedy as you like. If only you saw his calves,
you'd know that he can . . . wear heavy shackles.

BAL   (*to Harpax*) What do you say? Were you also used to
lying in a cradle as a baby?

SIMO   Of course.

BAL   (*still to Harpax*) Were you also used to doing—do you
know what I'm saying?[52]

SIMO   Of course he was used to it.

HAR   Are you two in your right mind?

---

[52] Veiled reference to masturbation.

BAL   quid hoc quod te rogo?
1180   noctu in uigiliam quando ibat miles, quom tu ibas simul,
       conueniebatne in uaginam tuam machaera militis?
HAR i in malam crucem.
BAL   ir' licebit tamen tibi hodie temperi.
HAR quin tu mulierem mi emittis? aut redde argentum.
BAL   mane.
HAR quid maneam?
BAL   chlamydem hanc commemora quanti conducta est.
HAR   quid est?
1185 SIMO quid meret machaera?
HAR   elleborum hisce hominibus opus est.
BAL   eho!
HAR mitte.
BAL   quid mercedis petasus hodie domino demeret?
HAR quid? "domino"? quid somniatis? mea quidem haec habeo omnia,
    meo peculio empta.
BAL   nemp' quod femina summa sustinent.
1189–90 HAR uncti hi sunt senes, fricari sese ex antiquo uolunt.
BAL responde, opsecro hercle, hoc uero serio quod te rogo:
    quid meres? quantillo argenti te conduxit Pseudolus?
HAR quis istic Pseudolust?
BAL   praeceptor tuos, qui te hanc fallaciam
    docuit, ut fallaciis hinc mulierem a me abduceres.

1182 tamen tibi *A*, tibi tamen *P*
1192 argenti te *CD*, argenti ote *B*, argento te *Camerarius*

---

53 Ridiculous metaphor for anal intercourse.

BAL   What about what I ask you? When the soldier went to   1180
keep watch at night and you were going with him, did
the soldier's sword fit into your scabbard?[53]

HAR   Go and be hanged.

BAL   No, you will have the opportunity to go and be hanged
in good time today.

HAR   Why don't you send out the woman to me? Or return the
money.

BAL   Wait.

HAR   What should I wait for?

BAL   Tell me how much this cloak was hired for.

HAR   What's that?

SIMO What's the sword worth?   1185

HAR   These people need hellebore![54]

BAL   (grabbing him) Hey!

HAR   Let go!

BAL   What pay does the hat earn for its owner today?

HAR   What? "Its owner"? What are you two dreaming about?
I own all these things, they were bought from my private
means.

BAL   Yes, the ones supported by the tops of your thighs.

HAR   These old men are oiled, they want to get a good old-   1190
fashioned rubdown.[55]

BAL   Please answer me in truth and seriously what I ask you:
what do you earn? For how little money did Pseudolus
hire you?

HAR   Who is that Pseudolus?

BAL   Your instructor, the one who taught you this trick, so that
you'd take the woman away from me with tricks.

[54] A plant supposed to cure some types of madness.
[55] Also a euphemism for a beating.

PLAUTUS

1195	HAR	quem tu Pseudolum, quas tu mi praedicas fallacias,
		quem ego hominem nullius coloris noui?
	BAL	non tu istinc abis?
		nihil est hodie hic sycophantis quaestus: proin tu Pseudolo
		nunties abduxisse alium praedam, qui occurrit prior Harpax.
	HAR	is quidem edepol Harpax ego sum.
	BAL	immo edepol esse uis.
1200		purus putus hic sycophanta est.
	HAR	ego tibi argentum dedi
		et dudum adueniens extemplo symbolum seruo tuo,
		eri imagine opsignatam epistulam, hic ante ostium.
	BAL	meo tu epistulam dedisti seruo? quoi seruo?
	HAR	Syro.
	BAL	non confidit sycophanta hic [nequam est] nugis: meditate malust.
1205		edepol hominem uerberonem Pseudolum, ut docte dolum
		commentust! tantundem argenti quantum miles debuit
		dedit huic atque hominem exornauit mulierem qui abduceret.
		nam illam epistulam ipsus uerus Harpax huc ad me attulit.
1209–10	HAR	Harpax ego uocor, ego seruos sum Macedoni militis;
		ego nec sycophantiose quicquam ago nec malefice
		neque istum Pseudolum mortalis qui sit noui nec scio.
	SIMO	tu, nisi mirum est, leno, plane perdidisti mulierem.

1204 nequam est nugis *P*, nugis *Leo*   meditatum malest *A*, meditatur male *P*, meditate malust *O. Skutsch*

372

HAR What Pseudolus and what tricks are you talking about, 1195
you whom I know as a man of no color?[56]

BAL Why don't you come off it? There's no gain for your
guiles here today. So tell Pseudolus that someone else
has taken the booty away, the Harpax who came earlier.

HAR But I am that Harpax.

BAL No, you want to be him. (*to Simo*) This chap is an out- 1200
and-out impostor.

HAR (*to Ballio*) I gave the money to you, and a while ago, im-
mediately on my arrival, I gave the token to your slave
here in front of the door, a letter sealed with my master's
picture.

BAL You gave the letter to my slave? Which slave?

HAR Syrus.

BAL This trickster doesn't rely on empty words alone, he's bad
in a well-thought-out way. (*suddenly having an idea*) 1205
Pseudolus really is a rascal! How cleverly he came up
with this trick! He gave the same amount of money the
soldier owed me to this chap and fitted him out so that
he'd take the woman away: the real Harpax brought that
letter to me in person.

HAR I am called Harpax, I am the slave of the Macedonian 1210
soldier; I am not doing anything in a tricky or nasty way,
and I don't know or understand who that Pseudolus is.

SIMO You, pimp, have clearly lost the woman, unless a miracle
occurs.

---

[56] An unclear phrase. Perhaps an *umbraticus* (*Curc.* 556) is meant,
a man living a sheltered life; or Harpax is referring to a man who does
not blush and hence has no shame; or Harpax wants to express that he
is not interested in who Ballio is and uses an alternative phrase to the
proverbial "not caring whether he is black or white" (Catull. 93.2, Cic.
Phil. 2.41).

BAL	edepol ne istuc magis magisque metuo quom uerba au-	

          dio.

1215   mihi quoque edepol iam dudum ille Syrus cor perfrige-
            facit,

       symbolum qui ab hoc accepit. mira sunt ni Pseudolust.

       eho tu, qua facie fuit dudum quoi dedisti symbolum?

HAR rufus quidam, uentriosus, crassis suris, subniger,

       magno capite, acutis oculis, ore rubicundo, admodum

1220   magnis pedibus.

BAL   perdidisti, postquam dixisti pedes.

       Pseudolus fuit ipsus. actum est de me. iam morior,
           Simo.

HAR hercle te hau sinam emoriri, nisi mi argentum redditur,
       uiginti minae.

SIMO   atque etiam mihi aliae uiginti minae.

BAL auferen tu id praemium a me quod promisi per iocum?

1225 SIMO de improbis uiris auferri praemium et praedam decet.

BAL saltem Pseudolum mihi dedas.

SIMO   Pseudolum ego dedam tibi?

       quid deliquit? dixin ab eo tibi ut caueres centiens?

BAL perdidit me.

SIMO   at me uiginti modicis multauit minis.

BAL quid nunc faciam?

HAR si mi argentum dederis, te suspendito.

1230 BAL di te perdant! sequere sis me ergo hac ad forum ut
           soluam.

HAR   sequor.

SIMO quid ego?

BAL   peregrinos apsoluam, cras agam cum ciuibus.

BAL   Yes, I'm becoming more and more afraid when I hear his
      words. That Syrus who received the token from him has   1215
      also been striking a chill to my heart for a while now. It'll
      be a wonder if it isn't Pseudolus. (*to Harpax*) Hey you,
      what did the chap look like you gave the token to a while
      ago?

HAR   Someone red-haired, paunchy, with fat calves, darkish,
      with a big head, sharp eyes, a ruddy face, and very big   1220
      feet.

BAL   (*to Harpax*) You've killed me now that you've mentioned
      his feet. It was Pseudolus himself. I'm done for. (*to Simo*)
      I'm dying now, Simo.

HAR   No, I won't let you die, unless I'm paid the money,
      twenty minas.

SIMO (*also to Ballio*) And I too another twenty minas.

BAL   Will you take away from me as your booty what I prom-
      ised in jest?

SIMO Booty and plunder ought to be taken away from crooks.   1225

BAL   At least you should hand over Pseudolus to me.

SIMO I should hand over Pseudolus to you? What wrong has
      he done? Didn't I tell you a hundred times that you
      should be on your guard against him?

BAL   He's ruined me.

SIMO But me he's penalized with the nice little sum of twenty
      minas.

BAL   What should I do now?

HAR   When you've given me the money, hang yourself.

BAL   May the gods ruin you! Do follow me this way then to   1230
      the forum so that I can pay you.

HAR   Yes.

SIMO (*to Ballio*) What about me?

BAL   I'll settle the demands of outsiders first and deal with the

Pseudolus mihi centuriata habuit capitis comitia,
qui illum ad me hodie allegauit mulierem qui abduc-
eret.
sequere tu. nunc ne exspectetis dum hac domum re-
deam uia;
1235   ita res gesta est: angiporta haec certum est consecta-
rier.
HAR   si graderere tantum quantum loquere, iam esses ad fo-
rum.
BAL   certum est mi hunc emortualem facere ex natali die.

IV. viii: SIMO

SIMO   bene ego illum tetigi, bene autem seruos inimicum
suom.
nunc mihi certum est alio pacto Pseudolo insidias dare
1240   quam in aliis comoediis fit, ubi cum stimulis aut flagris
insidiantur: at ego iam intus promam uiginti minas
quas promisi si effecisset; obuiam ei ultro deferam.
nimis illic mortalis doctus, nimis uorsutus, nimis malus;
superauit dolum Troianum atque Vlixem Pseudolus.
1245   nunc ibo intro, argentum promam, Pseudolo insidias
dabo.

1243 doctus‹t› *Ritschl*

citizens tomorrow.[57] Pseudolus has held a general assembly[58] over my life, since he sent that chap to me today to take the woman away. (*to Harpax*) Follow me, you. (*to the audience*) Now don't wait for me to return home this way. Things have gone so ill with me, I've decided to   1235
follow along these back alleys.

HAR   If you walked at the rate you talk, you'd be at the forum already.

BAL   I've decided to make this my death day instead of my birthday.

Exeunt BALLIO *and* HARPAX *to the right.*

SIMO   I've hit him hard, and again my slave has hit his enemy hard. Now I'm resolved to ambush Pseudolus in a different way from how it happens in other comedies, where   1240
they lie in ambush with cattle prods or whips: by contrast, I shall now bring out the twenty minas I promised if he succeeded. I'll take the initiative in giving it to him. He's a very smart, very clever, very wicked fellow; Pseudolus has surpassed the Trojan trick and Ulysses.[59]   1245
Now I'll go in, bring out the cash, and lay an ambush for Pseudolus.

Exit SIMO *into his house.*

[57] A formula of the praetor.

[58] The *comitia centuriata* are a general assembly in which magistrates are elected and capital punishments are discussed.

[59] Ulysses had the Trojan horse built, a wooden animal in which Greek warriors were hiding until it had been brought into Troy, where they came out and fought, which led to the city's downfall.

PLAUTUS

ACTVS V

v. i: PSEVDOLVS

PSEV   quid hoc? sicin hoc fit, pedes? statin an non?
        an id uoltis ut me hinc iacentem aliquis tollat?
        nam hercle si cecidero, uostrum erit flagitium.
        pergitin pergere? ah! seruiendum mi hodie est;
1250   magnum hoc uitium uino est:
        pedes captat primum, luctator dolosust.
        profecto edepol ego nunc probe habeo madulsam:
        ita uictu excurato, ita magnis munditiis ⟨et⟩ dis dignis,
        itaque in loco festiuo sumus festiue accepti.
1255   quid opust me multas agere ambages? hoc
        est homini quam ob rem uitam amet,
1257   hic omnes uoluptates, in hoc
1257ᵃ   omnes uenustates sunt:
        deis proxumum esse arbitror.
        nam ubi amans complexust amantem, ubi ad labra la-
           bella adiungit,
1260   ubi alter alterum bilingui manufesto inter se prehend-
           unt,
        ubi mamma mammicula opprimitur aut si lubet cor-
           pora conduplicant,
        manu candida cantharum dulciferum propinat amicis-
           suma amico,
        neque [ibi] esse alium alii odio ibi nec molestum
        nec sermonibus morologis uti,
1265   unguenta atque odores, lemniscos, corollas
        dari dapsilis, non enim parce promi,

1249 seuiendum *P*, seruiendum *Hermann*
1253 et *add. Studemund*   1260 alter *CD*, altera *B*

ACT FIVE

Enter PSEUDOLUS *from the right, wearing a garland and clearly tipsy.*

PSEU What's that? Is this the way to act, my feet? Will you stand or not? Or do you want someone to pick me up from here when I'm lying on the ground? Yes, if I fall, it'll be your fault. Are you continuing to continue? Ah! I must let you have your way today. Wine has this big fault: 1250 he catches the feet first, he's a sly wrestler. Indeed, now I really do have a jag; with such choice food, in such great elegance worthy of the gods, and in such a delightful place were we received delightfully. What need is there 1255 for me to beat around the bush? This is the reason why a man loves his life, here there are all joys, in this there are all charms; I consider it to be closest to the gods. Yes, when a male lover embraces his female lover, when he joins his lips to her little lips, when they openly grab each 1260 other in double-tongue embrace, when the male breast is pressed against the female or, if you like, when the bodies duplicate, when dearest girlfriend toasts the melliferous bowl to her boyfriend with her white hand, and no one annoys or bothers another there or uses stupid speeches, when perfumes and scents, ribbons and gar- 1265 lands are given in abundance—and not brought out spar-

---

1262 propinare micissimam (amicissimam D^2) *amicitiam* P, propinat amicissuma amico *Leo*
1263 ibi *del. Leo*

	uictum ceterum ne quis me roget:
1268	hoc ego modo atque erus minor
1268ᵃ	hunc diem sumpsimus prothyme,
1269	postquam opus meum
1270	omne ut uolui perpetraui
1270ᵃ	hostibus fugatis.
	illos accubantis, potantis, amantis
1272	cum scortis reliqui et meum scortum ibidem
1272ᵃ	suo cordi atque animo opsequentis. sed postquam
	exsurrexi, orant med ut saltem.
1274	ad hunc me modum intuli illis satis facete
1274ᵃ	nimis ex discipulina, quippe ego qui
1275	probe Ionica perdidici. sed palliolatim amictus
1275ᵃ	sic haec incessi ludibundus.
	plaudunt, "parum" clamitant mi ut reuortar.
1277	occepi denuo, hoc modo. nolui
1277ᵃ	idem. amicae dabam me meae,
1278	ut me amaret: ubi circumuortor, cado:
1278ᵃ	id fuit naenia ludo.
	itaque dum enitor, prox! iam paene inquinaui pallium.
1280	nimiae tum uoluptati edepol fui.
1280ᵃ	ob casum datur cantharus: bibi.
	commuto ilico pallium, illud posiui;
	inde huc exii, crapulam dum amouerem.
	nunc ab ero ad erum meum maiorem uenio foedus
	commemoratum.
	aperite, aperite! heus, Simoni me adesse aliquis nunti-
	ate!

1270 omne ut uolui *B*, ut uolui omne *CD*
1272ᵃ suo *post* animo *P, transp. Leo*

ingly, in case anyone should ask me about the rest of the
entertainment: that's how I and my young master spent
this day merrily after I completed my entire work the   1270
way I liked, having put my enemies to flight. I left them
reclining, drinking, and making love together with their
prostitutes, and I left my prostitute in the same place, all
enjoying themselves and having a good time. But after I
got up, they asked me to dance. I struck a pose for them
like this (*demonstrates*), in good form and very much
in the correct style, since I learned the Ionian dance[60]   1275
well. But dressed in a mantle I merrily strutted these
steps like this. (*demonstrates again*) They clapped and
shouted "encore" at me so that I'd return. I began again,
in this way (*demonstrates again*), yet I didn't want to. I
was showing off to my girlfriend so that she'd love me;
when I was doing a pirouette, I fell: that was the unhappy
end of my performance. And so while I was struggling
up, whoops! I almost soiled my mantle. Then they were   1280
really delighted. In return for my fall they gave me the
tankard; I drank. I put my mantle on at once and took
the old one off. I went out here so as to get rid of my
headache. Now I'm coming from my master to my old
master to remind him of our treaty. (*knocking at Simo's
door*) Open up, open up! Hey, someone announce to
Simo that I'm here! (*goes back a few steps*)

[60] A lascivious type of dance.

v. ii: SIMO. PSEVDOLVS

1285	SIMO	uox uiri pessumi me exciet foras.
		sed quid hoc? quo modo? quid uideo ego?
	PSEV	cum corona ebrium Pseudolum tuom.
	SIMO	libere hercle hoc quidem. sed uide statum.
		num mea gratia pertimescit magis?
1290		cogito saeuiter blanditerne alloquar.
1291		sed me hoc uotat uim facere nunc
1291ᵃ		quod fero, si qua in hoc spes sita est mihi.
	PSEV	uir malus uiro
		optumo obuiam it.
	SIMO	di te ament, Pseudole.
	PSEV	hae!
	SIMO	i in malam crucem.
1295	PSEV	quor ego afflictor?
	SIMO	quid tu, malum, in os igitur mi ebrius irructas?
	PSEV	molliter sis tene me, caue ne cadam: non uides
		me ut madide madeam?
	SIMO	quae istaec audacia est te sic interdius
		cum corolla ebrium ingrediri?
	PSEV	lubet.
1300	SIMO	quid, lubet? pergin ructare in os mihi?
	PSEV	suauis ructus mihi est. sic sine, Simo.
	SIMO	credo equidem potis esse te, scelus,
		Massici montis uberrumos quattuor
		fructus ebibere in hora una.

1294 *personae nota et* hae *A*, pfui *BC*, ssui *D*, fui *T*, fu *Ritschl*
1295 adflictor *P*, adflicte(r) *A*
1296 sis *P*, sic *A*
1299 ingrediri *A*, incedere *P*

Enter SIMO *from his house, concealing a purse.*

SIMO The voice of a real crook is bringing me out. But what's   1285
      that? How? What do I see?
PSEU Your Pseudolus, with a garland and drunk.
SIMO Confident enough, this! (*aside*) But look at the posture.
      He isn't getting any more nervous on my account, is he?   1290
      I'm thinking whether to address him harshly or coax-
      ingly. But what I'm carrying now forbids me to do vio-
      lence to him, in case there's any hope for me in him.
PSEU (*approaching him*) A bad man is walking toward the best
      of men.
SIMO May the gods love you, Pseudolus.
PSEU Burp!
SIMO Go and be hanged! (*hits him*)
PSEU Why am I being knocked about?   1295
SIMO Why the blazes are you belching in my face, drunk?
PSEU Please hold me gently, make sure I don't fall; can't you
      see that I'm drunk as a lord?
SIMO What impudence is that, that you strut around like this
      in daytime, with a garland and drunk?
PSEU I like it. (*belches again*)
SIMO What, you like it? Are you continuing to belch in my   1300
      face?
PSEU Belching is sweet to me. Let it be like this, Simo.
SIMO I do believe that you could drink up four very rich crops
      of Mount Massicus[61] in one hour, you crook.

---

[61] A mountain in Campania famous for its wine.

PS hau male mones P, sed dica tamen ha(u ma)
le mones A, hau male mones sed dic tamen *Acidalius*
1320 heu heu *AD*, heu heu heu *BCT*

PSEU Add "in winter."[62]

SIMO Not a bad reminder, but tell me nevertheless: from 1305
where should I say you're bringing your heavily laden
bark?

PSEU I've just been drinking heavily with your son. But Simo,
how well Ballio has been tricked! How I brought into
effect what I predicted!

SIMO You're the worst of men. 1310

PSEU The woman's doing this: she's reclining at table as a free
woman with your son.

SIMO I know every single detail of your performance.

PSEU Then why are you hesitating to give me the money?

SIMO You demand your right, I admit. Take it. (*shows it to
Pseudolus*)

PSEU But you said you wouldn't give it to me: you're giving it
nevertheless. Weigh me down with the bag and follow 1315
me this way.

SIMO Should I weigh that chap down?

PSEU I know you will.

SIMO What should I do to him? Is he really taking the money
away and mocking me, to boot?

PSEU Woe to the losers!

SIMO Then turn your shoulder.

PSEU Here you are!

SIMO I never thought it would come about that I'd be your
suppliant. Dear o dear! 1320

PSEU Stop it!

SIMO I'm in pain!

PSEU If you weren't in pain, I would be.

[62] Since the days are shorter in winter, the daytime hours were also
shorter in antiquity: in antiquity the day had twelve hours, both in
summer and in winter.

SIMO quid? hoc auferen, Pseudole mi, aps tuo ero?

PSEV   lubentissumo corde atque animo.

SIMO nonne audes, quaeso, aliquam partem mihi gratiam
       facere hinc de argento?

PSEV non; me dices auidum esse hominem, nam hinc num-
       quam eris nummo diuitior,

       nec te mei tergi misereret, si hoc non hodie effecissem.

1325 SIMO erit ubi te ulciscar, si uiuo.

PSEV   quid minitare? habeo tergum.

SIMO age sane igitur.

PSEV   redi.

SIMO   quid redeam?

PSEV   redi modo: non eris deceptus.

SIMO redeo.

PSEV   simul mecum i potatum.

SIMO   egone eam?

PSEV   fac quod te iubeo.

       si is, aut dimidium aut plus etiam faxo hinc feres.

SIMO   eo, duc me quo uis.

PSEV quid nunc? numquid iratus es aut mihi aut fi—

1330   lio propter has res, Simo?

SIMO   nil profecto.

PSEV   i hac.

SIMO te sequor. quin uocas
       spectatores simul?

PSEV hercle me isti hau solent
       uocare, neque ergo ego istos;

1335   uerum si uoltis applaudere atque approba—

1335ᵃ   re hunc gregem et fabulam, in crastinum

1335ᵇ   uos uocabo.

1322 de argento A, argenti P   1324 sei hoc P, hoc si A
1327 i *nisi in* W *non fertur*

SIMO What? Will you take this away from your master, Pseudo-
lus dear?

PSEU With the greatest pleasure and joy.

SIMO Please, don't you want to let me off some part of this
money?

PSEU No. You'll call me a greedy person: from here you'll
never be richer by one coin. You wouldn't have pity on
my back either if I hadn't succeeded today.

SIMO I'll have an opportunity to take revenge on you, as truly   1325
as I'm alive.

PSEU Why are you threatening me? I have a back.

SIMO Go ahead then. (*puts the purse around the neck of
Pseudolus and turns to go*)

PSEU Come back.

SIMO Why should I come back?

PSEU Just come back; you won't be deceived.

SIMO I'm coming back. (*does so*)

PSEU Go for a drink with me.

SIMO I should go?

PSEU Do what I tell you. If you go, I'll make sure that you'll
carry away half the money or even more.

SIMO I'm going, take me where you want.

PSEU Well then? You aren't angry with me or your son because   1330
of this, are you, Simo?

SIMO Not at all.

PSEU Go this way.

SIMO I'm following you. Why don't you invite the spectators as
well?

PSEU They don't normally invite me, so I don't reciprocate. But   1335
if you want to give us your applause and approve of this
troupe and play, I'll invite you for tomorrow.

RUDENS

INTRODUCTORY NOTE

The *Rudens* or "The Rope" is one of the plays whose prologue is spoken by a deity, in this case Arcturus, the brightest star in the constellation Boötes. Arcturus informs us that, like other constellations, he descends from heaven in daytime to see which humans are good and which are bad. The good receive divine reward, the bad retribution. Our play is set on the coast of Cyrene, a city in what is now Libya; here there is a good man called Daemones and a bad man called Labrax. Daemones is an Athenian who had to emigrate because he lost his money by helping others. Daemones and his wife have a daughter, but she was kidnapped when she was a small child and could not be retrieved. Labrax is a pimp who bought the daughter of Daemones from a pirate. He did not know whose child she was, and to stop her finding her parents again kept a little box with her valuable miniature tokens safely stowed away; such miniature tokens were often given to children in case they got lost, as a means of finding their relatives again. When Palaestra, the daughter of Daemones, was older, a young Athenian called Plesidippus fell in love with her and asked the pimp if he could buy her. An agreement was reached and Plesidippus paid a deposit. The pimp, however, did not intend to keep the agreement. Rather, he decided to emigrate to Sicily, as a guest of his, a certain

Charmides, told him that he could make great profit there.
Plesidippus was supposed to meet Labrax at the temple of
Venus, but Labrax loaded all his possessions, including
Palaestra and her companion Ampelisca, onto a ship and
left together with Charmides the night before our play
begins. As the constellation Boötes was in antiquity con-
sidered to cause storms, Arcturus raised one that damaged
the house of Daemones but, more important, destroyed
the ship of Labrax. The two girls managed to escape on
the ship's boat, whereas the two men had to try to swim to
the shore.

Our play begins with Daemones and a slave of his,
Sceparnio, repairing the house. While they are working,
they encounter Plesidippus and his friends, who have got
wind of Labrax's actions and are trying to find him. Neither
Daemones nor Sceparnio has seen anyone fitting the de-
scription given by Plesidippus, but since they spot people
trying to swim to the shore, Plesidippus and his friends
rush there. After Daemones and Sceparnio go back into
their house, Palaestra appears; because she has lost Am-
pelisca and cannot find any signs of human habitation,
she is in despair. Some time later we see Ampelisca, who
has also survived and is looking for her companion. They
eventually meet and find the temple of Venus, where they
are received hospitably by the priestess Ptolemocratia.

Next we come across fishermen describing their hard
lot. Trachalio, a slave of Plesidippus, asks them for infor-
mation about the pimp and about his master, but they
have not seen anyone. However, when Ampelisca is sent
to the house of Daemones, Trachalio meets her and hears
about the goings-on the night before. It becomes apparent
that he is in love with Ampelisca. He goes into the temple

to console Palaestra. Ampelisca knocks at the door and encounters Sceparnio, who immediately begins flirting, against Ampelisca's wishes. When he is finally persuaded to bring water and goes in, Ampelisca can see her master and Charmides in the distance and flees into the temple. Sceparnio unwillingly carries the water into the temple and comes out again, wondering aloud what the two girls are doing. Labrax, who is having an argument with Charmides, overhears him, inquires further, and realizes that these must be his girls. First Labrax and then Charmides enter the temple, the former to get the girls out, the latter merely to watch.

Meanwhile, Daemones reappears and narrates his dream, in which a monkey asked him to lend him a ladder to drag two swallows from their nest; he ended up fighting with the beast. Daemones cannot know what this indicates, but to the audience it is immediately clear that the swallows represent the girls and the monkey Labrax. And indeed, as soon as his narrative is finished, Trachalio appears and entreats him to rescue two girls who are being mistreated in the temple. Daemones brings along two slaves with clubs, who beat up the pimp thoroughly. Trachalio runs off to fetch his master in the meantime. When Plesidippus arrives, he drags the pimp off to court, with the full approval of Charmides, who by now hates his former host. Trachalio, on the other hand, goes to the shore.

After this we meet Gripus, a slave who works for Daemones and who went fishing that night despite the storm. He caught the pimp's trunk in his net, in which is the little casket with Palaestra's miniature tokens. Gripus wonders what may be in the trunk; his suspicion is that it holds great riches, and he dreams of becoming free and famous. However, before he can reach home he is detained by Trachalio, who holds him back by tugging at a rope attached to the net. This rope, a rather insignificant detail in the story, is what Plautus named his play for, just as he named his *Asinaria* or "Comedy of Asses" for some donkeys that were sold for a good sum of money but do not actually appear in the play. Trachalio, knowing that Palaestra's casket is in the trunk, tries to get Gripus to give up part of his booty but does not succeed. In the end all he can manage is to force him to go to an arbiter. Gripus brings him to Daemones, who he hopes will not take his find away from him. But Daemones hears Trachalio out and decides that Palaestra must be given a chance to recover her property. It turns out not only that she knows the contents of her casket well enough to list them one by one without hesitation, but also that these miniature tokens were given to her by Daemones and his wife, who are her parents. Daemones promises that he will give his daughter in marriage to Plesidippus and that he will make sure that Trachalio is manumitted and can marry Ampelisca. While Trachalio goes to town to bring back his master, Gripus tries to persuade his master to let him keep the remainder of the trunk's contents. Daemones, however, is determined to return the trunk and its contents to its owner, and Gripus feels his heart sink. Plesidippus comes back and goes into the house to make the engagement official, while Gripus vents his anger outside.

There he meets Labrax, who has lost his right to Palaestra in court. Gripus promises to get the trunk back for Labrax if he gets an Attic talent as reward, and Labrax happily agrees, without having any intention of paying him. Daemones does indeed return the trunk to Labrax immediately, but while doing so finds out about the pimp's promise and takes the talent himself. Gripus feels defrauded again. What he does not realize is how Daemones actually uses the money: he buys Ampelisca's freedom for half the talent, which is a generous sum, especially since Labrax had paid less for her originally, and with the other half of the money he intends to give Gripus his freedom. He does not tell Gripus explicitly that he will free him, but at the end of the play he invites him to dinner along with the pimp, and this invitation proves that Gripus is no longer a slave.

Plautus states explicitly (ll. 32–33) that the *Rudens* is based on an original by Diphilus, though we do not know which play it was. Marx (1928: 274) argues that the original was the *Epitrope* or "Arbitration," but this title is not attested securely and Daemones does not deliver any arbitration proper after his daughter has been recovered. While the title of the Greek original thus remains unclear, elements of Plautine intervention in the plot can be seen with greater certainty. To begin with, it is not unlikely that the characters Ampelisca, Charmides, and Sceparnio were introduced by Plautus. Ampelisca does not have any real function in the play and is a mere doublet of Palaestra; the only scene in which she actually does something is ll. 414–57, where she asks Sceparnio for water, but even that is unnecessary, as the priestess for whom she does so is already heating up some water in l. 411. Similarly, Charmides is no more than a doublet of Labrax, and it is entirely unbelievable that he can go into the temple in l. 592 in order to sleep and remain there undisturbed or at least without being mentioned until he reappears in l. 705 and then stand by silently till l. 867. Sceparnio does not have any important function in the play either. His dialogues with Ampelisca and Charmides are charming but do not advance the action. What is more, his appearance immediately after the prologue is actually rather odd. He comes out on his master's orders to dig up some earth, but is called back inside in l. 184, before he can have done any serious work.

In this same scene, Daemones, who in the prologue was commended for his humanity (ll. 35–38), is remarkably cruel: Sceparnio reports the shipwreck of two girls, and instead of going to the shore to rescue them, Daemones rebukes Sceparnio for his interest in their fate (ll. 177 and 181–83). Equally inconsistent is the appearance of Plesidippus, who wants to check if Labrax is waiting for him at the temple, even though he has been reliably informed that the pimp has set sail. Such oddities can perhaps be explained best if we assume that the passage in question is an addition by Plautus, who in general cared less about the internal consistency of his plots than did his Greek models but who was keen for such spectacular highlights. If so, the first appearance of Daemones in the Greek play may have been the passage in which he narrates his dream. This possibility becomes a likelihood if we consider that the play starts in the morning and that Daemones is most likely to tell us about his dream immediately after getting up, not in the middle of the day and after having been introduced to us already.

In this dream, the monkey, which stands for Labrax, asks Daemones if it can borrow a ladder in order to be able to reach the swallows (ll. 601–2). In our play Labrax does not ask Daemones for help, but it is likely that he did so in the Greek original, where the connection between dream and reality would thus have been closer. Therefore it seems that Plautus took over the dream from his Greek source without making sure that it still suited the passages that he changed.

Another passage that cannot have been in the Greek comedy in the form that we find in Plautus is the one in ll. 1045–1190, where at times we have five speakers, a state of affairs unlikely for a Greek play, where the maximum number of speakers at any given time was three.

However, the most remarkable changes Plautus introduced seem to have been toward the end of the play. Gripus says that he wants to post signs indicating that he found a trunk (ll. 1294–96) so that the owner can come and reclaim it, but in fact he knows that the pimp Labrax is the owner, which makes his statement rather pointless. But much more striking is the behavior of Daemones, whom we are supposed to think of as a particularly humane individual: Plesidippus frees his slave Trachalio for his help in securing Palaestra for him, but Gripus, who is after all the person who found the trunk that enabled Daemones to recognize his daughter, is not similarly rewarded. He does get his freedom, but he has to pay for it with half the talent he earned from the pimp; and Daemones also takes the other half away from him in order to free Ampelisca. Of course Daemones legally owns everything that comes to Gripus, but morally Gripus should have a say over the talent; Daemones appears to be generous only with what he has not earned himself. Without doubt Plautus has introduced changes here. If Ampelisca is indeed an invention by Plautus, at least part of Daemones' meanness toward Gripus is purely Plautine.

We do not know for certain when the *Rudens* was first staged; the various proposals differ from each other by up to thirty years. The most reliable criterion for dating would be references to historical events, but these are few and vague. In l. 86 the *Alcmene* by Euripides is mentioned, and the addition of the Greek author of the play indicates that this reference comes from Plautus rather than Diphilus. While we are in all likelihood dealing with a Roman adaptation of the Greek play, we know neither the Roman poet nor the date of the adaptation, so that this reference cannot help us any further. Similarly, the mention of enemies that Rome is at war with is very imprecise. If this is a reference to the Carthaginians, who were defeated near Zama by Scipio in 202 BC, this is a good *terminus ante quem*; however, this is far from certain. In l. 525 we hear of *uelitatio*; the special fighting technique of the *uelites* was first introduced in 211 BC, which is thus a *terminus post quem*, but as this is also the period in which Plautus wrote his first plays, the reference is not very helpful.

Internal criteria for dating Plautine plays are the number of sung passages and allusion to or citations from other plays. The *Rudens* contains an average number of songs, which is an indication that it belongs to the middle period of Plautus' career. Allusions and citations are more difficult to judge, partly because one has to be careful to exclude chance similarities and partly because, where direct influence is obvious, it is often far less clear in which direction the influence goes. Much has been made of the similarities between the dreams in the *Mercator* (ll. 225–70) and the *Rudens* (ll. 593–612), and Woytek has tried to demonstrate that the dream in the *Rudens* is in fact the model of the other dream. However, it is possible that both dreams come from their respective Greek originals and that the similarities occurred already there. And even if Woytek is right, it has to be admitted that the *Mercator* is not easy to date. Woytek also noticed similarities between the threats of suicide in *Rud.* 1288–89 and *Stich.* 638–40. The latter passage does indeed look like a pastiche of phrases, but whether the *Rudens* is the basis is not as obvious to me as it is to Woytek. If he is correct here, we have 200 BC, the date of the *Stichus*, as *terminus ante quem* for the *Rudens*. While it thus remains impossible to date the *Rudens* with any precision, most of the indications points to it being a play of the middle period.

SELECT BIBLIOGRAPHY

Editions and Commentaries

Fay, H. C. (1969), *Plautus: Rudens; Edited with Introduction, Notes and Vocabulary* (Bristol).

Marx, F. (1928), *Plautus Rudens: Text und Kommentar* (Berlin).

Sonnenschein, E. A. (1891), *T. Macci Plauti Rudens; Edited with Critical and Explanatory Notes* (Oxford).

Criticism

Jocelyn, H. D. (1966), "Plautus, *Rudens* 83–88," in *Classical Review* NS 16: 148.

Lefèvre, E. (1984), *Diphilos und Plautus: Der* Rudens *und sein Original* (Stuttgart).

——— (2006), *Plautus'* Rudens (Tübingen).

Scheidweiler, F. (1954), "Zum plautinischen Rudens," in *Rheinisches Museum für Philologie* NS 97: 160–65.

Skutsch, O. (1966), "Plautus, *Rudens*, 603 ff.," in *Classical Review* NS 16: 12–14.

Smitskamp, R. (ed.) (1979), "Housman on Plautus: Manuscript Notes in the *Rudens* of Friedrich Marx (1928)" (Leiden).

Woytek, E. (2001), "Sprach- und Kontextbeobachtung im Dienste der Prioritätsbestimmung bei Plautus: Zur Datierung von Rudens, Mercator und Persa," in *Wiener Studien* 114: 119–42.

RVDENS

ARGVMENTVM

Reti piscator de mari extraxit uidulum,
Vbi erant erilis filiae crepundia,
Dominum ad lenonem quae surrepta uenerat.
Ea in clientelam suipte imprudens patris
5 **N**aufragio eiecta deuenit. cognoscitur
Suoque amico Plesidippo iungitur.

THE ROPE

PLOT SUMMARY

With his net, a fisherman hauled a trunk from the sea, contain-
ing the recognition tokens of his master's daughter. She had
fallen into the hands of a master who was a pimp. Without
knowing it, she comes to be a dependant of her own father 5
when she is cast ashore in a shipwreck. She is recognized and
married to her boyfriend, Plesidippus.

PLAUTUS

PERSONAE

ARCTVRVS prologus
SCEPARNIO seruos
PLESIDIPPVS adulescens
DAEMONES senex
PALAESTRA mulier
AMPELISCA mulier
PTOLEMOCRATIA sacerdos Veneris
PISCATORES
TRACHALIO seruos
LABRAX leno
CHARMIDES senex
LORARII
GRIPVS piscator

RUDENS

CHARACTERS

ARCTURUS speaker of the prologue; brightest star in the constellation Boötes, which caused a storm the night before our play

SCEPARNIO a slave; insolent, works for Daemones

PLESIDIPPUS a young man; an Athenian in love with Palaestra

DAEMONES an old man; an Athenian of noble character

PALAESTRA a woman; slave of Labrax, turns out to be the daughter of Daemones

AMPELISCA a woman; slave of Labrax and companion of Palaestra

PTOLEMOCRATIA priestess of Venus; a kind, elderly woman

FISHERMEN poor people who provide Trachalio with information

TRACHALIO a slave; works for Plesidippus

LABRAX a pimp; thoroughly disreputable

CHARMIDES an old man; business partner of Labrax, of the same character

SLAVES WITH ROPES work for Daemones

GRIPUS a fisherman; slave of Daemones

PLAUTUS

SCAENA

Cyrenis

STAGING

The stage represents the coast near Cyrene. On the right we can see the farm of Daemones; the door opens into the farmyard, behind which is his house. On the left we can see a temple of Venus; there is an altar in front and a statue of Venus inside. Offstage on the right are the town and the harbor; offstage on the left is the seashore.

PLAUTUS

PROLOGVS

ARC   qui gentis omnis mariaque et terras mouet,
       eius sum ciuis ciuitate caelitum.
       ita sum ut uidetis: splendens stella candida,
       signum quod semper tempore exoritur suo
5   hic atque in caelo. nomen Arcturo est mihi.
       noctu sum in caelo clarus atque inter deos,
       inter mortalis ambulo interdius.
       et alia signa de caelo ad terram accidunt:
       qui est imperator diuom atque hominum Iuppiter,
10   is nos per gentis alios alia disparat
       qui facta hominum moresque, pietatem et fidem
       noscamus, ut quemque adiuuet opulentia.
       qui falsas litis falsis testimoniis
       petunt quique in iure abiurant pecuniam,
15   eorum referimus nomina exscripta ad Iouem;
       cottidie ille scit quis hic quaerat malum:
       qui hic litem apisci postulant periurio
       mali, res falsas qui impetrant apud iudicem,
       iterum ille eam rem iudicatam iudicat;
20   maiore multa multat quam litem auferunt.
       bonos in aliis tabulis exscriptos habet.
       atque hoc scelesti in animum inducunt suom,
       Iouem se placare posse donis, hostiis:

7 ambulo ⟨clam⟩ *Geppert*   10 alius *P*, alios *Lindsay*, aliud
Seyffert   11 que *solum in T*   22 ⟨si⟩ in *Müller*

PROLOGUE

Enter ARCTURUS *from the left, wearing a star on his head.*

ARC In the city of the celestials I am a fellow citizen of he who
wields sway over all peoples, seas, and lands. I am the
way you see me: resplendent with a shining star, a con-
stellation that always rises in its due season here and 5
in heaven. Arcturus is my name. By night I am in the
heaven, bright and among the gods, by day I walk among
mortals. Other constellations also descend from heaven
to earth: Jupiter, who is ruler of gods and men, dispatches 10
each of us to a different post among the peoples, so that
we may learn the deeds and characters of men, their
virtue and good faith, and how fortune furthers each. Of
those who bring fraudulent cases to court, supported by
fraudulent evidence, and of those who deny the receipt
of money before a magistrate on oath, we write down the 15
names and bring them back to Jupiter. Every day he
learns who is looking for trouble here. If bad people here
expect to win a lawsuit by perjury or succeed in pressing
false claims before a judge, he judges the judged matter
again; he penalizes them with a penalty bigger than the 20
action that they win. Good men he has listed on other
tablets. And yet the wicked convince themselves that
they can placate Jupiter with gifts and sacrifices. They

et operam et sumptum perdunt; id eo fit quia
25   nihil ei acceptum est a periuris supplici;
facilius si qui pius est a dis supplicans
quam qui scelestust inueniet ueniam sibi.
idcirco moneo uos ego haec, qui estis boni
29   quique aetatem agitis cum pietate et cum fide:
29ᵃ   ***
30   retinete porro, post factum ut laetemini.
nunc huc qua causa ueni argumentum eloquar.
primumdum huic esse nomen urbi Diphilus
Cyrenas uoluit. illic habitat Daemones
in agro atque uilla proxuma propter mare,
35   senex, qui huc Athenis exul uenit, hau malus;
neque is adeo propter malitiam patria caret,
sed dum alios seruat se impediuit interim,
rem bene paratam comitate perdidit.
huic filiola uirgo periit paruola.
40   eam de praedone uir mercatur pessumus,
is eam huc Cyrenas leno aduexit uirginem.
adulescens quidam ciuis huius Atticus
eam uidit ire e ludo fidicinio domum,
amare occepit: ad lenonem deuenit,
45   minis triginta sibi puellam destinat
datque arrabonem et iure iurando alligat.
is leno, ut se aequom est, flocci non fecit fidem
nec quod iuratus adulescenti dixerat.
ei erat hospes par sui, Siculus senex
50   scelestus, Agrigentinus, urbis proditor;
is illius laudare infit formam uirginis
et aliarum itidem quae eius erant mulierculae.
infit lenoni suadere ut secum simul
eat in Siciliam: ibi esse homines uoluptarios

waste their effort as well as their money. This happens
because no peace offering is welcome to him if it comes   25
from perjurers. If someone is virtuous, he will find fa-
vor for himself more easily by entreating the gods than
someone who is wicked. That is why I urge you, who are
good and who live your lives in virtue and honesty: *** go   30
on persevering, that you may rejoice afterward. Now I'll
tell you the plot summary, which is why I've come here.
To begin with, Diphilus wanted the name of this city to
be Cyrene. (*pointing to the farm*) Over there lives Dae-
mones, in the farm and farmhouse so close to the sea, an   35
old man who came here as an exile from Athens, not a
bad person; what's more, he is deprived of his homeland
not on account of any offense, but in rescuing others he
entangled himself and lost his well-earned fortune
through his kindness. He lost his daughter when she was
very little. A crook bought her from a pirate, and this   40
man, a pimp, brought the girl here to Cyrene. A certain
young man, a compatriot of hers from Athens, saw her
going home from music school. He fell in love with her.
He went to the pimp, arranged to buy the girl for thirty   45
minas, gave him a deposit, and bound him with an oath.
This pimp, true to type, didn't care at all about his prom-
ise or about what he'd told the young man on oath. He
had as a guest the counterpart of himself, an old man
from Sicily, a wicked fellow, from Agrigentum, the type   50
that would betray his city; he began to praise the looks
of that girl, and in the same way the looks of the other
women whom he had. He began to advise the pimp to
come to Sicily with him; he said that there were plea-

29^a *uersum excidisse apparet ex A*

55 dicit, potesse ibi eum fieri diuitem,
 ibi esse quaestum maxumum meretricibus.
 persuadet. nauis clanculum conducitur,
 quicquid erat noctu in nauem comportat domo
 leno; adulescenti qui puellam ab eo emerat
60 ait sese Veneri uelle uotum soluere
 —id hic est Veneris fanum—et eo ad prandium
 uocauit adulescentem huc. ipse hinc ilico
 conscendit nauem, auehit meretriculas.
 adulescenti alii narrant ut res gesta sit,
65 lenonem abiisse. ad portum adulescens uenit:
 illorum nauis longe in altum apscesserat.
 ego quoniam uideo uirginem asportarier,
 tetuli et ei auxilium et lenoni exitium simul:
 increpui hibernum et fluctus moui maritumos.
70 nam Arcturus signum sum omnium acerrumum:
 uehemens sum exoriens, quom occido uehementior.
 nunc ambo, leno atque hospes, in saxo simul
 sedent eiecti: nauis confracta est eis.
 illa autem uirgo atque altera itidem ancillula
75 de naui timidae desiluerunt in scapham.
 nunc eas ab saxo fluctus ad terram ferunt
 ad uillam illius, exul ubi habitat senex,
 quoius deturbauit uentus tectum et tegulas;
 et seruos illic est eius qui egreditur foras.
80 adulescens huc iam adueniet, quem uidebitis,
 qui illam mercatust de lenone uirginem.
 ualete, ut hostes uostri diffidant sibi.

68 et ei *T*, et *BCD*
70 omnium ‹unum› *Seyffert*
72 in saxo leno atque hospes *P, transp. Reiz*

sure-loving people there, that he could become rich   55
there, and that there was enormous profit for prostitutes
there. He convinced him. A ship was hired in secret and
the pimp brought all his property from home onto the
ship. To the young man who had bought the girl from
him he said he wanted to fulfill a vow to Venus—this here   60
is the temple of Venus (*points to it*)—and for this reason
he invited the young man here to lunch. He himself
embarked on the ship at once and sailed off with the
prostitutes. Others told the young man of the event, that   65
the pimp had left. The young man came to the harbor.
Their ship had gone far out on the sea. When I saw that
the girl was being carried off, I brought help to her and
at the same time destruction to the pimp. I raised a
blustering storm and moved the waves of the sea. For I,   70
Arcturus, am the fiercest constellation of all. I am violent
when I rise, and when I set I am even more violent. Now
both of them, the pimp and his guest, are sitting on the
cliff together, cast out; their ship has been wrecked. But
that girl and also a second one, her maid, were fright-   75
ened and jumped down from the ship onto the ship's
boat. Now the waves are carrying them away from the
cliff onto the land, to the farmhouse where that old man
lives in exile. The wind has blown off his roof and tiles.
And that chap who is coming out is his slave. Soon you'll   80
see the young man arrive here, the one who bought that
girl from the pimp. Fare well, so that your enemies may
lose heart.

Exit ARCTURUS *to the left.*

PLAUTUS

ACTVS I

I. i: SCEPARNIO

SCE   pro di immortales, tempestatem quoius modi
        Neptunus nobis nocte hac misit proxuma!
85   detexit uentus uillam. quid uerbis opust?
        non uentus fuit, uerum Alcumena Euripidi,
        ita omnis de tecto deturbauit tegulas;
        illustriorem fecit fenstrasque indidit.

I. ii: PLESIDIPPVS. SCEPARNIO. DAEMONES

PLE   et uos a uostris abduxi negotiis
90   neque id processit qua uos duxi gratia
        nec quiui ad portum lenonem prehendere.
        sed mea desidia spem deserere nolui:
        eo uos, amici, detinui diutius.
        nunc huc ad Veneris fanum uenio uisere,
95   ubi rem diuinam se facturum dixerat.
SCE   si sapiam, hoc quod me mactat concinnem lutum.
PLE   prope me hic nescioquis loquitur.
DAE   heus, Sceparnio!
SCE   qui nominat me?
DAE   qui pro te argentum dedit.
SCE   quasi me tuom esse seruom dicas, Daemones.

---

88 inlustrioris *P*, inlustriorem *Lambinus*
96 me mactat *P*, mandatumst *Seyffert*

---

[1] God of the sea.

[2] A lost play by one of the three greatest Greek writers of tragedy.
When Alcmene gave birth to Hercules, there was a thunderstorm (see
also the ending of Plautus' *Amphitruo* in Vol. 1).

ACT ONE

Enter SCEPARNIO *from the farmhouse, carrying a shovel.*

SCE Immortal gods, what a storm Neptune[1] sent us last night! The wind unroofed our farmhouse. What need is 85 there for words? It wasn't a wind, but the Alcmene by Euripides,[2] to judge from the way it blew off all the tiles from the roof. It made our house brighter and put windows into it.

Enter PLESIDIPPUS *from the right, followed by three friends; they all have swords and wear cloaks.*

PLE *(still at a distance, to his friends)* I've taken you away from your own affairs, but the thing for which I took you 90 didn't succeed and I couldn't get hold of the pimp at the harbor. Still, I didn't want to give up hope just for lack of energy on my part; that's why I've detained you longer, my friends. Now I'm coming here to look at the temple of Venus, where he said he was going to sacrifice. 95

SCE *(to himself)* If I had any sense, I'd sort out this mud that's wearing me out.

PLE Someone's speaking here near me.

Enter DAEMONES *from the farmhouse.*

DAE Hey there, Sceparnio!

SCE Who's calling me?

DAE The man who paid for you.

SCE As if you wanted to say that I'm your slave, Daemones.

100	DAE	luto usust multo, multam terram confode.
		uillam integundam intellego totam mihi,
		nam nunc pellucet ea quam cribrum crebrius.
	PLE	pater salueto, amboque adeo.
	DAE	saluos sis.
	SCE	sed utrum tu masne an femina es, qui illum patrem
105		uoces?
	PLE	uir sum equidem.
	SCE	quaere, uir, porro patrem.
	DAE	filiolam ego unam habui, eam unam perdidi:
		uirile sexus numquam ullum habui.
	PLE	at di dabunt.
	SCE	tibi quidem hercle, quisquis es, magnum malum,
		qui oratione [nos] hic occupatos occupes.
110	PLE	isticin uos habitatis?
	SCE	quid tu id quaeritas?
		quon furatum mox uenias, uestigas loca?
	PLE	peculiosum esse addecet seruom et probum,
		quem ero praesente ⟨haud⟩ praetereat oratio
		aut qui inclementer dicat homini libero.
115	SCE	et impudicum et impudentem hominem addecet
		molestum ultro aduenire ad alienam domum,
		quoi debeatur nil.
	DAE	tace, Sceparnio.
		quid opus⟨t⟩, adulescens?
	PLE	istic infortunium,
		qui praefestinet, ubi erus assit, praeloqui.
120		sed nisi molestum est paucis percontarier
		uolo ego ex te.

106 ⟨quam⟩ habui *Seyffert*   109 nos *del. Guyet*
111 an quo *P*, quon *Leo*   112 decet *P*, addecet *Bothe*

414

DAE   We need a lot of mud, dig up a lot of earth. I realize that   100
       I have to reroof the whole farmhouse: now it lets the light
       in in more places than a sieve.

PLE   (*approaching them*) My greetings, father—to both of
       you, in fact.

DAE   Hello.

SCE   (*to Plesidippus*) But are you a man or a woman, since you
       call him father?   105

PLE   I for one am a man.

SCE   Look for a father further off, if you're a man.

DAE   (*to Plesidippus*) I had one little daughter; I lost her, my
       only one. I've never had any child of the male sex.

PLE   But the gods will give you one.

SCE   To you they'll give a big thrashing, whoever you are, for
       keeping busy people busy here with your talk.

PLE   Do you two live over there?   110

SCE   Why are you asking about that? Are you looking for
       somewhere to come and burgle next?

PLE   A slave must be rich and reliable if the turn to speak
       doesn't pass him by in his master's presence or if he can
       be rude to a free man.

SCE   And a man must be indecent and shameless if he comes   115
       as a nuisance to a stranger's house of his own accord,
       even though nothing is owed to him.

DAE   Be quiet, Sceparnio. (*to Plesidippus*) What do you need,
       young man?

PLE   A thrashing for this chap, since he's in a hurry to speak
       first although his master is present. But if it isn't incon-   120
       venient, I want to question you briefly.

---

113 haud *add. Acidalius*   118 opus‹t› *Fleckeisen*

	DAE	dabitur opera atque in negotio.
	SCE	quin tu in paludem is exsicasque harundinem
		qui pertegamus uillam, dum sudum est?
	DAE	tace.
		tu si quid opus est dice.
	PLE	dic quod te rogo,
125		ecquem tu hic hominem crispum, incanum uideris,
		malum, periurum, palpatorem—
	DAE	plurumos,
		nam ego propter eius modi uiros uino miser.
	PLE	hic dico, in fanum Veneris qui mulierculas
		duas secum adduxit, quique adornaret sibi
130		ut rem diuinam faciat, aut hodie aut heri.
	DAE	non hercle, adulescens, iam hos dies complusculos
		quemquam istic uidi sacruficare, nec potest
		clam me esse si qui sacruficat: semper petunt
		aquam hinc aut ignem aut uascula aut cultrum aut
		ueru
135		aut aulam extarem aut aliquid—quid uerbis opust?
		Veneri paraui uasa et puteum, non mihi.
		nunc interuallum iam hos dies multos fuit.
	PLE	ut uerba praehibes, me periisse praedicas.
	DAE	mea quidem hercle causa saluos sis licet.
140	SCE	heus tu qui fana uentris causa circumis,
		iubere meliust prandium ornari domi.
	DAE	fortasse tu huc uocatus es ad prandium,
		ill' qui uocauit nullus uenit?
	PLE	admodum.
	SCE	nullum est periclum te hinc ire impransum domum:

---

[3] Probably a loose translation of Greek *bomolokhos*, "man who lurks about altars to get scraps from the sacrifices."

416

DAE You'll be attended to, even though we're in the midst of business.

SCE (*to Plesidippus*) Why don't you go into the marsh and cut reed for us to cover the farmhouse with, while the weather's good?

DAE (*to Sceparnio*) Be quiet. (*to Plesidippus*) You tell me if you need anything.

PLE Tell me what I ask of you, whether you've seen anybody 125 here with gray, curly hair, a wrongdoer, perjurer, con man—

DAE (*interrupting*) A lot: it's because of such men that I live so wretchedly.

PLE I mean here, someone who brought two women to the temple of Venus with him and who was getting ready to 130 sacrifice, either today or yesterday.

DAE Young man, I haven't seen anyone sacrificing for several days now, and it can't be without my noticing if anyone does: they always want to get water from here or fire or vessels or a knife or a spit or a pot for cooking entrails or 135 something—what need is there for words? I acquired my vessels and my well for Venus, not for myself. Now I've had a break for many days.

PLE To judge from what you say, you're telling me that I've died.

DAE So far as I am concerned you can be in good health.

SCE (*to Plesidippus*) Hey you, who go round temples for the 140 sake of your belly,[3] you'd better have a lunch prepared at home.

DAE (*to Plesidippus*) Perhaps you were invited here for lunch and the one who invited you didn't come?

PLE Exactly.

SCE It doesn't bother me if you go home without lunch. It's 145

417

145	Cererem te melius‹t› quam Venerem sectarier:
	amori haec curat; tritico curat Ceres.
PLE	deludificauit me ille homo indignis modis.
DAE	pro di immortales! quid illuc est, Sceparnio,
	hominum secundum litus?
SCE	ut mea opinio est
150	propter uiam illi sunt uocati ad prandium.
DAE	qui?
SCE	quia post cenam, credo, lauerunt heri.
DAE	confracta nauis in mari est illis.
SCE	ita est.
	at hercle nobis uilla in terra et tegulae.
DAE	hui!
154–	homunculi quanti estis! eiecti ut natant!
55 PLE	ubi sunt hisce homines, opsecro?
DAE	hac ad dexteram;
	uiden? secundum litus.
PLE	uideo. sequimini.
	utinam is sit quem ego quaero, uir sacerrumus.
	ualete.
SCE	si non moneas, nosmet meminimus.
160	sed, o Palaemon, sancte Neptuni comes,
	qui ‹et› Herculei socius esse diceris,
	quod facinus uideo!

145 melius‹t› *Reiz*
149 aut mea est opinio *P*, ut mea opinio est *Reiz*
156 hi *B*, *om. CD*, hisce *Marx*
161 et add. *Marx*   herculi *T*, hercule *CD*, herculis *B*, Herculei
Lindsay

better for you to follow Ceres[4] than Venus; the latter takes care of love, but Ceres takes care of wheat.

PLE   (*to Daemones*) That chap has ridiculed me outrageously.

DAE   (*to Sceparnio, while watching the sea*) Immortal gods! What's the meaning of those people along the shore, Sceparnio?

SCE   (*having a look as well*) In my opinion they've been invited for a lunch for the journey.[5]   150

DAE   How so?

SCE   Because I think they had a bath after dinner yesterday.

DAE   Their ship's been wrecked at sea.

SCE   Yes; just like our farmhouse and tiles on land.

DAE   Goodness! Poor devils, how little worth you are! How   155
hard they're swimming, having been thrown overboard!

PLE   Where are these people, please?

DAE   Here to the right. Can you see them? Along the shore.

PLE   I can. (*to his friends*) Follow me. If only it is the chap I'm looking for, the arch-villain. (*to Daemones and Sceparnio*) Take care of yourselves.

Exeunt PLESIDIPPUS and his friends to the left.

SCE   (*calling after him*) We keep that in mind ourselves, without your advice. (*to himself*) But, o Palaemon,[6] holy   160
friend of Neptune, you who are also called the companion of Hercules, what action do I see!

[4] Goddess of vegetation and the harvest.

[5] *Propter uiam*, "for the journey," is the name of an obscure sacrifice to Hercules made before embarking on a travel. As it was customary to wash before sacrifices, Sceparnio jokingly equates their shipwreck with a bath.   [6] Greek deity identified with the Roman Portunus, the god of harbors.

DAE   quid uides?

SCE   mulierculas
uideo sedentis in scapha solas duas.
ut afflictantur miserae! eugae eugae, perbene!

165   ab saxo auortit fluctus ad litus scapham
neque gubernator umquam potuit tam bene.
non uidisse undas me maiores censeo.
saluae sunt si illos fluctus deuitauerint.
nunc, nunc periclum est. <unda> eiecit alteram.

170   at in uado est, iam facile enabit. eugepae!
[uiden alteram illam ut fluctus eiecit foras?]
surrexit, horsum se capessit. salua res.
desiluit haec autem altera in terram e scapha.
ut prae timore in genua in undas concidit!

175   salua est, euasit ex aqua. iam in litore est.
sed dextrouorsum auorsa it in malam crucem.
hem! errabit illaec hodie.

DAE   quid id refert tua?

SCE   si ad saxum quo capessit ea deorsum cadet,

179–
80   errationis fecerit compendium.

DAE   si tu de illarum cenaturus uesperi es,
illis curandum censeo, Sceparnio;
si apud me esuru's, mihi dari operam uolo.

SCE   bonum aequomque oras.

DAE   sequere me hac ergo.

SCE   sequor.

I. iii: PALAESTRA

185 PAL   nimio hominum fortunae minus miserae memorantur

---

166 tam bene *T, om. BCD*   169 unda *add. Guyet*
171 *uersum del. Sonnenschein*   178 cadet *T,* cadit *BCD*

DAE   What do you see?

SCE   I can see two women sitting in a boat alone. How the
      poor wretches are being knocked about! Hurray, hurray,
      excellent! The wave has turned the boat away from the   165
      cliff toward the beach; a steersman could never have
      done it equally well. I don't think I've ever seen higher
      waves! They're safe if they keep clear of them. Now, now
      there's a risk. (*Palaestra falls overboard*) The wave has
      thrown one of them out! But she's in shallow water, she'll   170
      easily swim to land now. Hurray! [Can you see how the
      wave has thrown one of them overboard?] She's stood
      up, she's coming here. (*as Ampelisca leaves the boat*) All's
      well! This second one has jumped from the boat onto
      land. How she's fallen onto her knees in the waves out
      of fear! She's safe, she's left the water. Now she's on the   175
      shore. But she's turned to the right and is going to the
      devil! Ha! She'll go astray today.

DAE   What business of yours is this?

SCE   If she falls down the cliff where she's going, she'll go to   180
      the devil more quickly.

DAE   If you're going to eat from their supper, I think you
      should look after them, Sceparnio; if you're going to eat
      at my place, I want you to attend to me.

SCE   What you ask is right and fair.

DAE   Then follow me this way.

SCE   Yes.

Exeunt DAEMONES *and* SCEPARNIO *into the farmhouse.*
Enter PALAESTRA *from the left, wet and in rags.*

PAL   The fate of humans is described as much less wretched   185

quam in usu, experiundo is datur acerbum.

⟨satin⟩ hoc deo complacitum est, med hoc ornatu or-
   natam

in incertas regiones timidam eiectam?

hancine ego ad rem natam miseram me memorabo?

190 hancine ego partem capio ob pietatem praecipuam?

nam hoc mi haud labori est laborem hunc potiri,

si erga parentes aut deos me impiaui;

sed id si parate curaui ut cauerem,

tum hoc mi indecore, inique, immodeste

195 datis di; nam quid habebunt sibi signi impii posthac,

si ad hunc modum est innoxiis honor apud uos?

197 nam me si sciam ⟨in uos⟩ fecisse aut parentes

197ᵃ sceleste, minus me miserer;

sed erile scelus me sollicitat, eius me impietas male
   habet.

is nauem atque omnia perdidit in mari:

200 haec bonorum eius sunt reliquiae;

200ᵃ etiam quae simul

201 uecta mecum in scapha est excidit.

201ᵃ ego nunc sola sum.

quae mihi si foret salua saltem, labor

lenior esset hic mi eius opera.

nunc quam spem aut opem aut consili quid capessam?

205 ita hic sola solis locis compotita sum.

205ᵃ ∗∗∗

206 hic saxa sunt, hic mare sonat,

206ᵃ nec quisquam homo mi obuiam uenit.

206ᵇ ∗∗∗

hoc quod induta sum, summae opes oppido,

nec cibo nec loco tecta quo sim scio:

quae mihi est spes qua me uiuere uelim?

422

than the bitterness they are actually given through expe-
rience and practice. Has it really pleased the god that I
should have been thrown overboard into unknown re-
gions, dressed in this outfit and full of fear? Will I say
that I, wretch that I am, was born for this? Am I getting   190
this reward for my outstanding virtue? Well, meeting
with this suffering is no suffering to me, if I've sinned
against my parents or the gods; but if I've carefully taken
care to be on my guard against this, then, o gods, you're
giving me this in an unbecoming, unfair, unrestrained   195
way: how will the guilty be marked out hereafter if this
is the way you treat the innocent? Well, if I knew I'd
committed a wrong against you or my parents, I'd pity
myself less. But it's my master's crime that's troubling
me, it's his wickedness that's distressing me. He has lost
his ship and everything in the sea. (*pointing to herself*)   200
This is the remainder of his goods; even the girl who was
being carried on the boat together with me has fallen
overboard. I'm all alone now. If only she were safe, my
misfortune would be more bearable on her account.
Now what hope or help or what plan should I take? All   205
alone here, I have attained these lonely places. *** Here
are the cliffs, here the sea resounds, and no one is com-
ing toward me. *** What I'm wearing is the sum total of
my possessions, and I don't know with what food or shel-
ter I could be covered. What hope do I have on account

187 satin *add. Spengel*
191 aut *P*, haut *Scutarius*, sat *Müller*
192 parentem *P*, parentes *Fleckeisen*
197 in uos *add. Leo*   205ᵃ *uersus excidit in A*
206ᵇ *duo uersus exciderunt in A*

210   nec loci gnara sum nec prius hic fui.
saltem aliquem uelim qui mihi ex his locis
aut uiam aut semitam monstret, ita nunc
hac an illac eam incerta sum consili;
nec prope usquam hic quidem cultum agrum conspi-
           cor.

215   algor, error, pauor, me omnia tenent.
216   haec parentes mei hau scitis miseri
216[a]   me nunc miseram esse ita uti sum:
libera ego prognata fui maxume, nequiquam fui.
nunc qui minus seruio quam si serua forem nata?
nec quicquam umquam illis profui qui me sibi edux-
           erunt.

I. iv: AMPELISCA. PALAESTRA

220 AMP quid mi meliust, quid magis in rem est, quam a cor-
           pore uitam ut secludam?
ita male uiuo atque ita mi multae in pectore sunt curae
           exanimales.
ita res se habent: uitae hau parco, perdidi spem qua
           me oblectabam.
omnia iam circumcursaui atque omnibus latebris per-
           reptaui
quaerere conseruam, uoce, oculis, auribus ut peruesti-
           garem.
225   neque eam usquam inuenio nec quo eam nec qua
           quaeram consultum est,
nec quem rogitem responsorem quemquam interea
           conuenio,
nec magis solae terrae solae sunt quam haec loca atque
           hae regiones;
nec, si uiuit, eam uiua umquam quin inueniam desis-
           tam.

of which I'd wish to live? I don't know the place and I   210
haven't been here before. At least I'd like someone to
show me a way or a path out of this area: I'm uncertain
in my mind whether I should go this way or that. Nor can
I see cultivated land anywhere close by. The feelings of   215
being cold, being lost, and being afraid all hold me in
their grip. My poor parents, you don't know that I'm as
wretched now as I am. Beyond all question I was born
free, but in vain. How am I less of a slave now than if I'd
been born a slave? Nor have I ever been of any use to
those who raised me.

Enter AMPELISCA *from the left, also wet and in rags; she does
not notice her friend.*

AMP   What's better for me, what's more useful, than to take my   220
what's that's how unhappily I'm living
and that's how many paralyzing worries are in my breast.
The situation is like this: I don't care for my life, I've lost
the hope that I delighted in. I've already run around ev-
ery nook and cranny and I've crawled through every
hiding place to look for my fellow slave, in order to find
her with my voice, eyes, and ears. I can't find her any-   225
where and I have no idea where to go or in which way
to look for her; meanwhile I can't find anyone to reply
whom I could ask, and desert lands aren't more deserted
than this area and these regions. If she's alive, I'll never,
as long as I live, give up without finding her.

---

210 diu *P*, prius *Marx*
219 profuit *P*, profui *Camerarius*
220 a corpore *A*, corpore *P*   ut secludam *A*, secludam *CD*,
sedulam *B*

	PAL	quoianam uox mihi prope hic sonat?
230	AMP	pertimui, quis hic loquitur prope?
	PAL	Spes bona, opsecro, subuenta mihi.
		exime ex hoc miseram metu.
	AMP	certo uox muliebris auris tetigit meas.
	PAL	mulier est, muliebris uox mi ad auris uenit.
235		num Ampelisca opsecro est?
	AMP	ten, Palaestra, audio?
	PAL	quin uoco ut me audiat nomine illam suo?
		Ampelisca!
	AMP	hem quis est?
	PAL	ego Palaestra.
	AMP	dic ubi es?
	PAL	pol ego nunc in malis plurumis.
	AMP	socia sum nec minor pars mea est quam tua.
240		sed uidere expeto te.
	PAL	mihi es aemula.
	AMP	consequamur gradu uocem. ubi es?
	PAL	ecce me.
		accede ad me atque adi contra.
	AMP	fit sedulo.
	PAL	cedo manum.
	AMP	accipe.
	PAL	dic uiuisne, opsecro.
	AMP	tu facis me quidem uiuere ut nunc uelim,
245		quom mihi te licet tangere. ut uix mihi
		credo ego hoc, te tenere! opsecro, amplectere,
		spes mea. ut me omnium iam laborum leuas!

232 eximes *P*, exime *Pylades*
244 ut uiuere *P*, *transp. Reiz*

PAL	Whose voice can I hear nearby?	
AMP	I've become scared; who is speaking nearby?	230
PAL	Kind Hope, please come to my assistance! Free a poor girl from this fear.	
AMP	Certainly a woman's voice has touched my ears.	
PAL	It is a woman, a woman's voice is coming to my ears. Please, is it Ampelisca?	235
AMP	Can I hear you, Palaestra?	
PAL	Why don't I call her by her name so that she can hear me? (*loudly*) Ampelisca!	
AMP	Ha! Who is it?	
PAL	I'm Palaestra.	
AMP	Tell me, where are you?	
PAL	Goodness, right now I'm in very many troubles.	
AMP	I'm your partner: my share isn't smaller than yours. But I'm keen to see you.	240
PAL	You're my rival in this.	
AMP	Let's follow each other's voices, step by step. Where are you?	
PAL	(*spotting her*) Here I am. Come to me, approach me from the other side.	
AMP	I'm doing my best.	
PAL	Give me your hand.	
AMP	Take it. (*they shake hands*)	
PAL	Tell me whether you're alive, please.	
AMP	You make me want to live again, now that I can touch you. How I can hardly believe myself in this, that I'm holding you! Please embrace me, my hope. (*as they are holding each other tight*) How you're already relieving me from all my sufferings!	245

PAL   occupas praeloqui quae mea oratio est.

      nunc abire hinc decet nos.

AMP   quo, amabo, ibimus?

250 PAL   litus hoc persequamur.

AMP   sequor quo lubet.

      sicine hic cum uuida ueste grassabimur?

PAL   hoc quod est, id necessarium est perpeti.

      sed quid hoc, opsecro, est?

AMP   quid?

PAL   uiden, amabo,

      fanum [uidesne] hoc?

AMP   ubi est?

PAL   ad dexteram.

255 AMP uideo decorum dis locum uiderier.

PAL   hau longe abesse oportet homines hinc, ita hic lepidust
        locus.

      quisquis est deus, ueneror ut nos ex hac aerumna exi-
        mat,

      miseras, inopes, aerumnosas ut aliquo auxilio adiuuet.

I. v: PTOLEMOCRATIA. PALAESTRA. AMPELISCA

PTO   qui sunt qui a patrona preces mea expetessunt?

260   nam uox me precantum huc foras excitauit.

      bonam atque opsequentem deam atque hau grauatam

      patronam exsequontur benignamque multum.

PAL   iubemus te saluere, mater.

PTO   saluete,

      puellae. sed unde uos

265   ire cum uuida ueste dicam, opsecro,

265ᵃ   tam maestiter uestitas?

PAL   ilico hinc imus, hau longule ex hoc loco;

      uerum longe hinc abest unde aduectae huc sumus.

PAL   You're taking the words right out of my mouth. Now we
       ought to leave this place.

AMP   Where will we go, please?

PAL   Let's follow this shore.   250

AMP   I'm following you where you wish. Will we tramp around
       here like this, with wet clothes?

PAL   It's necessary to endure the present state of things. But
       what's this, please?

AMP   What?

PAL   Can you see this temple, please?

AMP   Where is it?

PAL   To the right.

AMP   I can see that the place seems worthy of the gods.   255

PAL   There ought to be people not far from here, given how
       pleasant this place is. (*loudly*) I entreat whichever god it
       is to relieve us from this toil and to support us wretched,
       destitute, miserable women with some help.

Enter PTOLEMOCRATIA *from the temple of Venus.*

PTO   Who are the people who seek favor from my patron-
       ess with prayers? Yes, the voices of people praying have   260
       called me out here. They're applying to a good and oblig-
       ing goddess and not a grudging patroness, but one who
       is very kind.

PAL   (*as they approach*) Our greetings to you, mother.

PTO   Greetings, my girls. But where should I say you've come   265
       from with wet clothes, please, dressed so gloomily?

PAL   We've come from right here, not far from this place; but
       the place from where we've traveled here is far away.

---

248 mest oratio *P*, mea oratio est *Reiz*   254 uidesne *del. Baier*

	PTO	nempe equo ligneo per uias caerulas
		estis uectae?
	PAL	admodum.
	PTO	ergo aequius uos erat
270		candidatas uenire hostiatasque: ad hoc
		fanum ad istunc modum non ueniri solet.
	PAL	quaene eiectae e mari sumus ambae, opsecro,
		unde nos hostias agere uoluisti huc?
		nunc tibi amplectimur genua egentes opum,
275		quae in locis nesciis nescia spe sumus,
		ut tuo recipias tecto seruesque nos
		miseriarumque te ambarum uti misereat,
		quibus nec locus<t> ullus nec spes parata,
		neque hoc amplius [quam] quod uides nobis quicquam
		est.
280	PTO	manus mi date, exsurgite a genibus ambae.
		misericordior nulla me est feminarum.
		sed haec pauperes res sunt inopesque, puellae:
283		egomet <meam> uix uitam colo;
283ᵃ		Veneri cibo meo seruio.
	AMP	Veneris fanum, opsecro, hoc est?
285	PTO	fateor. ego huius fani
285ᵃ		sacerdos clueo.
		uerum quicquid est comiter fiet a me,
		quo hoc copiae ualebit.
		ite hac mecum.
	PAL	amice benigneque honorem,
		mater, nostrum habes.
	PTO	oportet.

272 sumus *P*, simus *Bentley*   273 uoluisti *P*, uoluistis *Hermann*
278 locus<t> *Reiz*   279 quam *del. Reiz*
282 que *del. Hermann*   283 meam *add. Spengel*

430

PTO   Presumably you have traveled on a wooden steed across
      the azure main?

PAL   Exactly.

PTO   Then it would have been more appropriate for you to   270
      come dressed in white and with sacrificial victims; to
      this temple one doesn't normally come in the state you
      are in.

PAL   We've both been shipwrecked; please, where did you
      want us to bring sacrificial victims from? (*as they kneel
      before her*) Now we're clutching your knees, devoid of
      resources, we who are in an unknown place with un-   275
      known hope, that you may receive us under your roof
      and protect us and that you may feel pity for the pitiful
      state both of us are in; there's no place and no hope avail-
      able to us, and we don't have anything more than what
      you see.

PTO   Give me your hands, rise from your knees, both of you.   280
      (*they obey*) No woman is more compassionate than me.
      But my means are poor and meager, my girls. I barely
      keep myself alive; I serve Venus at my own expense.

AMP   Is this a temple of Venus, please?

PTO   Yes, it is. I bear the title of priestess of this temple. But   285
      everything will be done hospitably by me, so far as my
      means will allow. Come with me this way.

PAL   You treat us in a kind and friendly way, mother.

PTO   So I should.

Exeunt PTOLEMOCRATIA, PALAESTRA, *and* AMPELISCA *into
the temple.*

---

287 nunc copia *B*, non copia *CD*, hoc copiae *Marx*

ACTVS II

II. i: PISCATORES

290 PIS omnibus modis qui pauperes sunt homines miseri ui-
           uont,
         praesertim quibus nec quaestus est neque ⟨e⟩didicere
           artem ullam:
         necessitate quicquid est domi id sat est habendum.
         nos iam de ornatu propemodum ut locupletes simus
           scitis:
         hisce hami atque haec harundines sunt nobis quaestu
           et cultu.
295   ⟨cottidie⟩ ex urbe ad mare huc prodimus pabulatum:
         pro exercitu gymnastico et palaestrico hoc habemus;
         echinos, lopadas, ostreas, balanos captamus, conchas,
         marinam urticam, musculos, plagusias striatas;
         postid piscatum hamatilem et saxatilem aggredimur.
300   cibum captamus e mari: si euentus non euenit
         nec quicquam captum est piscium, salsi lautique pure
         domum redimus clanculum, dormimus incenati.
         atque ut nunc ualide fluctuat mare, nulla nobis spes
           est:
         nisi quid concharum capsimus, [in]cenati sumus pro-
           fecto.
305   nunc Venerem hanc ueneremur bonam, ut nos lepide
           adiuerit hodie.

II. ii: TRACHALIO. PISCATORES

TRA animum aduorsaui sedulo ne erum usquam praeteri-
       rem;
     nam quom modo exibat foras, ad portum se aibat ire,

RUDENS

ACT TWO

Enter FISHERMEN *from the right, carrying nets and other fishing equipment.*

FISHER People who are poor live wretchedly in all ways, espe- 290
cially those who have no trade and haven't learned any
skill. Out of necessity you must be content with whatever
you have. How rich *we* are you can tell pretty well from
our getup: these hooks and these fishing rods are our
profit and profession. Every day we come from town 295
here to the sea to forage. We have this instead of training
in athletics and wrestling. We try to catch sea urchins,
limpets, oysters, cockles, sea snails, sea nettles, mussels,
and fluted scallops. Then we take to hook and rock fish-
ing. We try to catch our food from the sea; if no result 300
results and nothing in the way of fish is caught, we sneak
back home salted and washed clean and we sleep with-
out dinner. And given how strongly the sea is heaving
now, we don't have any hope: unless we catch some mus-
sels, we've had all the dinner we're going to get. Let us 305
now venerate good Venus here that she may assist us
nicely today.

Enter TRACHALIO *from the right.*

TRA *(to himself)* I've taken care with all my heart not to go
past master anywhere; when he was going out just now,
he said he was going to the harbor, and he told me to

291 didicere *P*, edidicere *Marx*
295 cottidie *Camerarius ex libris ueteribus*
300 uenit *P*, euenit *Bothe*   304 incenati *P*, cenati *Reiz*

me huc obuiam iussit sibi uenire ad Veneris fanum.
sed quos percontor commode eccos uideo astare. ad-
    ibo.

310 saluete, fures maritumi, conchitae atque hamiotae,
famelica hominum natio. quid agitis? ut peritis?

PIS ut piscatorem aequom est, fame sitique speque falsa.

TRA ecquem adulescentem huc, dum hic astatis, expedite,
uidistis ire strenua facie, rubicundum, fortem,

315 qui tris secum homines duceret chlamydatos cum
    machaeris?

PIS nullum istac facie ut praedicas uenisse huc scimus.

TRA   ecquem
recaluom ad Silanum senem, statutum, uentriosum,
tortis superciliis, contracta fronte, fraudulentum,
deorum odium atque hominum, malum, mali uiti pro-
    brique plenum,

320 qui duceret mulierculas duas secum satis uenustas?

PIS cum istius modi uirtutibus operisque natus qui sit,
eum quidem ad carnuficem est aequius quam ad Ve-
    nerem commeare.

TRA at si uidistis, dicite.

PIS   huc profecto nullus uenit.
uale.

TRA   ualete. credidi: factum est quod suspicabar,

325 data uerba ero sunt, leno abit scelestus exulatum,

312 falsa *add. T*

313 expedite *add. T*

314 uidisti seni *BCD*, uidistis uenientem *T*, uidistis eire
Seyffert   hic posuit Lindsay (*post* 315 *in codicibus*)

315 semihomines *T*, secum homines *Mitscherlich*

434

meet him at the temple of Venus. But look, I can see
people I can ask, standing here just at the right time. I'll
approach. (*to the fishermen*) My greetings, thieves of the 310
sea, shellicans and hookamites, you starveling tribe of
people. How are you? How are you perishing?

FISHER As befits a fisherman, through hunger, thirst, and false
hope.

TRA Tell me, while you've been standing here, have you seen
any young man coming here, of determined appearance,
ruddy, and strong, who was taking three men with him, 315
with cloaks and swords?

FISHER We don't know of any man of the appearance you
describe coming here.

TRA Have you seen any old man with a bald forehead, like
Silenus,[7] good-sized, with a big belly, with twisted eye-
brows and a scowling forehead, a swindler, an object of
hate to gods and men, evil, full of evil, vice, and dis-
grace, who was taking two rather pretty women with 320
him?

FISHER Someone who is distinguished by virtues and accom-
plishments of that type ought to go to the hangman
rather than to Venus.

TRA But tell me if you've seen one.

FISHER Certainly no one came here. Goodbye.

Exeunt FISHERMEN *to the left.*

TRA (*calling after them*) Goodbye. (*to himself*) I thought
so; what I suspected has happened, my master's been 325

---

[7] The ugly and often drunken tutor and companion of Dionysus,
the god of wine.

PLAUTUS

in nauem ascendit, mulieres auexit: hariolus sum.
is huc erum etiam ad prandium uocauit, sceleris se-
  men.
nunc quid mi meliust quam ilico hic opperiar erum
  dum ueniat?
eadem, sacerdos Veneria haec si quid amplius scit,
si uidero, exquisiuero: faciet me certiorem.

330

II. iii: AMPELISCA. TRACHALIO

AMP intellego: hanc quae proxuma est ‹me› uillam Veneris
  fano
  pulsare iussisti atque aquam rogare.
TRA   quoia ad auris
  uox mi aduolauit?
AMP   opsecro, quis hic loquitur?
TRA   quem ego uideo?
  estne Ampelisca haec quae foras e fano egreditur?
AMP   estne hic

335 Trachalio quem conspicor, calator Plesidippi?
TRA ea est.
AMP   is est. Trachalio, salue.
TRA   salue, Ampelisca.
  quid agis tu?
AMP   aetatem hau malam male.
TRA   melius ominare.
AMP uerum omnis sapientis decet conferre et fabulari.
  sed Plesidippus tuos erus ubi, amabo, est?
TRA   heia uero,
340 quasi non sit intus!
AMP   nec pol est neque huc quidem ullus uenit.
TRA non uenit?
AMP   uera praedicas.

436

tricked, the crooked pimp has gone into exile, has gone
aboard a ship, and taken the women away. I'm a sooth-
sayer. He even invited my master here to lunch, that
fount of infamy. Now what's better for me than to wait
right here till my master comes? At the same time I'll
also ask the priestess of Venus if she knows anything   330
more, if I see her. She'll inform me.

Enter AMPELISCA *from the temple, carrying a pitcher.*

AMP (*into the temple*) I understand: you've told me to knock
     at the farmhouse that's right next to the temple of Venus
     and to ask for water.
TRA Whose voice has flown to my ears?
AMP Please, who is speaking here?
TRA Who do I see? Isn't this Ampelisca who is leaving the
     temple?
AMP Isn't this Trachalio I see, the attendant of Plesidippus?   335
TRA It's her.
AMP It's him. (*aloud*) My greetings, Trachalio.
TRA And mine to you, Ampelisca. How are you?
AMP I'm spending that time of life that's not bad badly.
TRA Speak a better omen.
AMP All wise people ought to communicate and speak the
     truth. But where's your master Plesidippus, please?
TRA Come off it! As if he weren't inside.   340
AMP He isn't and he hasn't come here at all.
TRA He hasn't come?
AMP You're telling the truth.

---

329 hanc sacerdos Veneria *P, corr. Leo*
331 me *add. Bentley*

	TRA	non est meum, Ampelisca.
		sed quam mox coctum est prandium?
	AMP	quod prandium, opsecro te?
	TRA	nemp' rem diuinam facitis hic.
	AMP	quid somnias, amabo?
	TRA	certe huc Labrax ad prandium uocauit Plesidippum
345		erum meum erus uoster.
	AMP	pol hau miranda facta dicis:
		si deos decepit et homines, lenonum more fecit.
	TRA	non rem diuinam facitis hic uos neque erus?
	AMP	hariolare.
	TRA	quid tu agis hic igitur?
	AMP	ex malis multis metuque summo
		capitalique ex periculo orbas auxilique opumque huc
350		recepit ad se Veneria haec sacerdos me et Palaestram.
	TRA	an hic Palaestra est, opsecro, eri mei amica?
	AMP	certo.
	TRA	inest lepos in nuntio tuo magnus, mea Ampelisca.
		sed istuc periclum pellubet quod fuerit uobis scire.
	AMP	confracta est, mi Trachalio, hac nocte nauis nobis.
355	TRA	quid, "nauis"? quae istaec fabula est?
	AMP	non audiuisti, amabo,
		quo pacto leno clanculum nos hinc auferre uoluit
		in Siciliam et quicquid domi fuit in nauem imposiuit?
		ea nunc perierunt omnia.
	TRA	oh, Neptune lepide, salue!
		nec te aleator nullus est sapientior profecto.
360		nimis lepide iecisti bolum: periurum perdidisti.
		sed nunc ubi est leno Labrax?
	AMP	periit potando, opinor:
		Neptunus magnis poculis hac nocte eum inuitauit.

TRA	That's not my habit, Ampelisca. But how soon will lunch be cooked?
AMP	What lunch, please?
TRA	Presumably you're sacrificing here.
AMP	What are you dreaming about, please?
TRA	Surely your master Labrax has invited my master Plesidippus here to lunch.
AMP	You aren't saying anything strange: if he deceived gods and men, he acted in keeping with the custom of pimps.
TRA	Aren't you sacrificing here, nor my master?
AMP	You're a clairvoyant.
TRA	Then what are you doing here?
AMP	When we were in many troubles and greatest fear, in danger to our lives and devoid of help and resources, this priestess of Venus took me and Palaestra in here to her.
TRA	Is Palaestra here, please, my master's girlfriend?
AMP	Certainly.
TRA	There's great charm in your message, my dear Ampelisca. But I'd love to know what danger you were in.
AMP	Our ship was smashed to pieces last night, my dear Trachalio.
TRA	What do you mean, "ship"? What story is that?
AMP	Haven't you heard, please, how the pimp wanted to carry us off to Sicily in secret and how he put everything he had at home aboard a ship? All this has now been lost.
TRA	Oh, charming Neptune, my greetings! Indeed no dicer is more cunning than you. You made your throw in ever so cleverly a way: you've destroyed a perjurer. But where's the pimp Labrax now?
AMP	He's died of drinking, I think: Neptune invited him to big goblets last night.

Line numbers in margin: 345, 350, 355, 360

PLAUTUS

TRA	credo hercle ἀναγκαίῳ datum quod biberet. ut ego amo te,	
	mea Ampelisca, ut dulcis es, ut mulsa dicta dicis!	
365	sed tu et Palaestra quo modo saluae estis?	
AMP	scibis faxo.	
	⟨de⟩ naui timidae ambae in scapham insiluimus, quia uidemus	
	ad saxa nauem ferrier; properans exsolui restim,	
	dum illi timent; nos cum scapha tempestas dextrouor- sum	
	differt ab illis; itaque nos uentisque fluctibusque	
370	iactatae exemplis plurumis miserae perpetuam noctem;	
	uix hodie ad litus pertulit nos uentus exanimatas.	
TRA	noui, Neptunus ita solet, quamuis fastidiosus	
	aedilis est: si quae improbae sunt merces, iactat omnis.	
374– AMP	uae capiti atque aetati tuae!	
75 TRA	tuo, mea Ampelisca . . .	
	sciui lenonem facere ⟨ego⟩ hoc quod fecit; saepe dixi;	
	capillum promittam optumum est occipiamque hario- lari.	
AMP	cauistis ergo tu atque erus ne abiret, quom scibatis?	
TRA	quid faceret?	
AMP	si amabat, rogas, quid faceret? asseruaret	
380	dies noctesque, in custodia esset semper. uerum ecas- tor	
	ut multi fecit, ita probe curauit Plesidippus.	
TRA	quor tu istuc dicis?	
AMP	res palam est.	
TRA	scin tu? etiam qui it lauatum	
	in balineas, quom ibi sedulo sua uestimenta seruat,	

366 nauis *P*, de naui *Fleckeisen*   376 ego *add. Pylades*

440

TRA   I do believe he was given something to drink under compulsion. How I love you, my dear Ampelisca, how sweet you are, what honeyed words you speak! But how come   365 you and Palaestra are safe?

AMP   I'll let you know. In our terror, we both jumped down from the ship onto its boat because we saw that the ship was being carried to the cliffs. I hurriedly untied the rope while the men were still panicking. The storm carried us with our boat to the right, away from them. And so we were tossed about by winds and waves in all sorts   370 of ways the entire night, poor us. It was only today that the wind carried us to the shore half dead.

TRA   I know, that's what Neptune is like, he's an ever-so-particular market inspector: if there's any bad merchandise, he throws the lot overboard.

AMP   Bad luck to your head and life!   375

TRA   To you, my dear Ampelisca . . . I knew the pimp would do what he did. I've often said it. It would be best for me to let my hair grow and begin soothsaying.[8]

AMP   Then were you and your master on your guard to stop him getting away, since you knew?

TRA   What should he have done?

AMP   You ask what he should have done, if he was in love? He should have watched over her day and night, he should   380 always have been on guard. But Plesidippus' care for her was as great as the value he set on her.

TRA   Why do you say that?

AMP   It's obvious.

TRA   Don't you know? Clothes are stolen from the man who goes to the baths even when he's watching over them

---

[8] Soothsayers typically let their hair grow long.

PLATUS

PLAUTUS

tamen surrupiuntur, quippe qui quem illorum opseruet
falsust;
385 fur facile quem opseruat uidet: custos qui fur sit nescit.
sed duce me ad illam ubi est.
AMP   i sane in Veneris fanum huc intro,
sedentem flentemque opprimes.
TRA   ut iam istuc mihi molestum est!
sed quid flet?
AMP   ego dicam tibi: hoc sese excruciat animi,
quia leno ademit cistulam ei quam habebat ubique
habebat
390 qui suos parentes noscere posset: eam ueretur
ne perierit.
TRA   ubinam ea fuit cistellula?
AMP   ibidem, in naui.
conclusit ipse in uidulum, ne copia esset eius
qui suos parentes nosceret.
TRA   o facinus impudicum,
quam liberam esse oporteat seruire postulare!
395 AMP nunc eam cum naui scilicet abiisse pessum in altum.
et aurum et argentum fuit lenonis omne ibidem.
TRA credo aliquem immersisse atque eum excepisse.
AMP   id misera maesta est
sibi eorum euenisse inopiam.
TRA   iam istoc magis usus facto est
ut eam intro consolerque eam, ne sic se excruciet
animi;
400 nam multa praeter spem scio multis bona euenisse.
AMP at ego etiam, qui sperauerint spem decepisse multos.

392 eius *P*, ei *Luchs*   395 eam *P*, eum *Bentley*
399 ne *P*, ut *Camerarius*

442

carefully, the reason being that he doesn't know who in the crowd he ought to watch. The thief can easily see the   385
man he's observing, the guard doesn't know who the thief is. But take me where she is.

AMP   Do go in here into the temple of Venus and you'll find her sitting and crying.

TRA   Now then, I don't like that! But why is she crying?

AMP   I'll tell you. She's tormenting herself because the pimp took away from her the box which she had and where she had the means to be able to recognize her parents. She's   390
afraid that it's perished.

TRA   Where was that box?

AMP   In the same place, on the ship. Our master shut it up in a trunk so that she wouldn't get a chance to get the means to recognize her parents.

TRA   What a shameless deed, to demand that a girl who ought to be free should be a slave!

AMP   Now of course it's gone to the bottom of the sea together   395
with the ship. All the pimp's gold and silver was there, too.

TRA   I expect someone plunged in and took it out.

AMP   The poor girl is sad that she's been deprived of these things.

TRA   Now it's all the more necessary that I should go in and console her, so that she won't torture herself like this: I   400
know that many good things have happened to many beyond their hope.

AMP   But I also know that hope has deceived many who have hoped.

TRA   ergo animus aequos optumum est aerumnae condi-
        mentum.
       ego eo intro, nisi quid uis.

AMP   eas. ego quod mihi imperauit
       sacerdos, id faciam atque aquam hinc de proxumo
         rogabo;

405   nam extemplo, si uerbis suis peterem, daturos dixit.
       nec digniorem censeo uidisse anum me quemquam,
       quoi deos atque homines censeam bene facere magis
         decere.
       ut lepide, ut liberaliter, ut honeste atque hau grauate
       timidas, egentis, uuidas, eiectas, exanimatas

410   accepit ad sese, hau secus quam si ex se simus natae!
       ut eapse ⟨sic⟩ succincta aquam calefactat, ut lauemus!
       nunc, ne morae illi sim, petam hinc aquam unde mi
         imperauit.
       heus ecquis in uilla est? ecquis hoc recludit? ecquis
         prodit?

II. iv: SCEPARNIO. AMPELISCA

SCE   quis est qui nostris tam proterue foribus facit iniuriam?
415 AMP ego sum.
SCE   hem! quid hoc boni est? eu edepol specie
                   lepida mulierem!
AMP   salue, adulescens.
SCE   et tu multum salueto, adulescentula.
AMP   ad uos uenio.

411 sic *add. Camerarius*

TRA   That's why self-possession is the best seasoning for sorrow. I'm going in, unless you want anything.

Exit TRACHALIO *into the temple.*

AMP   (*calling after him*) Do go. (*to the audience*) I'll do what the priestess told me and ask for water from here next door: she said they'd give it to me immediately if I ask in 405 her name. I don't think I've ever seen any more deserving old woman, anyone to whom I'd think gods and men ought to do more good turns. How charmingly, how generously, how considerately and not grudgingly she received us at her place when we were afraid, in need, wet, cast out, and half dead, just as if we were her own 410 daughters! How she herself, girded up like this, is heating the water so that we can wash! Now, in order not to waste her time, I'll ask for water from the place she told me. (*knocks on the door*) Hello, is anyone in the farmhouse? Is anyone opening the door? Is anyone coming out?

Enter SCEPARNIO *from the farmhouse, wearing a reed mat over his clothes to protect him from rain.*

SCE   Who is it who is doing an injustice to our door in such violent fashion?

AMP   It's me.   415

SCE   (*aside*) Oho! What good luck is this? Goodness, a pleasant-looking woman!

AMP   My greetings, young man.

SCE   And my warmest greetings to you, young girl.

AMP   I've come to you.

445

SCE   accipiam hospitio, si mox uenies uesperi,
item ut affectam; nam nunc nihil est qui te mane mu-
nerem.
sed quid ais, mea lepida, hilara?

AMP   aha! nimium familiariter
420   me attrectas.

SCE   pro di immortales! Veneris effigia haec quidem est.
ut in ocellis hilaritudo est, heia, corpus quoius modi,
subuolturium—illud quidem, "subaquilum" uolui
dicere.
uel papillae quoius modi, tum quae indoles in sauio
est!

AMP   non ego sum pollucta pago. potin ut me apstineas ma-
num?

425 SCE   non licet te sic placidule bellam belle tangere?

AMP   otium ubi erit, tum tibi operam ludo et deliciae dabo;
nunc quam ob rem huc sum missa, amabo, uel tu mi
aias uel neges.

SCE   quid nunc uis?

AMP   sapienti ornatus quid uelim indicium facit.

SCE   meus quoque hic sapienti ornatus quid uelim indicium
facit.

430 AMP   haec sacerdos Veneris hinc me a uobis iussit petere
aquam.

SCE   at ego basilicus sum: quem nisi oras guttam non feres.
nostro illum puteum periclo et ferramentis fodimus.

---

417 uenis *B*, ueni is *CD*, uenies *Lambinus*   uesperi *add. T*
418 adfectam *P*, adlectam *Scheidweiler*   inanem *B*, manem *CD*,
mane mulierem *T*, mane munerem *Hildebrand*
425 placide *P*, placidule *Fleckeisen*
430 petere aquam iussit a uobis *P*, *transp. Ussing*

SCE I'll receive you hospitably, like a sick person,[9] if you come soon, in the evening; now I don't have anything I can present you with, it's too early. But what do you say, my charming, cheerful girl? (*fondles her*)

AMP Ooh! You're touching me far too intimately.   420

SCE (*to the audience*) Immortal gods! This girl is the very picture of Venus. What charm there is in her eyes! Goodness! What a body! Ironed—I meant to say "bronzed."[10] What nipples! And what natural beauty there is in her mouth!

AMP I'm no dish for the whole village. Can't you keep your hands away from me?

SCE Am I not allowed to touch you gently like this, a pretty   425
girl, in a pretty way?

AMP When I have free time, I'll attend to you for jest and joy; now as for the reason why I've been sent here, please give me a yes or a no.

SCE What do you want now?

AMP (*pointing to her pitcher*) My getup shows a sensible person what I want.

SCE (*pointing to his groin*) This getup of mine also shows a sensible person what I want.

AMP This priestess of Venus from over here has told me to ask   430
you for water.

SCE But I am the boss; unless you coax me, you won't get a drop. We dug this well at our own expense and with our

---

[9] I.e., with all comforts and in bed.

[10] *Subaquilus*, "bronzed, tanned," superficially looks as if it came from *sub* + *aquila*, "a bit like an eagle." This similarity is the reason why Sceparnio comes up with the nonce formation *subuolturius*, "a bit like a vulture," here rendered as "ironed" to enable a pun with "bronzed."

		nisi multis blanditiis a me gutta non ferri potest.
	AMP	quor tu aquam grauare, amabo, quam hostis hosti commodat?
435	SCE	quor tu operam grauare mihi quam ciuis ciui commodat?
	AMP	immo etiam tibi, mea uoluptas, quae uoles faciam omnia.
	SCE	eugepae! saluos sum, haec iam me suam uoluptatem uocat.
		dabitur tibi aqua, ne nequiquam me ames. cedo mi urnam.
	AMP	cape.
		propera, amabo, efferre.
	SCE	manta, iam hic ero, uoluptas mea.
440	AMP	quid sacerdoti me dicam hic demoratam tam diu?
		ut etiam nunc misera timeo ubi oculis intueor mare!
442–50		sed quid ego misera uideo procul in litore?
		meum erum lenonem Siciliensemque hospitem,
		quos periisse ambos misera censebam in mari.
		iam illud mali plus nobis uiuit quam ratae.
		sed quid ego cesso fugere in fanum ac dicere haec
455		Palaestrae, in aram ut confugiamus prius quam ⟨is⟩ huc
		scelestus leno ueniat nosque hic opprimat?
		confugiam huc, ita res suppetit subit⟨aria⟩.

II. v: SCEPARNIO

SCE	pro di immortales! in aqua numquam credidi

455 is *add. Seyffert*
457 subit⟨aria⟩ *Ussing*

own tools. Not a drop can be got from me, except with much coaxing.

AMP   Why do you begrudge me water, please, something which stranger supplies to stranger?

SCE   Why do *you* begrudge me your service, something which   435
citizen supplies to citizen?

AMP   No, my darling, I'll do everything you want.

SCE   Hurray! I'm saved, now she calls me her darling. You'll
get the water, so that you don't love me for nothing. Give
me your pot.

AMP   (*handing it over*) Take it. Please be quick to bring it
out.

SCE   Wait, I'll be back in a moment, my darling.

Exit SCEPARNIO *into the farmhouse with the bucket.*

AMP   What should I tell the priestess has detained me here for   440
so long? How afraid I am even now when I look at the
sea with my eyes, poor me! But dear me! What can I see   450
in the distance on the shore? My master, the pimp, and
his guest from Sicily, both of whom I thought had died
in the sea, poor me! That's more trouble alive than we'd
reckoned on. But why am I hesitating to flee into the
temple and tell Palaestra about this, so that we may take   455
refuge at the altar before this criminal pimp comes here
and pounces on us? I'll take refuge here: it's an emer-
gency.

Exit AMPELISCA *into the temple.*
Enter SCEPARNIO *from the farmhouse with a full bucket.*

SCE   (*to himself*) Immortal gods! I never believed that there's

uoluptatem inesse tantam. ut hanc traxi lubens!
460   nimio minus altus puteus uisust quam prius.
ut sine labore hanc extraxi! praefiscini!
satin nequam sum, utpote qui hodie amare inceperim?
em tibi aquam, mea tu belliata. em sic uolo
te ferre honeste ut ego fero, ut placeas mihi.
465   sed ubi tu es, delicata? cape aquam hanc sis. ubi es?
amat hercle me, ut ego opinor. delituit mala.
ubi tu es? etiamne hanc urnam acceptura es? ubi es?
commodule melius⟨t⟩. tandem uero serio,
etiam acceptura es urnam hanc? ubi tu es gentium?
470   nusquam hercle equidem illam uideo. ludos me facit.
apponam hercle urnam iam ego hanc in media uia.
sed autem, quid si hanc hinc apstulerit quispiam,
sacram urnam Veneris? mi exhibeat negotium.
metuo hercle ne illa mulier mi insidias locet,
475   ut comprehendar cum sacra urna Veneria.
nempe optumo ⟨me⟩ iure in uinclis enicet
magistratus si quis me hanc habere uiderit.
nam haec litterata est, eapse cantat quoia sit.
iam hercle euocabo hinc hanc sacerdotem foras,
480   ut hanc accipiat urnam. accedam huc ad fores.
heus, exi, Ptolemocratia, cape hanc urnam tibi:
muliercula hanc nescioquae huc ad me detulit.
intro ferunda est. repperi negotium,
siquidem his mihi ultro aggerunda etiam est aqua.

462 satis *P*, satin *Bothe*
468 melius *P*, meliust *plerique edd.*
476 me *add. Camerarius*
481 eu si *B*, eus si (*cum spatio*) *CD*, heus exi *Seyffert*

so much joy in water. How happy I was to draw it up! The   460
well seemed a lot less deep than before. How I drew it
up without effort! Touch wood![11] Aren't I naughty, since
I've fallen in love today? (*holding out the pot*) Here's the
water for you, my pretty one. There, I want you to carry
it gracefully, the way I am carrying it, so that you will
please me. But where are you, playful girl? Take this   465
water, will you? Where are you? (*to the audience*) She
really loves me, I think. She's playing hide and seek, the
rogue. (*calling out*) Where are you? Aren't you going to
take this pot? Where are you? Better not go too far. Re-
ally, though, aren't you going to take this pot? Where on
earth are you? (*to the audience*) I can't see her anywhere.   470
She's making a fool of me. I'll place this pot in the middle
of the road now. But what if someone takes it away, the
sacred pot of Venus? He'd create trouble for me. I'm
afraid that that woman could be setting a trap for me so   475
that I'm caught with the sacred pot of Venus. No doubt
the magistrate would be perfectly entitled to chain me
up and kill me, if anyone sees me in possession of it: it's
lettered, it tells its own tale. Now I'll call this priestess
out so that she can take this pot. I'll go to the door here.   480
(*knocking on the door of the temple, loudly*) Hey there,
come out, Ptolemocratia, take this pot. Some woman
brought it here to my place. (*to himself*) I have to carry
it in. A nice job I've found, if I even have to bring them
water of my own accord.

Exit SCEPARNIO *into the temple.*

[11] *Praefiscini* is a formula used to avert bad luck that could arise
from praising oneself or being praised.

II. vi: LABRAX. CHARMIDES

485 LAB   qui homo ‹esse› sese miserum et mendicum uolet,
          Neptuno credat sese atque aetatem suam:
          nam si quis cum eo quid rei commiscuit,
          ad hoc exemplum amittit ornatum domum.
          edepol, Libertas, lepida es quae numquam pedem
490   uoluisti in nauem cum Hercule una imponere.
          sed ubi ille meus est hospes qui me perdidit?
          atque eccum incedit!

CHAR   quo malum properas, Labrax?
          nam equidem te nequeo consequi tam strenue.

LAB   utinam te prius quam oculis uidissem meis
495   malo cruciatu in Sicilia perbiteres,
          quem propter hoc mihi optigit misero mali.

CHAR utinam, quom in aedis me ad te adduxisti ‹tuas›,
          in carcere illo potius cubuissem die.
          deosque immortalis quaeso, dum uiuas, uti
500   omnis tui similis hospites habeas tibi.

LAB   Malam Fortunam in aedis te adduxi meas.
          quid mihi scelesto tibi erat auscultatio?
          quidue hinc abitio? quidue in nauem inscensio?
          ubi perdidi etiam plus boni quam mi fuit.

505 CHAR pol minime miror nauis si fracta est tibi,
          scelus te et sceleste parta quae uexit bona.

LAB   pessum dedisti me blandimentis tuis.

CHAR scelestiorem cenam cenaui tuam
          quam quae Thyestae quondam aut posita est Tereo.

---

485 esse *add. Bentley*
497 tuas *add. Camerarius*

---

[12] An obscure allusion.
[13] When Thyestes slept with the wife of his brother Atreus, Atreus

Enter LABRAX *from the left, followed by* CHARMIDES; *both are wet and in rags.*

LAB A man who wants to be wretched and a beggar should   485
entrust himself and his life to Neptune: if anyone has any
dealings with him, he sends him home in a plight like
this. Goodness, Liberty, you were smart never to want to   490
set foot on a ship together with Hercules.[12] But where's
that guest of mine who ruined me? And look, here he
comes!

CHAR Where the blazes are you rushing to, Labrax? I can't fol-
low you so energetically.

LAB If only you'd perished in torments in Sicily before I'd set   495
eyes on you! Because of you I got into this trouble, poor
me.

CHAR If only I'd slept in prison instead on that day when you
took me into your house! And I ask the immortal gods
that as long as you live all guests that you have may be   500
specimens like yourself.

LAB I brought you as Bad Luck into my house. What induced
a wretch like me to listen to you? Or what to go away
from here? Or what to go aboard a ship? There I lost
even more possessions than I had.

CHAR I'm not surprised at all if your ship was wrecked, since it   505
carried a rascal like you and your rascally acquired pos-
sessions.

LAB You've ruined me with your wheedling ways.

CHAR The dinner of yours that I ate was more criminal than
the one that was once put before Thyestes or Tereus.[13]

killed the sons of Thyestes and served them to him as a meal. Tereus
raped his wife's sister and kept her prisoner, but when his wife found
out, she killed her son and presented him to Tereus as a meal.

510 LAB   perii! animo male fit. contine quaeso caput.

     CHAR pulmoneum edepol nimis uelim uomitum uomas.

     LAB   eheu! Palaestra atque Ampelisca, ubi estis nunc?

     CHAR piscibus in alto, credo, praebent pabulum.

     LAB   mendicitatem mi optulisti opera tua,

515   dum tuis ausculto magnidicis mendaciis.

     CHAR bonam est quod habeas gratiam merito mihi,

         qui te ex insulso salsum feci opera mea.

     LAB   quin tu hinc is a me in maxumam malam crucem?

     CHAR eas. easque res agebam commodum.

520 LAB   eheu! quis uiuit me mortalis miserior?

     CHAR ego multo tanta miserior quam tu, Labrax.

     LAB   qui?

     CHAR   quia ego indignus sum, tu dignu's qui sies.

     LAB   o scirpe, scirpe, laudo fortunas tuas,

         qui semper seruas gloriam aritudinis.

525 CHAR equidem me ad uelitationem exerceo,

         nam omnia corusca prae tremore fabulor.

     LAB   edepol, Neptune, es balineator frigidus:

         cum uestimentis postquam aps te abii, algeo.

     CHAR ne thermopolium quidem ullum instruit,

530   ita salsam praehibet potionem et frigidam.

     LAB   ut fortunati sunt fabri ferrarii

         qui apud carbones assident! semper calent.

509 ante posita est et Tereo *P*, aut posita est Tereo *Nettleship*
521 tanta *ABCD*, tanto *B²*

---

14 Holding someone's head is supposed to help him not to vomit.

15 Lit. "from a saltless man into a salted one." Salt often stands for wit.

LAB I'm dead! I'm feeling sick. Please hold my head.[14] 510
CHAR I only hope you vomit up your lungs.
LAB Dear me! Palaestra and Ampelisca, where are you now?
CHAR They're providing food for the fish in the sea, I believe.
LAB You've brought me beggary by your intervention, when 515
     I listened to your boastful lies.
CHAR You should really feel very grateful to me; I've turned
     you from a dry man into a man of humor by my interven-
     tion.[15]
LAB Why don't you leave me alone and go and hang your-
     self?
CHAR You go. I was about to suggest the very same.
LAB Dear me! What mortal lives more wretchedly than me? 520
CHAR I am much more wretched than you, Labrax.
LAB How so?
CHAR Because I don't deserve it, but you do.
LAB O bulrush, bulrush, I congratulate you on your condi-
     tion; you always preserve your glory of being dry.
CHAR I'm practicing the fighting methods of the light-armed 525
     soldiers: all my words have a flourish in them from my
     trembling.[16]
LAB Really, Neptune, you are a cold bath attendant: since I
     left you, I've been freezing, even with my clothes on.
CHAR He hasn't even set up a hot-drink counter: he hands out 530
     cold and salty drink.
LAB How fortunate blacksmiths are, who sit next to hot coals!
     They're always warm.

[16] The *uelites* were a type of light-armed soldiers known for their
rapid attacks.

CHAR utinam fortuna nunc anetina uterer,
   ut quom exiissem ex aqua, arerem tamen.
535 LAB quid si aliquo ad ludos me pro manduco locem?
   CHAR quapropter?
   LAB   quia pol clare crepito dentibus.
   CHAR iure optumo me elauisse arbitror.
   LAB qui?
   CHAR quia auderem tecum in nauem ascendere,
   qui a fundamento mi usque mouisti mare.
540 LAB tibi auscultaui, tu promittebas mihi
   illi esse quaestum maxumum meretricibus,
   ibi me corruere posse aiebas ditias.
   CHAR iam postulabas te, impurata belua,
   totam Siciliam deuoraturum insulam?
545 LAB quaenam ballaena meum uorauit uidulum,
   aurum atque argentum ubi omne compactum fuit?
   CHAR eadem illa, credo, quae meum marsuppium,
   quod plenum argenti fuit in sacciperio.
   LAB eheu! redactus sum usque ad unam hanc tuniculam
550   et ad hoc misellum pallium. perii oppido!
   CHAR uel consociare mihi quidem tecum licet:
   aequas habemus partis.
   LAB   saltem si mihi
   mulierculae essent saluae, spes aliquae forent.
   nunc si me adulescens Plesidippus uiderit,
555   quo ab arrabonem pro Palaestra acceperam,
   iam is exhibebit hic mihi negotium.
   CHAR quid, stulte, ploras? tibi quidem edepol copia est
   dum lingua uiuet, qui rem soluas omnibus.

  537 ⟨e⟩lauisse *Fleckeisen* *si duplex hiatus displicet,* med *legendum* 538 *fortasse* quia ⟨enim⟩ *scribendum*
  555 quo ab *A,* a quo *P*

CHAR I wish I shared the ducks' lot now, so that when I came out of the water, I'd still be dry.

LAB What if I hire myself out somewhere as a muncher[17] for the games? 535

CHAR Why?

LAB Because I make a lot of noise with my teeth.

CHAR I fully deserve to have been cleaned out.

LAB How so?

CHAR For having consented to go aboard a ship with you, you who have stirred up the sea from its base.

LAB I listened to you, you promised me that there would 540 be enormous profit for prostitutes there, and you said I could shovel together wealth.

CHAR You dirty beast, did you expect you'd immediately swallow the whole island of Sicily?

LAB What whale swallowed my trunk, where all my gold and 545 silver were packed?

CHAR That same one, I believe, which swallowed my wallet, which was full of money in my traveling bag.

LAB Dear me! I've been reduced to this one little tunic and 550 that wretched little cloak. I'm utterly ruined!

CHAR I can enter into partnership with you if you like: we have equal shares.

LAB If at least my women were safe, I'd have some hopes. If young Plesidippus sees me now, from whom I received 555 a deposit for Palaestra, he'll instantly give me a hard time.

CHAR Why are you crying, you idiot? You are rich so long as your tongue lives, with which you pay everybody.

---

[17] The *manducus*, "muncher," was a figure in Atellan farce; he had champing jaws.

II. vii: SCEPARNIO. LABRAX. CHARMIDES

SCE   quid illuc, opsecro, negoti ‹est› quod duae mulierculae

560   hic in fano Veneris signum flentes amplexae tenent,

       nescioquem metuentes miserae? nocte hac aiunt prox-
        uma

       se iactatas atque eiectas hodie esse aiunt e mari.

LAB   opsecro hercle, adulescens, ubi istaec sunt quas memo-
       ras mulieres?

SCE   hic in fano Veneris.

LAB   quot sunt?

SCE   totidem quot ego et tu sumus.

565 LAB nemp' meae?

SCE   nemp' nescio istuc.

LAB   qua sunt facie?

SCE   scitula.

       uel ego amare utramuis possum, si probe appotus siem.

LAB   nemp' puellae?

SCE   nemp' molestus es. i uise, si lubet.

LAB   meas oportet intus esse hic mulieres, mi Charmides.

CHAR Iuppiter te perdat, et si sunt et si non sunt tamen.

570 LAB intro rumpam iam huc in Veneris fanum.

CHAR   in barathrum mauelim.

       opsecro, hospes, da mihi aliquid ubi condormiscam
        loci.

SCE   istic ubi uis condormisce; nemo prohibet, publicum
        est.

CHAR at uides me ornatus ut sim uestimentis uuidis:

559 est *add.* Fleckeisen

Enter SCEPARNIO *from the temple.*

SCE   (*to himself*) What does that mean, please, that two women here in the temple of Venus are clinging to her 560 statue, embracing it? They're afraid of someone, poor girls. They say that they were caught in a storm last night and that they were cast ashore today.

LAB   Please, young man, where are those women you mention?

SCE   Here in the temple of Venus.

LAB   How many are there?

SCE   As many as you and I are.

LAB   Surely they're mine?   565

SCE   Surely I don't know that.

LAB   What do they look like?

SCE   Pretty. I could make love to either of them if I were properly drunk.

LAB   Surely they're young?

SCE   Surely you're a nuisance. Go and see if you want to.

LAB   My women should be in here, my dear Charmides.

CHAR Whether they are or whether they aren't, may Jupiter ruin you all the same.

LAB   Now I'll burst into the temple of Venus here.   570

Exit LABRAX *into the temple.*

CHAR (*calling after him*) I'd rather you burst into the pit. (*to Sceparnio*) Please, kind stranger, give me someplace where I can sleep.

SCE   Sleep over there where you like; no one forbids it, it's common land.

CHAR But you can see how I'm dressed in wet clothes. Put me

459

recipe me in tectum, da mihi uestimenti aliquid aridi
575 dum arescunt mea; in aliquo tibi gratiam referam loco.
SCE tegillum eccillud, mihi unum id aret; id si uis dabo:
eodem amictus, eodem tectus esse soleo, si pluit.
tu istaec mihi dato: exarescent faxo.
CHAR   eho an te paenitet,
in mari quod ‹semel› elaui, ni hic in terra iterum
eluam?
580 SCE eluas tu an exunguare ciccum non interduim.
tibi ego numquam quicquam credam nisi si accepto
pignore.
tu uel suda uel peri algu uel tu aegrota uel uale.
barbarum hospitem mi in aedis nil moror. sat litium
est.
CHAR iamne abis? uenalis illic ductitauit, quisquis est;
585 non est misericors. sed quid ego hic asto infelix uui-
dus?
quin abeo huc in Veneris fanum, ut edormiscam hanc
crapulam,
quam potaui praeter animi quam lubuit sententiam?
quasi uinis Graecis Neptunus nobis suffudit mare,
itaque aluom prodi sperauit nobis salsis poculis;
590 quid opust uerbis? si inuitare nos paulisper pergeret,
ibidem obdormissemus: nunc uix uiuos amisit domum.
nunc lenonem quid agit intus uisam, conuiuam meum.

579 semel *add. Müller*

---

18 Charmides as a Sicilian is not a foreigner but also a Greek;
Sceparnio may be deliberately rude.
19 Inferior wine was mixed with seawater as preservative (cf. Cato
agr. 24). The following image is that of seawater as a laxative.

up in your house, give me some dry clothing until my 575
things are dry; I'll repay you sometime.

SCE (*pointing to the reed mat over his shoulders*) That mat is
the only dry thing I have. If you want it, I'll give it to you.
With that I'm usually clothed and covered when it rains.
Give me your clothes: I'll dry them.

CHAR Hey, aren't you content that I was cleaned out at sea
once, unless I'm cleaned out again here on dry land?

SCE I couldn't care less whether you're cleaned out or oiled 580
out. I'll never trust you with anything except after receiv-
ing a deposit. You may sweat or die from cold or be ill or
be well. I don't care for letting a foreign[18] guest into my
house. I have enough arguments as it is.

Exit SCEPARNIO into the farmhouse.

CHAR (*calling after him*) Are you leaving already? (*to himself*)
He's been a slave-dealer, whoever he is: he isn't compas- 585
sionate. But why am I standing around here, dripping,
wretch that I am? Why don't I go into the temple of
Venus here in order to sleep off my hangover which I got
by drinking against my inclinations? Neptune poured
seawater into us as if we were Greek wines,[19] and in this
way he hoped that our constipation would be relieved
with the briny goblets. What need is there for words? If 590
he'd continued to invite us for a bit longer, we'd have
fallen asleep there. Now he has sent us home, barely
alive. Now I'll see what the pimp, my host, is doing in-
side.

Exit CHARMIDES into the temple.

ACTVS III

III. i: DAEMONES

DAE   miris modis di ludos faciunt hominibus,
    mirisque exemplis somnia in somnis danunt:
595   ne dormientis quidem sinunt quiescere.
    uelut ego hac nocte quae processit proxuma
    mirum atque inscitum somniaui somnium.
    ad hirundininum nidum uisa est simia
599   ascensionem ut faceret ammolirier:
599ᵃ   ut in omnibus *** suis
600   neque eas eripere quibat inde. postibi
    uidetur ad me simia aggredirier,
    rogare scalas ut darem utendas sibi.
603   ego ad hoc exemplum simiae respondeo,
603ᵃ   ***

    natas ex Philomela ac [ex] Procne esse hirundines.
605   ago cum illa ne quid noceat meis popularibus,
    atque illa nimio iam fieri ferocior;
    uidetur ultro mihi malum minitarier.
    in ius uocat me. ibi ego nescioquo modo
    iratus uideor mediam arripere simiam;
610   concludo in uincla bestiam nequissumam.
    nunc quam ad rem dicam hoc attinere somnium
    numquam hodie quiui ad coniecturam euadere.
    sed quid hic in Veneris fano meae uiciniae
    clamoris oritur? animus mirat‹ur meus›.

599ᵃ *uestigia in A, non fertur in P*
603ᵃ *uersus excidit in A*
604 ex *del. Bothe*   ex Philomela Attica esse *Schoell*
614 mirat‹ur meus› *Camerarius*

RUDENS

ACT THREE

Enter DAEMONES *from the farmhouse.*

DAE   The gods mystify men in a strange fashion and give them
dreams in their sleep in strange ways: they don't even   595
allow those who are sleeping to rest. For instance, I
dreamed a strange and uncanny dream last night. I
dreamed that a monkey was trying to climb up to a swal-
lows' nest: as in all its ***, and it couldn't drag them away   600
from there. Then the monkey seems to approach me
and ask me to lend it a ladder. I answer the monkey like
this[20] *** that swallows were born from Philomela and
Procne.[21] I plead with it not to harm my compatriots, and   605
now it becomes a lot more insolent. It seems to take the
offensive and threaten me with a beating. It summons
me to court. There somehow I seem to grab the monkey
around the middle in my anger. I put that vilest of ani-   610
mals in chains. Now today I haven't been able to arrive
at an interpretation of what I should say this dream per-
tains to. But what noise arises here in the temple of
Venus in my neighborhood? It's very surprising.

[20] In the missing line he presumably said that he is an Athenian
citizen.

[21] Slightly imprecise; when Tereus wanted to kill his wife, Procne,
and her sister Philomela, Procne did indeed become a swallow, but
Philomela turned into a nightingale.

III. ii: TRACHALIO. DAEMONES

615 TRA   pro Cyrenenses populares! uostram ego imploro fidem,
           agricolae, accolae propinqui qui estis his regionibus,
           ferte opem inopiae atque exemplum pessumum pes-
               sum date.
           uindicate, ne impiorum potior sit pollentia
           quam innocentum, qui se scelere fieri nolunt nobilis.
620   statuite exemplum impudenti, date pudori praemium,
           facite hic lege potius liceat quam ui uicto uiuere.
           currite huc in Veneris fanum, uostram iterum imploro
               fidem,
           qui prope hic adestis quique auditis clamorem meum,
           ferte suppetias qui Veneri Veneriaeque antistitae
625   more antiquo in custodelam suom commiserunt caput,
           praetorquete iniuriae prius collum quam ad uos per-
               uenat.
    DAE   quid istuc est negoti?
    TRA   per ego haec genua te optestor, senex,
           quisquis es—
    DAE   quin tu ergo omitte genua et quid sit mi expedi
           ‹quod tu›multues.
    TRA   —teque oro et quaeso, si speras tibi
630   hoc anno multum futurum sirpe et laserpicium
           eamque euenturam exagogam Capuam saluam et sos-
               pitem,
           atque ab lippitudine usque siccitas ut sit tibi—
    DAE   sanun es?

626 peruen[i]at *Guyet*
629 ‹quod tu›multues *Lambinus*

464

Enter TRACHALIO *from the temple, shouting.*

TRA   Citizens of Cyrene! I implore your protection, you farm- 615
       ers and neighbors who are close to us here! Bring help
       to the helpless and bring this evil act to an evil end!
       Avenge wrongdoing so that the power of the wicked is
       not more powerful than that of the innocent, who don't
       want to become famous as victims of crime! Make an   620
       example of impudence, give decency its reward, make
       sure that one can live by law rather than coerced by
       brute force! Rush here into the temple of Venus, I im-
       plore your protection again, you who are close by and
       can hear my shouting! Bring help to those who have
       entrusted their lives to Venus and the high priestess of 625
       Venus according to ancient custom! Wring the neck of
       injustice before it reaches you!

DAE   What's the matter?

TRA   (*prostrating himself before Daemones*) I implore you by
       these knees of yours, old man, whoever you are—

DAE   (*interrupting*) Then let go of my knees and explain to me
       the reason for your disorderly behavior.

TRA   —and I beg and entreat you: as truly as you hope
       that you'll have much silphium[22] and silphium resin this 630
       year and that its export to Capua will be safe and sound,
       and so that you may have drought instead of discharge
       in your eyes throughout—

DAE   (*interrupting*) Are you in your right mind?

---

[22] Silphium (Lat. *sirpe*) is a now extinct plant that grew only around
Cyrene. It was used as a spice and for medicinal purposes. *Laserpicium*
is the plant's resin, harvested in a manner similar to asafetida. The stalks
of the plant are called *magydaris*.

	TRA	—seu tibi confidis fore multam magydarim,
		ut te ne pigeat dare operam mihi quod te orabo, senex.
635	DAE	at ego te per crura et talos tergumque optestor tuom,
		ut tibi ulmeam uberem esse speras uirgidemiam
		et tibi euenturam hoc anno uberem messem mali,
		ut mi istuc dicas negoti quid sit quod tumultues.
	TRA	qui lubet maledicere? equidem tibi bona [ex]optaui
		omnia.
640	DAE	bene equidem tibi dico, qui te digna ut eueniant pre-
		cor.
	TRA	opsecro, hoc praeuortere ergo.
	DAE	quid negoti est?
	TRA	mulieres
		duae innocentes intus hic sunt, tui indigentes auxili,
		quibus aduorsum ius legesque insignite iniuria hic
		facta est fitque in Veneris fano; tum sacerdos Veneria
645		indigne afflictatur.
	DAE	quis homo est tanta confidentia
		qui sacerdotem audeat uiolare? sed eae mulieres
		quae sunt? aut quid is iniqui fit?
	TRA	si das operam, eloquar.
		Veneris signum sunt amplexae. nunc ‹homo audacis-
		sumus›
		eas deripere uolt. eas ambas esse oportet ‹liberas›.
650	DAE	quis istic est qui deos tam parui pendit? ‹paucis ex-
		pedi.›

636 speras *D*, speres *BC*
639 [ex]optaui *Guyet*
646 uiolare audeat *P, transp. Pylades*
648 homo audacissumus *Lambinus e libris ueteribus*
649 liberas *add. Camerarius*

466

TRA —or as truly as you trust that you will have many sil-
phium stalks, do not begrudge attending to me in what
I ask of you, old man.

DAE (*angrily*) But I entreat you by your shins and your ankle 635
bones and your back: as truly as you hope that you'll have
a large harvest of elm rods and that you will get a large
crop of thrashing this year, tell me why you're causing
this disturbance.

TRA Why do you want to be rude to me? I for my part wished
you all good things.

DAE I for my part am polite to you: I pray that you get what 640
you deserve.

TRA Please, attend to this, then.

DAE What's the matter?

TRA (*pointing to the temple*) There are two innocent women
in here, in need of your help; here in the temple of Venus
a glaring wrong has been and is being done to them
against law and justice. And the priestess of Venus is 645
being knocked about in an outrageous way, too.

DAE Who has such audacity that he'd dare to do violence to
a priestess? But who are these women? Or what injustice
is happening to them?

TRA If you pay attention, I'll tell you. They're clinging to the
statue of Venus. Now the wicked man wants to drag them
off. Both of them ought to be free.

DAE Who is that man who has so little regard for the gods? 650
Tell me briefly.

---

650 paucis expedi *Lambinus e libris ueteribus*

PLAUTUS

TRA fraudis, sceleris, parricidi, periuri plenissumus,
     legerupa impudens, impurus, inuerecundissumus,
     uno uerbo apsoluam, leno est: quid illum porro prae-
       dicem?

DAE edepol infortunio hominem praedicas donabilem.

655 TRA qui sacerdoti scelestus faucis interpresserit.

DAE at malo hercle cum magno suo fecit. ite istinc foras,
     Turbalio, Sparax. ubi estis?

TRA   i opsecro intro, subueni
     illis.

DAE   iterum haud imperabo. sequimini hac.

TRA   age nunciam,
     iube oculos elidere, itidem ut sepiis faciunt coqui.

660 DAE proripite hominem pedibus huc itidem quasi occisam
     suem.

TRA audio tumultum. opinor, leno pugnis pectitur.
     nimis uelim improbissumo homini malas edentauerint.
     sed eccas ipsae huc egrediuntur timidae e fano mu-
     lieres.

656 malo cum magno suo fecit hercle *P, transp. Brix*

468

TRA   A man absolutely full of fraud, crime, parricide, and per-
jury, an impudent, dirty, completely shameless law-
breaker; I'll finish it in one word, he's a pimp. What else
should I call him?

DAE   Really, you're calling him someone who needs to be pre-
sented with a thrashing.

TRA   Yes, because the criminal throttled the priestess.   655

DAE   But doing this will cost him dearly. (*into the farmhouse*)
Come out from there, Turbalio and Sparax! Where are
you?

TRA   Please go in and come to their help.

DAE   (*again into the farmhouse*) I won't tell you a second
time!

Enter two SLAVES *from the farmhouse.*

DAE   (*to the slaves*) Follow me this way. (*points to the tem-
ple*)

TRA   (*to Daemones*) Go on now, tell them to gouge his eyes
out the way cooks do with cuttlefish.

DAE   (*to the slaves*) Drag him out here by his feet like a slaugh-   660
tered pig.

Exeunt DAEMONES *and the two* SLAVES *into the temple. There
is noise inside.*

TRA   I can hear an uproar. I think the pimp is being combed
with fists. I really hope they've knocked the teeth out of
the crook's jaws. But look, the women themselves are
coming out of the temple in their panic.

III. iii: PALAESTRA. TRACHALIO. AMPELISCA

PAL   nunc id est quom omnium copiarum atque opum,

665   auxili, praesidi uiduitas nos tenet.

        <nec salust ne>c uia est quae salutem afferat,

        <nec quam in p>artem ingredi persequamur

        scimus: tanto in metu nunc sumus ambae,

        <tanta> importunitas tantaque iniuria

670   orta in nos est modo hic intus ab nostro ero,

        quin scelestus sacerdotem anum praecipes

        reppulit, propulit perquam indignis modis

        nosque ab signo intumo ui deripuit sua.

        sed nunc sese ut ferunt res fortunaeque nostrae,

675   par moriri est. neque est melius morte in malis

        rebus miseris.

TRA   quid est? quae illaec oratio est?

        cesso ego has consolari. heus Palaestra!

PAL   qui uocat?

TRA   Ampelisca.

AMP   opsecro, quis <is> est qui uocat?

PAL   quis is est qui nominat?

TRA   si respexis, scies.

680 PAL   o salutis meae spes.

TRA   tace ac bono animo es.

680ᵃ me uide.

PAL   si modo id liceat, uis ne opprimat,

681   quae uis uim mi afferam ipsa adigit.

TRA   ah! desine,

681ᵃ nimis inepta es.

---

666 <nec salust ne>c *Lindsay*   667 <nec quam in p>artem *Leo*
669 tanta *add. Valla*   670 orta in *solum in* T
675 est moriri P, *transp. Reiz*   678 is *add. Leo*

RUDENS

Enter PALAESTRA *and* AMPELISCA *from the temple, without seeing Trachalio.*

PAL (*to the audience*) Now is the time that deprivation of all supplies and resources, of help and protection, holds us 665 in its grip. There's no salvation and no path that brings salvation, nor do we know in which direction we should attempt to go: that's how great the fear is that we're in, that's how great the oppression and injustice is that has 670 arisen against us from our master in here now. Yes, and the criminal hustled the old priestess backward and forward impetuously, in a very shameful way, and he pulled us away from the statue deep inside by force. But the way our situation and position is now, it's better to die. 675 In a bad and wretched situation nothing is better than death.

TRA (*to himself*) What's that? What does that speech mean? I'm not consoling them quickly enough. (*loudly*) Hey, Palaestra!

PAL Who's calling?

TRA Ampelisca!

AMP Please, who is it that's calling?

PAL Who is it that's naming us?

TRA If you look back, you'll know.

PAL (*to Trachalio*) O hope of my safety. 680

TRA Be quiet and take heart. Look at me.

PAL If only it were granted that violence shouldn't crush us, violence which forces me to do violence to myself!

TRA Ah! Stop it, you're being too silly.

	PAL	desiste dictis nunciam miseram me consolari;
		nisi quid re praesidium apparas, Trachalio, acta haec res est.
	AMP	certum est moriri quam hunc pati ⟨saeuire⟩ lenonem in me.
685		sed muliebri animo sum tamen: miserae ⟨quom uenit⟩ in mentem
		mihi mortis, metus membra occupat. edepol diem hunc acerbum!
	TRA	bonum animum habete.
	PAL	nam, opsecro, unde iste animus mi inuenitur?
	TRA	ne, inquam, timete; assidite hic in ara.
	AMP	quid istaec ara
		prodesse nobis ⟨plus⟩ potest quam signum in fano hic intus
690		Veneris, quod amplexae modo, unde abreptae per uim miserae?
	TRA	sedete hic modo, ego hinc uos tamen tutabor. aram habete hanc
		uobis pro castris, moenia ⟨haec⟩; hinc ego uos defensabo.
		praesidio Veneris malitiae lenonis contra incedam.
	PAL	tibi auscultamus et, Venus alma, ambae te opsecramus,
695		aram amplexantes hanc tuam lacrumantes, genibus nixae,
		in custodelam nos tuam ut recipias et tutere;
		illos scelestos qui tuom fecerunt fanum parui
		fac ut ulciscare nosque ut hanc tua pace aram opsidere
700		patiare: elautae ambae sumus opera Neptuni noctu,
		ne indignum id habeas neue idcirco nobis uitio uortas,
		si quippiam est minus quod bene esse lautum tu arbitrare.

PAL   Stop consoling a wretch like me with your words now; unless you bring us some protection in action, Trachalio, we're done for.

AMP   I'm resolved to die rather than let this pimp treat me cruelly. But still, I have a woman's mind; poor me, when 685 death comes to my mind, fear grips my limbs. Goodness, this day is bitter!

TRA   Take courage, you two.

PAL   Please, where should I find that courage?

TRA   Stop being afraid, I tell you. Sit down here by the altar.

AMP   How can that altar be of more use to us than the statue of Venus here inside the temple, which we were clinging 690 on to just now and which we were dragged away from by force, poor us?

TRA   Just sit here, you two, I'll still protect you from here. Have this altar as your camp, and this as your ramparts; from here I'll defend you. Under Venus' protection I'll defy the pimp's wickedness.

PAL   We'll obey you and, kind Venus, we both entreat you, clinging to this altar of yours in tears and kneeling, 695 that you may receive us into your protection and guard us. Do take revenge on those criminals who have slighted your temple and do allow us to sit by your altar by your leave. We were both cleaned out by Neptune's doing in the night, so don't take offense and don't find fault with 700 us if there's anything there that you consider unclean.

---

684 saeuire *add. Schoell*   685 quom uenit *add. Fleckeisen*
689 plus *add. Camerarius*
692 haec *add. Lambinus*
699 pot(iare) lau- *A*, aut hae *B*, aut ae *CDT*, patiare (e)lautae *edd.*
701 lautu *P*, lautum tu *Camerarius*

TRA Venus, aequom has petere intellego: decet aps te id im-
      petrari;
    ignoscere his te conuenit: metus has id ut faciant sub-
      igit.
    te ex concha natam esse autumant, caue tu harum con-
      chas spernas.
705   sed optume eccum exit senex patronus mihique et uo-
      bis.

    III. iv: DAEMONES. TRACHALIO. LABRAX. LORARII

DAE exi e fano, natum quantum est hominum sacrilegis-
      sume.
    uos in aram abite sessum. sed ubi sunt?
TRA   huc respice.
DAE optume, istuc uolueramus. iube modo accedat prope.
    tun legerupionem hic nobis cum dis facere postulas?
710   pugnum in os impinge.
LAB   iniqua haec patior cum pretio tuo.
DAE at etiam minitatur audax?
LAB   ius meum ereptum est mihi,
    meas mihi ancillas inuito me eripis.
TRA   habe iudicem
    de senatu Cyrenensi quemuis opulentum uirum,
    si tuas esse oportet niue eas esse oportet liberas
715   neu te in carcerem compingi aequom est aetatemque
      ibi
    te usque habitare, donec totum carcerem contriueris.
LAB non hodie isti rei auspicaui, ut cum furcifero fabuler.
    te ego appello.

702 ut *uel* ue A, *spatium P*, Venus *Schoell*   712 habe inuicem
T (*unde* habe iudicem *Lindsay*), *om. BCD*, *edo*** A, cedo arbitrum
Studemund   714 eas oportet esse *P, transp. Merula*
    715 est aequom *P, transp. Gimm*

474

TRA   Venus, I know that what they seek is fair; they ought to
       get it from you. You should forgive them; fear forces
       them to do this. People say you were born from a scallop;
       take care you don't despise their scallops.[23] But perfect,   705
       look, the old man, my and your patron, is coming out.

Enter DAEMONES *from the temple, followed by the two* SLAVES
dragging out LABRAX; CHARMIDES *follows at a distance.*

DAE   (*to Labrax*) Leave the temple, you most godless of all
       men ever born! (*to the girls*) You two, go to sit by the
       altar. (*looking around*) But where are they?

TRA   Look here. (*points to them*)

DAE   Perfect, that's what we wanted. Just let him come close.
       (*to Labrax*) Do you expect to break our law here with the
       blessing of the gods? (*to a slave*) Plunge your fist into his   710
       face. (*the slave obeys*)

LAB   It'll be at your cost that I'm suffering this outrage.

DAE   Is the brazen fellow even threatening me?

LAB   My rights have been torn away from me, you're tearing
       my slave girls away from me against my will.

TRA   Take any wealthy man from the senate of Cyrene as your
       arbitrator to judge whether they ought to be yours or
       whether they ought not to be free and whether you ought   715
       not to be put into prison and live there your entire life,
       until you've worn out the entire prison.

LAB   I didn't elect to devote myself today to conversation with
       a gallows bird. (*to Daemones*) I'm addressing you.

---

[23] Venus, born from the foam of the sea, is often depicted on a shell;
but the word, used of the girls, has a double meaning ("female geni-
talia").

DAE	cum istoc primum qui te nouit disputa.
LAB	tecum ago.
TRA	atqui mecum agendum est. suntne illae ancillae tuae?
720 LAB	sunt.
TRA	agedum ergo, tange utramuis digitulo minimo modo—
LAB	quid si attigero?
TRA	extemplo hercle ego te follem pugilatorium
	faciam et pendentem incursabo pugnis, periurissume.
LAB	mihi non liceat meas ancillas Veneris de ara abducere?
DAE	non licet: est lex apud nos—
LAB	mihi cum uostris legibus
725	⟨nil quicquam est⟩ commerci. equidem istas iam am-
	bas educam foras.
	tu, senex, si istas amas, huc arido argento est opus;
	si autem Veneri complacuerunt, habeat, si argentum
	dabit.
DAE	det tibi argentum? nunc adeo meam ut scias senten-
	tiam,
	occipito modo illis afferre uim ioculo pauxillulum,
730	ita ego te hinc ornatum amittam tu ipsus te ut non
	noueris.
	uos adeo, ubi ego innuero uobis, ni ei caput exoculas-
	sitis,
	quasi murteta iunci, item ego uos uirgis circumuin-
	ciam.
LAB	ui agis [mecum].
TRA	etiam uim probro das, flagiti flagrantia?
LAB	tun, trifurcifer, mihi audes inclementer dicere?

724 ⟨ita⟩ est *Lambinus*
725 nil quicquam est *add. Seyffert*
728 *incertum utrum* det *an* dei *habeat* A, do P

DAE First argue with the man who knows you.

LAB I'm concerned with you.

TRA But you have to be concerned with me. Are those your slave girls?

LAB Yes. 720

TRA Go on then, just touch one of them with your finger-tip—

LAB (*interrupting*) What if I do?

TRA I'll turn you into a punch ball at once and attack you with my fists while you hang, you monstrous perjurer.

LAB I shouldn't be allowed to take my own slave girls away from the altar of Venus?

DAE You aren't allowed to: there's a law among us—

LAB (*interrupting*) I have nothing to do with your laws. I'll 725 remove both of them. If you're in love with them, old man, you need to give me hard cash; and if Venus has taken a liking to them, she can have them if she gives me money.

DAE She should give you money? So that you may know my judgment now, just begin to do violence to them a little bit, as a joke, and I'll send you off in such a state that you 730 won't know yourself. (*to the slaves*) As for you, unless you knock the eyes out of his head when I give you the signal, I'll surround you with rods the way reeds surround myrtle groves.

LAB You're doing violence to me.

TRA Are you even finding fault with violence, you outrageous thug?

LAB Do you dare to speak to me uncivilly, you gallows bird?

---

730 tu ipsus te ut *P*, ut tu ipsu*** *A*
733 mecum *om. A*   proportas *P*, probro das *Leo*

735 TRA fateor, ego trifurcifer sum, tu es homo apprime probus:
      numqui minus hasce esse oportet liberas?

   LAB   quid, "liberas"?

   TRA atque eras tuas quidem hercle atque ex germana Grae-
         cia;
      nam altera haec est nata Athenis ingenuis parentibus.

   DAE quid ego ex te audio?

   TRA   hanc Athenis esse natam liberam.

740 DAE mea popularis, opsecro, haec est?

   TRA   non tu Cyrenensis es?

   DAE immo Athenis natus altusque educatusque Atticis.

   TRA opsecro, defende ciuis tuas, senex.

   DAE   o filia
      mea, quom hanc uideo, mearum me apsens miseri-
         arum commones;
      trima quae periit mi iam tanta esset, si uiuit, scio.

745 LAB argentum ego pro istisce ambabus quoiae erant domino
         dedi;
      quid mea refert Athenis natae haec an Thebis sient,
      dum mihi recte seruitutem seruiant?

   TRA   itane, impudens?
      tune hic, feles uirginalis, liberos parentibus
      sublectos habebis atque indigno quaestu conteres?

750   nam huic alterae quae patria sit profecto nescio,
      nisi scio probiorem hanc esse quam te, impuratissume.

   LAB tuae istae sunt?

   TRA   contende ergo uter sit tergo . . . uerior:
      ni offerrumentas habebis pluris in tergo tuo

    746 hae athenis natae *P, transp. Schoell*

478

TRA   (*with irony*) I admit it, I'm a gallows bird and you are a   735
       very fine fellow. Should they be any less free?

LAB   What, "free"?

TRA   And your owners, being girls from Greece proper:
       (*pointing to Palaestra*) this one was born in Athens to
       free parents.

DAE   What do I hear from you?

TRA   That this girl was born free in Athens.

DAE   Is she my compatriot, please?   740

TRA   Are you not from Cyrene?

DAE   No, I was born, raised, and brought up in Attic Athens.

TRA   Please defend your fellow citizens, old man.

DAE   O my daughter, when I see this girl, you remind me of
       my wretched situation in your absence; my girl that van-
       ished when she was three would be that big now, if she's
       alive, I know.

LAB   I gave their owner money for them both. What business   745
       of mine is it whether they were born in Athens or in
       Thebes, so long as they serve me well in slavery?

TRA   Really, you shameless creature? Will you, you maiden
       mouser, own children that were snatched away from
       their parents, and will you wear them out in your vile
       trade? Well, I don't know in fact what native city this   750
       other one has, except that I know she's more decent than
       you, you filthy creature.

LAB   They're yours?

TRA   Then compete which of us has a back that's . . . truer:[24]
       unless you have more scars on your back than any war-

---

[24] An unexpected joke. We expect him to say "neater" or "having fewer scars from beating," but he says "truer" to indicate why he has not been beaten.

quam ulla nauis longa clauos, tum ego ero mendacis-
    sumus:

755   postea aspicito meum, quando ego tuom inspectauero:

ni erit tam sincerum ut quiuis dicat ampullarius

optumum esse operi faciundo corium et sincerissu-
    mum,

quid causae est quin uirgis te usque ad saturitatem
    sauciem?

quid illas spectas? quas si attigeris, oculos eripiam tibi.

760 LAB   atqui, quia uotas, utramque iam mecum abducam
    simul.

DAE   quid facies?

LAB   Volcanum adducam, is Venerist aduorsarius.

TRA   quo illic it?

LAB   heus, ecquis hic est? heus!

DAE   si attigeris ostium,

iam hercle tibi fiet in ore messis mergis pugneis.

LOR   nullum habemus ignem, ficis uictitamus aridis.

765 TRA   ego dabo ignem, siquidem in capite tuo conflandi copia
    est.

LAB   ibo hercle aliquo quaeritatum lignum.

DAE   quid quom inueneris?

LAB   ignem magnum hic faciam.

DAE   quin inhumanum exuras tibi?

LAB   immo hasce ambas hic in ara ut uiuas comburam, id
    uolo.

761 quid Ω, qui *Trappes-Lomax per litteras*
763 messis in ore fiet Ω, *transp. Sonnenschein*
766 ignem *P*, *gnem *A*, lignum *Schoell*

ship has nails, I'll be the biggest liar. After that, when I've 755
inspected yours, look at mine: unless it's so unspoiled
that any wineskin-maker would say it's perfect for carry-
ing on his craft and absolutely unspoiled, do you have
any objection against me wounding you with rods till I'm
tired? Why are you looking at them? If you touch them,
I'll tear out your eyes.

LAB And yet, just because you forbid me to, I'll drag both off 760
with me at the same time now.

DAE What will you do?

LAB I'll bring Vulcan, he's the enemy of Venus.[25]

TRA Where is he going?

LAB (*unaware that the house he is approaching belongs to
Daemones*) Hello! Is anyone here? Hello!

DAE If you touch the door, I'll make hay in your face with a
fisty pitchfork this instant.

SLAVE (*to Labrax*) We don't have any fire, we live on dried
figs.[26]

TRA (*to Labrax*) I'll give you fire, if I can kindle it on your 765
head.

LAB I'll go somewhere to look for wood.

DAE What when you've found some?

LAB I'll make a big fire here.

DAE So that you can burn out your inhumanity with it?

LAB No, burning these two girls alive here on the altar, that's
what I want.

[25] Vulcan stands for fire; the pimp wants to smoke the girls out. The
unattractive Vulcan was the husband of Venus, who cheated on him
with Mars, which led to the enmity between the couple.
[26] Which do not require cooking.

PLAUTUS

TRA iam hercle ego te continuo barba arripiam, in ignem
      coniciam
770   teque ambustulatum obiciam magnis auibus pabulum.
DAE quom coniecturam egomet mecum facio, haec illa est
      simia
      quae has hirundines ex nido uolt eripere ingratiis,
      quod ego in somnis somniaui.
TRA   scin quid tecum oro, senex?
      ut illas serues, uim defendas, dum ego erum adduco
      meum.
775 DAE quaere erum atque adduce.
TRA   at hic ne—
DAE   maxumo malo suo
      si attigerit siue occeptassit.
TRA   cura.
DAE   curatum est, abi.
TRA hunc quoque asserua ipsum ne quo abitat; nam promi-
      simus
      carnufici aut talentum magnum aut hunc hodie sistere.
DAE abi modo, ego dum hoc c‹ur›abo recte.
TRA   iam ego reuenero.

III. v: DAEMONES. LABRAX. LORARII

780 DAE utrum tu, leno, cum malo lubentius
      quiescis an sic sine malo, si copia est?
LAB ego quae tu loquere flocci non facio, senex.
      meas quidem te inuito et Venere et summo Ioue
      de ara capillo iam deripiam.

779 *uersus deest in P*   kocc . . . tabo *A*, hoc curabo *Studemund*

482

TRA Now I'll seize you by your beard at once, throw you into the fire, and throw you before the big birds[27] as fodder   770 when you're half roasted.

DAE (*to himself*) Now that I come to consider it, this is that monkey that wants to drag these swallows from their nest against their will, which I dreamed about in my sleep.

TRA Do you know what I ask of you, old man? That you protect them and prevent violence against them while I bring my master here.

DAE Do look for your master and bring him here.   775

TRA But this chap shouldn't—

DAE (*interrupting*) It'll cost him dearly if he touches them or even begins to.

TRA Take care of it.

DAE It's taken care of, off you go.

TRA And watch him so that he doesn't slip away, either: we've promised the hangman either an Attic talent or to produce him in court today.

DAE Just go while I take care of it properly.

TRA I'll be back in a moment.

Exit TRACHALIO *to the left.*

DAE (*to Labrax*) Do you prefer to be peaceful with a beating,   780 pimp, or like this, without a beating, if you have the choice?

LAB I don't care a straw about what you say, old man. This minute I'll drag off my girls from the altar by their hair, against your will and that of Venus and of Jupiter above.

27 I.e., vultures.

	DAE	tangedum.
785	LAB	tangam hercle uero.
	DAE	agedum ergo, accede huc modo.
	LAB	iubedum recedere istos ambo illuc modo.
	DAE	immo ad te accedent.
	LAB	non hercle equidem censeo.
	DAE	quid ages si accedent propius?
	LAB	ego recessero.

uerum, senex, si te umquam in urbe offendero,
790   numquam hercle quisquam me lenonem dixerit
si te non ludos pessumos dimisero.

	DAE	facito istuc quod minitare; sed nunc interim,

si illas attigeris, dabitur tibi magnum malum.

	LAB	quam magnum uero?
	DAE	quantum lenoni sat est.
795	LAB	minacias ego flocci non faciam tuas,

equidem has te inuito iam ambas rapiam.

	DAE	tangedum.
	LAB	tangam hercle uero.
	DAE	tanges, at scin quo modo?

i dum, Turbalio, curriculo, affert‹o domo›
duas clauas.

	LAB	clauas?
	DAE	sed probas. propera cito.
800		ego te hodie faxo recte acceptum ut dignus es.
	LAB	eheu! scelestus galeam in naui perdidi;

796 kas *A*, eas *P*
798 affert‹o domo› *Leo*

DAE	Just touch them.
LAB	I shall indeed touch them. 785
DAE	Go on then, just come here.
LAB	(*as the two slaves approach him*) Just tell those two to go back there.
DAE	No, they'll come toward you.
LAB	I really don't think so.
DAE	What will you do if they come closer?
LAB	I'll go back. But, old man, if I ever meet you in town, no 790 one shall ever call me a pimp if I don't make great sport of you before I let you go.
DAE	Do what you're threatening me with; but now in the meantime you'll get a big thrashing if you touch them.
LAB	How big, though?
DAE	Enough for a pimp.
LAB	I don't care a straw about your threats; I'll drag both of 795 them away against your will.
DAE	Just touch them.
LAB	I shall indeed touch them.
DAE	You will touch them, but do you know how? (*to one of the slaves*) Go quickly, Turbalio, bring two cudgels from home.
LAB	Cudgels?
DAE	(*still to Turbalio*) And what's more, proper ones. Hurry quickly. 800

Exit TURBALIO *into the farmhouse.*

DAE	(*to Labrax*) I'll give you a proper reception today, as you deserve.
LAB	Poor me! I lost my helmet on the ship, fool that I am.

nunc mi opportuna hic esset, salua si foret.
licet saltem istas mi appellare?

DAE   non licet.

804–5   ehem! optume edepol eccum clauator [ad]uenit.

LAB   illud quidem edepol tinnimentum est auribus.

DAE   age accipe illinc alteram clauam, Sparax.
age, alter istinc, alter hinc assistite.
assistite ambo sic. audite nunciam:

810   si hercle illic illas hodie digito tetigerit
inuitas, ni istunc istis inuitassitis
usque adeo donec qua domum abeat nesciat,
periistis ambo. si appellabit quempiam,
uos respondetote istinc istarum uicem;

815   sin ipse abitere hinc uolet, quantum potest
extemplo amplectitote crura fustibus.

LAB   etiam me abire hinc non sinent?

DAE   dixi satis.
et ubi ille cum ero seruos huc aduenerit
qui erum accersiuit, itote extemplo domum.

820   curate haec sultis magna diligentia.

LAB   heu hercle! ne istic fana mutantur cito:
iam hoc Herculei est, Veneris fanum quod fuit,
ita duo destituit signa hic cum clauis senex.
non hercle quo hinc nunc gentium aufugiam scio,

825   ita nunc mi utrumque saeuit, et terra et mare.
Palaestra!

804–5 [ad]uenit *Bentley*
815 abire *CD*, abile *B*, abbitere *Acidalius*

486

Now it would come in handy if I still had it. Can I at least address them?

DAE No. 805

Enter TURBALIO *with two cudgels from the farmhouse.*

DAE Ah! Excellent, look, the man with the cudgels is coming.

LAB That means ringing for my ears.

DAE Come on, take the other cudgel from him, Sparax. Come on, one of you stand there, the other here. Stand like this, both of you. Now listen: if he touches them with a 810 finger against their wishes today and if you don't give him a taste of your cudgels until he doesn't know what way to go home, you're both dead. If he addresses anyone, you two must reply in their place from there. But if he 815 wants to go away himself, you must instantly compass about his shins with the clubs as quickly as possible.

LAB Won't they even let me go away from here?

DAE (*ignoring him*) I've said enough. And when that slave who went to fetch his master arrives here with him, go home at once. Attend to this with great care, will you? 820

Exit DAEMONES *into his house.*

LAB Poor me! Seriously, temples change quickly at your place: this one, which used to be a temple of Venus, is one of Hercules, to judge from how the old man has set up two statues with cudgels here.[28] I really don't know where on earth I should flee to now, both land and sea 825 are so savage to me. Palaestra!

[28] Hercules is typically depicted with a cudgel or club.

LOR   quid uis?

LAB   apage, controuorsia est,
     haec quidem Palaestra quae respondit non mea est.
     heus, Ampelisca!

LOR2   caue sis infortunio.

LAB   ultro te! signa ut homines satis recte monent.

830   sed uobis dico, heus uos! num molestiae est
     me adire ad illas propius?

LOR   nil . . . nobis quidem.

LAB   numquid molestum mihi erit?

LOR   nil, si caueris.

LAB   quid est quod caueam?

LOR   em! a crasso infortunio.

LAB   quaeso hercle abire ut liceat.

LOR   abeas, si uelis.

835 LAB   bene hercle factum. habeo uobis gratiam.
     non [ac]cedam potius.

LOR   illic astato ilico.

LAB   edepol proueni nequiter multis modis.
     certum est hasce hodie usque opsidione uincere.

III. vi: PLESIDIPPVS. TRACHALIO.
LABRAX. CHARMIDES. LORARII

PLE   meamne ille amicam leno ui, uiolentia

840   de ara deripere Veneris uoluit?

TRA   admodum.

PLE   quin occidisti extemplo?

TRA   gladius non erat.

PLE   caperes aut fustem aut lapidem.

829 ut potest ignaui *P*, ultro te! signa ut *Leo*
836 [ac]cedam *Seyffert*   astate *P*, astato *Gruterus*

SLAVE What do you want?

LAB Go away, I protest, this Palaestra who has answered isn't mine. Hey, Ampelisca!

SLAVE2 Watch out for trouble.

LAB Away with you! The statues give quite proper warnings, like humans. But I'm speaking to you two, hey, you! Is 830 there any harm in me coming closer to them?

SLAVE None . . . for us.

LAB Will it be harmful to me?

SLAVE Not if you watch out.

LAB What is it that I should watch out for?

SLAVE There you go! For a fat thrashing.

LAB I ask you to let me leave.

SLAVE Leave, if you wish.

LAB That's kind of you. I'm grateful to you. (*as he moves* 835 *away, the slaves approach*) I'd better not retreat.

SLAVE Stand still there at once.

LAB I've come off really miserably. I'm resolved to gain possession of the girls today by besieging them unremittingly.

Enter PLESIDIPPUS *and* TRACHALIO *from the left; Plesidippus is carrying a rope.*

PLE Did that pimp want to drag my girlfriend from the altar 840 of Venus with force and violence?

TRA Exactly.

PLE Why didn't you kill him at once?

TRA I didn't have a sword.

PLE You should have taken a club or a stone.

TRA	quid? ego quasi canem
	hominem insectarer lapidibus nequissumum?
LAB	nunc pol ego perii, Plesidippus eccum adest.
845	conuorret iam hic me totum cum puluisculo.
PLE	etiamne in ara tunc sedebant mulieres,
	quom ad me profectu's ire?
TRA	ibidem nunc sedent.
PLE	quis illas nunc illic seruat?
TRA	nescioquis senex,
	uicinus Veneris; is dedit operam optumam.
850	is nunc cum seruis seruat. ego mandaueram.
PLE	duc me ad lenonem recta. ubi illic est homo?
LAB	salue.
PLE	salutem nil moror. opta ocius:
	rapi te optorto collo mauis an trahi?
	utrumuis opta dum licet.
LAB	neutrum uolo.
855 PLE	abi sane ad litus curriculo, Trachalio,
	iube illos in urbem ire obuiam ad portum mihi,
	quos mecum duxi, hunc qui ad carnuficem traderent.
	post huc redito atque agitato hic custodiam.
	ego hunc scelestum in ius rapiam, ⟨exigam⟩ exulem.
860	age, ambula in ius.
LAB	quid ego deliqui?
PLE	rogas?
	quin arrabonem a me accepisti ob mulierem
	et eam hinc abduxti?
LAB	non auexi.
PLE	quor negas?

859 exigam *add. Schoell*
862 iam *P*, et eam *Pylades*   abduxisti *P*, auexti *Acidalius*

TRA   What? Should I have chased the good-for-nothing with stones like a dog?

LAB   (*aside*) Now I'm dead, look, Plesidippus is here. He'll 845 sweep me away to the last speck of dust now.

PLE   Were the women still sitting by the altar when you set out to come to me?

TRA   They're still sitting in the same place.

PLE   Who is watching over them now?

TRA   Some old man, the neighbor of Venus; he's been very helpful. He's now watching over them with slaves. I told 850 him to.

PLE   Take me to the pimp directly. Where is he?

LAB   My greetings.

PLE   I don't care for your greetings. Choose quickly: do you prefer to be pushed away with a rope around your neck or to be pulled away? Choose whichever you like while you can.

LAB   I don't fancy either.

PLE   Do go to the shore quickly, Trachalio, and tell the men I 855 took with me to come into town to meet me at the harbor, so that they can hand this chap over to the executioner. Then come back here and keep watch. I'll hustle this criminal away to court, I'll drive him into exile.

Exit TRACHALIO *to the left.*

PLE   (*to Labrax*) Come on, go to court. 860

LAB   What wrong have I done?

PLE   You ask? You, who took a deposit from me for the woman and took her away from here?

LAB   I didn't get her away.

PLE   Why do you deny it?

LAB	quia pol prouexi: auehere non quiui miser.	

LAB   quia pol prouexi: auehere non quiui miser.
    equidem tibi me dixeram praesto fore
865   apud Veneris fanum: ⟨num⟩quid muto? sumne ibi?
PLE   in iure causam dicito, hic uerbum sat est:
    sequere.
LAB   opsecro te, subueni mi, Charmides.
    rapior optorto collo.
CHAR   quis me nominat?
LAB   uiden me ut rapior?
CHAR   uideo atque inspecto lubens.
870 LAB   non subuenire mi audes?
CHAR   quis homo te rapit?
LAB   adulescens Plesidippus.
CHAR   ut nanctu's habe.
    bono animo meliust te in neruom correpere.
    tibi optigit quod plurumi exoptant sibi.
LAB   quid id est?
CHAR   ut id quod quaerant inueniant sibi.
875 LAB   sequere, opsecro, me.
CHAR   pariter suades qualis es:
    tu in neruom rapere, eo me opsecras ut te sequar.
    etiam retentas?
LAB   perii!
PLE   uerum sit uelim.
    tu, mea Palaestra et Ampelisca, ibidem ilico
    manete dum ego huc redeo.
LOR   equidem suadeo
880   ut ad nos abeant potius, dum recipis.
PLE   placet,
    bene facitis.

865 ⟨num⟩quid *Bentley*

LAB   Because I got her out to sea, but I couldn't get her away,
wretch that I am. Anyhow, I told you I'd be at the temple   865
of Venus: am I changing anything? Am I not there?

PLE   Defend yourself in court; there's been enough talk here.
Follow me. (*puts the rope around his neck and tries to
drag him off*)

LAB   I beg you, come to my help, Charmides! I'm being hus-
tled away with a rope round my neck.

CHAR Who is calling me?

LAB   Can't you see how I'm being hustled away?

CHAR I can and I watch it with pleasure.

LAB   Don't you want to come to my help?   870

CHAR Who is hustling you away?

LAB   Young Plesidippus.

CHAR Findings, keepings. It's better for you to crawl to prison
cheerfully. You've got what a lot of people wish for.

LAB   What's that?

CHAR To get what they're looking for.

LAB   I entreat you, follow me.   875

CHAR Your advice is of the same quality as you are: you are
being hustled away to prison and you entreat me to fol-
low you there. (*as Labrax tries to grab him*) Are you even
holding me back?

LAB   I'm dead!

PLE   I wish it were true. You, Palaestra, my love, and Am-
pelisca, wait there in the same spot till I come back
here.

SLAVE My advice is that they'd better go to our house till you   880
return.

PLE   Good idea! That's kind of you.

PLAUTUS

LAB	fures mi estis.
LOR	quid, "fures"? rape.
LAB	oro, opsecro, Palaestra.
PLE	sequere, carnufex.
LAB	hospes!
CHAR	non sum hospes, repudio hospitium tuom.
LAB	sicin me spernis?
CHAR	sic ago. ‹sat› semel bibo.
885 LAB	di te infelicent!
CHAR	isti capiti dicito.

credo alium in aliam beluam hominem uortier:
illic in columbum, credo, leno uortitur,
nam collus in columbari hau multo post erit;
in neruom ille hodie nidamenta congeret.
890 uerum tamen ibo ei aduocatus ut siem,
si qui mea opera citius . . . addici potest.

ACTVS IV

IV. i: DAEMONES

DAE bene factum et uolup est me hodie his mulierculis
tetulisse auxilium. iam clientas repperi,
atque ambas forma scitula atque aetatula.
895 sed uxor scelesta me omnibus seruat modis,
ne qui significem quippiam mulierculis.
sed Gripus seruos noster quid rerum gerat
miror, de nocte qui abiit piscatum ad mare.

884 sat *add. Fay*
888 in columbari collum *P*, in columbari collus *Priscianus, transp.*
Fleckeisen
896 quid *P*, qui *Acidalius*

LAB   You're robbers!

SLAVE What, "robbers"? (*to Plesidippus*) Hustle him away.

LAB   I beg and entreat you, Palaestra!

PLE   Follow me, you criminal.

LAB   (*to Charmides*) My friend!

CHAR I'm not your friend, I reject your friendship.

LAB   Do you despise me like this?

CHAR Yes, just like this. One drink is enough.

LAB   May the gods curse you!   885

PLESIDIPPUS drags LABRAX off to the right.

CHAR (*calling after him*) Speak for yourself. (*to the audience*)
      I believe that everyone turns into a different animal.
      That pimp is turning into a ringdove, I believe: in a little
      while his neck will be in a collar ring. He'll carry his
      material for a nest into prison today. But still, I'll go to   890
      be his advocate, to see if through my help he can some-
      how more quickly . . . be sentenced.

*Exit CHARMIDES to the right; exeunt PALAESTRA, AMPELISCA,
and the two SLAVES into the farmhouse.*

ACT FOUR

Enter DAEMONES from the farmhouse.

DAE   It was a good thing and I'm happy that I've brought these
      women help today. They're my dependants now, and
      both of pretty appearance and blooming youth. But my   895
      wretched wife is constantly watching me so that I can't
      get any message to the girls. But I wonder what our slave
      Gripus is up to; he went down to the sea to go fishing in

pol magis sapisset si dormiuisset domi,
900 nam nunc et operam ludos facit et retia,
ut tempestas est nunc atque ut noctu fuit.
in digitis hodie percoquam quod ceperit,
ita fluctuare uideo uehementer mare.
sed ad prandium uxor me uocat. redeo domum.
905 iam meas opplebit auris [sua] uaniloquentia.

IV. ii: GRIPVS

GRI Neptuno has ago gratias meo patrono,
qui salsis locis incolit pisculentis,
quom med ex suis [locis] pulchre ornatum expediuit
templis redducem, pluruma praeda onustum,
910 salute horiae, quae in mari fluctuoso
piscatu nouo me uberi compotiuit.
miroque modo atque incredibili hic piscatus mi lepide
  euenit,
nec piscium ullam unciam pondo hodie cepi, nisi hoc
  quod fero hic in rete.
914– nam ut de nocte multa impigreque exsurrexi,
15 lucrum praeposiui sopori et quieti:
tempestate saeua experiri expetiui
paupertatem eri qui et meam seruitutem
tolerarem, opera hau fui parcus mea.
920 nimis homo nihili est quis est piger nimisque id genus
  odi ego male.
uigilare decet hominem qui uolt sua temperi conficere
  officia.

900 retia *P*, retiam *Priscianus*   905 sua *del. Guyet*
908 me ex suis locis *P*, med ex suis *Reiz*
913 hodie pondo *P*, *transp. Pylades*

the middle of the night. He'd have been wiser to sleep at home: now he's wasting his effort and the nets, given 900 what the storm is like now and what it was like during the night. I'll cook his catch on my fingers today,[29] so violently can I see the sea surge. (*after some noise inside*) But my wife is calling me to lunch. I'm returning home. Now she'll fill my ears with her idle chatter. 905

Exit DAEMONES *into his house.*
Enter GRIPUS *from the left, carrying a net with a trunk in it; from the net a long rope is trailing.*

GRI To Neptune, my patron, who inhabits the salty places full of fish, I give thanks for releasing me from his regions for my return, equipped beautifully and laden with very great booty, leaving my fishing boat intact, which has put 910 me in possession of a new, rich catch of fish in the heaving sea. And in a strange and unbelievable way I got a lovely catch here, and yet I didn't catch one ounce of fish today, except for what I'm carrying here in my net. Yes, 915 when I got up energetically in the middle of the night, I preferred profit to sleep and rest. In the wild storm I strove to try to alleviate my master's poverty and my slavery, I didn't spare my effort. He who is lazy is abso- 920 lutely worthless, and I absolutely hate that type. A man who wants to do his duties in good time ought to stay

[29] I.e., he will catch nothing.

918 sententiam *P*, seruitutem *Camerarius*
920 quis *BCD*, qui *W*

non enim illum exspectare ⟨id⟩ oportet, dum erus se
    ad suom suscitet officium.
nam qui dormiunt lubenter sine lucro et cum malo qui-
    escunt.
nam ego nunc mihi, qui impiger fui,

925   repperi ut piger si uelim siem:
925ᵃ   hoc ego in mari quicquid hic inest
926   repperi. [quicquid inest,] graue quidem est;
926ᵃ   aurum hic ego inesse reor; nec mi conscius est ullus
    homo. nunc haec
occasio tibi, Gripe, optigit ut liberet extemplo prae-
    tor te.
nunc sic faciam, sic consilium est: ad erum ueniam
    docte atque astu[te].
pauxillatim pollicitabor pro capite argentum ut sim
    liber.

930   iam ubi liber ero, igitur demum instruam agrum atque
    aedis, mancupia,
nauibus magnis mercaturam faciam, apud reges rex
    perhibebor.
post animi causa mi nauem faciam atque imitabor Stra-
    tonicum,
oppida circumuectabor. ubi nobilitas mea erit clara,
oppidum magnum communibo; ei ego urbi Gripo in-
    dam nomen,

935   monumentum meae famae et factis, ibi[que] regnum
    magnum instituam.
magnas res hic agito in mentem instruere. hunc nunc
    uidulum condam.
sed hic rex cum aceto pransurust et sale sine bono pul-
    mento.

awake. He ought not to wait until his master wakes him
for his duty. Yes, those who like sleeping rest without
profit and with thrashing. Well, I, who was energetic,
have now found the means to be lazy if I wish: I've found 925
this in the sea, whatever is in here. It really is heavy; I
believe there's gold in here. And nobody knows what I've
done. Now, Gripus, you've got this chance for the prae-
tor[30] to free you. Now I'll act like this, my plan goes like
this: I'll approach my master adroitly and with cunning.
Little by little I'll promise him money for myself so that
I may be free.[31] As soon as I'm free, I'll organize a farm 930
and a house and slaves, I'll do trade with big ships, I'll
be considered a king among kings. Later I'll build myself
a ship for my enjoyment and imitate Stratonicus;[32] I'll
sail around the cities. When my fame is well known, I'll
set up a big city. This city I shall call Gripus, as a memo- 935
rial to my fame and deeds. There I shall set up a great
kingdom. I'm arranging to organize great things here in
my mind. Now I'll put away this trunk. But this king's
going to have lunch with vinegar and salt and without a
tasty relish.

[30] Roman magistrate with chiefly judicial functions. Manumissions
in Greece were less formal.   [31] Gripus does not want to indicate
how rich he is so that his master cannot demand too high a sum for his
release.   [32] Greek musician of the fourth century who traveled to
present his art.

922 id *add. Seyffert*   926 quicquid inest *del. Questa*
927 tibi occasio *P*, *transp. Fay*   liberes ex populo praeter te *P*,
liberet te ex populo praetor *Fleckeisen*, liberet extemplo praetor te
Lindsay in apparatu   928 astu[te] *Reiz*
935 ibi[que] *Sonnenschein*

IV. iii: TRACHALIO. GRIPVS

938	TRA	heus, mane.
	GRI	quid maneam?
	TRA	dum hanc tibi
938ᵃ		quam trahis rudentem complico.
939	GRI	mitte modo.
	TRA	at pol ego te adiuuo,
939ᵃ		nam bonis quod bene fit hau perit.
940	GRI	turbida tempestas heri fuit,
941		nil habeo, adulescens, piscium,
941ᵃ		ne tu mihi esse postules;
942		non uides referre me uuidum
942ᵃ		retem sine squamoso pecu?
943	TRA	non edepol piscis expeto
943ᵃ		quam tui sermonis sum indigens.
944	GRI	enicas iam me odio, quisquis es.
944ᵃ	TRA	non sinam ego abire hinc te. mane.
945	GRI	caue sis malo. quid tu, malum, nam me retrahis?
	TRA	audi.
	GRI	non audio.
	TRA	at pol qui audies post.
	GRI	quin loquere quid uis.
947	TRA	eho manedum. est operae pretium
947ᵃ		quod tibi ego narrare uolo.
948	GRI	eloquere: quid id est?
	TRA	uide num
948ᵃ		quispiam consequitur prope nos.
	GRI	ecquid est quod mea referat?
	TRA	scilicet.
950		sed boni consili ecquid in te mihi est?

942ᵃ retem *Priscianus*, rete *P*   947 modo *P*, manedum *Leo*

Enter TRACHALIO *from the left.*

TRA Hey, wait. (*grabs the rope*)
GRI What should I wait for? (*keeps walking*)
TRA Till I fold up this rope for you which you're dragging
along.
GRI Just let go.
TRA But I'm helping you, since a good deed done to good
men doesn't perish.
GRI Yesterday the weather was stormy; I don't have any fish, 940
young man, don't imagine that I do. Can't you see that
I'm carrying back a wet net without any scaly livestock?
TRA I'm not looking for fish as much as I'm in need of a con-
versation with you.
GRI You're killing me with your tedium, whoever you are.
TRA I won't let you go away from here. Wait! (*pulls on the
rope*)
GRI Watch out for trouble, will you? Why the blazes are you 945
holding me back?
TRA Listen.
GRI I won't.
TRA But you will later. (*pulls again*)
GRI Say what you want.
TRA Hey, just wait. What I want to tell you is worth your
while.
GRI Tell me, what is it?
TRA Look if anyone's following close to us.
GRI Is it something that matters to me?
TRA Of course. But do you have some discretion in you? 950

GRI   quid negoti est modo dice.

TRA   dicam, tace,

952–53   si fidem modo das mihi te non fore infidum.

954–55   GRI   do fidem tibi, fidus ero, quisquis es.

TRA   audi.

956   furtum ego uidi qui faciebat;

956ᵃ   no[ue]ram dominum, id quoi fiebat,

957   post ad furem egomet deuenio

957ᵃ   feroque ei condicionem hoc pacto:

958   "ego istuc furtum scio quoi factum est;

958ᵃ   nunc mi si uis dare dimidium,

959   indicium domino non faciam."

959ᵃ   is mi nihil etiam respondit.

960   quid inde aequom est dari mihi? dimidium

961   uolo ut dicas.

GRI   immo hercle etiam plus,

961ᵃ   nam nisi dat, domino dicundum

962   censeo.

TRA   tuo consilio faciam.

962ᵃ   nunc aduorte animum; namque hoc om-

962ᵇ   ne attinet ad te.

GRI   quid factum est?

TRA   uidulum istum quoius est noui ego hominem iam
      pridem.

GRI   quid est?

TRA   et quo pacto periit.

GRI   at ego quo pacto inuentust scio

965   et qui inuenit hominem noui et dominus qui nunc est
      scio.

   nihilo pol pluris tua hoc quam quanti illud refert mea:

   ego illum noui quoius nunc est, tu illum quoius antehac
      fuit.

   hunc homo feret a me nemo, ne tu te speres potis.

GRI Just tell me what's the matter.

TRA I'll tell you, be quiet, so long as you give me your word
that you'll play fair.

GRI I do, I'll play fair, whoever you are. (*stops*) 955

TRA Listen. I saw someone who was committing a theft. I
knew the owner to whom this was being done. Then I
come to the thief myself and bring him my terms in this
way: "I know who this was stolen from. Now if you're
willing to give me half, I won't inform the owner." He
still hasn't given me any reply. What is a fair part I should 960
be given from it? I want you to say half.

GRI No, even more: if he doesn't give it to you, I think the
owner has to be told.

TRA I'll follow your advice. Now pay attention, because all
this has to do with you.

GRI What's happened?

TRA I've known the man whose trunk this is for a long time
now.

GRI What's that?

TRA And how it got lost.

GRI But I know how it was found and I'm familiar with the 965
man who found it and I know who the owner is now. And
this is no more any of your business than what you say is
any of mine. I know the man who it belongs to now, you
the one who it belonged to before. No one will take this
away from me, so don't expect that you can.

951 dic *P*, dice *Reiz*
956[a] no[ue]ram *Lindsay in apparatu*
961 amplius *P*, plus *Seyffert*

TRA   non ferat si dominus ueniat?
GRI   dominus huic, [nemo] ne frustra sis,
970   nisi ego nemo natust, hunc qui cepi in uenatu meo.
TRA   itane uero?
GRI   ecquem esse dices in mari piscem meum?
      quos quom capio, siquidem cepi, mei sunt; habeo pro
          meis,
      nec manu asseruntur neque illinc partem quisquam
          postulat.
      in foro palam omnis uendo pro meis uenalibus.
975   mare quidem commune certo est omnibus.
TRA   assentio:
      qui minus hunc communem quaeso mi esse oportet
          uidulum?
      in mari inuentust communi.
GRI   esne impudenter impudens?
      nam si istuc ius sit quod memoras, piscatores perierint.
      quippe quom extemplo in macellum pisces prolati
          sient,
980   nemo emat, suam quisque partem piscium poscant sibi,
      dicant in mari communi captos.
TRA   quid ais, impudens?
      ausu's etiam comparare uidulum cum piscibus?
      eadem tandem res uidetur?
GRI   in manu non est mea:
      ubi demisi retem atque hamum, quicquid haesit ex-
          traho.
985   meum quod rete atque hami nancti sunt meum potis-
          sumum est.
TRA   immo hercle haud est, siquidem quod uas excepisti.
GRI   philosophe!
TRA   sed tu enumquam piscatorem uidisti, uenefice,

504

TRA If the owner were to come, he wouldn't take it away?

GRI Don't be mistaken: no owner exists for this apart from 970
myself; I caught it in my hunt.

TRA Really?

GRI Will you say that any fish in the sea belongs to me? When
I catch them, if indeed I do, they do belong to me. I treat
them as mine, and no one puts a legal claim to them or
demands a share of them. I sell them all on the market,
in public, as my stock in trade. The sea is certainly shared 975
between all.

TRA I agree: why, please, should this trunk not be shared with
me? It was found in the shared sea.

GRI Aren't you shamelessly impudent? If what you say were
right, fishermen would be dead. As soon as fish was
brought to the market, no one would buy it, everybody 980
would claim his share of fish, and they would say it was
caught in the shared sea.

TRA What do you say, you shameless creature? Have you even
dared to compare the trunk to fish? Does it really seem
the same thing?

GRI It doesn't depend on me: when I let down the net and
the hook, I pull out whatever sticks to them. What my 985
net and my hooks have got is mine and mine alone.

TRA No, it isn't, if you catch some container.

GRI Philosopher!

TRA But have you, you crook, ever seen a fisherman catch a

---

969 nemo *del. Reiz*

977 commune est GR ne *P*, communi GR esne *Leo*

984 retem *CD Priscianus*, rete *B*

uidulum piscem cepisse aut protulisse ullum in forum?
non enim tu hic quidem occupabis omnis quaestus
    quos uoles:

990   et uitorem et piscatorem te esse, impure, postulas.
uel te mihi monstrare oportet piscis qui sit uidulus,
uel quod in mari non natum est neque habet squamas
    ne feras.

GRI   quid? tu numquam audisti esse antehac uidulum pis-
    cem?

TRA   scelus,
nullus est.

GRI   immo est profecto; ego qui sum piscator scio;
995   uerum rare capitur, nullus minus saepe ad terram
    uenit.

TRA   nil agis, dare uerba speras mihi te posse, furcifer.

GRI   quo colore est, hoc colore capiuntur pauxilluli;
sunt alii puniceo corio, magni item; atque atri.

TRA   scio.
tu hercle, opino[r], in uidulum te bis conuortes, nisi
    caues:

1000   fiet tibi puniceum corium, postea atrum denuo.

GRI   quod scelus hodie hoc inueni!

TRA   uerba facimus, it dies.
uide sis quoius arbitratu nos uis facere.

GRI   uiduli
arbitratu.

TRA   ⟨itane?

GRI⟩   ita enim uero.

TRA   stultus es.

GRI   salue, Thales.

---

    999 opino[r] *Bothe*   piscem *P*, bis *Leo*   1002 facere uis *P*,
transp. Gruterus   1003 itane GRI *add. Seyffert*

trunk-fish or bring one to market? No, you won't occupy
all occupations you want here: you piece of dirt, you   990
expect to be both a trunk maker and a fisherman. Either
you ought to show me how a trunk can be a fish or you
ought not to take what wasn't born in the sea and doesn't
have scales.

GRI   What? Have you never heard before that there's a trunk-
fish?

TRA   You criminal, there's no such thing.

GRI   Yes, there is; I, who am a fisherman, know it. But it's   995
caught rarely, no fish is landed less often.

TRA   You aren't getting anywhere, you expect you can fool me,
you crook.

GRI   With the color it has, they're caught when they're tiny;
others have a scarlet skin and are big at the same time;
and there are black ones.

TRA   I know. I think *you* will turn into a trunk twice, if you
don't watch out: your skin will become scarlet and later   1000
black in turn.[33]

GRI   (*aside*) What a load of trouble I've found today!

TRA   We're talking idly, the day is going. Decide under whose
arbitration you want us to settle the matter.

GRI   Under the trunk's arbitration.

TRA   Really?

GRI   Yes, really.

TRA   You're an idiot.

GRI   My greetings, Thales.[34]

[33] From beating.
[34] One of the Seven Sages, proverbially clever.

TRA tu istunc hodie non feres, nisi das sequestrum aut arbi-
     trum
1005   quoius haec res arbitratu fiat.
GRI   quaeso, sanun es?
TRA elleborosus sum.
GRI   [at] ego cerritus, hunc non amittam tamen.
TRA uerbum etiam adde unum, iam in cerebro colaphos ap-
     strudam tuo;
     iam ego te hic, itidem quasi peniculus nouos exurgeri
     solet,
     ni hunc amittis, exurgebo quicquid umoris tibi est.
1010 GRI tange: affligam ad terram te itidem ut piscem soleo
     polypum.
     uis pugnare?
TRA   quid opust? quin tu potius praedam diuide.
GRI hinc tu nisi malum frunisci nil potes, ne postules.
     abeo ego hinc.
TRA   at ego hinc offlectam nauem, ne quo abeas. mane.
     si tu proreta isti naui es, ego gubernator ero.
1015 GRI mitte rudentem, sceleste.
TRA   mittam: omitte uidulum.
GRI numquam hercle hinc hodie ramenta fies fortunatior.
TRA non probare pernegando mihi potes, nisi pars datur
     aut ad arbitrum reditur aut sequestro ponitur.
GRI quemne ego excepi in mari—
TRA   at ego inspectaui e litore.
1020 GRI —mea opera, labore, et rete et horia?
TRA   numqui minus,
     si ueniat nunc dominus quoiust, ego qui inspectaui
     procul
     te hunc habere, fur sum quam tu?

1006 at *del. Guyet*

TRA	You won't take this away today, unless you provide a third party[35] or an arbitrator under whose arbitration this matter can be settled.	1005
GRI	Please, are you in your right mind?	
TRA	I'm crazy.	
GRI	And I am mad, yet I won't let go of this.	
TRA	Just add one word and I'll bury my fists in your brains. If you don't let go of it, I'll squeeze you out here, whatever liquid you have in you, just as a new sponge is normally squeezed out.	
GRI	Touch me: I'll knock you to the ground just as I normally do with an octopus. Do you want to fight?	1010
TRA	What's that necessary for? You should divide the booty instead.	
GRI	From here you can't get anything except for a beating, so don't expect to. I'm going away. (*moves again*)	
TRA	(*pulling at the rope*) But I will turn the ship in my direction so that you won't go away anywhere. Wait. If you're the man at the prow of this ship, I'll be the steersman.	
GRI	Let go of the rope, you criminal.	1015
TRA	I will: let go of the trunk.	
GRI	You'll never become one scrap richer from here today.	
TRA	You can't gain your point against me by obstinate refusal, unless I'm given a share or we go to an arbitrator or it's entrusted to a third party.	
GRI	One that I caught in the sea—	
TRA	(*interrupting*) But I observed you from the shore.	
GRI	—with my own effort, work, net, and fishing boat?	1020
TRA	Since I observed from a distance that you have it, am I any less a thief than you, if the owner it belongs to should come now?	

[35] He would keep the trunk until its ownership was decided.

	GRI	nihilo.
	TRA	mane, mastigia:

quo argumento socius non sum et fur sum? facdum ex
te sciam.

	GRI	nescio neque ego istas uostras leges urbanas scio,
1025		nisi quia hunc meum esse dico.
	TRA	et ego item esse aio meum.
	GRI	mane, iam repperi quo pacto nec fur nec socius sies.
	TRA	quo pacto?
	GRI	sine me hinc abire, tu abi tacitus tuam uiam;

nec tu me quoiquam indicassis neque ego tibi quic-
quam dabo;

tu taceto, ego mussitabo: hoc optumum atque aequis-
sumum est.

| 1030 | TRA | ecquid condicionis audes ferre? |
| | GRI | iam dudum fero: |

ut abeas, rudentem amittas, mihi molestus ne sies.

	TRA	mane dum refero condicionem.
	GRI	te, opsecro hercle, aufer modo.
	TRA	ecquem in his locis nouisti?
	GRI	oportet uicinos meos.
	TRA	ubi tu hic habitas?
	GRI	porro illic longe usque in campis ultumis.
1035	TRA	uin qui in hac uilla habitat, eius arbitratu fieri?
	GRI	paulisper remitte restem dum concedo et consulo.
	TRA	fiat.
	GRI	eugae! salua res est, praeda haec perpetua est mea.

ad meum erum arbitrum uocat me hic intra praesepis
meas;

numquam hercle hodie abiudicabit ab suo triobolum.

GRI   No less than me.

TRA   Wait, you villain: how is it that I'm not a partner but am a thief? Let me know.

GRI   I don't know, and I don't know those city laws of yours, ex-   1025
cept that I claim that this belongs to me.

TRA   And I say in the same way that it belongs to me.

GRI   Wait, I've found a way now how you can be neither thief nor partner.

TRA   How?

GRI   Let me go away from here, and you go away your way silently. You mustn't report me to anyone and I won't give you anything. You be silent and I will hold my tongue. That's best and fairest.

TRA   Do you want to make me some offer?   1030

GRI   I've already made it: that you should go away, let go of the rope, and not be a nuisance to me.

TRA   Wait while I make you a counteroffer.

GRI   Please, just be off yourself.

TRA   Do you know anyone in this area?

GRI   I ought to know my neighbors.

TRA   Where do you live here?

GRI   Out there, in the distance, in the fields way back.

TRA   Do you want the matter to be settled under the arbitra-   1035
tion of the man who lives in this farmhouse? (*points to
the house of Daemones*)

GRI   Let the rope slack off for a little while I withdraw and take counsel.

TRA   (*doing so*) Okay.

GRI   (*aside*) Hurray! It's safe, this booty is mine for good. He's calling me to my master as arbitrator, here on my home ground. He'll never take as little as three obols away from his own slave by his verdict today. Really, that chap   1040

1040   ne iste hau scit quam condicionem tetulerit. eo ad arbi-
              trum.

TRA   quid igitur?

GRI   quamquam istuc esse ius meum certo scio,
        fiat istuc potius quam nunc pugnem tecum.

TRA   nunc places.

GRI   quamquam ad ignotum arbitrum me appellis, si adhi-
              bebit fidem,
        etsi ignotust, notus⟨t⟩: si non, notus ignotissumust.

IV. iv: DAEMONES. GRIPVS. TRACHALIO.
PALAESTRA. AMPELISCA

1045 DAE serio edepol, quamquam uobis ⟨uolo⟩ quae uoltis, mu-
              lieres,
        metuo propter uos ne uxor mea med extrudat aedibus,
        quae me paelices adduxe dicet ante oculos suos.
        uos confugite in aram potius quam ego.

AMP + PAL   miserae periimus.

DAE ego uos saluas sistam, ne timete. sed quid uos foras
1050   prosequimini? quoniam ego assum, faciet nemo ini-
              uriam;
        ite, inquam, domum ambo nunciam. ex praesidio prae-
              sides!

GRI   o ere, salue.

DAE   salue, Gripe. quid fit?

TRA   tuosne hic seruos est?

1040 ibo *P*, eo *Sonnenschein*

1044 etsist ignotus *P*, etsi ignotust *Acidalius*   notus⟨t⟩ *Sonnen-schein*

1045 uolo *add. Gruterus*

doesn't know what offer he's made. I'm going to an arbi-
trator.

TRA Well then?

GRI Even though I know for sure that that is my right, I'd
rather do what you want than fight with you now.

TRA Now that's better of you.

GRI Even though you're forcing an unknown arbitrator on
me, he's known, if he displays good faith, even though
he's unknown. Otherwise, this known man is most un-
known.

Enter DAEMONES, PALAESTRA, *and* AMPELISCA *from the farm-
house.*

DAE Seriously, even though I want for you what you want   1045
yourselves, my women, I'm afraid that my wife will
throw me out of the house because of you; she'll say I've
brought in mistresses before her very eyes. You flee to
the altar rather than me.

AMP + PAL Poor us, we're dead.

DAE I'll make sure you're safe, stop being afraid.

Enter two SLAVES *from the house.*

DAE (*to the slaves*) But why are you following me out? Since   1050
I am with them, no one will do them an injustice. Both of
you, I'm telling you, go home now. Guards, off guard!

Exeunt SLAVES *into house.*

GRI (*as he approaches*) My greetings, master.

DAE And mine to you, Gripus. How are things?

TRA Is this your slave?

GRI   hau pudet.
TRA   nil ago tecum.
GRI   ergo abi hinc sis.
TRA   quaeso responde, senex:
tuos hic seruost?
DAE   meus est.
TRA   em istuc optume, quando tuost.
1055   iterum te saluto.
DAE   et ego te. tune es qui hau multo prius
abiisti hinc erum accersitum?
TRA   ego is sum.
DAE   quid nunc uis tibi?
TRA   nempe hic tuos est?
DAE   meus est.
TRA   istuc optume, quando tuost.
DAE   quid negoti est?
TRA   uir scelestus illic est.
DAE   quid fecit tibi
uir scelestus?
TRA   homini ego isti talos suffringi uolo.
1060 DAE   quid est? qua de re litigatis nunc inter uos?
TRA   eloquar.
GRI   immo ego eloquar.
TRA   ego, opinor, rem facesso.
GRI   si quidem
sis pudicus, hinc facessas.
DAE   Gripe, animum aduorte ac tace.
GRI   utin istic prius dicat?
DAE   audi. loquere tu.
GRI   alienon prius
quam tuo dabis orationem?
TRA   ut nequitur comprimi!

GRI I'm not ashamed of it.

TRA I'm not dealing with you.

GRI Then go away from here, will you?

TRA Please answer, old man: is this your slave?

DAE Yes.

TRA There, it's good news that he's yours. I'm greeting you again.

DAE And I you. Aren't you the one who went away a little earlier to fetch his master?

TRA Yes, I'm the one.

DAE What do you want now?

TRA Surely this is your slave?

DAE Yes.

TRA It's good news that he's yours.

DAE What's the matter?

TRA That chap is a criminal.

DAE What did the criminal do to you?

TRA I want his ankle bones to be broken.

DAE What is it? Why are you quarreling with each other now?

TRA I'll tell you.

GRI (*to Daemones*) No, *I* will tell you.

TRA *I* am the plaintiff, I believe.

GRI If you had any sense of decency, you'd be plainly off.

DAE Gripus, pay attention and be quiet.

GRI So that he can speak first?

DAE (*to Gripus*) Listen. (*to Trachalio*) You, speak.

GRI Are you letting a stranger speak before your own slave?

TRA (*to Daemones*) How impossible it is to restrain him! As I

1060 nunc litigatis *P*, *transp. Camerarius*

1065   ita ut occepi dicere, illum quem dudum ⟨e fano foras⟩
            lenonem extrusisti, hic eius uidulum eccillum ⟨tenet⟩.
GRI   non habeo.
TRA   negas quod oculis uideo?
GRI   at ne uideas uelim.
            habeo, non habeo: quid tu me curas quid rerum
               geram?
TRA   quo modo habeas, id refert, iurene anne iniuria.
1070 GRI   ni istum cepi, nulla causa est quin me condones cruci;
            si in mari reti prehendi, qui tuom potiust quam meum?
TRA   uerba dat. hoc modo res gesta est ut ego dico.
GRI   quid tu ais?
TRA   quod primarius uir dicat: comprime hunc sis, si tuost.
GRI   quid? tu idem mihi uis fieri quod erus consueuit tibi?
1075   si ille te comprimere solitus⟨t⟩, hic noster nos non so-
            let.
DAE   uerbo illo modo ille uicit. quid nunc tu uis? dic mihi.
TRA   equidem ego nec partem posco mi istinc de istoc ui-
            dulo
            nec meum esse hodie umquam dixi; sed isti inest cis-
            tellula
            huius mulieris, quam dudum dixi fuisse liberam.
1080 DAE   nemp' tu hanc dicis quam esse aiebas dudum popula-
            rem meam?
TRA   admodum; et ea quae olim parua gestauit crepundia
            istic in ista cistula insunt, quae istic inest in uidulo.

      1065 e fano foras *add. Schoell*
      1066 tenet *add. Guyet*
      1071 retia *BCD*, reti *Z*
      1075 solitus⟨t⟩ *Fleckeisen*

began to say, look, this chap's holding that trunk of that pimp you threw out of the temple not long ago.

GRI   I don't have it.

TRA   You deny what I can see with my eyes?

GRI   But I wish you couldn't see. I've got it, I haven't got it; why do you care what I'm doing?

TRA   Whether you've got it lawfully or not, that's what matters.

GRI   If I didn't draw it up myself, there's no reason why you 1070
shouldn't put me on the cross; if I got hold of it in the
sea with my own net, how is it yours rather than mine?

TRA   (*to Daemones*) He's fooling you. The matter happened
the way I'm telling you.

GRI   What do you say?

TRA   What any man of the first rank would say: (*to Daemones*)
squash him please, if he belongs to you.

GRI   What? Do you want the same done to me that your master does to you? Even if he does squash you, this one of 1075
ours doesn't do it to us.[36]

DAE   (*to Trachalio*) He just got the better of you with that
word. What do you want now? Tell me.

TRA   I for one neither demand a share for myself from that
trunk nor have I ever said today that it belongs to me;
but in there, there's a box belonging to the woman who
not long ago I said was born free.

DAE   Presumably you mean the one who not long ago you said 1080
was my compatriot?

TRA   Exactly. And the tokens she wore when she was little are
there in that box that's there in the trunk. This isn't of

[36] *Comprimere*, here translated as "squash," means both "keep in check" and "bugger."

PLAUTUS

          hoc neque isti usu est et illi miserae suppetias feret,
          si id dederit qui suos parentes quaerat.
DAE   faciam ut det. tace.
1085 GRI nihil hercle ego sum isti daturus.
TRA   nil peto nisi cistulam
          et crepundia.
GRI   quid si ea sunt aurea?
TRA   quid istuc tua?
          aurum auro expendetur, argentum argento exaequa-
               bitur.
GRI   fac sis aurum ut uideam, post ego faciam ut uideas cis-
               tulam.
DAE   caue malo ac tace tu. tu perge ut occepisti dicere.
1090 TRA unum te opsecro ut ted huius commiserescat mulieris
          si quidem hic lenonis eius est uidulus, quem suspicor;
          hic nisi de opinione certum nil dico tibi.
GRI   uiden? scelestus aucupatur.
TRA   sine me ut occepi loqui.
          si scelesti illius est hic quoius dico uidulus,
1095   haec poterunt nouisse: ostende his iube.
GRI   ain? ostendere?
DAE   haud iniquom dicit, Gripe, ut ostendatur uidulus.
GRI   immo hercle insignite inique.
DAE   quidum?
GRI   quia, si ostendero,
          continuo hunc nouisse dicent scilicet.
TRA   scelerum caput,
          ut tute es item omnis censes esse, periuri caput?

     1087 exaequabitur *B*, -bimus *C*, -bimur *D*

518

any use to that chap and he'll bring help to the poor girl, if he gives her the means to look for her parents.

DAE I'll have him give it to her. Be quiet.

GRI I won't give her anything.   1085

TRA I'm not demanding anything except for the box and the tokens.

GRI What if they're made of gold?

TRA What does that matter to you? Gold will be compensated for with the same weight of gold, silver will be counter-balanced with silver.

GRI Let me see the gold, then I'll let you see the box.

DAE (*to Gripus*) You, watch out for trouble and be quiet. (*to Trachalio*) You, continue to speak as you've begun.

TRA The one thing I beg of you is that you have pity on this   1090 woman, if this is indeed this pimp's trunk, which I sus-pect it is. Here I say this by conjecture, not from certain knowledge.

GRI (*to Daemones*) Can't you see? The criminal's setting a trap.

TRA Let me speak as I've begun. If this is the trunk of that villain who I say it belongs to, they'll be able to recognize   1095 it. Have him show it to them.

GRI Do you say so? Show it?

DAE What he says is not unfair, Gripus, that the trunk should be shown.

GRI No, it's utterly unfair.

DAE How so?

GRI Because if I show it, they'll instantly say that they recog-nize it, of course.

TRA You fount of iniquity, do you think everybody is like you, you fount of perjury?

1100	GRI	omnia ego istaec facile patior, dum hic hinc a me sentiat.
	TRA	atqui nunc aps te stat, uerum hinc cibit testimonium.
	DAE	Gripe, aduorte animum. tu paucis expedi quid postulas.
	TRA	dixi equidem, sed si parum intellexti, dicam denuo.
		hasce ambas, ut dudum dixi, ita esse oportet liberas:
1105		haec Athenis parua fuit uirgo surrupta.
	GRI	dic mihi,
		quid id ad uidulum attinet, seruae sint istae an liberae?
	TRA	omnia iterum uis memorari, scelus, ut defiat dies.
	DAE	apstine maledictis et mi quod rogaui dilue.
	TRA	cistellam isti inesse oportet caudeam in isto uidulo,
1110		ubi sunt signa qui parentes noscere haec possit suos,
		quibuscum periit parua Athenis, sicuti dixi prius.
	GRI	Iuppiter te dique perdant! quid ais, uir uenefice?
		quid, istae mutae sunt, quae pro se fabulari non queant?
	TRA	eo tacent quia tacita est melior mulier semper quam loquens.
1115	GRI	tum pol tu pro portione nec uir nec mulier mihi es.
	TRA	quidum?
	GRI	quia enim nec loquens es nec tacens umquam bonus.
		quaeso, enumquam hodie licebit mihi loqui?

1100 istaec ego *P, transp. Bothe*
1101 ibi *P*, cibit *Acidalius*
1106 pertinet *B*, pertinent *CD*, attinet *Fleckeisen*
1111 parua periit *P, transp. Sonnenschein*
1114 tacita bonast *P*, tacitast melior *Bentley*

GRI I easily put up with all your words, so long as this man is 1100
on my side. (*points to Daemones*)

TRA But now he's only standing on your side, but he'll ask for
evidence from here. (*points to the trunk*)

DAE Gripus, pay attention. (*to Trachalio*) You, tell me briefly
what you demand.

TRA I've told you, but if you didn't understand it fully I'll
say it again. These two girls ought to be free, as I said
a while ago. (*pointing to Palaestra*) This one was kid- 1105
napped from Athens when she was a little girl.

GRI Tell me, what does it have to do with the trunk whether
they're slaves or free?

TRA You want everything to be told again, you crook, so that
the day will run out.

DAE Refrain from your rude words and explain what I've
asked.

TRA There in that trunk there ought to be a little box made
of rushes, containing the proofs with which this girl can 1110
recognize her parents; they're the proofs with which she
disappeared from Athens as a little girl, as I said be-
fore.

GRI May Jupiter and the gods ruin you! What do you say, you
poisoner? What, are they dumb so that they can't speak
for themselves?

TRA They're silent because a woman is always better silent
than speaking.

GRI Then you don't have your fair share of either man or 1115
woman.

TRA How so?

GRI Because you're never any good, either speaking or silent.
(*to Daemones*) Please, will I ever be allowed to speak
today?

DAE   si praeterhac
⟨unum⟩ uerbum faxis hodie, ego tibi comminuam
caput.

TRA ut id occepi dicere, senex, eam te quaeso cistulam

1120   ut iubeas hunc reddere illis; ob eam si quid postulat
sibi mercedis, dabitur: aliud quicquid ibi est habeat
sibi.

GRI nunc demum istuc dicis, quoniam ius meum esse intel-
legis:
dudum dimidiam petebas partem.

TRA   immo etiam nunc peto.

GRI uidi petere miluom, etiam quom nihil auferret tamen.

1125 DAE non ego te comprimere possum sine malo?

GRI   si istic tacet,
ego tacebo; si iste loquitur, sine me pro parti loqui.

DAE cedo modo mihi uidulum istum, Gripe.

GRI   concredam tibi:
ac si istorum nil sit, ut mi reddas.

DAE   reddetur.

GRI   tene.

DAE audi nunciam, Palaestra atque Ampelisca, hoc quod lo-
quor.

1130   estne hic uidulus ubi cistellam tuam inesse aiebas?

PAL   is est.

GRI perii hercle ego miser! ut prius quam plane aspexit
ilico
eum esse dixit!

PAL   faciam ego hanc rem ⟨ex procliui pla⟩nam tibi.
cistellam isti inesse oportet caudeam in isto uidulo.
ibi ego dicam quicquid inerit nominatim: tu mihi

1118 unum *add. Camerarius*

522

DAE   If you utter a single word in addition to this today, I'll smash your head.

TRA   As I've begun to say, old man, I ask you to have him return this box to them; if he demands any reward for it, he shall receive it. Whatever else there is he can have for himself.   1120

GRI   Now at last you're saying that, since you realize that it's my right; a while ago you were demanding half.

TRA   Yes, and I'm still demanding it now.

GRI   I have seen a kite pounce, without carrying off anything after all.

DAE   Can't I restrain you without a beating?   1125

GRI   If he is quiet, I will be quiet. If he speaks, let me speak on my part.

DAE   Just give me that trunk, Gripus.

GRI   I'll entrust it to you, but on condition that you return it to me if there's nothing in what he says.

DAE   It will be returned.

GRI   Here you are. (*hands it over*)

DAE   Listen now to what I say, Palaestra; you too, Ampelisca. Is this the trunk in which you said your little box is?   1130

PAL   It is.

GRI   I'm dead, poor me! How she immediately said that it's the one, before looking at it properly!

PAL   I'll make this difficulty straightforward for you. A little box made of rushes ought to be there in that trunk. I'll tell you all that is in there by name. You mustn't show me   1135

1126 pro re mea parte *P*, pro parte *Leo*, pro re mea *Camerarius*
1127 istum uidulum *P, transp. Pylades*
1130 *fortasse* uidlus *aut* aibas *legendum*
1132 ‹ex procliui pla›nam *Gulielmus*

1135   nullum ostenderis; si falsa dicam frustra dixero,
              uos tamen istaec quicquid isti inerit uobis habebitis;
              sed si erunt uera, tum opsecro te ut mea mi reddantur.
DAE   placet.
              ius merum oras meo quidem animo.
GRI   at meo hercle ‹iniuriam›.
              quid si ista aut superstitiosa aut hariola est atque omnia
1140   quicquid insit uera dicet? idne habebit hariola?
DAE   non feret nisi uera dicet: nequiquam hariola‹bi›tur.
              solue uidulum ergo, ut quid sit uerum quam primum
                sciam.
TRA   hoc habet.
GRI   solutust.
DAE   aperi.
PAL   uideo cistellam.
DAE   haecine est?
PAL   istaec est. o mei parentes, hic uos conclusos gero,
1145   huc opesque spesque uostrum cognoscendum condidi.
GRI   tum tibi hercle deos iratos esse oportet, quisquis es,
              quae parentes tam in angustum tuos locum compe-
                geris.
DAE   Gripe, accede huc; tua res agitur. tu, puella, istinc
              procul
              dicito quid insit et qua facie, memorato omnia.
1150   si hercle tantillum peccassis, quod posterius postules
              te ad uerum conuorti, nugas, mulier, magnas egeris.
GRI   ius bonum oras.

1138 iniuriam *add. Camerarius*
1140 insit *P*, inerit *Müller*   in me *P*, idne *Lindsay*, anne *Valla*
1141 hariola‹bi›tur *Pylades*

anything. If I make mistakes, I'll make my claims void, and you will still have for yourself whatever is in there. But if it's correct, then I ask you that my things be returned to me.

DAE   Agreed. What you ask is only fair in my opinion.

GRI   But in mine it's unfair. What if she's a witch or a soothsayer and names everything that's in there correctly? 1140
Will a soothsayer obtain it?

DAE   She won't get it unless she names things rightly: she'll get nowhere by soothsaying. Untie the trunk then, so that I may know the truth as soon as possible. (*Gripus obeys*)

TRA   He's had it!

GRI   It's untied.

DAE   Open it. (*Gripus obeys*)

PAL   I can see the little box.

DAE   Is it this one? (*takes it out*)

PAL   It's that one. O my dear parents, here I'm carrying you shut in, here I placed my means and hopes of recogniz- 1145
ing you.

GRI   Then the gods should really be angry with you, whoever you are, for shutting up your parents in such a narrow place.

DAE   Gripus, come here; it's your case that's on. You, girl, say from there from a distance what's inside and what it looks like; state everything. If you make the smallest mistake, 1150
you'll waste your effort completely, woman, in case you suppose you can correct yourself later.

GRI   What you ask is fair and good.

PLAUTUS

TRA	edepol hau te orat, nam tu iniuriu's.
DAE	loquere nunciam, puella. Gripe, animum aduorte ac tace.
PAL	sunt crepundia.
DAE	ecca uideo.
GRI	perii in primo proelio.

1155 mane, ne ostenderis.

DAE	qua facie sunt? responde ex ordine.
PAL	ensiculust aureolus primum litteratus.
DAE	dicedum in eo ensiculo litterarum quid est?
PAL	mei nomen patris. post altrinsecust securicula ancipes, itidem aurea, litterata: ibi matris nomen in securicula est.
DAE	mane.

1160 dic, in ensiculo quid nomen est paternum?

PAL	Daemones.
DAE	di immortales, ubi loci sunt spes meae?
GRI	immo edepol meae?
TRA	pergite, opsecro, continuo.
GRI	placide, aut ite in malam crucem.
DAE	loquere matris nomen hic quid in securicula siet.
PAL	Daedalis.
DAE	di me seruatum cupiunt.
GRI	at me perditum.

1165 DAE filiam meam esse hanc oportet, Gripe.

1158 itidem *Priscianus*, item *P*

526

TRA   She can't be asking you because you're no good.[37]

DAE   Speak now, girl. Gripus, pay attention and be quiet.

PAL   There are little tokens.

DAE   Yes, I can see them.

GRI   I've perished at the beginning of the battle. (*to Daemo-*   1155
      nes) Wait, don't show them.

DAE   (*to Palaestra*) What do they look like? Answer one by
      one.

PAL   First there's a little sword made of gold, with letters on
      it.

DAE   (*as he takes it out*) Tell me, what letters are on this
      sword?

PAL   My father's name. Then on the other side there's a little
      two-headed ax, also made of gold and with letters on it.
      There, on the little ax, is my mother's name.

DAE   Wait. Tell me, what's your father's name on the little   1160
      sword?

PAL   Daemones.

DAE   Immortal gods, where are my hopes?

GRI   No, where are mine?

TRA   (*to Daemones and Palaestra*) Please, continue at once.

GRI   Gently, or go and be hanged.

DAE   (*to Palaestra*) Tell me what your mother's name is on the
      little ax. (*takes it out*)

PAL   Daedalis.

DAE   The gods want me saved.

GRI   But me, lost.

DAE   This girl must be my daughter, Gripus.   1165

---

[37] Joke based on the ambiguity in Gripus' statement: *ius bonum
oras* can literally mean "you ask for good justice" or "you ask a good
man for justice."

GRI   sit per me quidem.
qui te di omnes perdant, qui me hodie oculis uidisti
    tuis,
meque adeo scelestum, qui non circumspexi centiens,
prius me ne quis inspectaret quam rete extraxi ex aqua!

PAL post sicilicula argenteola et duae conexae maniculae et
1170   sucula.

GRI   quin tu i dierecta cum sucula et cum porculis.

PAL et bulla aurea est pater quam dedit mi natali die.

DAE ea est profecto. contineri quin complectar non queo.
filia mea, salue. ego is sum qui te produxi pater,
ego sum Daemones et mater tua eccam hic intus Dae-
    dalis.

1175 PAL salue, mi pater insperate.

DAE   salue. ut te amplector lubens!

TRA uolup est quom istuc ex pietate uostra uobis contigit.

DAE capedum, hunc si potes fer intro uidulum, age, Tra-
    chalio.

TRA ecce Gripi scelera! quom istaec res male euenit tibi,
Gripe, gratulor.

DAE   age eamus, mea gnata, ad matrem tuam,
1180   quae ex te poterit argumentis hanc rem magis exqui-
    rere,
quae te magis tractauit magisque signa pernouit tua.

PAL intro eamus omnes, quando operam promiscam damus.
sequere me, Ampelisca.

---

[38] Palaestra seems to refer to a windlass, commonly called "little
sow" (*sucula*) in Latin, and not to a pig-shaped toy. The "little piglets"
(*porculi*) that Gripus refers to are simply mentioned by association,
though this is also a technical term for clutching devices in a windlass
(sometimes called *dogs* in English).

GRI   Let her be, for all I care. (*to Trachalio*) May all the gods ruin you, all those who have set eyes on me today, and me too, wretch that I am, because I didn't look around a hundred times to check that no one was watching me before I pulled it out of the water with my net!

PAL   (*to Daemones*) Then there's a little sickle made of silver and two little connected hands and a little sow.   1170

GRI   Go and be hanged with your little sow and your little piglets.[38]

PAL   (*ignoring him*) And there's a golden locket which my father gave me on my birthday.

DAE   It really is her. I can't keep myself from embracing you. My daughter, greetings to you. I am the father who brought you up, I am Daemones, and look, your mother Daedalis is inside.

PAL   Greetings to you, my unhoped-for father.   1175

DAE   Greetings. How happy I am to embrace you! (*does so*)

TRA   I'm glad that that has happened to you as a reward for your virtue.

DAE   Take this trunk and bring it in, if you can, go on, Trachalio.

TRA   Behold the misfortunes of Gripus! I congratulate you, Gripus, because this has turned out so badly for you.

Exit TRACHALIO *into the farmhouse with the trunk.*

DAE   Come on, my daughter, let's go to your mother, who will   1180 be able to find further proofs of this from you; she handled you more and knows your characteristics better.

PAL   Let's all go inside, since we're all doing our best together. Follow me, Ampelisca.

AMP   quom te di amant uoluptati est mihi.

GRI   sumne ego scelestus qui illunc hodie excepi uidulum?

1185   aut quom excepi, qui non alicubi in solo apstrusi loco?

credebam edepol turbulentam praedam euenturam
    mihi,

quia illa mihi tam turbulenta tempestate euenerat.

credo edepol ego illic inesse argenti et auri largiter.

quid meliust quam ut hinc intro abeam et me suspen-
    dam clanculum,

1190   saltem tantisper dum apscedat haec a me aegrimonia?

IV. v: DAEMONES

DAE   pro di immortales! quis me est fortunatior,

qui ex improuiso filiam inueni meam?

satin si quoi homini di esse bene factum uolunt,

aliquo illud pacto optingit optatum piis?

1195   ego hodie ⟨qui⟩ nec speraui nec credidi,

is improuiso filiam inueni tamen;

et eam de genere summo adulescenti dabo

ingenuo, Atheniensi et cognato meo.

ego eum adeo arcessi huc ad me quam primum uolo

1200   iussique exire huc eius seruom, ut ad forum

iret; nondum egressum esse eum, id miror tamen.

accedam, opinor, ad fores. quid conspicor?

uxor complexa collo retinet filiam.

nimis paene inepta atque odiosa eius amatio est.

IV. vi: DAEMONES. TRACHALIO

1205 DAE   aliquando osculando meliust, uxor, pausam fieri;

      1195 qui *add.* Sonnenschein
      1200 seruom eius *P, transp.* Acidalius

AMP   I'm happy that the gods love you.

Exeunt DAEMONES, PALAESTRA, *and* AMPELISCA *into the farmhouse.*

GRI   Aren't I a wretch because I caught that trunk today? Or   1185
      rather because I didn't put it away somewhere in a lonely
      place when I caught it? I believed that there was a storm
      brewing in that prize of mine because I'd got it in such
      stormy weather. I do believe that there's a lot of silver
      and gold in there. What's better than for me to go inside
      and hang myself secretly, at least until I get over this   1190
      distress?

Exit GRIPUS *into the farmhouse.*
Enter DAEMONES *from the farmhouse after some time has passed.*

DAE   Immortal gods! Who is luckier than me, since I found
      my daughter unexpectedly? If the gods want to do some-
      one a good turn, do the virtuous really get that desire
      fulfilled in some way? I, who neither hoped for it nor   1195
      believed it, even so found my daughter unexpectedly
      today. And I'll give her to a freeborn young man from an
      excellent family, an Athenian and relative of mine. I want
      him to be brought here to me as soon as possible, and I   1200
      told his slave to come out here to go to the forum. I'm
      surprised he hasn't come out yet, though. I'll go to the
      door, I think. (*peers in*) What do I see? My wife is cling-
      ing to our daughter's neck and holding her back. Her
      petting is getting on for being out of place and tedious.
DAE   (*into the house*) It's better to put a stop to your kissing at   1205

atque adorna, ut rem diuinam faciam, quom intro
aduenero,
Laribus familiaribus, quom auxerunt nostram familiam.
sunt domi agni et porci sacres. sed quid istum remora-
mini,
mulieres, Trachalionem? atque optume eccum exit fo-
ras!

1210 TRA   ubi ubi erit, [tamen] iam inuestigabo et mecum ad te
adducam simul
Plesidippum.

DAE   eloquere ut haec res optigit de filia;
eum roga ut relinquat alias res et huc ueniat.

TRA   licet.

DAE   dicito daturum meam illi filiam uxorem—

TRA   licet.

DAE   —et patrem eius me nouisse et mi esse cognatum.

TRA   licet.

1215 DAE   sed propera.

TRA   licet.

DAE   iam hic fac sit, cena ut curetur.

TRA   licet.

DAE   omnian licet?

TRA   licet. sed scin quid est quod te uolo?
quod promisisti ut memineris, hodie ut liber sim.

DAE   licet.

TRA   fac ut exores Plesidippum ut me ⟨manu⟩ emittat.

DAE   licet.

1210 tamen iam *B*, tamen *CD*, iam *Guyet*
1215 sis *P*, sit *Acidalius*
1218 manu *add. Camerarius*

some point, my wife. And get ready so that I can sacrifice to the household gods[39] when I come in, because they've increased our household. We have unblemished lambs and pigs ready. But why are you delaying Trachalio, my women? Excellent, look, he's coming out!

Enter TRACHALIO *from the farmhouse.*

TRA   Wherever he is, I'll find Plesidippus now and bring him   1210
       to you along with me.
DAE   Tell him how this happened about my daughter; ask him
       to leave everything else aside and to come here.
TRA   Okay.
DAE   Say that I'll give him my daughter in marriage—
TRA   (*interrupting*) Okay.
DAE   —and that I know his father and that he's my relative.
TRA   Okay.
DAE   But be quick.   1215
TRA   Okay.
DAE   Make sure that he is here instantly so that dinner can be
       seen to.
TRA   Okay.
DAE   Okay to everything?
TRA   Okay. But do you know what I want from you? To re-
       member what you promised me, so that I'm free today.
DAE   Okay.
TRA   Make sure that you persuade Plesidippus to set me
       free.
DAE   Okay.

[39] In the Latin, Daemones speaks imprecisely; the household gods did not consist of several *Lares* but of one *Lar* and two *Penates*.

	TRA	et tua filia facito oret: facile exorabit.
	DAE	licet.
1220	TRA	atque ut mi Ampelisca nubat, ubi ego sim liber.
	DAE	licet.
	TRA	atque ut gratum mi beneficium factis experiar.
	DAE	licet.
	TRA	omnia⟨n⟩ licet?
	DAE	licet: tibi rursum refero gratiam.

              sed propera ire in urbem actutum et recipe te huc rur-
                sum.

	TRA	licet.

              iam hic ero. tu interibi adorna ceterum quod opust.

	DAE	licet.
1225		Hercules istum infelicet cum sua licentia!

              ita meas repleuit auris quicquid memorabam "licet."

IV. vii: GRIPVS. DAEMONES

	GRI	quam mox licet te compellare, Daemones?
	DAE	quid est negoti, Gripe?
	GRI	de illo uidulo,

              si sapias, sapias; habeas quod di dant boni.

1230	DAE	aequom uidetur tibi, ut ego alienum quod est
		meum esse dicam?
	GRI	quodne ego inueni in mari?
	DAE	tanto illi melius optigit qui perdidit;
		tuom esse nihilo magis oportet uidulum.
	GRI	isto tu pauper es quom nimis sancte piu's.
1235	DAE	o Gripe, Gripe, in aetate hominum plurumae

        1222 omnia⟨n⟩ *Camerarius*
        1229 dant boni *B*, danunt dant boni *C*, boni danunt dant *D*

TRA And have your daughter ask him: she'll easily persuade
     him.
DAE Okay.
TRA And have Ampelisca marry me when I'm free.   1220
DAE Okay.
TRA And have me find my good turn repaid by your actions.
DAE Okay.
TRA Okay to everything?
DAE Okay: I'm paying you back in your own coin. But be
     quick to go to the city at once and return here again.
TRA Okay. I'll be back here in a moment. Meanwhile, you
     should get everything else that's necessary ready.

Exit TRACHALIO *to the right.*

DAE (*calling after him*) Okay. (*to the audience*) May Hercules   1225
     curse him with his okaying! He's really filled my ears with
     his "okay," whatever I said.

Enter GRIPUS *from the farmhouse.*

GRI How soon can I speak to you, Daemones?
DAE What's the matter, Gripus?
GRI About that trunk, if you were wise, you'd be wise; you'd
     keep the good things the gods give you.
DAE Does it seem right to you that I should say that some-   1230
     thing belonging to someone else belongs to me?
GRI Something I found in the sea?
DAE So much the better for the man who lost it. The trunk
     shouldn't be yours any the more for that reason.
GRI You're poor precisely because you're terribly over-
     virtuous.
DAE O Gripus, Gripus, very many snares are set in the life of   1235

fiunt trasennae, ubi decipiuntur dolis.
atque edepol in eas plerumque esca imponitur:
quam si quis auidus poscit escam auariter,
decipitur in trasenna auaritia sua.
1240 ill' qui consulte, docte atque astute cauet,
diutine uti bene licet partum bene.
mi istaec uidetur praeda praedatum irier,
ut cum maiore dote abeat quam aduenerit.
egone ut quod ad me allatum esse alienum sciam
1245 celem? minime istuc faciet noster Daemones.
semper cauere hoc sapientis aequissumum est
ne conscii sint ipsi malefici[is] suis.
ego mi collusim nil moror ullum lucrum.
GRI spectaui ego pridem comicos ad istunc modum
1250 sapienter dicta dicere, atque is plaudier,
quom illos sapientis mores monstrabant poplo:
sed quom inde suam quisque ibant diuorsi domum,
nullus erat illo pacto ut illi iusserant.
DAE abi intro, ne molestu's, linguae tempera.
1255 ego tibi daturus nil sum, ne tu frustra sis.
GRI at ego deos quaeso ut, quicquid in illo uidulo est,
si aurum, si argentum est, omne id ut fiat cinis.
DAE illuc est quod nos nequam seruis utimur.
nam illic cum seruo si quo congressus foret,
1260 et ipsum sese et illum furti astringeret;
dum praedam habere se censeret, interim
praeda ipsus esset, praeda praedam duceret.

1247 malefici[is] *Gulielmius*
1248 cum lusi *P*, conlusim *Exon*

men where they're deceived with tricks. And mostly a
bait is placed in them. If any voracious man greedily goes
for the bait, he's caught in the net through his own
greed. The man who is on his guard wisely, cleverly, and   1240
astutely can for a long time make use of what he's gained
appropriately. It seems to me that that plunder which
you recommend will be taken as plunder, so that it leaves
with a bigger dowry than the one it came with. Should I
conceal what I know has been brought to me as belong-   1245
ing to someone else? Our Daemones will certainly not
do that. Sensible masters really must be on their guard
all the time that they aren't themselves partners in crime
with their slaves. I don't care for any profit derived from
collusion.

GRI   I've watched comic actors before say wise words like that   1250
       and receive applause when they showed those wise stan-
       dards of behavior to the people. But when they all went
       to their homes on their different ways, nobody behaved
       the way they'd told them to.

DAE   Go in, stop being a nuisance, and control your tongue. I'm   1255
       not going to give you anything, make no mistake about
       it.

GRI   But I ask the gods that whatever is in that trunk, whether
       it's gold or silver, may turn to dust and ashes in its en-
       tirety.

Exit GRIPUS *into the farmhouse.*

DAE   That's why we have such bad slaves. Indeed, if he'd fallen
       in with some other slave, he'd have implicated both him-   1260
       self and that other in theft; and while believing that he
       had booty, he would be the booty himself; the booty

537

nunc hinc intro ibo et sacruficabo, postibi
iubebo nobis cenam continuo coqui.

IV. viii: PLESIDIPPVS. TRACHALIO

1265 PLE iterum mi istaec omnia itera, mi anime, mi Trachalio,
mi liberte, mi patrone potius, immo mi pater.
repperit patrem Palaestra suom atque matrem?

TRA   repperit.

PLE et popularis est?

TRA   opino[r].

PLE   et nuptura est mi?

TRA   suspicor.

PLE censen hodie despondebit eam mi, quaeso?

TRA   censeo.

1270 PLE quid? patri etiam gratulabor quom illam inuenit?

TRA   censeo.

PLE quid matri eius?

TRA   censeo.

PLE   quid ergo censes?

TRA   quod rogas
censeo.

PLE   dic ergo quanti censes?

TRA   egone? censeo.

PLE assum equidem, ne censionem semper facias.

TRA   censeo.

1266 immo potius *P, transp. Reiz*   1268 opino[r] *Bothe*

---

[40] Plesidippus uses the word *censere*, "reckon," in a different sense: the verb can also describe making the census, in which the property and class of citizens are determined.   [41] Yet another meaning of the word: *censio* also stands for the fine a censor gives to defaulters.

would take him as booty. Now I'll go in and sacrifice, then I'll have us a dinner cooked straightaway.

Exit DAEMONES into the farmhouse.
Enter PLESIDIPPUS and TRACHALIO from the right.

PLE   Repeat all this to me again, my life, my dear Trachalio,   1265
      my freedman, or rather my patron, no, my father. Has
      Palaestra found her father and mother?

TRA   She has.

PLE   And is she my compatriot?

TRA   I think so.

PLE   And is she going to marry me?

TRA   I suspect so.

PLE   Do you reckon that he'll betroth her to me today,
      please?

TRA   I reckon.

PLE   Well then? Will I also congratulate her father on finding   1270
      her?

TRA   I reckon.

PLE   How about her mother?

TRA   I reckon.

PLE   What do you reckon, then?

TRA   What you ask I reckon.

PLE   Tell me then, how much do you reckon?[40]

TRA   I? I reckon.

PLE   I for one am present, so don't always make your reckoning.[41]

TRA   I reckon.

PLE	quid si curram?
TRA	censeo.
PLE	an sic potius placide?
TRA	censeo.
1275 PLE	etiamne eam adueniens salutem?
TRA	censeo.
PLE	etiam patrem?
TRA	censeo.
PLE	post eius matrem?
TRA	censeo.
PLE	quid postea?
	etiamne adueniens complectar eius patrem?
TRA	non censeo.
PLE	quid matrem?
TRA	non censeo.
PLE	quid eampse illam?
TRA	non censeo.
PLE	perii! dilectum dimisit. nunc non censet quom uolo.
1280 TRA	sanus non es. sequere.
PLE	duc me, mi patrone, quo lubet.

ACTVS V

V. i: LABRAX

LAB	quis me est mortalis miserior qui uiuat alter hodie,
	quem ad recuperatores modo damnauit Plesidippus?

1275 etiam[ne] *Sonnenschein*

---

[42] I.e., he has finished the census and will not say *censeo*, "I reckon," any longer.

PLE	What if I run?
TRA	I reckon.
PLE	Or rather gently like this?
TRA	I reckon.
PLE	Should I also greet my girl on my arrival?
TRA	I reckon.
PLE	Her father, too?
TRA	I reckon.
PLE	Then her mother?
TRA	I reckon.
PLE	What after that? Should I also embrace her father on my arrival?
TRA	I reckon not.
PLE	What about her mother?
TRA	I reckon not.
PLE	What about herself?
TRA	I reckon not.
PLE	I'm ruined! He's stopped the review.[42] Now that I want to he doesn't reckon.
TRA	You aren't in your right mind. Follow me.
PLE	Take me where you want, my dear patron.

1275

1280

Exeunt TRACHALIO *and* PLESIDIPPUS *into the farmhouse.*

ACT FIVE

Enter LABRAX *from the right.*

LAB What other mortal alive is more wretched than me to-
     day? Plesidippus has just got me condemned before the

abiudicata a me modo est Palaestra. perditus sum.
nam lenones ex Gaudio credo esse procreatos,

1285 ita omnes mortales, si quid est mali lenoni, gaudent.
nunc alteram illam quae mea est uisam huc in Veneris
    fanum,
saltem ut eam abducam, de bonis quod restat reliqui-
    arum.

V. ii: GRIPVS. LABRAX

GRI numquam edepol hodie ad uesperum Gripum inspici-
    etis uiuom
    nisi uidulus mihi redditur.

LAB   perii quom mentionem

1290 fieri audio usquam uiduli: ⟨est⟩ quasi palo pectus tun-
    dat.

GRI istic scelestus liber est: ego qui in mari prehendi
    rete atque excepi uidulum, ei dari negatis quicquam.

LAB pro di immortales! suo mihi hic sermone arrexit auris.

GRI cubitum hercle longis litteris signabo iam us-
    quequaque,

1295 si quis perdiderit uidulum cum auro atque argento
    multo,
    ad Gripum ut ueniat. non feretis istum, ut postulatis.

LAB meum hercle illic homo uidulum scit qui habet, ut ego
    opinor.
    adeundus mi illic est homo. di, quaeso, subuenite.

GRI quid me intro reuocas? hoc uolo hic ante ostium ex-
    tergere.

1290 est *add. Lindsay*

assessors.[43] Palaestra has been taken away from me by
the court. I'm ruined. Yes, I do believe that pimps were
born from Joy, given how all people rejoice if anything   1285
bad happens to a pimp. Now I'll go here to the temple
of Venus to see that other girl that belongs to me, so that
I can at least take her away, the remnant that's left of my
property.

Enter GRIPUS *from the farmhouse, carrying a rusty spit and a
brush.*

GRI   (*into the house*) You'll never see Gripus alive until to-
      night unless the trunk is returned to me.
LAB   (*aside*) I'm dead whenever I hear a trunk being men-   1290
      tioned: it's as if it beat my chest with a pole.
GRI   (*muttering to himself*) That criminal is free; yet you re-
      fuse to give anything to me, who caught the trunk in the
      sea with my net and took it out.
LAB   (*aside*) Immortal gods! With his talk he's made me prick
      up my ears.
GRI   (*still to himself*) I'll post signs everywhere with letters
      three feet high: if anyone has lost a trunk with a lot of   1295
      gold and silver, he should come to Gripus. You folks
      won't get it as easily as you expect to.
LAB   (*still aside*) That chap knows who has my trunk, I think.
      I need to approach him. O gods, please come to my
      help.
GRI   (*reacting to a noise from within*) Why are you calling me
      in? I want to rub this clean out here in front of the

[43] The *recuperatores* or "assessors" were a board of three or five
men dealing with disputes between citizens and outsiders.

1300   nam hoc quidem pol e robigine, non est e ferro factum,
        ita quanto magis extergeo, rutilum atque tenuius fit.
        nam hoc quidem uenenatum est uerum: ita in manibus
           consenescit.

LAB   adulescens, salue.

GRI   di te ament cum irraso capite.

LAB   quid fit?

GRI   uerum extergetur.

LAB   ut uales?

GRI   quid tu? num medicus, quaeso, es?

1305 LAB   immo edepol una littera plus sum quam medicus.

GRI   tum tu
        mendicus es?

LAB   tetigisti acu.

GRI   uidetur digna forma.
        sed quid tibi est?

LAB   hac proxuma nocte in mari ⟨mi⟩ et alii
        confracta est nauis, perdidi quicquid erat miser ibi
           omne.

GRI   quid perdidisti?

LAB   uidulum cum auro atque argento multo.

1310 GRI   ecquid meministi in uidulo qui periit quid ibi infuerit?

LAB   quid refert, qui periit?

GRI   tamen—

LAB   sine hoc, aliud fabulemur.

GRI   quid si ego sciam qui inuenerit? uolo ex te scire signa.

LAB   octingenti nummi aurei in marsuppio infuerunt,
        praeterea centum minaria Philippa in pasceolo sorsus.

    1302 quidem hoc *P, transp. Bothe*   1307 mi *add. Seyffert*
    1313 nummi octingenti *P, transp. Benoist*
    1314 mna *P,* denaria *Nonius,* minaria *Leo*   philipp[i]a *Seyffert*

door; this is made of rust, not of iron: the more I rub it,   1300
the redder and thinner it gets. Yes, this spit is bewitched,
to judge from how it crumbles away under my hands.

LAB   My greetings, young man.

GRI   May the gods love you with your uncropped head.

LAB   What are you up to?

GRI   Rubbing this spit clean.

LAB   How are you?

GRI   What about you? Tell me, are you a medical?

LAB   No, I'm two letters[44] more than a medical.   1305

GRI   Then are you a mendicant?

LAB   You've hit the nail on the head.

GRI   You look the part. But what's wrong with you?

LAB   Last night the ship belonging to me and someone else
was wrecked at sea; whatever I had in it, I've lost it all.

GRI   What have you lost?

LAB   A trunk with a lot of gold and silver.

GRI   Do you remember what was in the trunk that got lost?   1310

LAB   (*slyly*) What does it matter? It got lost.

GRI   Still—

LAB   (*interrupting*) Let it be, let's talk about something else.

GRI   What if I should know who found it? I want you to give
me proof that it's yours.

LAB   There were eight hundred gold staters in a wallet, and
what's more, a hundred Philippic[45] minas approximately
in a pouch.

---

[44] "One letter more" in the Latin because the words are *medicus* ("medical, doctor") and *mendicus* ("mendicant, beggar"), respectively.

[45] The only function of the adjective *Philippic* here is to point out great monetary value.

1315	GRI	magna hercle praeda est, largiter mercedis indipiscar;
		di⟨ui⟩ homines respiciunt: bene ego hinc praedatus ibo.
		profecto est huius uidulus. perge alia tu expedire.
	LAB	talentum argenti commodum magnum inerit in crumina,
		praeterea sinus, cantharus, epichysis, gaulus, cyathus.
1320	GRI	papae! diuitias tu quidem habuisti luculentas.
	LAB	miserum istuc uerbum et pessumum est, "habuisse" et nihil habere.
	GRI	quid dare uelis qui istaec tibi inuestiget indicetque? eloquere propere celeriter.
	LAB	nummos trecentos.
	GRI	tricas!
	LAB	quadrigentos.
	GRI	tramas putidas!
	LAB	quingentos.
	GRI	cassam glandem!
1325	LAB	sescentos.
	GRI	curculiunculos minutos fabulare.
	LAB	dabo septingentos.
	GRI	os calet tibi, nunc id frigefactas.
	LAB	mille dabo nummum.
	GRI	somnias.
	LAB	nihil addo.
	GRI	abi igitur.
	LAB	audi:
		si hercle abiero hinc, hic non ero. uin centum et mille?

1316 di⟨ui⟩ *Lindsay in apparatu*   di me omnes *Weise*

| GRI | (*aside*) It's a big booty, I'll get a huge reward. The gods look favorably on men: I'll leave enriched with spoil. It is indeed his trunk. (*to Labrax*) You, continue with the other contents. | 1315 |

GRI (*aside*) It's a big booty, I'll get a huge reward. The gods look favorably on men: I'll leave enriched with spoil. It is indeed his trunk. (*to Labrax*) You, continue with the other contents. 1315

LAB In a purse there will be a silver talent of full weight, and in addition there will be a wine bowl, a goblet, a jug, a water bowl, and a ladle.

GRI Dear me! You have had striking riches. 1320

LAB That phrase is wretched and awful, "to have had" and to have nothing.

GRI What would you be willing to give to someone for tracking those things down and informing you? Tell me fast and quickly.

LAB Three hundred sesterces.[46]

GRI Rubbish!

LAB Four hundred.

GRI Rotten rags!

LAB Five hundred.

GRI An empty acorn!

LAB Six hundred. 1325

GRI You're talking chopped-up weevils.

LAB I'll make it seven hundred.

GRI You must have burned your mouth; that's why you're now cooling it.

LAB I'll make it a thousand sesterces.

GRI You're dreaming.

LAB I'm not adding anything.

GRI Then go away.

LAB Listen: if I go away, I won't be here. Do you want one thousand one hundred?

[46] The Latin simply has "coins." No high value is intended, so presumably sesterces are meant.

| | GRI | dormis. |

GRI   dormis.

LAB eloquere quantum postules.

GRI   quo nihil inuitus addas:

1330   talentum magnum. non potest triobolum hinc abesse.
          proin tu uel aias uel neges.

LAB   quid istic? necessum est, uideo:
          dabitur talentum.

GRI   accededum huc: Venus haec uolo arroget te.

LAB quod tibi lubet id mi impera.

GRI   tange aram hanc Veneris.

LAB   tango.

GRI per Venerem hanc iurandum est tibi.

LAB   quid iurem?

GRI   quod iubebo.

1335 LAB praei uerbis quiduis. [id] quod domi est, numquam ulli
          supplicabo.

GRI tene aram hanc.

LAB   teneo.

GRI   deiera te mi argentum daturum
          eodem die, ⟨tui⟩ uiduli ubi sis potitus.

LAB   fiat.
          Venus Cyrenensis, testem te testor mihi,
          si uidulum illum quem ego in naui perdidi

1340   cum auro atque argento saluom inuestigauero
          isque in potestatem meam peruenerit,
          tum ego huic—

GRI   "⟨tum ego huic⟩ Gripo," inquito et me tangito.

LAB —tum ego huic, Gripo dico, Venus, ut tu audias,
          talentum argenti magnum continuo dabo.

1335 id *del. Bentley*   1337 tui *add. Seyffert*
1342 tum ego huic *add. Schoell*

GRI   You're fast asleep.

LAB   Tell me how much you demand.

GRI   A sum to which you needn't add anything against your
       will: a full talent. Not even three obols can be missing   1330
       from it. So tell me yes or no.

LAB   Oh well. It can't be helped, I see. You'll get a talent.

GRI   Come here; I want Venus to bind you over by an oath.
       (*walks toward the altar*)

LAB   Command me what you like.

GRI   Touch this altar of Venus.

LAB   Yes. (*does so*)

GRI   You have to swear by Venus.

LAB   What should I swear?

GRI   What I tell you.

LAB   Dictate anything you like. I'll never beg anyone for   1335
       something I have a plentiful stock of.

GRI   Hold this altar.

LAB   Yes. (*does so*)

GRI   Swear that you'll give me the money on the same day that
       you get hold of your trunk.

LAB   Yes. (*solemnly*) Venus of Cyrene, I call you as my witness:
       if I track down that trunk I lost on the ship safely, with   1340
       the gold and silver, and if it comes into my power, then
       I shall give this man—

GRI   (*interrupting*) Say "then I shall give this man, Gripus,"
       and touch me.

LAB   —then I shall give him, I mean Gripus, Venus, so that
       you may hear, a full silver talent at once.

1345	GRI	⟨sed⟩ si fraudassis, dic ut te in quaestu tuo
		Venus eradicet, caput atque aetatem tuam.
		tecum hoc habeto tamen, ubi iuraueris.
	LAB	illaec aduorsum si quid peccasso, Venus,
		ueneror te ut omnes miseri lenones sient.
1350	GRI	tamen fiet, etsi tu fidem seruaueris.
		tu hic opperire, iam ego faxo exibit senex;
		eum tu continuo uidulum reposcito.
	LAB	si maxume mi illum reddiderit uidulum,
		non ego illic hodie debeo triobolum.
1355		meus arbitratust lingua quod iuret mea.
		sed conticiscam: eccum exit et ducit senem.

V. iii: GRIPVS. DAEMONES. LABRAX

GRI	sequere hac.
DAE	ubi istic leno est?
GRI	heus tu, em tibi! hic habet uidulum.
DAE	habeo et fateor esse apud me, et, si tuos est, habeas
	tibi.
	omnia, ut quicque infuit, ita salua sistentur tibi.
1360	tene, si tuost.
LAB	o di immortales! meus est. salue, uidule.
DAE	tuosne est?
LAB	rogitas? si quidem hercle Iouis fuit, meus est tamen.

1345 sed *add. Bothe*
1359 quicquid *CD*, quit quit *B*, quidque *Reiz*   infuere *P*, infuit
Fleckeisen

| GRI | But if you commit an offense, say that Venus may ruin you in your trade, you, your person, and your life. Have this for yourself anyway once you've sworn. | 1345 |

LAB   If I commit any offense against that, Venus, I entreat you that all pimps may be wretched.

| GRI | It'll happen anyway, even if you keep your word. You wait here, I'll make sure that the old man will come out in a minute; demand the trunk back from him at once. | 1350 |

Exit GRIPUS *into the farmhouse.*

| LAB | Even if he returns that trunk to me, I don't owe him as little as three obols today. It's for me to decide what my tongue swears. But I'll fall silent: look, he's coming out and bringing the old man. | 1355 |

Enter GRIPUS *and* DAEMONES *from the farmhouse, the latter carrying the trunk.*

GRI   Follow me this way.

DAE   Where is that pimp?

GRI   (*to Labrax*) Hey you, here you are! He has the trunk.

| DAE | (*also to Labrax*) I do have it and I admit that it's with me, and, if it belongs to you, you can have it for yourself. Everything will be returned safe and sound to you the way it was inside. Take it, if it belongs to you. (*hands it over*) | 1360 |

LAB   Immortal gods! It does belong to me. My greetings, trunk.

DAE   Does it belong to you?

LAB   You ask? Even if it used to belong to Jupiter, it still belongs to me.

DAE omnia insunt salua; una istinc cistella excepta est modo
cum crepundiis, quibuscum hodie filiam inueni meam.
LAB quam?
DAE   tua quae fuit Palaestra, ea filia inuenta est mea.
1365 LAB bene mehercle factum est. quom istaec res tibi ex sen-
            tentia
pulchre euenit, gaudeo.
DAE   istuc facile non credo tibi.
LAB immo hercle, ut scias gaudere me, mihi triobolum
ob eam ne duis, condono te.
DAE   benigne edepol facis.
LAB immo tu quidem hercle uero.
GRI   heus tu! iam habes uidulum.
1370 LAB habeo.
GRI   propera.
LAB   quid properabo?
GRI   reddere argentum mihi.
LAB neque edepol tibi do nec quicquam debeo.
GRI   quae haec factio est?
non debes?
LAB   non hercle uero.
GRI   non tu iuratus mihi es?
LAB iuratus sum et nunc iurabo, si quid uoluptati est mihi:
ius iurandum rei seruandae, non perdendae conditum
    est.
1375 GRI cedo sis mihi talentum magnum argenti, periurissume.
DAE Gripe, quod tu istum talentum poscis?
GRI   iuratust mihi
dare.

DAE   Everything is inside, safe and sound; only one little box with tokens has been taken out of it; with them I've found my daughter today.

LAB   What daughter?

DAE   The girl who was your Palaestra has been found to be my daughter.

LAB   Excellent. I'm happy that this turned out well for you, according to your wish.   1365

DAE   I don't believe you easily in that.

LAB   No, so that you can be sure that I'm happy, you needn't give me a three-obol piece for her, I let you off.[47]

DAE   (*with irony*) That's kind of you.

LAB   No, kind of you, really.

GRI   Hey you! Now you have the trunk.

LAB   I do.   1370

GRI   Hurry up.

LAB   Hurry up with what?

GRI   Paying me the money.

LAB   I won't give it to you and I don't owe you anything.

GRI   What's the meaning of this? You don't owe me?

LAB   No, I don't.

GRI   Didn't you swear me an oath?

LAB   I did swear and I'll swear now, if the fancy takes me; the oath was invented for preserving property, not for losing it.

GRI   Kindly give me the full silver talent, you awful perjurer.   1375

DAE   Gripus, what's that talent of yours which you're demanding?

GRI   He swore he'd give me one.

---

[47] The pimp has no right to any money for a freeborn girl anyway.

LAB   lubet iurare. tun meo pontifex periurio es?

DAE qua pro re argentum promisit hic tibi?

GRI   si uidulum
hunc redegissem in potestatem eius, iuratus⟨t⟩ dare
1380   mihi talentum magnum argenti.

LAB   cedo quicum habeam iudicem,
ni dolo malo instipulatus sis siue etiamdum siem
quinque et uiginti annos natus.

GRI   habe cum hoc.

LAB   alio est opus.

DAE iam ab istoc auferre haud ausim, si istunc condemnau-
      ero.
promisisti⟨n⟩ huic argentum?

LAB   fateor.

DAE   quod seruo ⟨meo⟩
1385   promisisti meum esse oportet, ne tu, leno, postules
te hic fide lenonia uti: non potes.

GRI   iam te ratu's
nactum hominem quem defrudares? dandum huc ar-
      gentum est probum:
id ego continuo huic dabo adeo me ut hic emittat
      manu.

DAE quando ergo erga te benignus ⟨ego⟩ fui atque opera
      mea
1390   haec tibi sunt seruata—

GRI   immo hercle mea, ne tu dicas tua.

1379 iuratus⟨t⟩ *Lambinus*
1381 siue *Priscianus*, niue *P*
1383 aut sim *P*, haut ausim *Lindsay*, haut potis sim *Leo*
1384 promisisti⟨n⟩ *Reiz*   meo *add. Pylades*
1389 ego *add. Guyet*

LAB I like swearing. Are you a high priest appointed to take cognizance of my perjury?[48]

DAE What did he promise you the money for?

GRI If I restored this trunk to him, he swore he'd give me a 1380 full silver talent.

LAB Name someone with whom I can go before an arbitrator to see if you didn't make conditions in bad faith and if I have reached the age of twenty-five yet.[49]

GRI Go with him.

LAB I need a different one.

DAE (*aside*) I wouldn't dare to take anything away from him (*points to Gripus*) now if I judge against him (*points to Labrax*). (*to Labrax*) Did you promise this man money?

LAB I admit it.

DAE What you promised to my slave ought to belong to me, 1385 so don't expect to use pimp's honor, pimp: you can't.

GRI (*to Labrax*) Did you think now you'd got hold of someone you could cheat? You have to give me a nice sum of money; I'll give that to this man at once so that he can set me free.

DAE (*also to Labrax*) Since I was benevolent toward you and these things were preserved for you through my ef- 1390 fort—

GRI (*interrupting*) No, through mine, don't say through yours.

---

[48] The *pontifex* or "high priest" had to make atonement for others' perjuries to prevent divine retribution from affecting the entire community. [49] Gripus as a slave cannot speak for himself before an arbitrator. Labrax also refers to the *lex Plaetoria*, a law according to which minors under the age of twenty-five must not be involved in financial dealings.

DAE   si sapies, tacebis. tum te mihi benigne itidem addecet
        bene merenti bene referre gratiam.
LAB   nemp' pro meo
        iure oras?
DAE   mirum quin tuom ius meo periclo aps te expetam.
GRI   saluos sum, leno labascit, libertas portenditur.
1395   DAE   uidulum istunc ille inuenit, illud mancupium meum
           est;
        ego tibi hunc porro seruaui cum magna pecunia.
LAB   gratiam habeo et de talento nulla causa est quin feras,
        quod isti sum iuratus.
GRI   heus tu! mihi dato ergo, si sapis.
DAE   tacen an non?
GRI   tu meam rem simulas agere, tibi mu⟨nis uiam⟩.
1400   non hercle istoc me interuortes, si aliam praedam per-
           didi.
DAE   uapulabis uerbum si addes isto unum.
GRI   uel hercle enica,
        non tacebo umquam alio pacto nisi talento comprimor.
LAB   tibi operam hicquidem dat. tace.
DAE   concede hoc tu, leno.
LAB   licet.
GRI   palam age, nolo ego murmurillum nec susurrum fieri.
1405   DAE   dic mihi: quanti illam emisti tuam alteram muliercu-
        lam,
        Ampeliscam?
LAB   mille nummum denumeraui.

1399 mu⟨nis uiam⟩ *Koch*   1401 istuc *P*, isto *Spengel*

---

[50] The Latin simply has *nummi*, "coins." The default value of the
nummus is one sesterce piece, but this price would be too low for a

DAE   (*to Gripus*) You'd better be quiet. (*to Labrax*) Then you should in the same way kindly return the favor, since I've deserved well of you.

LAB   Presumably you're asking in recognition of my right?

DAE   Odd that I'm not putting myself to the trouble of asking you to make a concession to yourself.

GRI   I'm safe, the pimp is wavering, it's an omen that my freedom is approaching.

DAE   (*to Labrax*) That man found that trunk; he's my slave; I   1395 have preserved it for you further, with a great sum of money.

LAB   I'm grateful to you and I don't object to you getting the talent that I swore I'd give him.

GRI   Hey you! Better give it to me.

DAE   Will you be quiet or not?

GRI   You pretend to be looking after my interest, but you're building a road for yourself. You shan't swindle me out   1400 of that, even if I've lost the other booty.

DAE   You'll get a thrashing if you add one more word to that.

GRI   You can even kill me, I'll never be quiet unless I'm silenced with a talent.

LAB   It's your interest he's looking after. Be quiet.

DAE   You, pimp, walk over here.

LAB   Okay.

GRI   (*calling after them*) Act openly, I don't want any muttering or whispering to take place.

DAE   (*to Labrax*) Tell me: for how much did you buy that other   1405 woman of yours, Ampelisca?

LAB   I paid down two thousand drachmas.[50]

female slave. A thousand didrachmas corresponds to twenty minas, which is a reasonable sum. Daemones offers half a talent, which is thirty minas.

DAE   uin tibi
      condicionem luculentam ferre me?

LAB   sane uolo.

DAE diuiduom talentum faciam.

LAB   bene facis.

DAE   pro illa altera,
      libera ut sit, dimidium tibi sume, dimidium huc cedo.

1410 LAB maxume.

DAE   pro illo dimidio ego Gripum emittam manu,
      quem propter tu uidulum et ego gnatam inueni.

LAB   bene facis,
      gratiam habeo magnam.

GRI   quam mox mi argentum ergo redditur?

DAE res soluta est, Gripe. ego habeo.

GRI   at ego me hercle mauolo.

DAE nihil hercle hic tibi est, ne tu speres. iuris iurandi uolo
1415   gratiam facias.

GRI   perii hercle! nisi me suspendo occidi.
      numquam hercle iterum defrudabis me quidem post
        hunc diem.

DAE hic hodie cenato, leno.

LAB   fiat, condicio placet.

DAE sequimini intro. spectatores, uos quoque ad cenam
        uocem,
      ni daturus nil sim nec sit quicquam pollucti domi,
1420   niue adeo uocatos credam uos esse ad cenam foras.
      uerum si uoletis plausum fabulae huic clarum dare,
      comissatum omnes uenitote ad me ad annos sedecim.
      uos hic hodie cenatote ambo.

LAB + GRI   fiat.

DAE   plausum date.

1413 hercle at ego me *P, transp. Studemund*

DAE   Do you want me to make you an advantageous offer?

LAB   I do indeed.

DAE   I'll share the talent.

LAB   That's kind of you.

DAE   Take half for that other one, so that she may be free, and give half to me.

LAB   By all means.   1410

DAE   For that half I'll set Gripus free; because of him you found your trunk and I my daughter.

LAB   That's kind of you, thank you very much.

GRI   (*approaching them*) How soon am I paid my money, then?

DAE   The issue has been resolved, Gripus. I have it.

GRI   But I prefer having it myself.

DAE   There's nothing in here for you, don't have any hopes. I want you to let him off his oath.   1415

GRI   I'm ruined! Unless I hang myself I'm dead. You'll never cheat me again after this day.

DAE   Have dinner here today, pimp.

LAB   Yes, I like the invitation.

DAE   Follow me in, you two. Spectators, I'd also invite you to dinner, were it not for the fact that I'm not going to give any and that I don't have any meal at home, and were it   1420 not for the fact that I believe you've been invited out for dinner. But if you want to give this play your loud applause, you can all come for drinks at my place in sixteen years' time. (*to Labrax and Gripus*) Both of you, dine here today.[51]

LAB + GRI   Yes.

DAE   (*to the audience*) Give us your applause.

[51] Slaves do not dine with free men; the invitation indicates that Gripus is now free.

METRICAL APPENDIX

POENVLVS

arg. 1–209 ia^6
210–29 ba^4
230 ba^2 + ba^c
231 ba^3
231^a tr^4∧
232 an^7
233–37 ba^4
238 v^r
239 ia^7
240–43 ba^4
244 ba^2 + ba^c
245 ba^c
245^a–46 ba^3
247 ba^2
248–50 ba^4
251 an^4∧ + an^4
252 ba^4
253 ba^1 + ia^2
254 cr^3
254^a ith
255–57 ba^4
258 ba^1 + ba^c

259 ba^4
260 ba^3
261–409 tr^7
410–503 ia^6
504–608 tr^7
609 extra metrum
609^a–14 tr^7
615–816 ia^6
817–20 ia^8
821–22 ia^7
823–929 tr^7
930–49 ia^6 ?
950–1173 ia^6
1174–75 an^8
1176–76^a an^4
1177 cr^2 + cr^c
1177^a an^4
1178 an^8
1179–83 an^4
1183^a an^2
1183^b an^4∧
1184–86 an^7

METRICAL APPENDIX

1187–90 an^8

1191 an^4

1191^a an$^{4\wedge}$

1191^b–92 c^r

1192^a–94 ia^8

1195 ia^6

1196 ia^4

1196^a ia^6

1197 an$^{4\wedge}$

1197^a–98^a ia^4

1199 ia^7

1200 an^4 + c^r

1201–25 tr^7

1226–73 ia^7

1274–1303 tr^7

1304–97 ia^6

1398–1422 tr^7

PSEVDOLVS

arg. 1 + 2, 1–128 ia^6

129 extra metrum

130–32 ia^6

133–37 an^8

138 tr^7

139 tr^4

140 tr^7

141 c^r

142–44 tr^8

145 tr^7

146–52 ia^8

153 ia^7

154 ia^8

155–56 ia^7

157–58 ia^8

159–60 ia^7

161–64 tr^8

165–68 an^8

169–70 ia^8

171–72 ia^7

173 tr^8

174–80 an^8

181 an^7

182–84 an^8

185–86 ia^8

187 ia$^{4\wedge}$

188–92 ia^8

193 ia^6

194–95 tr sy^{6metr}

195^a tr$^{4\wedge}$

196 tr^7

197–98 tr^8

199–200 tr^7

201 tr^8

202–2^a tr$^{4\wedge}$

203–4^a tr sy^{8metr}

205 extra metrum

205^a–7 ia^4

208 ia^6

209–10 tr^8

211–13 tr^4∧

214 tr^7

215 tr^8

216–17 tr^4∧

218 tr^8

219 ia^7

220 tr^7

221 tr^8

222 tr^4∧

223 tr^7

224 tr^4∧

225 tr^8

226 tr^7

227 ia^8

228 tr^8

229 tr^7

230 an^8

231 an^7

232 an^8

233–38 an^7

239 an^4

239^a an^4∧

240 an^4 + ia^2

240^a–42 tr^4

243 tr^8

244–48 ba^4

249 tr^8

250–54 ba^4

255 tr^8

256–57 ba^4

258 cr^c + cr^c

259–60 cr^4

261 cr^2 + cr^c

262 cr^1 + tr^4∧

263 cr^2 + cr^c

264 cr^1 + ith

265–393 tr^7

394–573^a ia^6

574–76 an^8

577 cr^c

578 an^8

579 tr^4∧

580 an^8

581–82 ba^8

583 an^8

584–85^a tr^7

586 an^8

586^a c^r

587–88 an^8

589 v^r

590 tr^8

591 an^4

592 an^8

593 an^7

594–98 an^8

599 an^4∧

600–600^a ia^4

601–1^a an^4

602–2^a wil

602^b c^r

603 gl
603^a ith
603^b c^r
604–766 tr^7
767–904 ia^6
905–8^a an sy$^{16\mathrm{metr}}$
909–9^a an$^4\wedge$
910–12 an^8
913–13^a an^4
914 ia^8
915 ia^7
916–18 an$^4\wedge$
919–19^a ia^4
920–21 cr^4
922 tr^2 + ith
923–25^a ia^4
926–30 cr^4
931 an^4
931^a c^r
932–35 cr^4
935^a c^r
936–37 an^7
938 an^4 + c^r
938^a c^r
939 an^4
939^a an$^4\wedge$
940 an^7
941–42 an^8
943–46 an^7
947–48 an^8
949 an^4 + c^r
950 an$^4\wedge$

950^a ith
951–96 tr^7
997 ia^8
998–1102 ia^6
1103–4 an^8
1105–6 ba^4
1107 tr^7
1108 cr^2
1109 cr^c + cr^c
1110 an$^4\wedge$
1111 tr^4
1112 cr^c + tr$^4\wedge$
1113 ia^4 + tr$^4\wedge$
1114–15 c^r + ia^2
1116–18 cr^4
1119 cr^3
1120–23^a tr sy$^{13\mathrm{metr}}$
1124–25 tr^7
1126–30 ba^4
1131 ba^3 + ia^2
1131^a tr$^4\wedge$
1132–34^a tr sy$^{10\mathrm{metr}}$
1135–1245 tr^7
1246–47 ba^4
1248–49 cr^2 + ith
1250 ith
1251–52 ba^4
1253 an^7
1254 v^r
1255 c^r + c^r
1256–57 ia^4
1257^a ia$^4\wedge$

1258 $\text{ia}^2 + \text{ia}^2$	1292–93 cr^c
1259–60 tr^8	1294 $\text{cr}^2 + \text{cr}^c$
1261–62 an^8	1295 an^7
1263 ba^4	1296 cr sy$^{\text{5metr}}$
1264 $\text{ba}^c + \text{ba}^c$	1297 c^r
1265–66 ba^4	1298–99 cr^4
1267 $\text{ba}^c + \text{ba}^c$	1300 $\text{cr}^2 + \text{cr}^c$
1268 $\text{cr}^c + \text{cr}^c$	1301 $\text{cr}^2 + \text{thy}$
1268^a $\text{cr}^1 + \text{ith}$	1302 $\text{cr}^c + \text{cr}^c$
1269 cr^c	1303–4 cr^4
1270 tr^4	1305 ia^4
1270^a ith	1306–7 cr^4
1271–72^a ba^4	1308–8^a cr^c
1273 ba^3	1309 $\text{cr}^2 + \text{cr}^c$
1274 $\text{ion}^4{\wedge}$	1310–10^a cr^c
1274^a–75^a ion sy$^{\text{10metr}}$	1311 $\text{cr}^2 + \text{cr}^c$
1276 $\text{ba}^c + \text{ba}^2$	1312 $\text{cr}^2 + \text{thy}$
1277 cr^4	1313 tr^7
1277^a cr^3	1314 $\text{cr}^3 + \text{tr}^2$
1278 cr^4	1315–16 an^8
1278^a $\text{an}^4{\wedge}$	1317–20 $\text{an}^4{\wedge}$
1279 tr^7	1320^a $\text{ia}^4{\wedge}$
1280–80^a $\text{cr}^c + \text{cr}^c$	1321 an^7
1281–82 ba^4	1322–23 an^8
1283–84 tr^8	1324–27 an^7
1285 $\text{cr}^2 + \text{cr}^c$	1328 an^8
1286 $\text{cr}^2 + \text{thy}$	1329–30 ba sy$^{\text{8metr}}$
1287–88 $\text{cr}^2 + \text{cr}^c$	1331–33 cr^2
1289–90 cr^4	1334 $\text{ia}^4{\wedge}$
1291 ia^4	1335–35^a cr sy$^{\text{7metr}}$
1291^a $\text{cr}^2 + \text{cr}^c$	1335^b tr^2

METRICAL APPENDIX

RVDENS

arg., 1–184 ia^6
185 v^r
186 ba^2 + c^r
187 an^4 + c^r
188 ia$^{4\wedge}$ + an^2
189 an^4 + an^2
190 an$^{4\wedge}$ + an$^{4\wedge}$
191–94 ba^4
195–96 v^r
197 ba^4
197^a ia$^{4\wedge}$
198 an^7
199 cr^4
200 cr^3
200^a cr^c
201 cr^3
201^a cr^c
202 cr^4
203 cr^2 + thy
204 ba^4
205 ba^3 + ia^2
205^a ?
206 ia^4
206^a ia^2 + cr^c
206^b ?
207–8 cr^4
209 cr^2 + thy
210 cr^2 + cr^c
211 cr^c + cr^2

212 cr^2 + sp^2
213–14 cr^4
215 cr^2 + thy
216 cr^2 + sp^2
216^a an$^{4\wedge}$
217 tr^8
218 an$^{4\wedge}$ + c^r
219 ia^7
220–24 an^8
225–28 an^7
229 cr^2 + ia^2
230 cr^c + ia^2
231 cr^c + cr^c
232 tr^2 + ia^2
233–36 cr^4
237 cr^2 + tr^2
238–52 cr^4
253 cr^2 + ith
254 ia^4
255 ia^6
256 ia^8
257–58 tr^7
259–63 ba^4
264 ba^1 + ia^2
265 cr^c + cr^2
265^a ia$^{4\wedge}$
266–71 cr^4
272–73 cr^2 + cr^c
274–77 cr^4

566

278–82 ba^4

283–83^a ia^4

284–85 ia^4∧

285^a c^r

286 ba^4

287 ia^4∧

288 ba^4

289 ia^4∧

290–413 ia^7

414–41 tr^7

442–558 ia^6

559–92 tr^7

593–614 ia^6

615–63 tr^7

664–66 cr^4

667 cr^2 + tr^2

668 cr^2 + sp^2

669–73 cr^4

674 cr^3 + tr^2

675–76 cr^4

677 cr^2 + tr^4∧

678 cr^2 + cr^c

679–81 cr^4

681^a tr^2

682–705 ia^7

706–79 tr^7

780–905 ia^6

906–11 ba^4

912–13 an^8

914–18 ba^4

919 an^4

920 tr^7

921–22 an^8

923 tr^8

924–25^a cr^c + cr^c

926 cr^2

926^a–32 an^8

933 an^7

934 an^8

935 an^7

936 an^8

937 an^7

938–44^a ia^4

945–46 ia^4 + ith

947–48^a wil

949–51 cr^4

952–55 wil + cr^c

956–62^a an^4

962^b an^4∧

963–1190 tr^7

1191–1204 ia^6

1205–26 tr^7

1227–64 ia^6

1265–80 tr^7

1281–1337 ia^7

1338–56 ia^6

1357–1423 tr^7

INDEX OF PROPER NAMES

The index is limited to names of characters in the plays, and of characters, persons, towns, countries, regions, peoples, languages, works of literature, feasts, and deities mentioned in the plays. Names for which established English forms or translations exist are listed under the English forms, for instance, *Jupiter* or *Underworld*.

INDEX OF PROPER NAMES